Contents

GW00546390

Finding questions

Question index 4
Topic index 7

Using your BPP Practice and Revision Kit 8

Passing ACCA exams

Revising and taking ACCA exams 11
How to revise 12
How NOT to revise 13
How to PASS your exams...14
How to FAIL your exams 15
Using your BPP products..16

Passing 3.5

Revising 3.5 19
Passing the 3.5 exam 21
Recent exams 24
Useful websites 30
Syllabus mindmap 31

Planning your question practice

BPP's question plan..35
Build your own exams...39

Questions and answers

Questions 43
Answers 117

Exam practice

Mock exam 1
- Questions 303
- Plan of attack 311
- Answers 312

Mock exam 2
- Questions 327
- Plan of attack 335
- Answers 336

Mock exam 3 (December 2006)
- Questions 353
- Plan of attack 363
- Answers 364

ACCA examiner's answers
- June 2006 exam 381
- December 2006 exam 391

Review form & free prize draw

3

Question index

The headings in this checklist/index indicate the main topics of questions, but questions often cover several different topics.

The single preparation question gives you a firm foundation for further exam standard questions that assume knowledge of this topic.

		Marks	Time allocation Mins	Page number Question	Answer
Part A: Models of strategic management					
1	Question with analysis: Bartok Fuel	20	36	43	117
2	Aurora Lighting plc	20	36	45	119
3	*Preparation question: Planning components*	–	–	46	120
4	Introducing strategic management	20	36	46	122
5	Gould & King (6/06)	20	36	47	124
Part B: Strategic analysis and options					
6	Question with analysis: Fancy Packaging (6/02)	20	36	48	127
7	Lawson Engineering (12/05)	20	36	50	131
8	Five forces	20	36	50	134
9	Classics on the cheap	20	36	51	136
10	Question with answer plan: Grow or buy? (12/02)	20	36	53	137
11	Question with student answer: McGeorge Holdings (6/03)	20	36	53	140
12	KPG Systems	20	36	54	144
13	Airtite (6/06)	20	36	54	145
14	Pharmia plc	20	36	55	148
15	Qualispecs	20	36	56	151
16	Question with answer plan: Digwell	20	36	57	153
17	MegaMart (6/04)	20	36	57	157
18	Salt and Soap (6/04)	20	36	58	159

	Marks	Time allocation Mins	Page number Question	Answer

Part C: Implementing strategy

	Marks	Mins	Question	Answer
19 Environmental strategy (6/05)	20	36	59	162
20 Question with analysis: Apex culture (6/02)	20	36	60	164
21 Supaserve (12/05)	20	36	62	166
22 Global Imaging (6/06)	20	36	62	168
23 IT Project (M&S, 6/98, amended)	20	36	63	171
24 Westport University (M&S, 6/99, amended)	20	36	63	172
25 Ashkol Furniture (6/03)	20	36	64	174
26 Smalltown	20	36	64	176
27 Helen's Cakes (6/05)	20	36	65	179
28 Lakeside Business School (12/04)	20	36	65	182
29 Connie Head (6/04)	20	36	66	184
30 Isabella Correlli (M&S, 12/00, amended)	20	36	67	186
31 Question with analysis: Fashion retailer (M&S, 12/00, amended)	20	36	68	190
32 Auto Direct (6/05)	20	36	69	192
33 Focus Bank (12/04)	20	36	70	194
34 Smith Norman (12/03)	20	36	70	196
35 La Familia Amable (12/05)	20	36	71	199
36 Rameses International (12/02)	20	36	72	201
37 John Hudson (12/01)	20	36	72	203
38 Pamper Products	20	36	73	205
39 Sykes Engineering (6/03)	20	36	74	207
40 Question with analysis: Service performance (6/02)	20	36	75	209

Part D: Global strategy

	Marks	Mins	Question	Answer
41 Excalibur Sportswear (12/01)	20	36	77	212
42 Question with analysis: Global marketing (12/02)	20	36	78	214
43 Prestige Packaging (12/03)	20	36	80	216
44 Asia Invest (12/04)	20	36	80	219

	Marks	Time allocation Mins	Page number Question	Page number Answer

Case studies

	Marks	Mins	Question	Answer
45 Question with analysis: Lionel Cartwright (12/01)	60	108	81	222
46 Question with student answer: Bethesda Heights (6/02)	60	108	87	228
47 World-Wide Agricultural (12/02)	60	108	89	237
48 Hair Care (6/03)	60	108	91	242
49 Polymat Tapes (12/03)	60	108	94	249
50 NMS (6/04)	60	108	97	254
51 Elite Plastic Packaging (12/04)	60	108	100	261
52 LRP	60	108	103	268
53 Screen Books	60	108	105	271
54 Universal Roofing Systems (6/05)	60	108	106	276
55 Datum Paper Products (12/05)	60	108	109	283
56 Churchill Ice Cream (6/06)	60	108	112	290

Mock exam 1

Questions 57 to 60

Mock exam 2

Questions 61 to 64

Mock exam 3 (December 2006)

Questions 65 to 68

Planning your question practice

Our guidance from page 35 shows you how to organise your question practice, either by attempting questions from each syllabus area or **by building your own exams** – tackling questions as a series of practice exams.

Topic index

Listed below are the key Paper 3.5 syllabus topics and the numbers of the questions in this Kit covering those topics.

If you need to concentrate your practice and revision on certain topics or if you want to attempt all available questions that refer to a particular subject, you will find this index useful.

Syllabus topic	Question numbers
Benchmarking	11
Change management	20, 32, 49
Core competences	33
Critical success factors	40
Cultural analysis	7, 20, 38
Decision trees	14
Environmental analysis	3, 6, 8, 45
Ethics, corporate governance and social responsibility	16, 17, 46, 47, 52
Five forces	8
Global strategy	41, 43, 42, 51
Human resource management	30
Levels of strategy	3
Marketing	21, 24, 25, 26, 27, 34, 50
Marketing research	6, 24, 26
Mission, goals and objectives	2, 3, 12, 13, 46, 50
New product development	49, 53
Organisation structure	35, 37, 54, 52
Outsourcing	10, 31, 33
Performance measurement and balanced scorecard	13, 28, 38, 40
Porter's diamond	44
Portfolio analysis	11
Position audit	7
Project management	19
Quality management	22, 44
Stakeholders	16, 28, 46
Strategic analysis	5, 7, 9, 12, 13, 18, 36, 45, 46, 47, 48, 49, 50, 51, 52, 53, 54, 55, 56
Strategic failure	38, 48,
Strategic models	1, 2, 4, 45
Strategic options	15, 21, 36, 44, 45, 46, 47, 48, 49, 50, 51, 52, 53, 54, 55, 56
Strategic use of IT	31
Value chain	5, 9, 48

Using your BPP Practice and Revision Kit

Tackling revision and the exam

You can significantly improve your chances of passing by tackling revision and the exam in the right ways. Our advice is based on recent feedback from ACCA examiners.

- We look at the dos and don'ts of revising for, and taking, ACCA exams
- We focus on Paper 3.5; we discuss revising the syllabus, what to do (and what not to do) in the exam, how to approach different types of question and ways of obtaining easy marks

Selecting questions

We provide signposts to help you plan your revision.

- A full **question index**
- A **topic index** listing all the questions that cover key topics, so that you can locate the questions that provide practice on these topics, and see the different ways in which they might be examined
- **BPP's question plan** highlighting the most important questions and explaining why you should attempt them
- **Build your own exams**, showing how you can practise questions in a series of exams

Making the most of question practice

At BPP we realise that you need more than just questions and model answers to get the most from your question practice.

- Our **Top tips** provide essential advice on tackling questions, presenting answers and the key points that answers need to include
- We show you how you can pick up **Easy marks** on questions, as we know that picking up all readily available marks often can make the difference between passing and failing
- We summarise **Examiner's comments** to show you how students who sat the exam coped with the questions
- We include ACCA's **marking guides** to show you what the examiner rewards
- We refer to the **BPP 2006 Study Text** for detailed coverage of the topics covered in each question
- A number of questions include **Analysis** and **Helping hands** attached to show you how to approach them if you are struggling
- We include **annotated student answers** to some questions to highlight how these questions can be tackled and ways answers can be improved.
- In a bank at the end of this Kit we include the **examiner's answers** to the 2006 exams. Used in conjunction with our answers they provide an indication of all possible points that could be made, issues that could be covered and approaches to adopt.

Attempting mock exams

There are three mock exams that provide practice at coping with the pressures of the exam day. We strongly recommend that you attempt them under exam conditions. **Mock exams 1 and 2** reflect the question styles and syllabus coverage of the exam; **Mock exam 3** is the actual December 2006 exam. To help you get the most out of doing these exams, we not only provide help with each answer, but also guidance on how you should have approached the whole exam.

Passing ACCA exams

Revising and taking ACCA exams

To maximise your chances of passing your ACCA exams, you must make best use of your time, both before the exam during your revision, and when you are actually doing the exam.

- Making the most of your revision time can make a big, big difference to how well-prepared you are for the exam

- Time management is a core skill in the exam hall; all the work you've done can be wasted if you don't make the most of the three hours you have to attempt the exam

In this section we simply show you what to do and what not to do during your revision, and how to increase and decrease your prospects of passing your exams when you take them. Our advice is grounded in feedback we've had from ACCA examiners. You may be surprised to know that much examiner advice is the same whatever the exam, and the reasons why many students fail don't vary much between subjects and exam levels. So if you follow the advice we give you over the next few pages, you will **significantly** enhance your chances of passing **all** your ACCA exams.

How to revise

☑ Plan your revision

At the start of your revision period, you should draw up a **timetable** to plan how long you will spend on each subject and how you will revise each area. You need to consider the total time you have available and also the time that will be required to revise for other exams you're taking.

☑ Practise Practise Practise

The **more exam-standard questions** you do, the **more likely you are to pass** the exam. Practising full questions will mean that you'll get used to the time pressure of the exam. When the time is up, you should note where you've got to and then try to complete the question, giving yourself practice at everything the question tests.

☑ Revise enough

Make sure that your revision covers the breadth of the syllabus, as in most papers most topics could be examined in a compulsory question. However it is true that some topics are **key** – they often appear in compulsory questions or are a particular interest of the examiner – and you need to spend sufficient time revising these. Make sure you also know the **basics** – the fundamental calculations, proformas and report layouts.

☑ Deal with your difficulties

Difficult areas are topics you find dull and pointless, or subjects that you found problematic when you were studying them. You mustn't become negative about these topics; instead you should build up your knowledge by reading the **Passcards** and using the **Quick quiz** questions in the Study Text to test yourself. When practising questions in the Kit, go back to the Text if you're struggling.

☑ Learn from your mistakes

Having completed a question you must try to look at your answer critically. Always read the **Top tips guidance** in the answers; it's there to help you. Look at **Easy marks** to see how you could have quickly gained credit on the questions that you've done. As you go through the Kit, it's worth noting any traps you've fallen into, and key points in the **Top tips** or **Examiner's comments** sections, and referring to these notes in the days before the exam. Aim to learn at least one new point from each question you attempt, a technical point perhaps or a point on style or approach.

☑ Read the examiners' guidance

We refer throughout this Kit to **Examiner's comments**; these are available on ACCA's website. As well as highlighting weaknesses, examiners' reports as often provide clues to future questions, as many examiners will quickly test again areas where problems have arisen. ACCA's website also contains articles by examiners which you **must** read, as they may form the basis of questions on any paper after they've been published.

Read through the examiner's answers to the 2006 exams included at the back of the Kit. In general these are far longer and more comprehensive than any answer you could hope to produce in the exam, but used in conjunction with our more realistic solutions, they provide a useful revision tool, covering all possible points and approaches.

☑ Complete all three mock exams

You should attempt the **Mock exams** at the end of the Kit under **strict exam conditions**, to gain experience of selecting questions, managing your time and producing answers.

How NOT to revise

☒ Revise selectively

Examiners are well aware that some students try to forecast the contents of exams, and only revise those areas that they think will be examined. Examiners try to prevent this by doing the unexpected, for example setting the same topic in successive sittings or setting topics in compulsory questions that have previously only been examined in optional questions.

☒ Spend all the revision period reading

You cannot pass the exam just by learning the contents of Passcards, Course Notes or Study Texts. You have to develop your **application skills** by practising questions.

☒ Audit the answers

This means reading the answers and guidance without having attempted the questions. Auditing the answers gives you **false reassurance** that you would have tackled the questions in the best way and made the points that our answers do. The feedback we give in our answers will mean more to you if you've attempted the questions and thought through the issues.

☒ Practise some types of question, but not others

Although you may find the numerical parts of certain papers challenging, you shouldn't just practise calculations. These papers will also contain written elements, and you therefore need to spend time practising written question parts.

☒ Get bogged down

Don't spend a lot of time worrying about all the minute detail of certain topic areas, and leave yourself insufficient time to cover the rest of the syllabus. Remember that a key skill in the exam is the ability to **concentrate on what's important** and this applies to your revision as well.

☒ Overdo studying

Studying for too long without interruption will mean your studying becomes less effective. A five minute break each hour will help. You should also make sure that you are leading a **healthy lifestyle** (proper meals, good sleep and some times when you're not studying).

How to PASS your exams

☑ Prepare for the day

Make sure you set at least one alarm (or get an alarm call), and allow plenty of time to get to the exam hall. You should have your route planned in advance and should listen on the radio for potential travel problems. You should check the night before to see that you have pens, pencils, erasers, watch, calculator with spare batteries, also exam documentation and evidence of identity.

☑ Select the right questions

You should select the optional questions you feel you can answer **best**, basing your selection on the topics covered, the requirements of the question, how easy it will be to apply the requirements and the availability of easy marks.

☑ Plan your three hours

You need to make sure that you will be answering the correct number of questions, and that you spend the right length of time on each question – this will be determined by the number of marks available. Each mark carries with it a **time allocation** of **1.8 minutes**. A 25 mark question therefore should be selected, completed and checked in 45 minutes. With some papers, it's better to do certain types of question first or last.

☑ Read the questions carefully

To score well, you must follow the requirements of the question, understanding what aspects of the subject area are being covered, and the tasks you will have to carry out. The requirements will also determine what information and examples you should provide. Reading the question scenarios carefully will help you decide what **issues** to discuss, **techniques** to use, **information** and **examples** to include and how to **organise** your answer.

☑ Plan your answers

Five minutes of planning plus twenty-five minutes of writing is certain to earn you more marks than thirty minutes of writing. Consider when you're planning how your answer should be **structured,** **w**hat the **format** should be and **how long** each part should take.

Confirm before you start writing that your plan makes **sense,** covers **all relevant points** and does not include **irrelevant material.**

☑ Show evidence of judgement

Remember that examiners aren't just looking for a display of knowledge; they want to see how well you can **apply** the knowledge you have. Evidence of application and judgement will include writing answers that only contain **relevant** material, using the material in scenarios to **support** what you say, **criticising** the **limitations** and **assumptions** of the techniques you use and making **reasonable recommendations** that follow from your discussion.

☑ Stay until the end of the exam

Use any spare time to **check and recheck** your script. This includes checking you have filled out the candidate details correctly, you have labelled question parts and workings clearly, you have used headers and underlining effectively and spelling, grammar and arithmetic are correct.

How to FAIL your exams

☒ Don't do enough questions

If you don't attempt sufficient questions on the paper, you are making it harder for yourself to pass the questions that you do attempt. If for example you don't do a 20 mark question, then you will have to score 50 marks out of 80 marks on the rest of the paper, and therefore have to obtain 63% of the marks on the questions you do attempt. Failing to attempt all of the paper is symptomatic of poor time management or poor question selection.

☒ Include irrelevant material

Markers are given detailed mark guides and will not give credit for irrelevant content. Therefore you should **NOT** braindump all you know about a broad subject area; the markers will only give credit for what is **relevant**, and you will also be showing that you lack the ability to **judge what's important.** Similarly forcing irrelevant theory into every answer won't gain you marks, nor will providing uncalled for features such as situation analyses, executive summaries and background information.

☒ Fail to use the details in the scenario

General answers or reproductions of old answers that don't refer to what is in the scenario in **this** question won't score enough marks to pass.

☒ Copy out the scenario details

Examiners see **selective** use of the right information as a key skill. If you copy out chunks of the scenario which aren't relevant to the question, or don't use the information to support your own judgements, you won't achieve good marks.

☒ Don't do what the question asks

Failing to provide all the examiner asks for will limit the marks you score. You will also decrease your chances by not providing an answer with enough **depth** – producing a single line bullet point list when the examiner asks for a discussion.

☒ Present your work poorly

Markers will only be able to give you credit if they can read your writing. There are also plenty of other things that will make it more difficult for markers to reward you. Examples include:

- Not using black or blue ink
- Not showing clearly which question you're attempting
- Scattering question parts from the same question throughout your answer booklet
- Not showing clearly workings or the results of your calculations

Paragraphs that are too long or which lack headers also won't help markers and hence won't help you.

Using your BPP products

This Kit gives you the question practice and guidance you need in the exam. Our other products can also help you pass:

- **Learning to Learn Accountancy** gives further valuable advice on revision

- **Passcards** provide you with clear topic summaries and exam tips

- **Success CDs** help you revise on the move

- **i-Pass CDs** offer tests of knowledge against the clock

- **Learn Online** is an e-learning resource delivered via the Internet, offering comprehensive tutor support and featuring areas such as study, practice, email service, revision and useful resources

You can purchase these products by visiting www.bpp.com/mybpp.

Visit our website www.bpp.com/acca/learnonline to sample aspects of Learn Online free of charge.

BPP
LEARNING MEDIA

Passing 3.5

Revising 3.5

Business strategy differs from most other subjects studied for accountancy qualifications in that it contains very little in the way of firm rules and procedures. There are several models and mnemonics that can be very useful, but their employment in the real world of business is always a matter of judgement and experience. Indeed, as the Examiner has pointed out, 'there are no right answers' to the questions he sets.

Candidates' success in this examination depends on advancing arguments supported by reference to both theory and the information given in the question settings. Many candidates find this very demanding; they can learn the theory but tend to be poor at applying it to the problems presented by the Examiner. Probably, this is partly because more than one theory may be applicable and partly because the theories themselves provide little guidance on how best to use them in any given set of circumstances. There are no templates or standard methods, unfortunately.

This means that success in Paper 3.5 depends heavily on developing the techniques involved in actually producing answers to questions. These involve the skills of analysis and synthesis to a very high level indeed. **Practice at answering questions is thus a most important part of preparation for this exam**.

Answering questions

There are several different processes involved in answering a scenario question.

(a)   The information contained in the question must be absorbed and understood.

(b)   The question requirements must be thoroughly understood and any possible ambiguities considered.

(c)   Models and theories must be examined for relevance to the scenario.

(d)   Practical risks, limitations, explanations and courses of action must be considered; these should be derived from the models and theories and applicable to the problems in the scenario.

(e)   A coherent answer must be planned and then written out.

If you think about this model you will see that it is supported by our general comments above. The conclusions we draw are that there are two main aspects to your revision for Paper 3.5. These are first, ensuring that you have the necessary knowledge of theory and second, ensuring that you can write answers that will be awarded sufficient marks to pass. **Most candidates spend far too much time on the first and not nearly enough on the second**. Question practice should therefore be the main constituent of your revision.

If you have followed a reasonably complete course of study, careful revision of your BPP Passcards should provide you with sufficient revision of basic knowledge. The detailed revision plan provided later in this Kit includes Passcard chapter references for each revision period. You should review this material quickly and then move on to question practice.

Using questions for revision

Look again at our analysis of the processes involved in answering a question. You should use your question practice to enhance your abilities at all of them.

If you are worried that you do not have the basic theory at your fingertips, by all means refer back to your Passcards and even, sparingly, to the Study Text; it is perfectly acceptable, at first, to tackle a question in slow time and to use it to help you remember important ideas. In fact, it is a very good idea to do so, since most people learn this sort of thing best by applying it in practical setting. However, you must push yourself constantly to make less and less reference to your books so that by the time your revision is complete you do not need them at all.

With each question you attempt, consciously remind yourself about the need to understand both the scenario and the requirements. You have 36 minutes for a 20 mark question and you should be prepared to spend several minutes on this process.

Computations in Paper 3.5

Success in Paper 3.5 forms part of your professional qualification as an accountant. However, as you must be aware, this does not mean that it is notably quantitative in nature. In fact, the exam is heavily biased towards the kind of problem that requires a discursive, written solution. In past exams, the Examiners have offered a significant amount of numerical data in the setting to question 1 and up to about twenty marks have been available for work involving computations. However, even in these parts of the exam, the emphasis has been laid at least as heavily on **making sensible use of the results of computations** as on performing the computations in the first place

The typical Paper 3.5 computation **does not require any abstruse theoretical knowledge or complex techniques**, such as you might expect in the financial strategy paper, nor will you be expected to carry out any extensive financial or cost accounting work that would be more suited to papers in those subjects. The typical Paper 3.5 computational element is unlikely to require more than basic arithmetic, including some use of ratios and percentages. The difficult part, just as in real life, is **deciding what computations are relevant and how to make the best use of the insights they provide**.

That said, a very useful technique for making a start on question 1 is to calculate a few ratios and percentages: this will often give you a very rapid route into the essence of the problems underlying the scenario.

Question practice

Question practice under timed conditions is essential, so that you can get used to the pressures of answering exam questions in **limited time** and practise not only the key techniques but allocating your time between different requirements in each question. Our list of recommended questions includes both 60 mark Section A and 20 mark Section B questions; it's particularly important to do a number of Section A questions in full to see how the numerical and written elements balance in longer questions.

Passing the 3.5 exam

The examiner

The examiner for Paper 3.5 is Ralph Bedrock, who was previously Assessor for this exam. He has recently retired from an academic post at Nottingham Trent University. In his 'Examiner's approach', published on the ACCA website (www.acca.co.uk/students/professionalscheme/paper3_5/3-5examapproach) he emphasises the need for 'judgement and technique' in order to make a valid contribution to strategic management.

The examiner makes several other interesting points.

(a) Questions in Section B may be based on any part of the syllabus. '**This makes question spotting a dangerous technique**'.

(b) Questions are unlikely to require knowledge of obscure academic models: they 'must be familiar with a small number of models **and know how to apply them**' (our emphasis).

(c) Marketing will continue to be important in the exam; in contrast to the previous Examiner's policy, HRM and IS are also likely topics for questions.

(d) '**Reading is a critical strategic skill**. Every opportunity should be taken to access papers, articles and books where strategy is considered. When you are required to show strategic insight, **there are no right answers**. Your judgement and technique will be displayed in the way you present arguments. This, in turn, will reflect your reading' (our emphasis).

We have now had sufficient material from this Examiner to be able to make some suggestions about what you can expect. The first thing to say is that the format and feel if the exam show great continuity with the pattern established by the previous Examiner.

A second important point is that the Examiner is sometimes rather imprecise in his question requirements. A good example is question 1(c) in the December 2005 exam. A related problem is that he sometimes asks you to do things you simply cannot achieve using the information in the scenario: examples are question 3 in the December 2005 exam and question 2(a) in the December 2004 exam.

We discuss how to deal with these, and other problems of interpretation in the Top tips accompanying each answer.

One final comment we can make is that the Examiner seems particularly fond of the McKinsey 7S model of the organisation. Do not attempt to use this in all of your answers, but you may find it useful for questions that you are finding particularly difficult to get to grips with.

The Examination

It is a good idea to think about the nature of any examination before the day you sit it. You must be sure you know what the Examiner wants from you in terms of number of answers and which questions are compulsory and so on. Paper 3.5 is quite simple in this respect. You **must do** question 1 and you must answer two questions from Section B.

Note that Section A is crucial. You are highly unlikely to pass on the strength of your answer to Question 1 alone, but **you are highly likely to fail if you do not make a creditable attempt at it**.

You must have a clear view of your overall preference about the order in which you will attempt questions before you enter the exam room. This is something you must do for yourself. Many people will advise that because Question 1 is so important you should definitely answer it first. Other people find that answering a shorter question first builds their confidence, especially if it is on a topic they are confident about. Only you can decide.

However, we would advise you that **it would be very risky to leave question 1 to the end**. This is a recipe for running out of time. While there are certain to be several separate requirements, you cannot deal with them in isolation from each other; you must make sure you do not end up repeating yourself by using ideas too early, for example. So you must allow sufficient time to complete **all** the requirements. If you leave question 1 to the end, you may not manage to do this.

You do not have a lot of choice in this examination. The overall requirements and the likely nature of the questions mean that you will be examined on much of a very wide syllabus. Do not despair if you find you are probing the boundaries of your knowledge. Most of your contemporaries will be in the same boat. Make sure you cover the essentials, use common sense and experience as much as possible, relate your answers to the settings and **do not** ramble or dump theory.

The aim is not to cover pages with ink. Write concisely. This will release time for planning and checking. You **must** allow time to think.

A very important thing to remember in this exam is that there is bound to be more than one way of answering most of the questions: uniquely correct answers are uncommon in a subject like this. If you can analyse data sensibly, apply theory appropriately and reach reasonable conclusions **you will pass**.

Tackling questions

You'll improve your chances by following a step-by-step approach along the following lines.

Step 1   Read the requirement

Identify the knowledge areas being tested and see precisely what the examiner wants you to do. This will help you focus on what's important in the scenario.

Step 2   Check the mark allocation

This shows the depth of answer anticipated and helps you allocate time.

Step 3   Read the scenario/preamble

Identify which information is relevant to which part, also which data will have to be used in calculations. Be careful to select the right alternatives when you're given a choice, and to identify irrelevant information that you won't be using in the calculations.

Step 4   Plan your answer

Marshal the theoretical material that you think is relevant and relate it to the information given in the scenario. Produce a lit of points you will make and decide on a logical order to market them in.

Step 5   Write your answer

Stick carefully to the time allocation for each question, and for each part of each question.

Step 6   Read it through

Most people are very reluctant to do this but it is **very** important. You **will** find errors of grammar, spelling and fact and places were you have not been clear. Put these things right ad press on.

Gaining the easy marks

Not all questions in this exam have easy marks, but most do. Very frequently, easy marks will be found by examining the question scenario in the light of an appropriate theory or model. However, be careful: generally speaking, there are very few marks available for **explaining** those theories and models.

An important aspect of scoring well is to **state the obvious**. Do not assume that the marker will take anything for granted. If, for example, it is very clear that an organisation has neglected its cost control, say so. But do not expect marks for merely reproducing what is in the question: there must be an element of analysis or deduction supporting what you say, even if it is very simple.

Another aspect of scoring the easy marks is time management. Make sure you answer all the parts of a question: the easy marks are not all in part (a). If you are running out of time, you can glean a few marks by writing brief notes – not bullet points, but short paragraphs that demonstrate some thought.

Recent exams

Format of the paper

Section A: 1 compulsory question   60
Section B: Choice of 2 from 3 questions (20 marks each)   40
                                                                                  ———
                                                                                  100

Time allowed: 3 hours

Additional information

The Study Guide provides more detailed guidance on the syllabus.

Analysis of recent papers

The analysis below shows the topics which have been examined in the current syllabus and includes the Pilot Paper.

December 2006

Section A

1   A clothing manufacturer is facing strategic decline and is considering changes to its production and distribution methods.

       (a)   Analysis of strategy and performance over three years, utilising results data provided
       (b)   Use of strategic alliances to develop foreign markets
       (c)   Costs and benefits of continuing the existing divisional split
       (d)   Changing management style in order to improve organisational culture

Section B

2   Advantages and disadvantages of an e-business strategy and using it to support a niche business
3   Assessing the strategic and social-responsibility implications of major franchise-based product development
4   Strategic considerations and critical success factors for a newly formed manufacturing company

---

Examiner's comments were not available at the time of going to print.

This paper is Mock exam 3 in this Kit.

June 2006

Question in this Kit

Section A

1   An ice cream manufacturing and retailing company has failed twice to enter foreign   56
     markets and has now set clear strategic targets for its UK operations.

     (a)   Advantages and disadvantages of current strategies
     (b)   Achievability and compatibility of the stated strategic goals
     (c)   Impact of the stated goals on the marketing mix
     (d)   Reasons for failure of international ventures

Section B

2   Features of a business plan; advantages and disadvantages of strategic planning   5
3   Environmental analysis in the low cost air travel industry and the use of scenario
     planning   13
4   HRM: linking the plan to overall strategy and outsourcing the function   22

Examiner's comments. Using too many models lends to superficial analysis and poor answers. Using a few models well is the route to a good mark.

Once again there is evidence that answering Question 1 last can lead to unnecessary time pressure and a poor answer.

December 2005

Question in this Kit

Section A

1   A paper products manufacturing company wishes to expand further: two options,   55
     acquisition and new construction, have been identified.

     (a)   Assess strategic fit with possible acquisition target
     (b)   Steps to build a shared culture
     (c)   Advantages and disadvantages of new construction
     (d)   Integration problems

Section B

2   Adding value in a new, low cost hotel chain; use of franchising to expand   35
                                                                                            7
3   Resource based strategy and balanced score card

4   Market segmentation for a grocery e-commerce venture; strategic impact of shift to
     e-commerce.   21

Examiner's comments. There is an increasing tendency for candidates to answer their chosen Section B questions before tackling question 1. This seems to lead to unnecessary time pressure and poor marks for the compulsory question. Linking chosen theory to a question setting is a vital skill: simply explaining a model, even if relevant, will produce a weak answer.

June 2005

Question in this Kit

Section A

1   A family-owned replacement roofs and windows company has grown rapidly and   54
      seeks further expansion.

      (a)   Service performance
      (b)   Strategic evaluation
      (c)   Implementation issues and change management
      (d)   'Excellence'

Section B

2   Distribution channels for bakery goods: advantages, disadvantages and marketing   27
      mix adjustments.

3   New car sales business model: managing change and assessing staff attitudes   32

4   Corporate environmental strategy: project management to achieve commitment;
      achieving both competitive advantage and social responsibility.   19

Examiner's comments. There was evidence of time pressure, with a significant number of candidates failing to answer all parts of the questions. The compulsory case study may have contributed to this pressure as it was fairly complex and had a comprehensive financial section, which needed careful analysis.

December 2004

Question in this Kit

Section A

1   An operating company within a divisional organisation wishes to expand overseas.   51

      (a)   Evaluation of possible market entry strategies

      (b)   Discussion of the organisation's approach to strategic management

      (c)   Communication, co-ordination and control issues in global expansion

      (d)   The potential contribution of accountants to the strategic management
              process

Section B

2   Environmental analysis – factors encouraging inward investment; using quality to   44
      gain competitive advantage

3   Evaluation of outsourcing a bank's customer enquiry service; achieving competitive   33
      advantage by understanding core competences

4   Reconciling stakeholder views on new strategy; using the balanced scorecard for this   28
      purpose

Examiner's comments. As previously, some candidates relied on common sense rather than appropriate strategic models and concepts: this approach rarely produces good marks. Relatively few candidates failed to understand the scenarios or the questions but far too many signed off report format answers with their real identities. This should not be done.

BPP
LEARNING MEDIA

June 2004

Question in this Kit

Section A

1   The founder of a small, innovative ICT business is under pressure from both the   50
     demands of growth and deteriorating business conditions

     (a)   Purpose of a mission statement and its potential contribution
     (b)   Reasoned analysis of the company's situation and problems
     (c)   Assessment of founder's exit options
     (d)   Differences between consumer and business-to-business marketing

Section B

2   Situation analysis report showing the relevance of marketing; advantages of a niche   18
     strategy

3   Corporate governance issues in a company dominated by one person; role and   17
     advantages of non-executive directors

4   Role and contribution of appraisal and performance management   29

Examiner's comments. Time management and examination technique often made the difference between a pass and a fail. The number of marks available is a guide to the required extent and depth of the answer. Appearance is important in report form questions and legibility helps the marker to award marks.

December 2003

Question in this Kit

Section A

1   A UK manufacturing company is failing to make progress because of poor marketing   49
     and excessive overheads (sound familiar?). An external consultant is asked to report

     (a)   Product portfolio review
     (b)   Strategic options available and preferred strategy
     (c)   Change from technology driven to marketing driven culture
     (d)   Steps to create better new product development system

Section B

2   Conflict over graduate training in an accountancy firm: understanding and resolving
3   Marketing as an element of strategy in a financial services company   34
4   Organic growth options for globalisation; international marketing research   43

Examiner's comments. There is no single correct sequence in which to attempt questions but leaving question 1 until last seems to add time pressure for some candidates. Text messages language may be unfamiliar to markers and lead to loss of marks.

June 2003

Question in this Kit

Section A

1   The owners of a company distributing hairdressing products are seeking increased
     growth

        (a)   Situation analysis and future trends   48

        (b)   Strategy generation and assessment

        (c)   Identification of potential for decline within the business

        (d)   Analysis of past growth using the value chain.

Section B

2   Product portfolio review and benchmarking at a consumer goods company   11

3   Marketing strategy for entry into a new consumer market; strategies for competitive   25
     advantage

4   Misbehaviour by CEO of public company; promoting ethical behaviour and cultural   39
     change

> **Examiner's comments.** This paper made use of more academic models than usual and candidates who applied
> them well scored higher marks than normal. The converse was also true.
>
> Too many candidates seemed to rely on Question 1 to achieve a pass mark and seem to pay too little attention to
> the optional questions.

December 2002

Question in this Kit

Section A

1   Strategic review of manufacturing company; strategic evaluation; factors influencing   47
     success in mergers; ethical problems

Section B

2   Reasons why strategies fail; successful implementation of strategy   36

3   Manufacturing or buying in goods for resale; problems of outsourcing non-core   10
     activities

4   Polycentrism and geocentrism in international operations; factors encouraging a   42
     policy of customisation

> **Examiner's comments.** Over-reliance on clearly important areas of the syllabus leads many candidates to failure.
> The examination tests the whole syllabus, not just the core areas.
>
> Candidates should aim to analyse the numerical data with greater rigour. Calculation of a few financial ratios is not
> enough.

June 2002

Question in this Kit

Section A

1   Stakeholders' goals and objectives in a hospital; identification of strategic problems;   46
     assessment of strategic options; social responsibility in the context of health care

Section B

2   Overseas marketing; obtaining and using market intelligence   6
3   Acquisition: potential problems; integrating a new business into a group   20
4   Package holiday operations: critical success factors and performance indicators   40

Examiner's comments. Many candidates showed that they did not understand the marketing function (which is essential knowledge). Some used lists too prominently and some displayed poor breadth of syllabus knowledge.

December 2001

Question in this Kit

Section A

1   Benefits and problems of emergent strategy; performance and critical success   45
     factors; collecting strategic information; methods of growth

Section B

2   Segmentation bases, strategies for market followers
3   Organisation structure; influences and application   37
4   Undertaking overseas marketing: factors and control of overseas resources   41

Pilot paper

Section A

1   Analysis of strategic challenges; control of a decentralised conglomerate; disposal of
     a subsidiary as a strategic option

Section B

2   Launching a new professional partnership; cost-based pricing
3   Commercial priorities and ethics; performance indicators
4   Management style and organisational change

Useful websites

The websites below provide additional sources of information of relevance to your studies for *Audit and Internal Review*.

- ACCA   www.accaglobal.com
- BPP   www.bpp.com
- Financial Times   www.ft.com
- The Economist   www.economist.com
- Wharton Business School   http://knowledge.wharton.upenn.edu

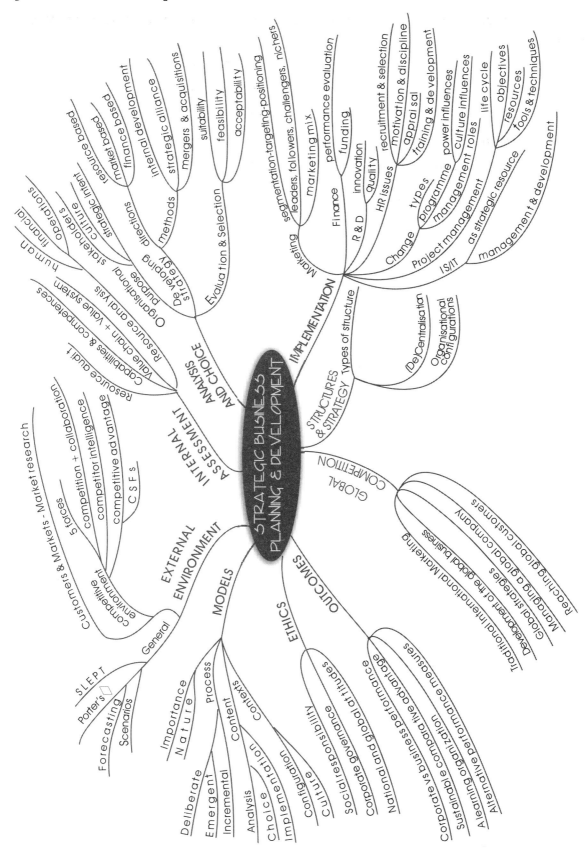

Syllabus mindmap

STRATEGIC BUSINESS PLANNING & DEVELOPMENT

INTERNAL ASSESSMENT AND CHOICE

- Organisational analysis
  - Resource and analysis
  - Value chain + value system
    - human
    - financial
    - operations
  - Capabilities & competences
  - Resource audit
- Developing strategy
  - purpose
  - stakeholders
  - strategic intent
  - culture
  - resource based
  - market based
  - finance based
  - internal development
  - strategic alliance
  - mergers & acquisitions
- Strategy methods, directions
- Evaluation & Selection
  - suitability
  - feasibility
  - acceptability

EXTERNAL ENVIRONMENT

- Customers & Markets - Market research
- 5 forces
  - competition + collaboration
  - competitor intelligence
  - competitive advantage
  - CSFs
- General
  - competitive environment
  - SLEPT
  - Porter's
  - Scenarios
  - Forecasting

MODELS

- Importance
- Nature
  - Process
  - Deliberate
  - Emergent
  - Incremental
- Content
  - Analysis
  - Contexts
  - Choice
  - Implementation
  - Configuration
  - Culture

IMPLEMENTATION

- Marketing
  - segmentation-targeting-positioning
  - leaders, followers, challengers, nichers
  - marketing mix
- Finance
  - performance evaluation
  - funding
- R & D
  - innovation
  - Quality
- HR issues
  - recruitment & selection
  - motivation & discipline
  - appraisal
  - training & development
  - power influences
  - culture influences
  - management roles
- Change
  - types
  - programme
  - management
  - life cycle
- Project management
  - as strategic resource
  - objectives
  - resources
  - tools & techniques
- IS/IT
  - management & development

STRUCTURES & STRATEGY

- Types of structure
- (De)Centralisation
- Organisational configurations

GLOBAL COMPETITION

- Development of the global business
- Traditional international Marketing
- Global strategies
- Managing a global business
- Reaching global customers

OUTCOMES

- Corporate vs business advantage
- National and global performance
- Sustainable competitive advantage
- A learning organization
- Alternative performance measures

ETHICS

- Corporate governance
- Social responsibility
- Culture and global attitudes

BPP LEARNING MEDIA

Planning your question practice

Planning your question practice

We have already stressed that question practice should be right at the centre of your revision. Whilst you will spend some time looking at your notes and Paper 3.5 Passcards, you should spend the majority of your revision time practising questions.

We recommend two ways in which you can practise questions.

- Use **BPP's question plan** to work systematically through the syllabus and attempt key and other questions on a section-by-section basis

- **Build your own exams** – attempt questions as a series of practice exams

These ways are suggestions and simply following them is no guarantee of success. You or your college may prefer an alternative but equally valid approach.

BPP's question plan

The BPP plan below requires you to devote a **minimum of 30 hours** to revision of Paper 3.5. Any time you can spend over and above this should only increase your chances of success.

Step 1   **Review your notes** and the chapter summaries in the Paper 3.5 **Passcards** for each section of the syllabus.

Step 2   **Answer the key questions** for that section. These questions have boxes round the question number in the table below and you should answer them in full. Even if you are short of time you must attempt these questions if you want to pass the exam. You should complete your answers without referring to our solutions.

Step 3   **Attempt the other questions** in that section. For some questions we have suggested that you prepare **answer plans** rather than full solutions. Planning an answer means that you should spend about 20% of the time allowance for the questions brainstorming the question and drawing up a list of points to be included in the answer.

Step 4   Attempt **Mock exams 1, 2 and 3** under strict exam conditions.

Syllabus section	2007 Passcards chapters	Questions in this Kit	Comments	Done ☑
Revision period 1				
Strategic management	1	4	This is quite a simple question but it covers some important basic concepts	☐
Models Applications	1	2	A long scenario but a very good question on a large area.	☐
	1,2	5(b)	This is an exam standard question with fairly demanding requirements.	☐
Revision period 2				
Mission	3	12(a)	A very neat exam standard part-question. Note the words used in the requirement and think about what 'explain' and 'consider' mean.	☐
Analysis scenarios	3	13	This is a very recent question and gives an idea of how the examiner's mind works. Think about the deeper aspects of environmental analysis in particular.	☐
	3	50	This is your first case study, so take it slowly. Think carefully about each part and plan it before writing it up in full. If you are at a loss as to how to start, look at the numeric data and calculate some ratios and annual changes in percentage terms. This will almost certainly give you some ideas and insights.	☐
Revision period 3				
Ethics and corporate governance	4	17	Corporate governance is a hot topic and this question covers some very important ground.	☐
		52(c)	This question is about more fundamental ethical matters that are likely to provide overtones to any question on corporate governance and managerial conduct. Make sure you take a firm line.	☐
Stakeholders	14	16	This is a good question to practice seeing more than one point of view. You may ultimately come down on the side of one particular group in such a question, but you will need to show that you have considered and understood any conflicting views where this is appropriate	☐
		40	Note form answer only. Make sure you know what critical success factors are.	☐
Revision period 4				
External environment	5	8	Applies Porter's model in a very specific way. Plan an answer and review the solution we provide.	☐
	17,18	41 (a)	A fairly simple scenario to check your understanding. Note form answer only.	☐

BPP
LEARNING MEDIA

Syllabus section	2007 Passcards chapters	Questions in this Kit	Comments	Done ☑
Revision period 5 Internal analysis and structure	6, 9	9	Once again, you should prepare a full answer, ensuring that you link your remarks closely to Wordsworth.	☐
		52	Plan the whole question – prepare full answers for part (b). Take care to answer the questions set.	☐
Revision period 6 Strategic analysis and options	7,8	48(a) 48(b)	Treat these two parts as a single question. You will need to study the scenario carefully to be able to produce a good answer, so allow yourself an extra 15 minutes reading time. Analyse the numerical data carefully for evidence. Choose a relevant model to guide your analysis of the current position.	☐
		49	Tackle this case study under exam conditions. Allow yourself 108 minutes to produce your answer, then review our solution.	☐
		14	The mathematical techniques you studied at lower levels are still examinable! Attempt the decision tree.	☐
Revision period 7 Change	11	20	The word 'change' is not mentioned in the requirements, but that is what this question is about. In part (b) avoid extensive explanation of change management models. Say what needs to be done at Apex finance.	☐
		29	Lawin's models are essential for Paper 3.5. Apply them here.	☐
Revision period 8 Operations	12	54	A good, testing question covering both strategy and operations.	☐
		33	Plan an answer and review the solution.	☐
Revision period 9 Global strategy	17, 18	43	Modes of entry is a fundamental topic in global strategy and you must be familiar with it. Part (b) is to some extent about environmental analysis.	☐
		41	Produce note form answers to these questions	☐
		42		☐
		44		☐
Revision period 10 IT	15	31	Despite being quite old, this question is very representative of the way the examiner is likely to approach the topic of IT.	☐

Syllabus section	2007 Passcards chapters	Questions in this Kit	Comments	Done ☑
Project management	10	19	This is a good question that covers project management in a way typical of the examiner.	☐
		28	Apply general skills to this specific area.	☐
Revision period 11 HRM	13	30	Recruitment and retention are important HRM topics. Make sure you find practical recommendations that are relevant to the scenario.	☐
	14	29	Notice that, unusually, it is part (a) that specifically refers to the subject organisation, while part (b) does not. Despite this, this is a good basic question to test your knowledge.	☐
		32	A rather specific but very up-to date question.	☐
Revision period 12			Attempt Mock Exam 1 in 3 hours without a break. Then take a short rest and review your answers. Remember that there are no definitive correct answers in this subject. However, there will usually be important specific matters to cover. The suggested solutions will help you here.	☐
Revision period 13			Attempt Mock Exam 2 as above.	☐
Revision period 14			Attempt Mock Exam 3 as above.	☐

Build your own exams

Having revised your notes and the BPP Passcards, you can attempt the questions in the Kit as a series of practice exams. You can organise the questions in the following ways:

- Either you can attempt complete old papers; recent papers are listed below.

	3.5							
	Jun'02	Dec'02	Jun'03	Jun'04	Dec'04	Jun'05	Dec'05	Jun'06
Section A								
1	46	47	48	50	51	54	55	56
Section B								
2	6	36	11	18	44	27	35	5
3	20	10	25	17	33	32	7	13
4	40	42	39	29	28	19	21	22

- Or you can make up practice exams, either yourself or using the mock exams that we have listed below.

	Practice exams					
	1	2	3	4	5	6
Section A						
1	49	50	51	54	55	56
Section B						
2	34	10	15	44	28	10
3	43	16	18	35	21	42
4	30	29	33	37	7	39

- Whichever practice exams you use, you must attempt **Mock exams 1, 2 and 3** at the end of your revision.

Questions

MODELS OF STRATEGIC MANAGEMENT

Questions 1 to 5 cover Models of Strategic Management, the subject of Part A of the BPP Study Text for Paper 3.5

1 Question with analysis: Bartok fuel   36 mins

Bartok Fuel is a private company run by two brothers, David and Sean Bartok. The company was founded in the 1940s by their father, Gerald, who started life with a petrol station and car repair workshop. After some years, Gerald expanded by buying a tanker and starting to distribute household fuel to customers. This part of the business has grown successfully and now has some 50 tankers and an annual turnover of £3million.

In the 1940s, the car repair business included the manufacture of car windscreens. From this grew an element of the business, called Bartok Glass, which now makes sealed glass window units for the construction industry and has a turnover of about £2 million.

During the 1950s and 1960s Gerald had purchased a number of sites from which petrol was sold. These sites are still owned by the company but are now leased to other companies and used for a variety of purposes. The original garage no longer exists, but the company still operates a car dealership and repair workshop in the centre of Woking. This part of the business started in the 1970s and for some time was fairly profitable, particularly when it was a Jaguar dealership run by Gerald's younger son, Sean. However, due to changes in the market place, the Jaguar franchise had to be sold and the business now sells Fiat and Kia cars.

The fuel distribution and glass businesses continue to be fairly profitable under the management of the older brother David, but the car business is facing hard times. The car retail business is notoriously cut-throat, with margins as low as 2-3% and very high targets set by the manufacturers. The car dealership also deals in second hand cars and this area is slightly more profitable. This division now employs about 50 people.

David is the managing director of the company and at a recent board meeting he put forward a number of proposals for improving the profitability of the car dealership and garage. One suggestion is that the site should be sold for its development potential and the car dealership brought to an end.

A further option brought up by David is the potential for entering the emerging Far East market for fuel distribution. He has recently met a Malaysian entrepreneur who was visiting the UK, who is making considerable profits in this area and is looking for investment from a new partner. David is very keen on this option and is trying to push it through.

Required

(a)   Describe the approach to strategy that Bartok Fuel appears to have had in the past.   **(4 marks)**

(b)   Could the management of Bartok Fuel adopt the rational model of strategic planning? What difficulties might they encounter?   **(10 marks)**

(c)   What factors should the Board to consider before making any decisions on the proposals to dispose of the Woking site for development and to enter the Far East fuel distribution market?   **(6 marks)**

(Total = 20 marks)

1 Question with analysis: Bartok fuel

36 mins

Origin of the business	Bartok Fuel is a private company run by two brothers, David and Sean Bartok. The company was founded in the 1940s by their father, Gerald, who started life with a **petrol station and car repair workshop**. After some
Diversification	years, Gerald expanded by **buying a tanker** and starting to distribute household fuel to customers. This part of the business has **grown successfully** and now has some 50 tankers and an annual turnover of £3million.
Organic growth	In the 1940s, the car repair business included the manufacture of car windscreens. From this grew an element of the business, called Bartok Glass, which now makes sealed glass window units for the
Market development	**construction industry** and has a turnover of about £2 million.
Fixed assets – property portfolio	During the 1950s and 1960s Gerald had purchased a number of sites from which petrol was sold. These sites are still **owned by the company** but are now leased to other companies and used for a variety of purposes. The original garage no longer exists, but the company still operates a car dealership and repair workshop in the centre of Woking. This part of the business started in the 1970s and for some time was
Up market	fairly profitable, particularly when it was a Jaguar dealership run by Gerald's younger son, Sean. However, due to changes in the market place, the **Jaguar** franchise had to be sold and the business now sells
A long way down market	**Fiat and Kia** cars.
Is it worth continuing?	The fuel distribution and glass businesses continue to be fairly profitable under the management of the older brother David, but the car business is facing hard times. The car retail business is notoriously cut-throat, with **margins as low as 2–3%** and very high targets set by the manufacturers. The car dealership also deals in second hand cars and this area is slightly more profitable. This division now employs about 50 people.
David is in charge	**David is the managing director** of the company and at a recent board meeting he put forward a number of proposals for improving the profitability of the **car dealership and garage**. One suggestion is that the site
Sean's part of the business	should be sold for its development potential and the car dealership brought to an end.
	A further option brought up by David is the potential for entering the emerging **Far East market** for fuel distribution. He has recently met a Malaysian entrepreneur who was visiting the UK, who is making considerable profits in this area and is looking for investment from a new partner. David is very keen on this option and is trying to push it through.

Initial impression – ridiculous!

Means: how have they made strategy?	*Required*
	(a) Describe the **approach to strategy** that Bartok Fuel appears to have had in the past. **(4 marks)**
Model disadvantages and scenario problems	(b) Could the management of Bartok Fuel adopt the rational model of strategic planning? What **difficulties** might they encounter? **(10 marks)**
	(c) What factors should the Board to consider before making any **decisions** on the proposals to dispose of the Woking site for development and to enter the Far East fuel distribution market? **(6 marks)**

(Total = 20 marks)

Two decisions, one easily manageable, the other requiring much more information and consideration

LEARNING MEDIA

2 Aurora Lighting plc

36 mins

Aurora Lighting plc is a company which designs, manufactures and installs lighting systems for large buildings, such as theatres, hospitals, and scientific laboratories (eg where certain wavelengths of light must be excluded to avoid damage to the experimental process). The business was founded by Dawn and Helmut Wagner in 1985. It has two activities.

(a)   Aurora designs and builds bespoke lighting systems to its customers' specifications.
(b)   Aurora manufactures standard lighting systems which can be purchased from a catalogue.

For a while, demand grew rapidly. The company's products and services were in great demand, and the company's sales revenue grew at a rate of about 20% per annum on average. Profits did not follow this trend. Whilst the company made gross margins of about 30%, net profits increased at a lower rate than sales. This was caused by several factors.

(a)   The company's expansion led it to occupy expensive new premises in north London.

(b)   Research and development costs of a new standard range of lighting equipment that came on stream just as the commercial property market collapsed.

(c)   The company has recently started to employ qualified architects to assist liaison with developers, architects' practices and contractors.

(d)   The company has had to employ more electrical engineers to cope with the demand for specialist lighting systems.

Such was the initial demand in the UK that the company neglected exports. However, Helmut was always careful to design the company's products to take German technical standards into account and some sales were made in Germany. Borealis, however, has been less in demand than the firm's bespoke services, in which products are made strictly to a client's specification.

In the early days of the company, Helmut and Dawn both felt that the firm needed a mission statement, especially as Borealis was only on the drawing board, and Helmut regarded this as the company's raison d'etre. Their mission was brief:

'Aurora will develop and market a standard range of high quality, value for money lighting equipment, employing the most advanced materials and using information technology in the product and in the design process.'

The strategic plan was first devised in 19X1. There have been some revisions: Borealis has been slower to grow than was hoped. It was hoped that a net profit margin of at least 8% would be achieved at all times. Borealis was anticipated to win 25% of the UK market by 19X7. In fact, it has only gained 10% of the market, at the moment. Competition is severe, and margins are lower than expected, but Helmut believes that the quality of the range will win through in the end.

Helmut feels that events have driven the mission off course a bit, but he still feels that once the European economies have emerged from recession Borealis should be back on course. The managers of the Borealis production line complain about lack of resources. The expansion of the manufacturing division was done at the Borealis production director's insistence.

In 19X7, Aurora was floated on the London Alternative Investment Market and subsequently went for a full listing on the Stock Exchange. The firm introduced an employee share option scheme. Dawn and Helmut have retained 51% of the shares, but wish to raise more capital: the share price has been falling recently despite the growth in profits and despite the briefings that Dawn and Helmut are happy to give investment analysts.

After they report their profits for 20X4, Helmut is dismayed to read the following in the *Financial News*.

'Shareholders can't really complain. A net profit margin of 15% is high for a firm in this sector, and Aurora's ability to spread its wings in Germany has convinced some wavering sceptics about the firm's strategy in the medium term. But doubts as to whether this results from good management or just good luck continue to depress the share price, especially as Phelps lighting system's division is muscling in on the bespoke market that Aurora has dominated until now.'

Required

(a) Does Aurora Lighting plc have a coherent approach to making strategies? **(4 marks)**

(b) With reference to appropriate models of strategic management, analyse the strategic management process in Aurora Lighting plc. **(10 marks)**

(c) What sort of goals and objectives are found in Aurora Lighting plc? How do they relate to the way in which strategy is made and managed? **(6 marks)**

(Total = 20 marks)

3 Preparation question: planning components

(a) Describe the different components of strategic planning at its corporate, tactical and operational levels, and show the relationship between these components.

(b) Distinguish between operational and non-operational goals.

(c) Briefly explain the segments into which the business environment can be analysed.

Guidance note

This question identifies the different kinds of goals, some of which can compromise the planning process.

4 Introducing strategic management

36 mins

N Ltd is a small family-controlled manufacturing company. In its 40-year history, the company has grown to the extent that it now employs 35 staff, producing a wide and diverse range of household goods and utensils. The company has increased in size from its small original base. However, it has never employed a strategic management approach for its development and has relied on operational decision-making to determine priorities. N Ltd has never gathered any information relating to its markets. In recent years, the company has experienced a reduction in turnover and profitability and is assessing how it might redress the situation.

The directors of N Ltd have now decided to introduce a strategic management approach which will assist in the selection of appropriate strategies for future development of the company.

Required

(a) Explain how strategic management differs from operational management. **(8 marks)**

(b) Discuss the cultural and organisational changes which N Ltd will need to implement in order to successfully introduce strategic management. **(12 marks)**

(Total = 20 marks)

5 Gould & King (6/06)

36 mins

David Gould set up his accounting firm, providing accounting services to small businesses, in 2001. Within three years his fee income was in excess of £100K a year and he had nearly 100 clients most of whom had been gained through word of mouth. David recognised that these small or micro businesses, typically employing ten or fewer people, were receiving less than satisfactory service from their current accountants. These accounting firms typically had between five and ten partners and operated regionally and not nationally. Evidence of poor service included limited access to their particular accountant, poor response time to clients' enquiries and failure to identify opportunities to save clients money. In addition bad advice, lack of interest in business development opportunities for the client and poor internal communication between the partners and their staff contributed to client dissatisfaction. David has deliberately kept the costs of the business down by employing three part-time accountants and relying on his wife to run the office.

David had recently met Ian King who ran a similar sized accounting firm. The personal chemistry between the two and complementary skills led to a partnership being proposed. Gould and King Associates, subject to securing the necessary funding, is to be launched in September 2006. David is to focus on the business development side of the partnership and Ian on the core services provided. Indicative of their creative thinking is David's conviction that accounting services are promoted very inadequately with little attempt to communicate with clients using the Internet. He is also convinced that there are real opportunities for the partnership to move into new areas such as providing accountancy services for property developers, both at home and abroad. Ian feels that the partnership should set up its own subsidiary in India, enjoying the benefits of much cheaper accountancy staff and avoiding the costs and complications of outsourcing their core accounting services. Ian sees fee income growing to £2 million in five years' time.

David has been asked by his bank to provide it with a business plan setting out how the partnership intends to grow and develop.

Required

(a)   Write a short report for David giving the key features that you consider to be important and that you would expect to see in the business plan for the Gould and King partnership that David has to present to his bank.

(12 marks)

There is considerable evidence that small firms are reluctant to carry out strategic planning in their businesses.

(b)   What are the advantages and disadvantages for Gould and King Associates in creating and implementing a strategic plan?

(8 marks)

(Total = 20 marks)

6 Question with analysis: Fancy Packaging (6/02)   36 mins

Eddie Lomax is the Marketing Director of The Fancy Packaging Company, a wholly owned subsidiary of the Acme Paper Company plc. Acme is a major industrially integrated European corporation comprising timber interests, pulp and paper production, as well as down-stream consumer focused activities such as publishing and paper products (paper plates, computer paper and note paper). Fancy Packaging was set up in the 1960s when conglomerates and operations in many different industries were popular. The subsidiary concentrates on the European market and produces packaging material, either paper or cardboard, focusing on the fast moving consumer goods sectors. The nature of this packaging is more decorative than protective.

The Fancy Packaging Company is now operating in a much more hostile environment. Firstly, there is increasing competition from other European suppliers, particularly those from the old Soviet bloc who currently have a lower cost base. Secondly, the demand for this decorative type of packaging is falling. There are a number of reasons for this but two stand out. There is an increasing trend to strip out frivolous packaging which adds little value. There is a growing fashion amongst some consumers to avoid conspicuous wastage and the dissipation of the world's scarce natural resources. This trend has developed as a result of the growing adverse public reaction to the increases in environmental pollution. Issues such as global warming have had a knock-on effect in alerting consumers to the dangers of resource wastage. A second reason for the decline in the demand for packaging is the increasing price competition within the fast moving consumer goods industries. Manufacturers are now looking for ways to reduce costs and not just differentiate their products. Packaging appears to be one of the areas where cost savings may be found.

Eddie Lomax believes that the potential for growth in Europe is not only limited but that the current level of sales is now threatened. He is convinced that the company must look to other non-European countries for survival. However the company has no experience in sales outside Europe and so he has approached a marketing research consultancy for guidance.

Required

(a)   Prepare a brief report to Eddie Lomax stating the key areas of information that would be of importance prior to deciding which overseas markets should be focused upon.   **(12 marks)**

(b)   Recommend a methodology for obtaining the required information by a company (Acme) which has, up to now, had little experience in marketing research.   **(8 marks)**

(Total = 20 marks)

6 Question with analysis: Fancy Packaging (6/02)   36 mins

SBU, subject to imposed targets	Eddie Lomax is the Marketing Director of The Fancy Packaging Company, a **wholly owned subsidiary** of the Acme Paper Company plc. Acme is a major industrially integrated European corporation comprising timber interests, pulp and paper production, as well as down-stream consumer focused activities such as
Less popular now	publishing and paper products (paper plates, computer paper and note paper). Fancy Packaging was set up in the 1960s when conglomerates and operations in many different industries **were popular**. The subsidiary concentrates on the European market and produces packaging material, either paper or cardboard, focusing
A very specific market	on the **fast moving consumer goods** sectors. The nature of this packaging is more decorative than protective.

Product life cycle?

A major threat – can it be met?	The Fancy Packaging Company is now operating in a much more hostile environment. Firstly, there is increasing competition from other European suppliers, particularly those from the old Soviet bloc who currently have a **lower cost base**. Secondly, the **demand for this decorative type of packaging is falling**. There are a number of reasons for this but two stand out. There is an increasing trend to strip out frivolous packaging which adds little value. There is a growing fashion amongst some consumers to avoid
Bad publicity	conspicuous wastage and the dissipation of the world's scarce natural resources. This trend has developed as a result of the growing adverse public reaction to the increases in environmental pollution. Issues such as
Fancy packaging's customers	global warming have had a knock-on effect in alerting consumers to the dangers of **resource wastage**. A second reason for the decline in the demand for packaging is the increasing price competition within the
Bargaining power of customers	**fast moving consumer goods industries**. Manufacturers are now looking for ways to **reduce costs** and not just differentiate their products. Packaging appears to be one of the areas where cost savings may be found.

Eddie Lomax believes that the potential for growth in Europe is not only limited but that the current level of sales is now threatened. He is convinced that the **company must look to other non-European countries for survival**. However the company has no experience in sales outside Europe and so he has approached a marketing research consultancy for guidance.

Seems sensible

Required

Explain environmental analysis: PEST, five forces	(a) Prepare a brief report to Eddie Lomax stating the **key areas of information** that would be of importance prior to deciding **which overseas markets** should be focused upon. **(12 marks)**

(b) Recommend a **methodology** for obtaining the required information by a company (Acme) which has, up to now, had little experience in marketing research. **(8 marks)**

(Total = 20 marks)

How to go about solving the problems of lack of information

7 Lawson Engineering (12/05)

36 mins

Joe Lawson is founder and Managing Director of Lawson Engineering, a medium sized, privately owned family business specialising in the design and manufacture of precision engineering products. Its customers are major industrial customers in the aerospace, automotive and chemical industries, many of which are globally recognised companies. Lawson prides itself on the long-term relationships it has built up with these high profile customers. The strength of these relationships is built on Lawson's worldwide reputation for engineering excellence, which has tangible recognition in its gaining prestigious international awards for product and process innovation and quality performance. Lawson Engineering is a company name well known in its chosen international markets. Its reputation has been enhanced by the awarding of a significant number of worldwide patents for the highly innovative products it has designed. This in turn reflects the commitment to recruiting highly skilled engineers, facilitating positive staff development and investing in significant research and development.

Its products command premium prices and are key to the superior performance of its customers' products. Lawson Engineering has also established long-term relationships with its main suppliers, particularly those making the exotic materials built into their advanced products. Such relationships are crucial in research and development projects, some of which take a number of years to come to fruition. Joe Lawson epitomises the 'can do' philosophy of the company, always willing to take on the complex engineering challenges presented by his demanding customers.

Lawson Engineering now faces problems caused by its own success. Its current location, premises and facilities are inadequate to allow the continued growth of the company. Joe is faced with the need to fund a new, expensive, purpose-built facility on a new industrial estate. Although successful against a number of performance criteria, Lawson Engineering's performance against traditional financial measures has been relatively modest and unlikely to impress the financial backers Joe wants to provide the necessary long-term capital.

Joe has become aware of the increasing attention paid to the intangible resources of a firm in a business. He understands that you, as a strategy consultant, can advise him on the best way to show that his business should be judged on the complete range of assets it possesses.

Required

(a)   Using models where appropriate, provide Joe with a resource analysis showing why the company's intangible resources and related capabilities should be taken into account when assessing Lawson Engineering's case for financial support. **(12 marks)**

(b)   What are the advantages and disadvantages of using a balanced scorecard to better assess the overall performance of Lawson Engineering? **(8 marks)**

(Total = 20 marks)

8 Five forces

36 mins

E, a well known cosmetics manufacturer, obtains worldwide sales for its global branded products. The directors pride themselves on having a clear understanding of E's consumer market which consists of both men and women. Its products mainly comprise deodorants, perfume, after-shave lotions, facial and body washes.

In carrying out an analysis of its competitive environment, the Marketing Director has applied Porter's Five Forces model and analysed the factors which affect E under each heading as follows.

- *Threat of entry:* Little threat as although major competitors exist, the size of E presents a large entry barrier.

- *Power of buyers:* Very important as the customer world wide have much choice from different competitors' products.

- *Power of suppliers:* Little threat as most suppliers of materials are small scale and E could easily source from other suppliers if necessary. Labour is relatively cheap in E's production facilities in developing world locations.

- *Substitute products:* There are many alternative products offered by competitors but there is little by way of a substitute for cosmetics, and therefore this poses little threat.

- *Rivalry among competitors:* There is strong competition in the cosmetics market with new products constantly being developed, and therefore this is a major threat.

The Marketing Director is reasonably confident that he has judged the impact of these competitive forces correctly as they apply to E. However, he would like some re-assurance of this. He has asked you, as Management Accountant, to provide some appropriate indicators by which the strength of the five competitive forces as they apply to E can be judged.

Required

Draft a report to the Marketing Director recommending suitable indicators which could be used to judge the strength of the five competitive forces as they apply to E. Discuss why you consider your recommendations to be appropriate. Include in your discussion consideration of whether or not you agree with his judgement regarding the impact of each force on E.

(20 marks)

9 Classics on the cheap   36 mins

Adapted from Tony James, 'Classics on the Cheap', Air UK Flagship, Issue no 45, August-September 1993, Stansted, Essex

Clive Reynard piles twenty glossy new paperbacks on the desk of his executive office. A year ago, a comparable array of similarly printed paperbacks - Austen, Hardy, Dickens etc - would have cost the reader around £150. But the books on Clive Reynard's desk retail in total for £20.00. Why?

The answer contains one of the most spectacular and audacious success stories in recent British publishing. As hardback sales shrink by around 15% a year and dozens of small firms fall victim to the recession, a publisher employing only ten full-time staff is bucking every trend by selling books by the million.

It was in June last year that Wordsworth editions, started five years earlier as a luxury book publisher, launched twelve classic paperback titles, apparently in headlong collision with market leaders, Penguin, Everyman and Oxford University Press.

Wordsworth sold two million books at £1.00 each, a phenomenal success achieved in a slump market. By the end of its first year in paperbacks, Wordsworth Editions had published nearly sixty classics, each with a minimum initial print run of 75,000. Most go almost immediately into at least one 30,000 reprint, ten of the first twelve titles sold out in a month, and they are best sellers internationally.

'We produce books for hard times,' says Reynard, head-hunted from Oxford University press and now Wordsworth's senior general editor. 'People want to read but increasingly cannot afford to spent the current £6-plus on a paperback. With our books they don't have to.'

All of which begs the question: why not?

Wordsworth's answer was to produce out-of-copyright books in huge quantities. The profit per unit is low, but there are a lot of units. The profit margin on a 1,500 page book selling for £1 is poor, but Wordsworth prove that it's there.

No one denies Wordsworth were in deep trouble two years ago. 'We began selling remainders, other people's mistakes,' remembers Michael Trayler, who started the company in 1987. A move into large colour books started promisingly but with hindsight there was too much dependence on the US market and when this suddenly went soft, the effect was calamitous.

Trayler and editorial director Marcus Clapham returned from America convinced disaster was closing in on Wordsworth unless something drastic was done. One day Mike said: 'Why don't we do classics for £1?' A crucial decision was not to tie products to the UK's price fixing scheme, the *Net Book Agreement*, but to allow shops to price as they pleased. (**Tutor's hint**. The *Net Book Agreement* is now suspended, enabling supermarkets to sell books at discount.) Despite such generosity, few retailers made concessions to Wordsworth's tight budget. W H Smith, the national book-selling chain, a major customer from the start, took between fifty and sixty per cent of every £1.

Smaller retailers are offered books in quantity for around 65p each but still fix their own profit margins. Some stores may offer six books for £5, others have been know to charge as much as £1.99 for the 1,642 page War and Peace or as little as 99p for the 951 pages of Vanity Fair. Paperback wholesalers and freelance sales reps looking for non-traditional markets which would sell a lot of books, suggested a range of supermarkets and service stations.

'If you're selling a classic book for about the price of a quality Sunday newspaper there is theoretically no limit to your outlets,' Trayler maintains. 'But without rapid turnover, you're dead.' A shoestring philosophy was essential from the start. Trayler vetoed an advertising budget: 'When you're selling a book at £1 that £1 does the advertising for you.' Staffing was kept to a minimum. Wordsworth's head office is above a shop in Ware, Herts, and executive staff are expected to travel economy class, answer their own phones and type their own letters.

'Our secret is that we're not greedy,' Reynard says. 'This is reflected in the price of our books. We're often asked why we don't double the price to £2 and make a lot more money. The danger is that someone would then come in and undercut us. At the moment no one can produce books any cheaper than we do. It simply wouldn't be worth the effort.'

Cheap or not, titles wouldn't sell unless the quality was good. Most of the books are printed and bound in Britain and the text is not abridged. But it is the ingenious legal manipulation of the copyright laws which keeps Wordsworth editions alive and viable. 'We give daily thanks for the two words 'public domain',' Trayler says.

In most countries, copyright expires fifty years after an author's death, and the work moves into the public domain, anyone can reproduce it for nothing. 'Selling books for £1 we simply could not afford an author's royalty,' says Reynard. 'When you are dealing with margins like ours there is a magnifying effect which would transform, say, 1p royalty per copy into an enormous percentage of our unit cost.' 'We don't see ourselves in direct competition with Penguin Classics or Oxford University Press,' says Reynard. 'Our editions are not for schools and universities but for people who wish to read the classics inexpensively.'

Required

(a)   Describe Wordsworth's *current* competitive strategy.   **(8 marks)**

(b)   Undertake a value chain analysis and identify those aspects of Wordsworth's organisation which underpin its success.   **(12 marks)**

(Total = 20 marks)

10 Question with answer plan: Grow or buy? (12/02)   36 mins

Mark Roberts is the owner of Greenfield Nurseries, a company specialising in growing plants for sale to garden centres and to specialist garden designers. With the growth in home ownership and an increase in leisure time this sector of the economy has seemed recession-proof. The company has grown over the past ten years and with 30 employees and several glasshouses it has a turnover of almost £1 million. The company is located on one relatively large site near to a rapidly expanding urban area. There is currently within the site no physical room for expansion. If the company is to increase its profits as a garden nursery it must either acquire additional land for growing plants or it must direct more of its sales to the ultimate user (the general public) away from sales to other intermediaries (the garden centres) and so obtain higher margins.

Mark is annoyed when he sees garden centres putting large margins on his products for re-sale. Why are these profits not coming to Greenfield Nurseries he wonders? He is now contemplating re-focusing his activities on selling plants and not producing them. It has been suggested that he turns his growing areas into a garden centre. He also should buy from other specialist nurseries, transforming his glass house space into selling areas. There is a large market nearby, with several new housing developments, all generating a huge demand for horticultural products. Mark has read that the further one moves downstream in the business chain – into dealing directly with the consumer – the greater is the profit margin. He is very tempted by this strategy, but he is not fully convinced of the wisdom of such a move.

Required

(a) Examine the arguments that may be used to support or reject such a 'buy instead of grow' strategy for Greenfield Nurseries. **(13 marks)**

(b) 'Outsourcing' has become a popular strategy for many companies in attempting to reduce their commitment to non-core activities. Identify the main management problems such a policy might generate. **(7 marks)**

(Total = 20 marks)

11 Question with student answer: McGeorge Holdings (6/03)
36 mins

McGeorge Holdings plc is a large, international consumer goods company specializing in household cleaning products and toiletries. It has many manufacturing and sales facilities throughout the world. Over several years it has offered an increasingly wide range of products appealing to differing market segments based on both socio-demographic and geographic criteria. However this product spread has not only resulted in increased sales volume but production, marketing and distribution costs have also increased disproportionately. McGeorge's costs are now about 20% higher than those of its nearest competitors. In such a competitive market it is difficult to pass on these extra costs to the customer.

In order to regain a competitive position Adrian Reed, the Managing Director of McGeorge Holdings, has been advised to reduce the range of products and the product lines. Advisors have suggested that a cut back in the product mix by about 20% could increase profits by at least 40%. Reed is keen to implement such a product divestment strategy but he fears that this cutting back could alienate customers. He needs to know which products need to be removed and which products are important to the survival of the company. He is unhappy about the overall performance of his company's activities. Benchmarking has been recommended as a method of assessing how his company's performance compares with that of his competitors.

Required

(a) Using appropriate analytical models discuss how Adrian Reed might select the products to be removed from the portfolio as part of his product divestment strategy. **(10 marks)**

(b) Examine how benchmarking can be carried out and discuss its limitations. **(10 marks)**

(Total = 20 marks)

53

12 KPG systems

36 mins

KPG systems was set up 10 years ago by its owner, a computer specialist, Andy Rowe. Andy is an entrepreneur with a high degree of technical ability and no fear of taking risks in emerging high-tech markets. In the last 10 years the business has grown from Andy's original ideas to one employing 100 people. KPG Systems provides network management systems to large international companies. The approach of the business, which has appealed to potential customers, is to recognise that no two information systems are the same and to customise its products and service to meet their individual needs. As an adjunct to providing these systems, technical support has become another key business element, although there have been some problems with providing a national network of service support.

KPG systems is a very small player in this market and its success has been due to Andy Rowe's drive, initiative and risk taking. One particular problem that has been noted is the lack of creative marketing strategies and plans compared to the heavy investment of its largely much larger competitors in market, product and competitor research. This has resulted in problems with suppliers, as KPG has sometimes found it difficult to predict sales accurately and therefore has had disruption to its manufacturing due to lack of components.

A further problem facing all players in this market has been the start of a major global downturn in the economy, which has meant fewer orders being placed by large companies and pressure being put on the business by its providers of finance.

The business is still run on a day-to-day basis by Andy but there are now various functional departments in operation, including manufacturing; sales and marketing; research and development; and administration. Andy is now at the point of not really knowing where the business is going in the future.

Required

(a)   Explain to Andy the purpose of a mission statement and consider how a mission statement could be of use to KPG even at this late stage of the business development.   **(10 marks)**

(b)   Use an appropriate model to analyse the current position of KPG systems.   **(10 marks)**

(Total = 20 marks)

13 Airtite (6/06)

36 mins

Airtite was set up in 2000 as a low cost airline operating from a number of regional airports in Europe. Using these less popular airports was a much cheaper alternative to the major city airports and supported Airtite's low cost service, modelled on existing low cost competitors. These providers had effectively transformed air travel in Europe and, in so doing, contributed to an unparalleled expansion in airline travel by both business and leisure passengers. Airtite used one type of aircraft, tightly controlled staffing levels and costs, relied entirely on online bookings and achieved high levels of capacity utilisation and punctuality. Its route network had grown each year and included new routes to some of the 15 countries that had joined the EU in 2004. Airtite's founder and Chief Executive, John Sykes, was an aggressive businessman ever willing to challenge governments and competitors wherever they impeded his airline and looking to generate positive publicity whenever possible.

John is now looking to develop a strategy which will secure Airtite's growth and development over the next 10 years. He can see a number of environmental trends emerging which could significantly affect the success or otherwise of any developed strategy. 2006 had seen fuel costs continue to rise reflecting the continuing uncertainty over global fuel supplies. Fuel costs currently account for 25% of Airtite's operating costs. Conversely, the improving efficiency of aircraft engines and the next generation of larger aircraft are increasing the operating efficiency of newer aircraft and reducing harmful emissions. Concern with fuel also extends to pollution effects on global warming and climate change. Co-ordinated global action on aircraft emissions cannot be ruled out, either in the form of higher taxes on pollution or limits on the growth in air travel. On the positive side European governments are anxious to continue to support increased competition in air travel and to encourage low cost operators competing against the over-staffed and loss-making national flag carriers.

The signals for future passenger demand are also confused. Much of the increased demand for low cost air travel to date has come from increased leisure travel by families and retired people. However families are predicted to become smaller and the population increasingly aged. In addition there are concerns over the ability of countries to support the increasing number of one-parent families with limited incomes and an ageing population dependent on state pensions. There is a distinct possibility of the retirement age being increased and governments demanding a higher level of personal contribution towards an individual's retirement pension. Such a change will have a significant impact on an individual's disposable income and with people working longer reduce the numbers able to enjoy leisure travel.

Finally, air travel will continue to reflect global economic activity and associated economic booms and slumps together with global political instability in the shape of wars, terrorism and natural disasters.

John is uncertain as to how to take account of these conflicting trends in the development of Airtite's 10-year strategy and has asked for your advice.

Required

(a)   Using models where appropriate, provide John with an environmental analysis of the conditions affecting the low cost air travel industry. **(12 marks)**

(b)   Explain how the process of developing scenarios might help John better understand the macro-environmental factors influencing Airtite's future strategy. **(8 marks)**

(Total = 20 marks)

14 Pharmia plc   36 mins

Pharmia plc is a drugs manufacturing company. It is operating in an intensively competitive market and prices are being forced down all over the world.

To maintain its position, Pharmia plc utilises the concept of the product portfolio. Currently, there are 34 new products in the portfolio, at various stages of development. Pharmia plc cannot predict if any of these will become a major product. However, its belief is that 'There are a number of runners in the race and the more you have the greater the chance there is of picking a winner'.

The company has also stated that it is a 'Research and Development (R&D) driven company'. Therefore Pharmia plc always tries to ensure that there is adequate investment in R&D. The other major aspect of its corporate strategy is a belief in aggressive marketing, occasioned by the circumstances of the global market.

A product manager of Pharmia plc has been unexpectedly given £5 million extra funding and has the following options available.

(i)   Tyrix is a drug in the early stages of development. If £5 million is invested now, it will reduce the time required before the drug is ready to be sold.

(ii)   Medvac has been successfully introduced into the market. It is having to compete against two rival products. An investment of £5 million would pay for an advertising campaign which it is thought would increase its market share.

(iii)   Sonprex is a mature product and is probably going to be superseded in the near future. An investment of £5 million would enable it to be repackaged and allow some promotional activities to be undertaken.

The following information has been provided by the marketing department.

Investment	Product	Outcome	Probability	Discounted payoff £ million
£5m	Tyrix	Success	3%	150
		Failure	97%	Nil
£5m	Medvac	Market share		
		+30%	1/6	48
		+15%	1/3	27
		+10%	1/2	(10)
£5m	Sonprex	Success	1	14

The options are mutually exclusive and must be undertaken completely or not at all. The payoffs are calculated before the cost of the investment.

Required

(a)   Present the expected values of the outcomes of the three options in the form of a decision tree.   **(6 marks)**

(b)   Evaluate the appropriateness of the use of expected values and subjective probabilities for this decision.

(6 marks)

(c)   Advise the product manager as to which drug should receive the investment.   **(8 marks)**

(Total = 20 marks)

15 Qualispecs   36 mins

Qualispecs has a reputation for quality, traditional products. It has a group of optician shops, both rented and owned, from which it sells its spectacles. Recently, it has suffered intense competition and eroding customer loyalty, but a new chief executive has joined from one of its major rivals Fastglass.

Fastglass is capturing Qualispecs' market through partnership with a high-street shopping group. These shops install mini-labs in which prescriptions for spectacles are dispensed within an hour. Some competitors have successfully experimented with designer frames and sunglasses. Others have reduced costs through new computer-aided production methods.

Qualispecs has continued to operate as it always has, letting the product 'speak for itself' and failing to utilise advances in technology. Although production costs remain high, Qualispecs is financially secure and has large cash reserves. Fortunately, the country's most popular sports star recently received a prestigious international award wearing a pair of Qualispecs' spectacles.

The new Chief Executive has established as a priority the need for improved financial performance. Following a review she discovers that:

(i)   targets are set centrally and shops report monthly. Site profitability varies enormously, and fixed costs are high in shopping malls;

(ii)   shops exercise no control over job roles, working conditions, and pay rates;

(iii)   individual staff pay is increased annually according to a pre-determined pay scale.

Everyone also receives a small one-off payment based on group financial performance.

Market analysts predict a slowdown in the national economy but feel that consumer spending will continue to increase, particularly among 18-30 year olds.

Required

(a) Produce a corporate appraisal of Qualispecs, taking account of internal and external factors, and discuss the key strategic challenges facing the company. **(12 marks)**

(b) Corporate appraisal offers a 'snapshot' of the present. In order to focus on the future, there is a need to develop realistic policies and programmes. Recommend, with reasons, strategies from your appraisal that would enable Qualispecs to build on its past success. **(8 marks)**

(Total = 20 marks)

16 Question with answer plan: Digwell 36 mins

Eastborough is a large region with a rugged, beautiful coastline where rare birds have recently settled on undisturbed cliffs. Since mining ceased 150 years ago, its main industries have been agriculture and fishing. However, today, many communities in Eastborough suffer high unemployment. Government initiatives for regeneration through tourism have met with little success as the area has poor road networks, unsightly derelict buildings and dirty beaches. Digwell Explorations, a listed company, has a reputation for maximizing shareholder returns and has discovered substantial tin reserves in Eastborough. With new technology, mining could be profitable, provide jobs and boost the economy. A number of interest and pressure groups have, however, been vocal in opposing the scheme.

Digwell Explorations, after much lobbying, has just received government permission to undertake mining. It could face difficulties in proceeding because of the likely activity of a group called the Eastborough Protection Alliance. This group includes wildlife protection representatives, villagers worried about the potential increase in traffic congestion and noise, environmentalists, and anti-capitalism groups.

Required

(a) Discuss the ethical issues that should have been considered by the government when granting permission for mining to go ahead. Explain the conflicts between the main stakeholder groups. **(10 marks)**

(b) By use of some (mapping) framework, analyse how the interest and power of pressure and stakeholder groups can be understood. Based on this analysis, identify how Digwell Explorations might respond to these groups. **(10 marks)**

(Total = 20 marks)

17 MegaMart (6/04) 36 mins

MegaMart plc is a medium sized retailer of fashion goods with some 200 outlets spread throughout the UK. A publicly quoted company on the London Stock Market, it has pursued a growth strategy based on the aggressive acquisition of a number of smaller retail groups. This growth has gone down well with shareholders, but a significant slowdown in retail sales has resulted in falling profits, dividends and, as a consequence, its share price. MegaMart had been the creation of one man, Rex Lord, a high profile entrepreneur, convinced that his unique experience of the retail business gained through a lifetime working in the sector was sufficient to guide the company through its current misfortunes. His dominance of the company was secured through his role as both Chairman and Chief Executive of the company. His control of his board of directors was almost total and his style of management such that his decisions were rarely challenged at board level. He felt no need for any non-executive directors drawn from outside the company to be on the board. Shareholders were already asking questions on his exuberant lifestyle and lavish entertainment, at company expense, which regularly made the headlines in the popular press. Rex's high profile personal life also was regularly exposed to public scrutiny and media attention.

As a result of the downturn in the company's fortunes some of his acquisitions have been looked at more closely and there are, as yet, unsubstantiated claims that MegaMart's share price had been maintained through premature disclosure of proposed acquisitions and evidence of insider trading. Rex had amassed a personal fortune through the acquisitions, share options and above average performance related bonuses, which had on occasion been questioned at the Shareholders' Annual General Meeting. His idiosyncratic and arrogant style of management had been associated with a reluctance to accept criticism from any quarter and to pay little attention to communicating with shareholders.

Recently, there has been concern expressed in the financial press that the auditors appointed by MegaMart, some twenty years ago, were also providing consultancy services on his acquisition strategy and on methods used to finance the deals.

Required

(a)   What corporate governance issues are raised by the management style of Rex Lord?   **(12 marks)**

(b)   Rex Lord has consistently resisted the appointment of independent, non-executive directors to the board of MegaMart plc. What advantages might the company gain through the appointment of such directors?

(8 marks)

(Total = 20 marks)

18 Salt and Soap (6/04)   36 mins

David Kirk is the recently appointed Sales and Marketing Director of the Salt and Soap Company, a medium-sized business supplying salt and soap products to the major supermarket chains operating in the UK. Salt was bought in bulk and then repackaged into convenient packet sizes using the supermarket's own brand. On the soap side, the company manufactured a range of cleaning materials, including soda crystals and soap flakes, with, again, the majority of its sales coming from supplying the supermarkets with their own label products. The use of soda and soap as 'natural' cleaning materials was now an insignificant part of the UK market for detergents and cleansers dominated by global manufacturers with powerful brand names.

The company's reliance on the supermarket majors was now causing some problems. The power of the supermarkets was such that 70% of the company's products were now for own label brands. The supermarkets were looking to drive costs down and impose price cuts on suppliers such as Salt and Soap. There was little opportunity to add to the product range supplied and one of their major supermarket customers was looking to reduce its cleaning product range by 15%. On the positive side, Salt and Soap now had a virtual monopoly of 'natural' cleaning products in the shape of soap flakes and soda crystals. These cleansing products were environmentally friendly, as they did not cause disposal and other problems associated with household detergents. Soda based products could also be used as safe disinfecting agents in 'commercial catering' where hygiene was of paramount importance; and also in gardens to clean concrete slabs, ponds and ornaments. David was aware that household users were buying these products from hardware stores and garden centres and he could access these new markets and uses through specialist wholesalers and thus reduce Salt and Soda's heavy dependence on own label supermarket customers.

David has commissioned you as a marketing consultant to assess the relevance of marketing to a small company heavily dependent on a small number of large retail customers.

Required

(a)   Provide David with a brief report using appropriate analytical tools assessing Salt and Soap's current position and showing the relevance of marketing to the company.   **(12 marks)**

(b)   What are the advantages of Salt and Soap becoming a 'niche player' in the new markets it is looking to develop?   **(8 marks)**

(Total = 20 marks)

19 Environmental strategy (6/05)

36 mins

Graham Smith is Operations Director of Catering Food Services (CFS) a £1·5 billion UK based distributor of foods to professional catering organisations. It has 30 trading units spread across the country from which it can supply a complete range of fresh, chilled and frozen food products. Its customers range from major fast food chains, catering services for the armed forces down to individual restaurants and cafes. Wholesale food distribution is very much a price driven service, in which it is very difficult to differentiate CFS's service from its competitors.

Graham is very aware of the Government's growing interest in promoting good corporate environmental practices and encouraging companies to achieve the international quality standard for environmentally responsible operations. CFS operates a fleet of 1,000 lorries and each lorry produces the equivalent of its own weight in pollutants over the course of a year without the installation of expensive pollution control systems. Graham is also aware that his larger customers are looking to their distributors to become more environmentally responsible and the 'greening' of their supply chain is becoming a real issue. Unfortunately his concern with developing a company-wide environmental management strategy is not shared by his fellow managers responsible for the key distribution functions including purchasing, logistics, warehousing and transportation. They argued that time spent on corporate responsibility issues was time wasted and simply added to costs.

Graham has decided to propose the appointment of a project manager to develop and implement a company environmental strategy including the achievement of the international quality standard. The person appointed must have the necessary project management skills to see the project through to successful conclusion.

You have been appointed project manager for CFS's 'environmentally aware' project.

Required

(a) What are the key project management skills that are necessary in achieving company-wide commitment in CFS to achieve the desired environmental strategy? **(15 marks)**

(b) How could pursuing a corporate environmental strategy both add to CFS's competitive advantage and be socially responsible? **(5 marks)**

(Total = 20 marks)

20 Question with analysis: Apex culture (6/02)   36 mins

Carol Brindle is the Managing Director of Apex Finance Ltd, a company specialising in financial services. The company has thirty offices in different geographic locations within the United Kingdom. The company acts for a variety of local businesses in the preparation of accounts and managing the raising of finance for capital investment and it has recently become involved in helping to provide venture capital. These offices also offer tax planning and investment advice to the general public. The culture of the company is rather aggressive and most of the staff are young, ambitious and recently qualified. There is a strong tendency towards centralisation with procedures and policies being imposed from a central management function. The company sought not only to standardise work outputs but also the working practices within its operations, leaving little discretion to its employees.

Recently, in pursuing a strategy of growth, Apex has bought a group of companies, offering similar types of services but in geographic areas where Apex is not represented. The style of management within the purchased group is dissimilar to that operating within Apex. In the acquired group the culture is more relaxed, with staff encouraged to manage and motivate themselves. Most staff have considerable experience and can be trusted to use their own initiative. Carol is naturally concerned that the acquisition might not be successfully integrated..

Required

(a)   Identify the major problems which may occur if this acquisition is not managed carefully.   **(10 marks)**

(b)   Assess the factors which need to be taken into consideration if the new acquisition is to be successfully incorporated into the group.   **(10 marks)**

(Total = 20 marks)

20 Question with analysis: Apex culture (6/02)   36 mins

Highly technical; great competence required; subject to regulation

Very similar to the subjects of Herzberg's original study: highly qualified professionals

Consider all aspects of the business, not just the staff

Change management

Carol Brindle is the Managing Director of Apex Finance Ltd, a company specialising in financial services. The company has thirty offices in different geographic locations within the United Kingdom. The company acts for a variety of local businesses in the **preparation of accounts** and managing the **raising of finance** for capital investment and it has recently become involved in helping to provide **venture capital**. These offices also offer **tax planning** and **investment advice** to the general public. The **culture of the company is rather aggressive** and most of the staff are **young, ambitious and recently qualified**. There is a strong tendency towards centralisation with procedures and policies being imposed from a central management function. The company sought not only to **standardise work outputs** but also the **working practices** within its operations, leaving little discretion to its employees.

Because of the need for accuracy and consistency

Synergy

Recently, in pursuing a strategy of growth, Apex has bought a group of companies, offering similar types of services but in **geographic areas where Apex is not represented**. The style of management within the purchased group is dissimilar to that operating within Apex. In the acquired group **the culture is more relaxed**, with staff encouraged to manage and motivate themselves. Most staff have **considerable experience and can be trusted to use their own initiative**. Carol is naturally concerned that the **acquisition might not be successfully integrated**.

Contrast

Many mergers fail over culture

Required

(a)   Identify the **major problems** which may occur if this acquisition is not managed carefully. **(10 marks)**

(b)   Assess the **factors which need to be taken into consideration** if the new acquisition is to be successfully incorporated into the group.

(10 marks)

(Total = 20 marks)

21 Supaserve (12/05)   36 mins

Chris Jones is Managing Director of Supaserve, a medium-sized supermarket chain faced with intense competition from larger competitors in their core food and drink markets. They are also finding it hard to respond to these competitors moving into the sale of clothing and household goods. Supaserve has a reputation for friendly customer care and is looking at the feasibility of introducing an online shopping service, from which customers can order goods from the comfort of their home and have them delivered, for a small charge, to their home.

Chris recognises that the move to develop an online shopping service will require significant investment in new technology and support systems. He hopes a significant proportion of existing and most importantly, new customers, will be attracted to the new service.

Required

(a)   What bases for segmenting this new market would you recommend and what criteria will help determine whether this segment is sufficiently attractive to commit to the necessary investment?   **(10 marks)**

(b)   Assess the likely strategic impact of the new customer delivery system on Supaserve's activities and its ability to differentiate itself from its competitors.   **(10 marks)**

(Total = 20 marks)

22 Global Imaging (6/06)   36 mins

Global Imaging is a fast growing high tech company with some 100 employees which aims to double in size over the next three years. The company was set up as a spin out company by two research professors from a major university hospital who now act as joint managing directors. They are likely to leave the company once the growth objective is achieved.

Global Imaging's products are sophisticated imaging devices facing a growing demand from the defence and health industries. These two markets are very different in terms of customer requirements but share a related technology. Over 90% of sales are from exports and the current strategic plan anticipates a foreign manufacturing plant being set up during the existing three-year strategic plan. Current management positions are largely filled by staff who joined in the early years of the company and reflect the heavy reliance on research and development to generate the products to grow the business. Further growth will require additional staff in all parts of the business, particularly in manufacturing and sales and marketing.

Paul Simpson, HR manager at Global Imaging is annoyed. This stems from the fact that HR is the one management function not involved in the strategic planning process shaping the future growth and direction of the company. He feels trapped in a role traditionally given to HR specialists, that of simply reacting to the staffing needs brought about by strategic decisions taken by other parts of the business. He feels even more threatened by one of the joint managing directors arguing that HR issues should be the responsibility of the line managers and not a specialist HR staff function. Even worse, Paul has become aware of the increasing number of companies looking to outsource some or all of their HR activities.

Paul wants to develop a convincing case why HR should not only be retained as a core function in Global Imaging's activities, but also be directly involved in the development of the current growth strategy.

Required

Paul has asked you to prepare a short report to present to Global Imaging's board of directors:

(a)   Write a short report for Paul Simpson on the way a Human Resource Plan could link effectively with Global Imaging's growth strategy.   **(12 marks)**

(b)   What advantages and disadvantages might result from outsourcing Global Imaging's HR function?

(8 marks)

(Total = 20 marks)

23 IT project (M&S, 6/98, amended)   36 mins

The organisation for which you work is about to evaluate a proposal for a major upgrade in its information technology support for office administration staff. Currently the work of these staff is fragmented, lacking integration and cohesion. The proposed upgrade will enable information transfer to be more readily achieved and should improve both the efficiency and effectiveness of the office administration. The suggestion is for each of the fifty staff members to have a high specification personal computer (PC) with associated software (word processing, spreadsheets etc.). All PCs will be linked into a local area network comprising several fileservers to handle shared applications, plus network links into Internet services. At the present time about thirty staff have access to PCs of a variety of types and specifications which are running a number of stand-alone applications. There is limited access on some machines to networked shared services. The capital cost of this proposed upgrade is estimated to be in the region of £250,000.

The Finance Director has asked you to take charge of the proposed project. He wishes the project to focus on two main issues: the cost justification of the expenditure in relation to competing IT project proposals and, if a go-ahead is given, and the achievement of a smooth transition in moving staff and applications to the new office support system. However, he is worried that the review might concentrate exclusively on monetary considerations, such as discounted cash flow, and he feels that this approach would be both simplistic and unsuitable.

Required

(a)   The new office support system is believed to be technically feasible but has not yet been cost justified. Explain how you might undertake a non-technical evaluation of the proposed investment of £250,000 in office information technology. Your evaluation should cover the treatment of both financial and non-financial criteria.   **(12 marks)**

(b)   Outline an approach which you might propose to adopt in planning for and executing an implementation of the new office support system.   **(8 marks)**

(Total = 20 marks)

24 Westport University (M&S, 6/99, amended)   36 mins

Westport University is a medium-sized educational institution, having achieved university status six years ago. It is located in a large city with a considerable commercial and manufacturing infrastructure. The university has tended to concentrate on vocational courses such as engineering, science and business and management studies. Because of its relative newness it is not a popular university having not yet acquired a strong academic reputation. With a recent growth in university places available, coupled with a small decline in student demand, Westport is currently unable to operate at full capacity. In order to avoid redundancies the university is looking for alternative courses to help them generate both income and students. Bill Loftus is the commercial manager for the business and finance faculty. He recognises that the faculty has a reasonably strong reputation for its degree programmes including an accountancy degree. However this is a full-time programme at undergraduate level. There are currently no postgraduate degrees in accountancy nor any facility for studying professional accountancy qualifications.

Bill realises that accountancy is growing in popularity and that to practice as an accountant and to progress in the profession one has to be a member of one of the professional accountancy bodies. However he also recognises that much of this training is pursued on a part-time basis by students who are already working within a financial environment. Although this area appears to be one with potential, the head of the faculty is unwilling to put resources into offering professional accountancy training until more research has been carried out.

Required

Acting in the position of Bill Loftus:

(a)   Present a report to the head of faculty, detailing what research into the professional accountancy training market needs to be carried out, and commenting on the method of research to be used.   **(10 marks)**

(b)   Assuming that the university approves the venture to develop professional accountancy training, identify the main marketing strategies that could be used to attract students to the programmes.   **(10 marks)**

(Total = 20 marks)

25 Ashkol Furniture (6/03)   36 mins

Salim Brommer is the Marketing Director of Ashkol Furniture Supplies, a medium-sized company which specializes in manufacturing office furniture. The company makes its products in India, so benefiting from relatively low labour costs. However it has recently experienced intense competition from suppliers who have even lower cost bases. Salim has decided that his company will benefit if he focuses on those customers who can provide higher profit margins.

He has decided to target domestic customers in Europe. Increasingly private households, particularly those with computers, are converting spare rooms into office-style areas. Additionally there has been a noticeable trend towards working from home. This saves employers incurring the costs of office provision, and also employees save on travel and can also work at times convenient to themselves. However Ashkol has no experience of dealing with these types of customer. The company now needs to develop a suitable marketing strategy to succeed in this new area and maintain a sustainable competitive advantage.

Required

(a)   Using a suitable model of your choice develop a marketing approach which Salim might use to enter this new market.   **(12 marks)**

(b)   Discuss how strategies can be used to create and sustain competitive advantage.   **(8 marks)**

(Total = 20 marks)

26 Smalltown   36 mins

The Smalltown Horticulture Society is a not-for-profit organisation with 300 members. It is owned by its members who each pay an annual subscription of £7 a year, and it has £12,000 in the bank. It has no debts and its only assets are a typewriter and some stationery. It rents its premises. The society's purpose is to 'promote a greater understanding of Horticulture'.

The society has held an annual flower show since 1905. Until 1970 the show was very well supported. It was held on the Wednesday and Thursday of the final week in September and attracted an attendance of around 8,000 people. Such a level of attendance enabled the society to cover the costs of the show and also to make a surplus. It used the surplus to finance its other activities, for instance providing free seeds to local elderly people.

Since 1970 the attendances have declined, and since 1990 the show has been put on to a single date basis as the admission receipts were insufficient to pay for the hire of the premises for two days. However attendances have further continued to decline and the latest show was 'very disappointing' (Society Chairman).

Following this, the chairman made a statement in which he called for 'the folk of Smalltown to become involved with the show like they used to be'. He observed that at the same time as the Smalltown show was being held, another society held a much bigger show in a town some sixty miles away. This show made a profit and was very well attended. Some Smalltown residents travelled to the other show but did not attend the Smalltown one.

The chairman concluded that 'unless we get better support in future, we will not be able to continue with the show and the people of Smalltown will lose out'.

Required

(a) Provide a brief report for the members of the Smalltown Horticulture Society, which comments on the extent to which the broad principles of the marketing concept have been utilised by the Society. **(8 marks)**

(b) Recommend strategies which would enable the society to fulfil its purpose in the future. Your recommendations should include a consideration of the role of market research for the society and be drafted to respect the culture of the society. **(12 marks)**

(Total = 20 marks)

27 Helen's Cakes (6/05)   36 mins

Helen Bradshaw, a recent graduate with a degree in catering management, has spotted a market opportunity during her first job with a large supermarket chain. She knows there is a growing market for distinctive, quality cakes in the bakery sections of the supermarket chains, as well as in supplying independent individual premium cake shops, and also for catering wholesalers supplying restaurants and hotels.

Helen is very determined to set up her own business under the brand name of 'Helen's Cakes', and has bought some equipment – industrial food mixers, ovens, cake moulds – and also rented a small industrial unit to make the cakes. Helen has created three sets of recipes – one for the premium cake shop market, one for the supermarkets and one for the catering wholesalers but is uncertain which market to enter first. Each channel of distribution offers a different set of challenges. The premium cake shop market consists of a large number of independent cake shops spread through the region, each looking for daily deliveries, a wide product range and low volumes. The supermarkets are demanding good quality, competitive prices and early development of a product range under their own brand name. The catering wholesalers require large volumes, medium quality and low prices.

Helen has learnt that you are a consultant specialising in start-up enterprises and is looking to you for advice.

Required

(a) Acting as a consultant, prepare a short report for Helen advising her on the advantages and disadvantages each channel offers and the implications for a successful start-up. **(12 marks)**

(b) How might the marketing mix vary between the three channels Helen is considering using? **(8 marks)**

(Total = 20 marks)

28 Lakeside Business School (12/04)   36 mins

The senior management team at Lakeside Business School is facing a new challenge. As one of the major faculties within Lakeside University, it has a wide undergraduate and postgraduate portfolio and as one of the new universities it is anxious to improve its position in the national higher education league tables. The problem concerns electronic learning and the challenge it presents to both staff and students. Electronic or e-learning is being encouraged by a number of factors affecting the education environment. The Business School is tasked with increasing its student numbers while, at the same time, facing reduced funding from central government to support such expansion. E-learning, which reduces face-to-face contact with lecturers, offers a means of using staff more effectively. As a result, it increases the independent learning time available to students and provides much more flexibility to the students as to when they choose to learn.

There are a number of disadvantages however. The design and maintenance of e-learning provision requires considerable investment in electronic hardware and software, technician support and academic staff time in converting their material into electronically accessible modules. Commitment to, and conviction about the benefits of e-learning is far from total for both staff and students. The university has committed significant funds to staff development for e-learning, but only the more computer literate members of staff have taken advantage of the courses available. As a consequence, the impact of e-learning is very varied – some modules are at the cutting edge, while others remain largely taught by traditional methods. Student representatives at course committee meetings have already commented critically on this variation. Students themselves vary considerably in their familiarity with and use of electronic learning. Attendance at traditional lectures has dropped significantly as a result of the lecture material being easily accessible on the relevant module's website.

The Business School's senior management team is being pressed by the university authorities to commit to the university's e-learning system. However, they are very wary of imposing e-learning on their staff in the face of known resistance. The impression given to current and prospective students, in an increasingly competitive and international marketplace, is far from impressive. The current partial and unsystematic use of e-learning is becoming a significant competitive disadvantage.

Required

(a)   What approaches could the senior management team use to reconcile the different stakeholders and their views of e-learning?   **(10 marks)**

(b)   What advantages and disadvantages could the balanced scorecard bring to resolving the problem?

(10 marks)

(Total = 20 marks)

29 Connie Head (6/04)   36 mins

Connie Head was the recently appointed HR manager in a medium sized accounting firm. Her appointment was a belated recognition by the senior partners of the firm that their ambitious corporate growth goals were linked to the performance of the individual business units and the accountants working in those units. Connie was convinced that performance management and an appraisal system were integral elements in helping the firm achieve its strategic objectives. This reflected her experience of introducing an appraisal system into the corporate finance unit for which she was responsible. The unit had consistently outperformed its growth targets and individual members of the unit were well motivated and appreciative of the appraisal process.

However, the senior partner of the firm remained unconvinced about the benefits of appraisal systems. He argued that accountants, through their training, were self-motivated and should have the maximum freedom to carry out their work. His experience of appraisal systems to date had shown them to lack clarity of purpose, be extremely time consuming, involve masses of bureaucratic form filling and create little benefit for the supervisors or their subordinates. Certainly, he was resistant to having his own performance reviewed through an appraisal system. Connie, however, was convinced that a firm-wide appraisal system would be of major benefit in helping the achievement of growth goals.

Required

(a)   Evaluate the extent to which an effective appraisal system could help the accounting firm achieve its goals.

(12 marks)

(b)   Using models where appropriate, assess the contribution, if any, of performance management to the strategic management process.   **(8 marks)**

(Total = 20 marks)

30 Isabella Correlli (M&S, 12/00, amended)   **36 mins**

Isabella Correlli is employed as a personnel manager for a medium-sized financial services firm. She is responsible for overseeing most of the operational activities within the Human Resource (HR) function of the firm – training, payroll, appraisals and discipline. Because the company employs many staff working in specialist areas such as investment advice, pensions and insurance selling it has seemed appropriate that recruitment and selection should be left to a professional agency which understands the business. However, over the past three years the company has suffered from an unusually high staff turnover. It has been noted that many of the recruits in these specialist areas have left within two years of joining the firm. Isabella's line manager is concerned about this trend. She has pointed out to her that the cost of both recruitment and training is very high and yet, almost before these staff have time to pay back the company's investment in them, they have moved on to other companies. The manager has asked Isabella to investigate this problem and propose solutions for her to examine, with the possibility of implementation.

Isabella has examined her files and begun a detailed evaluation of the situation. Her first finding has been that many of the recruits which the specialist agency has provided do not always appear suitable. Many have had a history of frequently changing jobs and appear to show no commitment to one firm. Others have had poor medical histories. Isabella also has decided to pay particular attention to exit interviews and annual appraisals. She has looked again at records and now makes sure that she is present at any current exit interviews because the pace of resignations has not shown any evidence of slackening. Unfortunately most meetings for both appraisals and exit interviews have not been well-structured. There is no clear evidence as to why staff are unhappy with their work. One thing does seem clear though. Money is not seen to be a major influencing factor for a move. Many leavers have been going to other companies for salaries not much higher than those being paid by Isabella's firm.

Isabella is convinced that the problem is with the initial recruitment and suggests that, in future, all the recruitment processes should be carried out in-house where the will be greater control in selection. Her line-manager is not so convinced. She believes that the problem could well originate within the company.

Required

(a)   Assuming the role of Isabella Correlli write a report to your line-manager which:

    (i)   justifies the case for recruitment being carried out in-house   **(6 marks)**

    (ii)   identifies the key criteria for selecting suitable candidates.   **(5 marks)**

(b)   It is important that the firm should improve its staff retention rate from both a cost and a morale perspective.

    Discuss ways in which Isabella's organisation can reduce this unacceptable level of staff turnover and, at the same time, provide a more highly motivated workforce.   **(9 marks)**

(Total = 20 marks)

31 Question with analysis: Fashion retailer (M&S, 12/00, amended)

36 mins

Paul Singh operates in the fashion clothing industry, owning 20 retail stores selling mainly to the teenage and youth market. This industry segment, comprising many small firms, each with a few retail stores, has very few large scale competitors. Paul's business has grown at a rapid rate with him acquiring his first store only five years ago. Despite this growth in business there has never been any associated integration of activities. Paul has been too busy growing his company to pay attention to consolidation and efficiency. However, he has now realised that despite this fast expansion his profits have not grown at the same rate as turnover. This part of the fashion business operates with very slim margins. The products are cheap but with the ever changing demand for fashion garments there are few opportunities for individual stores to hold stock for long periods of time. This has prevented Paul from taking advantage of economies of purchasing.

Each of his stores has tended to be run in isolation. He has left his local managers to decide on buying stock and on merchandising. His view has been that these managers are nearer to the customers and therefore they will know the fashion trends better. This appears to have worked with regard to turnover but he now needs to operate in a more cost-conscious manner. His computing system is being used in a old-fashioned way. It focuses on providing store accounts and is really only used by the small financial team (largely unqualified or still studying) located at the Head Office. Paul has been talking to friends who are operating in similar but non-competitive environments, and they have told him how useful they have found the up-to-date computer-based information systems. He has decided to investigate the opportunity of using information systems as a strategic tool.

Required

(a)   Using a suitable model to support your arguments explain how the strategic use of information systems could provide Paul with a competitive edge in this currently fragmented industry.   **(10 marks)**

(b)   It has been suggested to Paul that a suitable way of overcoming his IT problem might be to outsource the IT function. However, he has a fear of losing control.

Write a briefing paper to Paul, identifying the key issues associated with the proposal to outsource the IT system.   **(10 marks)**

(Total = 20 marks)

31 Question with analysis: Fashion retailer (M&S, 12/00, amended)

36 mins

Small/medium size business

Easy to make a start

Should there be?

Efficiency is required

Dis-economies of scale

Paul Singh operates in the fashion clothing industry, owning **20 retail stores** selling mainly to the teenage and youth market. This industry segment, comprising many small firms, each with a few retail stores, has **very few large scale competitors**. Paul's business has grown at a rapid rate with him acquiring his first store only five years ago. Despite this growth in business there has **never been any associated integration of activities**. Paul has been too busy growing his company to pay attention to consolidation and **efficiency**. However, he has now realised that despite this fast expansion his **profits have not grown at the same rate as turnover**. This part of the fashion business operates with very **slim margins**. The products are cheap but with the ever changing demand for fashion garments there are few opportunities for individual stores to hold stock for long periods of time. This has prevented Paul from taking advantage of **economies of purchasing**.

Bulk purchase discounts needed but not achieved

A hint!

Is this good enough?

Using information to create value

Each of his stores has tended to be run in isolation. He has left his local managers to decide on **buying stock** and on merchandising. His view has been that these managers are nearer to the customers and therefore they will know the fashion trends better. This appears to have worked with regard to turnover but he now needs to operate in a more cost-conscious manner. His computing system is being used in a **old-fashioned way**. It focuses on providing store accounts and is really only used by the small financial team (largely **unqualified or still studying**) located at the Head Office. Paul has been talking to friends who are operating in similar but non-competitive environments, and they have told him how useful they have found the up-to-date computer-based information systems. He has decided to investigate the opportunity of using information systems as a **strategic tool**.

Required

Note! McFarlan?

(a) **Using a suitable model** to support your arguments explain how the strategic use of information systems could provide Paul with a competitive edge in this currently fragmented industry.

(10 marks)

(b) It has been suggested to Paul that a suitable way of overcoming his IT problem might be to **outsource the IT** function. However, he has a fear of losing control.

Standard questions

Write a briefing paper to Paul, identifying the key issues associated with the proposal to outsource the IT system.

(10 marks)

(Total = 20 marks)

32 Auto Direct (6/05)

36 mins

Mark Howe, Managing Director of Auto Direct, is a victim of his own success. Mark has created an innovative way of selling cars to the public which takes advantage of the greater freedom given to independent car distributors to market cars more aggressively within the European Union. This reduces the traditional control and interference of the automobile manufacturers, some of whom own their distributors. He has opened a number of showrooms in the London region and by 2004 Auto Direct had 20 outlets in and around London. The concept is deceptively simple; Mark buys cars from wherever he can source them most cheaply and has access to all of the leading volume car models. He then concentrates on selling the cars to the public, leaving servicing and repair work to other specialist garages. He offers a classic high volume/low margin business model.

Mark now wants to develop this business model onto a national and eventually an international basis. His immediate plans are to grow the number of outlets by 50% each year for the next three years. Such growth will place considerable strain on the existing organisation and staff. Each showroom has its own management team, sales personnel and administration. Currently the 20 showrooms are grouped into a Northern and Southern Sales Division with a small head office team for each division. Auto Direct now employs 250 people.

Mark now needs to communicate the next three-year phase of the company's ambitious growth plans to staff and is anxious to get an understanding of staff attitudes towards the company and its growth plans. He is aware that you are a consultant used to advising firms on the changes associated with rapid growth and the way to generate positive staff attitudes to change.

Required

(a)   Using appropriate strategies for managing change provide Mark with a brief report on how he can best create a positive staff response to the proposed growth plans.   **(12 marks)**

(b)   What research techniques could Mark use to get an accurate assessment of staff attitudes to the proposed changes?   **(8 marks)**

(Total = 20 marks)

33 Focus Bank (12/04)   36 mins

Focus Bank, a global banking group with operations in some 70 countries worldwide, is facing an interesting dilemma – to what extent should it outsource its customer enquiry service function? Changes in technology have meant it has moved rapidly to set up its own call centres to handle customer enquiries and gain the benefits of increased staff productivity and higher levels of customer service. The increasing competitiveness in banking has meant that increasingly it has to outsource its customer service activities to outsourcing partners in parts of the world with lower labour costs. This in turn is bringing resistance from staff unions to the export of jobs and criticism from customers of poor service as a result of lower understanding and helpfulness from the call centres. The argument is centred around which competences and resources the bank should retain and develop and what activities can be more efficiently outsourced.

Required

(a)   What are the strategic and operational advantages and disadvantages of moving the customer enquiry service to an outside provider?   **(14 marks)**

(b)   What competitive advantage might the bank gain from a better understanding of its core competences?   **(6 marks)**

(Total = 20 marks)

34 Smith Norman (12/03)   36 mins

Julia Lowe was two years into her job as Marketing Manager at Smith Norman Associates, a medium sized independent financial services company. One of the main services offered by the firm was that of risk management to its client companies. As an insurance broker, Smith Norman Associates looked to organise the most effective insurance package for its industrial and commercial clients with the large, and increasingly international insurance companies. Julia was the first Marketing Manager at Smith Norman and faced considerable resistance amongst some of the senior managers in the firm. The financial advice provided by the senior staff relied heavily on their personal relationship with the financial directors in the companies looking to manage their business risks. Smith Norman's account managers had yet to be convinced of the need for a centralised marketing function in a financial services company, relying on personal one-to-one relationships.

The company had three separate divisions, each with its own marketing budget. There had been arguments at board level over both the size of the marketing spend – a two year campaign had to date cost £200K – and the basis on which the budget should be allocated between the divisions. Equally disturbing to Julia was the reluctance of some of the divisional heads to spend their marketing budget. Any underspending went immediately to the bottom line and this increase in profit was reflected in increased end-of-year bonuses.

She had, however, the support of both the Chairman and Managing Director of the firm, who recognised that the financial services industry was becoming increasingly competitive and developing an effective brand and reputation required a positive marketing strategy. Many of the services which they provided were difficult to differentiate. Julia now has to produce a report showing the relevance of marketing to Smith Norman and the reasons why the company should support an increased level of marketing spend over the next two years.

Required

(a)   Explain why marketing should form an important part of Smith Norman Associates' overall financial services strategy. **(12 marks)**

(b)   What measures might Julia use to demonstrate the effectiveness of the marketing activity to date? **(8 marks)**

(Total = 20 marks)

35 La Familia Amable (12/05)   36 mins

Ramon Silva is a Spanish property developer, who has made a considerable fortune from the increasing numbers of Europeans looking to buy new homes and apartments in the coastal regions of Mediterranean Spain. His frequent contact with property buyers has made him aware of their need for low cost hotel accommodation during the lengthy period between finding a property to buy and when they actually move into their new home. These would-be property owners are looking for inexpensive hotels in the same locations as tourists looking for cheap holiday accommodation.

Closer investigation of the market for inexpensive or budget hotel accommodation has convinced Ramon of the opportunity to offer something really different to his potential customers. He has the advantage of having no preconceived idea of what his chain of hotels might look like. The overall picture for the budget hotel industry is not encouraging with the industry suffering from low growth and consequent overcapacity. There are two distinct market segments in the budget hotel industry; firstly, no-star and one-star hotels, whose average price per room is between 30 and 45 euros. Customers are simply attracted by the low price. The second segment is the service provided by two-star hotels with an average price of 100 euros a night. These more expensive hotels attract customers by offering a better sleeping environment than the no-star and one-star hotels. Customers therefore have to choose between low prices and getting a poor night's sleep owing to noise and inferior beds or paying more for an untroubled night's sleep. Ramon quickly deduced that a hotel chain that can offer a better price/quality combination could be a winner.

The two-star hotels typically offer a full range of services including restaurants, bars and lounges, all of which are costly to operate. The low price budget hotels offer simple overnight accommodation with cheaply furnished rooms and staffed by part-time receptionists. Ramon is convinced that considerable cost savings are available through better room design, construction and furniture and a more effective use of hotel staff. He feels that through offering hotel franchises under the 'La Familia Amable' ('The Friendly Family') group name, he could recruit husband and wife teams to own and operate them. The couples, with suitable training, could offer most of the services provided in a two-star hotel, and create a friendly, family atmosphere – hence the company name. He is sure he can offer the customer twostar hotel value at budget prices. He is confident that the value-for-money option he offers would need little marketing promotion to launch it and achieve rapid growth.

Required

(a)   Provide Ramon with a brief report, using strategic models where appropriate, showing where his proposed hotel service can add value to the customer's experience.   **(12 marks)**

(b)   What are the advantages and disadvantages of using franchising to develop La Familia Amable budget hotel chain?   **(8 marks)**

(Total = 20 marks)

36 Rameses International (12/02)   36 mins

Jeanette Singh is the Strategic Policy Director of Rameses International, a large marketing company specialising in buying a variety of manufactured products from Western Europe and the USA for re-sale in Africa and in the Middle East. It was acting in the capacity of a large export house. In recent years the company had met strong opposition from other companies who were providing a similar sales service, in particular from the strong manufacturing companies who resented companies such as Rameses re-selling their products and obtaining profits which they considered to be rightly theirs.

Rameses International had initiated a number of strategies over the last year in order to minimise their problems. These strategies have varied from seeking a wider range of products to re-sell from a broader supply-base (more suppliers), attempting to have closer collaborative agreements with major suppliers to minimise any potential conflict, and attempting to operate in more markets. None of these strategies has worked.

Jeanette has been asked by the Board of Rameses to investigate the reasons for the failure of these strategies.

Required

(a)   Acting in the role of Jeanette Singh prepare a brief report to the Board, identifying major reasons why selected strategies might not be successful.   **(12 marks)**

(b)   Identify the issues that have to be considered before a strategy can be successfully implemented. **(8 marks)**

(Total = 20 marks)

37 John Hudson (12/01)   36 mins

John Hudson is the managing director of ALG Technology, a medium-sized high tech company operating in several geographic markets. The company provides software and instrumentation, mainly for military projects but it also does have civilian interests. It currently has four key projects: (1) a command, communication and control system for the army's gunnery regiments, (2) avionics for the fighter aircraft within the airforce, (3) an air traffic control system for a regional airport and (4) radar installations for harbour authorities in the Middle East. All these projects were expected to have a life expectancy of at least five years before completion. However Hudson was worried because each of these projects was increasingly falling behind schedule and the contracts which he had negotiated had late delivery penalties.

Hudson is convinced that a significant cause of the problem is the way that the company is organised. It has been shown that a competitive advantage can be obtained by the way a firm organises and performs its activities. Hudson's organisation is currently structured on a functional basis, which does not seem to work well with complex technologies when operating in dynamic markets. The functional structure appears to result in a lack of integration of key activities, reduced loyalties and an absence of team work. Hudson has contemplated moving towards a divisionalised structure, either by product or by market so as to provide some element of focus, but his experience has suggested that such a structure might create internal rivalries and competition which could adversely affect the performance of the company. Furthermore there is a risk that such a structure may lead to an over-emphasis on either the technology or the market conditions. He is seeking a structure which encourages both integration and efficiency. Any tendency towards decentralisation, whilst encouraging initiative and generating motivation may result in a failure to pursue a cohesive strategy, whereas a move towards centralisation could reduce flexibility and responsiveness.

BPP
LEARNING MEDIA

The company is already relatively lean and so any move towards delayering, resulting in a flatter organisation is likely to be resisted. Furthermore the nature of the market – the need for high technical specifications and confidentiality – is likely to preclude outsourcing as a means of achieving both efficiency and rapidity of response.

Required

(a) Provide an alternative organisational structure for ALG Technology, discussing both the benefits and problems which such a structure might bring. **(10 marks)**

(b) Evaluate the main factors which can influence organisational design relating these, where possible, to ALG Technology. **(10 marks)**

(Total = 20 marks)

38 Pamper Products   36 mins

Pamper Products Ltd was purchased as part of a management buy-out in 1996 by two brothers, Peter and David Sample. The company buys nail care and cosmetic products from a variety of suppliers in order to supply chemists and other retailers. Peter Sample was the Sales Director of the business before the buy-out and David was an accountant working in practice at the time.

David organised the finance by re-mortgaging both of their houses and borrowing further from the bank. He has continued to deal with the financial and administrative areas of the company whereas Peter is totally involved with suppliers and customers.

Peter was always an excellent salesman and his commitment to customer service is second to none. He deals personally with all of the major customers and has an excellent relationship with them.

Peter has a similar commitment to his suppliers. He has tried to limit the number of suppliers, but as the company has grown he has been forced to deal with a growing supplier base. Most of the purchases are from either the Far East or Europe. Initial concentration on a few major suppliers has ensured that Pamper Products has been able to have exclusive access to some products.

The company buys its products from a variety of manufacturers but markets them under its own brand name; it is able to charge premium prices for these products as a result of having created a trusted brand.

The company has gone from strength to strength in the years since the management buy-out with turnover increasing on average by over 20% per annum. This has led to an increased number of suppliers and an increase in staff from seven in 1996 to 22 currently. The company has also expanded physically and has recently rented a new warehouse, investing in a state of the art stock control system and a new computer system.

The initial bank loan was paid off according to its terms by 2001 but recently a further loan has had to be taken out in order to finance the expansion.

Peter is committed to even further expansion but David is concerned that the company's systems and finances cannot keep up with the rate of sales growth and would prefer a period of consolidation. As an accountant David is happy with the financial controls and performance measures that he has built into the system, but is concerned that possibly other non-financial measures might be just as important, particularly as the company continues to expand.

Required

(a) Explain to David the most common reasons why companies may fail and suggest ways in which Pamper Products Ltd could avoid them. **(10 marks)**

(b) Using the balanced scorecard approach, suggest other non-financial performance indicators that Pamper Products Ltd could use to monitor its overall performance as it continues to expand. **(10 marks)**

(Total = 20 marks)

39 Sykes Engineering (6/03)

36 mins

Jerome Sykes is the grandson of the founder of Sykes Engineering Group plc. This company is now a publicly quoted company with 2,000 employees, and although Jerome, the Chairman and Managing Director, only owns less than 2% of the equity of the Group he behaves as if it is his personal possession. His behaviour is becoming increasingly autocratic, involving himself in all levels of decision-making. This personalised decision-making has not brought consistency, clarity or rationality to the strategy process. Instead the company has suffered from confused improvisation, uncertainty and wild swings in corporate direction. Unfortunately this culture appears to have influenced many managers below Board level.

The Board of Directors has now been forced into action after extensive media coverage has criticized the company for a number of accounting irregularities over several years, the bribing of key foreign customers and sexual and racial harassment. This has inevitably adversely affected the share price. The key financial institutions who have invested in the Group are now demanding the removal of Jerome Sykes from office.

Required

(a)   Discuss actions which might have been taken earlier to have prevented such a situation from developing within the Sykes Engineering Group. **(10 marks)**

(b)   The culture of the company is now in need of change. Discuss ways in which change could be implemented within this seemingly dysfunctional company. **(10 marks)**

(Total = 20 marks)

40 Question with analysis: Service performance (6/02) 36 mins

Michael Medici has just been appointed as the Managing Director of Sun and Sand Travel Ltd. This is a small package holiday company travel, accommodation and on-site services all being pre-booked and included in the package price) focusing on the mass and cheaper end of the market. Company sales have grown at an annual rate of 10% over the past five years but profits have not risen at the same rate. The company has used price as its main competitive tool and the company has been more concerned with bottom-line financial results than with customer service.

Medici has spent the first two months of his work at Sun and Sand Travel Ltd, acting as a 'trouble shooter'. Customer complaints have risen to a record high. Almost 20% of recent customers have registered complaints including poor accommodation, flight delays and time of travel changes. The company is also facing hostile media criticism: both the press and television media are publicising the difficulties of the company. The outlook is not good: advance bookings are 30% lower than a year ago. Medici realises that the obsession with profit at the expense of other criteria has been both foolish and short termist. He recognises that if you do not get the service right then the profits will inevitably suffer.

Medici has set up a working party to advise him on what to do to improve the situation. One of the recommendations of the working party is to use performance indicators other than profit to assess how well the company is performing.

Required

(a)   Assess which performance indicators are particularly relevant for Sun and Sand Travel Ltd.   **(10 marks)**

(b)   Identify and discuss the critical success factors required of a company operating in this market segment.
(10 marks)

(Total = 20 marks)

40 Question with analysis: Service performance (6/02) 36 mins

Service business

Pressure on margins

Dis-economies of scale

Michael Medici has just been appointed as the Managing Director of Sun and Sand Travel Ltd. This is a small **package holiday company** (travel, accommodation and on-site services all being pre-booked and included in the package price) focusing on the **mass and cheaper end of the market**. Company sales have grown at an annual rate of 10% over the past five years but **profits have not risen at the same rate**. The company has used **price as its main competitive tool** and the company has been more concerned with bottom-line financial results than with customer service.

Very high

It will be difficult to survive on that basis

Service marketing mix emphasis on people

Medici has spent the first two months of his work at Sun and Sand Travel Ltd, acting as a 'trouble shooter'. Customer complaints have risen to a record high. Almost **20% of recent customers have registered complaints** including poor accommodation, flight delays and time of travel changes. The company is also facing hostile media criticism: both the press and television media are publicising the difficulties of the company. The outlook is not good: advance bookings are **30% lower than a year ago**. Medici realises that the obsession with profit at the expense of other criteria has been both foolish and short termist. He recognises that if you do not get the **service** right then the profits will inevitably suffer.

Medici has set up a working party to advise him on what to do to improve the situation. One of the recommendations of the working party is to use **performance indicators other than profit** to assess how well the company is performing.

Good idea – balanced scorecard?

Required

(a)   Assess which **performance indicators** are particularly relevant for Sun and Sand Travel Ltd.

(10 marks)

(b)   Identify and discuss the **critical success factors** required of a company operating in this market segment.

(10 marks)

(Total = 20 marks)

Must be aware of the relationship between these. One would normally start by identifying the CSFs and then create performance measures to track them so it *may* be a good idea to think about part (b)first

GLOBAL STRATEGY

Questions 41 to 44 cover Global Strategy, the subject of Part D of the BPP Study Text for Paper 3.5.

41 Excalibur Sportswear (12/01)   36 mins

Excalibur Sportswear is a United Kingdom marketing firm, selling high quality sports clothing within the UK. The firm has been set up by Simon Smith, who until recently was a world-class athlete. Smith, although selling his products exclusively in the UK, is sourcing production overseas, taking advantage of the cheaper labour costs and materials available elsewhere. Smith has used his reputation and his network of contacts to persuade footballers, tennis and golf professionals to wear his products. The logo and brand name of Excalibur are now becoming well known throughout the world as a result of the famous sports personalities being seen on TV wearing the company's products.

Despite this apparent success Excalibur is facing financial difficulties. In order to achieve the favourable exposure the company has spent heavily on advertising. The biggest expenditure has been the payment of promotional expenses to the world-famous sports stars, so that they will be seen wearing the company's products, particularly at events which are likely to be televised throughout the world. Compared with most of its competitors, Excalibur's costs were too high compared with its revenues. The company needed to sell more. The competitors' revenues were higher because they sold their products on a world-wide basis. Smith has decided that his company should look at its market as a global one and not as a national market. Expanding sales should not prove to be a problem for Excalibur. Most of the production is sub-contracted for foreign manufacturers so an expansion of capacity will have minimal financial impact on the marketing company. Similarly as most of the sales are through independent retail outlets there will be few increased costs for Excalibur as a result of the development of sales on a global basis. Naturally marketing costs, in particular those concerned with advertising, will rise.

Initial marketing research has confirmed the belief that Excalibur's products will be acceptable in many foreign markets. Many of the issues which can frequently threaten companies who decide to move into foreign markets are seen as favourable or at least benign. Trade barriers on such sports clothing products are relatively low. Although the company has no expertise in selling products overseas the fact that key activities – production and distribution – are outsourced, should make the challenge for Excalibur less testing. Finally, when seeking to establish markets overseas a shortage of finance is often a problem. Excalibur's bank is optimistic about the enterprise and is willing to provide market development finance.

Nevertheless Simon Smith is unhappy about relying on outsiders to provide critical inputs into the organisation. He believes that there is an increased risk of poorer quality and control affecting the company's reputation. Although existing suppliers and distributors have performed adequately he believes that a large expansion of Excalibur's activities, as proposed, might be beyond their capacity and any new suppliers may be of a lower standard. He is therefore contemplating setting up his own manufacturing facilities and distribution networks.

Required

(a) Evaluate the key factors which might encourage Excalibur to become involved in overseas marketing and even become a 'global' organisation.   **(12 marks)**

(b) Explain how risk, control and resource commitments might change for Simon Smith's firm as it attempts to take more control of its activities.   **(8 marks)**

(Total = 20 marks)

42 Question with analysis: Global marketing (12/02)   36 mins

Kirkbride Weston Inc is a US-based multinational company. It specialises in producing fork-life vehicles and has recently diversified into producing equipment for fully automated warehousing. It has traditionally considered each of its markets (it currently has business in 25 separate countries) as individual and has consequently customised not only the products to suit each market, but also the promotional strategies with localised brand names and distribution networks. As a result the company has been able to increase its share of the world market by appealing to local tastes, but this has been at a cost. This strategy of customisation has meant fragmented production lines, uneconomic distribution networks and a confused corporate image. Despite a regular increase in sales volume, profitability has been falling, as a result of the increased costs brought about by this excessive customisation.

Adrian Green is a new member of the company's marketing department, and having recently qualified from a prestigious business school has written a report for his line manager, basing his findings on work he had done during his studies. His main conclusion is that the company needs to move away from its 'polycentric' strategy and operate a more globally focused 'geocentric' strategy. In essence he is recommending that the company 'thinks globally but acts locally'. Adrian's line manager is impressed with this report and has forwarded it to the Marketing Director who, in turn, has presented the ideas to the main Board. The Board have asked that Adrian should explain his ideas more fully.

Required

(a) Acting in the role of Adrian Green provide a briefing report for the Board of Kirkbride Weston Inc explaining the different orientations of polycentric and geocentric companies.   **(12 marks)**

(b) Discuss the major factors which might encourage a company to pursue a policy of customisation.

(8 marks)

(Total = 20 marks)

42 Question with analysis: Global marketing (12/02)   36 mins

| Quality engineering required |

Kirkbride Weston Inc is a US-based multinational company. It specialises in producing **fork-lift vehicles** and has recently diversified into producing equipment for **fully automated warehousing**. It has traditionally considered each of its markets (it currently has business in 25 separate countries) as individual and has consequently **customised** not only the products to suit each market, but also the promotional strategies with localised brand names and distribution networks. As a result the company has been able to increase its share of the world market by appealing to local tastes, but this has been at a cost. This strategy of customisation has meant fragmented production lines, uneconomic distribution networks and a confused corporate image. Despite a regular increase in sales volume, profitability has been falling, as a result of the increased costs brought about by this excessive customisation.

| What are the advantages and disadvantages of this approach? The rest of the para sums it up! |

Adrian Green is a new member of the company's marketing department, and having recently qualified from a prestigious business school has written a report for his line manager, basing his findings on work he had done during his studies. His main conclusion is that the company needs to move away from its **'polycentric' strategy** and operate a more globally focused 'geocentric' strategy. In essence he is recommending that the company **'thinks globally but acts locally'**. Adrian's line manager is impressed with this report and has forwarded it to the Marketing Director who, in turn, has presented the ideas to the main Board. The Board have asked that Adrian should explain his ideas more fully.

| What is this exactly? |

| A well known phrase! Who said it? What did he mean? |

Required

| Text book stuff. You know it or you don't |

(a)   Acting in the role of Adrian Green provide a briefing report for the Board of Kirkbride Weston Inc explaining the **different orientations of polycentric and geocentric companies**.   **(12 marks)**

(b)   Discuss the **major factors** which might encourage a company to pursue a policy of customisation.
(8 marks)

(Total = 20 marks)

| The scenario has outlined some reasons for not doing it. When would it be a good idea? |

43 Prestige Packaging (12/03)

36 mins

David Upton, Managing Director of Prestige Packaging Ltd, a medium sized UK manufacturing company, was faced with an interesting dilemma. The company produced a unique, easy opening packaging process which had found a ready market in Europe with large multinational food and tobacco companies. The packaging process had a significant competitive advantage over its rivals and the company had ensured its technological superiority was protected by patents. However, dealing with global customers meant it was under pressure to become a global supplier with some form of presence in America and the Far East. Having a global presence would help secure its technological leadership and its increased size would help prevent its American and Korean competitors moving into the European market.

Various strategic options were open to the company. Acquiring a similar packaging company in an appropriate location was unlikely, as few companies were for sale. Furthermore, Prestige Packaging's technological advantage meant that a joint venture was not a realistic short term possibility. Eventually the decision was taken to choose some form of internal or organic growth; either a company sales office in a number of key markets, or a manufacturing operation handling the final stages of the manufacturing process and buying semi-finished material from the parent company or, finally, the appointment of an agent or distributor to look after its interests in these distant markets.

David has asked for your assistance in evaluating the risk and benefits associated with these alternative ways of expanding its international operations.

Required

(a)   Evaluate the advantages and disadvantages of the three stated organic options open to Prestige Packaging in its move to become a global company.   **(12 marks)**

(b)   What information should David use in coming to an informed decision?   **(8 marks)**

(Total = 20 marks)

44 Asia Invest (12/04)

36 mins

Salem Malik is head of Asia Invest, a government funded agency set up to attract foreign direct investment to help accelerate the industrial development of this Asian country. The government has ambitious plans to become a recognised force in global automobile manufacture within six years and recognises the need to get the major automobile companies to commit to setting up plants in the country. Creating a supportive environment for such companies would seem to be a prerequisite for the companies to locate in the country. Equally he recognises the intense competition between countries for such investment and the need for appropriate policies to create an attractive environment.

(a)   Using an appropriate model carry out an environmental analysis that will highlight the factors Salem should take into account when trying to attract such investment.   **(12 marks)**

The global automobile manufacturers are insisting on levels of service and quality that indigenous suppliers have not had to meet before.

(b)   In what ways can quality be used to gain competitive advantage in this industry?   **(8 marks)**

(Total = 20 marks)

45 Question with analysis: Lionel Cartwright (12/01)   108 mins

Lionel Cartwright considers himself to be an entrepreneur. He has been involved in many business ventures, each with minimal planning. He claims that this allows him to respond quickly to changing circumstances. His father had left him a small road haulage firm – three lorries – but he soon sold this to a larger operator when he recognised that operating margins were low and competition was severe. With the money received he bought a fast-food franchise, realising that this was where there was likely to be substantial growth. However, the franchisor required Lionel to limit both his ambitions and ideas for expansion to the development of this single franchise site. Lionel did not like this constraint and sold out and moved on. He then invested his money in an internet firm, having identified the potential in this market. Unfortunately for Lionel his investment in the company was insufficiently large to permit him to have much say in the management of the company so he again sold out. He demonstrated his opportunism because he managed to sell his investment before the technology shares had fallen on the global stock exchanges. Lionel now has a cash sum of about £12 million seeking a suitable investment.

It is clear form Lionel's track record that he enjoys involvement in the management of businesses and he also prefers some element of control. He appears to have a skill in identifying potential growth markets and he also seems to have an intuitive knowledge of the market place. He is currently showing an interest again in the food/restaurant retailing market and he is looking at organic foods and juices (produce grown without the use of synthetic fertilisers or pesticides). He has noticed a growing trend in the USA for outlets selling fresh vegetable and fruit juices which are squeezed to the customer's demand, either to be consumed on premises or taken away for consumption, as is the case with many fast-food chains. This development is all part of the growing health-conscious climate. Lionel believes that the European market is ready for such a venture and this is his initial objective. He has already opened four outlets in central London. To acquire the leases, fit out the premises, train labour and buy stock plus some initial expenditure on marketing has already cost Lionel £3 million. He realises that to become profitable he must open several more outlets so as to gain from both the experience curve and from economies of scale. He estimates that about 30 outlets will provide him with the necessary critical mass. He believes that these outlets could be anywhere in Europe, given the right environment. He is confident that he has identified a transnational segment for a health focused nutritious juice – a segment of the market which is uniform, regardless of nationality. This is based upon the youth market which tends to have common tastes in both entertainment and leisure activities throughout Europe – France, Italy, Germany and the UK appear to be acceptable target areas. However this segment is believed to be relatively sophisticated and affluent so outlets, therefore, will need to be in expensive city-centre areas or in other similar type areas which this target market group might regularly visit.

One of the problems facing Lionel's new venture and one of the pressures pushing him towards expansion is the need for regular access to suitable organic raw materials. These are in short supply. With large UK supermarkets generating increasing competitive demand for organic produce Lionel is finding it difficult to find reliable, quality suppliers. His current demand is too low and he needs to guarantee his suppliers a larger volume of orders so as to maintain their interest. He can only do this if he can rapidly expand the number of outlets he has or if he increases the volume sold through each outlet. The latter option is not really feasible. The area which each outlet covers is limited and to expand demand might mean either lowering the image which the outlet has developed and/or lowering the price of the products. Given the relative elasticities of demand, although the volumes of sales may rise, the profitability of each outlet may actually fall.

Another problem which Lionel is facing is obtaining suitable sites for his outlets. It is essential that these are in the appropriate locations. His current ones are in central London where there is a young and affluent market and also where the tourist trade is high. Future sites need to be acquired if expansion is to be achieved. If he goes into the rest of Europe they will need to be in major city centres or in similar type sophisticated tourist areas. It is inevitable that the availability of these sites will be limited and the cost of acquisition will be expensive. In addition the juice enterprise needs to be marketed in a sympathetic way. The target clientele, being young, mobile and affluent will be easily deterred from buying the product if the marketing lacks subtlety. Consequently any rush towards expansion by using aggressive marketing techniques must be tempered with caution. It will be too easy to down-grade the enterprise's image, so damaging it in the eyes of its potential customers.

Lionel had made an effort to understand his core competences and he hoped that these would match the critical success factors needed for this industry. He believed that he had the necessary market knowledge, his operation was small enough to be flexible and responsive to sudden changes in market circumstances and he felt that he had the level of motivation required to be successful in such a fast-moving, consumer, non-durable industry.

After one year's operations the results from the four London outlets compared with a chain of similar outlets in the USA seem to demonstrate that Lionel's ambitions may be over-optimistic. Whilst recognising that the enterprise is still young (although there is the novelty attraction and also no near competition) the profits are nowhere near as attractive as those being obtained from a larger chain (20 outlets) in the USA. [See details in Table 1.]

If Lionel is to achieve his ambition of setting up a profitable chain of retail juice outlets he must seek expansion without alienating his customer-base. He can do this gradually and internally by funding any expansion through retained earnings. He could also attempt to acquire another retail/fast food chain and adapt it to this new format. Finally, he could seek some sort of alliance whereby he achieves expansion, using other people's efforts and resources, particularly financial ones. This could involve licensing or franchising agreements. Each of these modes of expansion has its own advantages, but there are also disadvantages associated with each.

Table 1

Details of performance of individual outlets in USA and in the United Kingdom

All figures refer to the calendar year 2000 (£'000 where appropriate)

	UK outlet	USA outlet
Sales	600	750
Cost of materials	200	200
Labour costs	125	125
Rental/lease costs	125	85
Stocks held	30	20
Wasted materials as a % of sales	22	9
Varieties of products available for juicing (actual numbers)	14	25
Marketing costs allocated per unit	60	35
Administration costs allocated per outlet	20	10
Customers per week (actual numbers)	2,000	2,500
Size of store (square metres)	275	250
Numbers of staff	10	15
Number of hours open as a % of total hours available within any given week	40	65
Waiting time (from order to service) in minutes	15	8
Profit	70	295

Required

(a)   It appears that Lionel is a follower of the emergent school of strategy formulation as distinct from the rational model (planning) approach. Discuss the benefits that such an opportunistic approach may bring Lionel and comment on any problems he may experience with such an approach to setting strategy.

(15 marks)

(b)   Assess the performance of the UK outlets compared with their US equivalents, as indicated in Table 1, and identify from your analysis any critical success factors which may be currently lacking in Lionel's enterprise.

(15 marks)

(c)   What external information would you recommend that Lionel should have obtained prior to his decision to enter this market? Consider appropriate academic models Lionel might have utilised to obtain this information.

(10 marks)

(d)   Discuss both the advantages and disadvantages of

   (i)   internal growth;
   (ii)   acquisition; and
   (iii)   franchising

as methods whereby Lionel can achieve the expansion which he believes is necessary for his fresh juice outlets.

(20 marks)

(Total = 60 marks)

45 Question with analysis: Lionel Cartwright (12/01) 108 mins

Opportunist	Lionel Cartwright **considers himself to be an entrepreneur. He has been involved in many business ventures, each with minimal planning**. He claims that this allows him to **respond quickly to changing circumstances**. His father had left him a small road haulage firm – three lorries – but he soon **sold this to a larger operator** when he recognised that **operating margins were low and competition was severe**.
Does he do anything?	
Sensible	With the money received he bought a fast-food franchise, realising that this was where there was likely to be **substantial growth**. However, the franchisor required Lionel to limit both his ambitions and ideas for expansion to the development of this single franchise site. Lionel **did not like this constraint** and sold out and moved on. He then invested his money in an internet firm, having identified the potential in this market.
Important	
Personality	
Should have foreseen this	Unfortunately for Lionel his investment in the company was **insufficiently large** to permit him to have much say in the management of the company so he again sold out. He demonstrated his opportunism because he managed to sell his investment **before the technology shares had fallen** on the global stock exchanges.
Luck?	Lionel now has a cash sum of about **£12 million** seeking a suitable investment.
Can gear up	

It is clear form Lionel's track record that he enjoys involvement in the management of businesses and he also prefers some element of control. He **appears to have a skill in identifying potential growth markets** and he also seems to have an **intuitive knowledge of the market place**. He is currently showing an interest again in the food/restaurant retailing market and he is looking at organic foods and juices (produce grown without the use of synthetic fertilisers or pesticides). He has noticed a growing trend in the USA for outlets selling fresh vegetable and fruit juices which are squeezed to the customer's demand, either to be consumed on premises or taken away for consumption, as is the case with many fast-food chains. This development is all part of the **growing health-conscious climate**. Lionel believes that the European market is ready for such a venture and this is his initial objective. He has already opened **four outlets in central London**. To acquire the leases, fit out the premises, train labour and buy stock plus some initial expenditure on marketing has already cost Lionel **£3 million**. He realises that to **become profitable** he must open several more outlets so as to gain from both the experience curve and from economies of scale. He estimates that about **30 outlets** will provide him with the necessary critical mass. He believes that these outlets could be **anywhere in Europe**, given the right environment. He is confident that he has identified a transnational segment for a health focused nutritious juice – a segment of the market which is uniform, regardless of nationality. This is based upon the **youth market which tends to have common tastes** in both entertainment and leisure activities throughout Europe – France, Italy, Germany and the UK appear to be acceptable target areas. However this segment is believed to be relatively sophisticated and affluent so outlets, therefore, will need to be in **expensive city-centre areas** or in other similar type areas which this target market group might regularly visit.

Important (margin)
Real world accuracy here (margin)
Basic data (margin)
>50% growth: finance needed (margin)
Not yet profitable, then (margin)
Foreign experience needed (margin)
Caution (margin)

> Does it?

One of the problems facing Lionel's new venture and one of the pressures pushing him towards expansion is the need for regular access to **suitable organic raw materials. These are in short supply**. With large UK supermarkets generating increasing competitive demand for organic produce Lionel is finding it difficult to find reliable, quality suppliers. His current demand is too low and **he needs to guarantee his suppliers a larger volume of orders** so as to maintain their interest. He can only do this if he can rapidly expand the number of outlets he has or if he **increases the volume sold through each outlet**. The latter option is not really feasible. The area which each outlet covers is limited and to expand demand might mean either lowering the image which the outlet has developed and/or lowering the price of the products. Given the relative elasticities of demand, **although the volumes of sales may rise, the profitability of each outlet may actually fall**.

Fundamental (margin)
Back to growth (margin)
Preferable – would work the assets harder (margin)

> Basic reasoning sound, but is there room for small adjustments?

Another problem which Lionel is facing is obtaining suitable sites for his outlets. It is essential that these are in the appropriate locations. His current ones are in central London where there is a young and affluent market and also where the tourist trade is high. Future sites need to be acquired if expansion is to be achieved. If he goes into the rest of Europe they will need to be in major city centres or in similar type sophisticated tourist areas. It is inevitable that the **availability of these sites will be limited and the cost of acquisition will be expensive** . In addition the juice enterprise needs to be marketed in a sympathetic way. The target clientele, being young, mobile and affluent will be easily deterred from buying the product if the marketing lacks subtlety. Consequently any rush towards expansion by using aggressive marketing techniques must be tempered with caution. It will be too easy to down-grade the enterprise's image, so damaging it in the eyes of its potential customers.

True in the real world

Lionel had made an effort to understand his **core competences** and he hoped that these would match the **critical success factors** needed for this industry. He believed that he had the necessary market knowledge, his operation was small enough to be **flexible and responsive** to sudden changes in market circumstances and he felt that he had the **level of motivation** required to be successful in such a fast-moving, consumer, non-durable industry.

Good idea

After one year's operations the results from the four London outlets compared with a chain of similar outlets in the USA seem to demonstrate that Lionel's ambitions may be over-optimistic. Whilst recognising that the enterprise is still young (although there is the novelty attraction and also no near competition) the profits are nowhere near as attractive as those being obtained from a larger chain (20 outlets) in the USA. [See details in Table 1.]

How fair is the comparison?

If Lionel is to achieve his ambition of setting up a profitable chain of retail juice outlets he must seek expansion without alienating his customer-base. He can do this gradually and internally by funding any expansion through **retained earnings** . He could also attempt to **acquire another retail/fast food chain** and adapt it to this new format. Finally, he could seek some sort of alliance whereby he achieves expansion, using other people's efforts and resources, particularly financial ones. This could involve **licensing or franchising agreements** . Each of these modes of expansion has its own advantages, but there are also disadvantages associated with each.

Three possible routes – basis for a requirement, no doubt

Table 1

Getting to grips with the numbers: (1) Gross and net margins; (2) Cost categories as percentages of total costs; (3) Operating ratios: sales/m^2; sales/employee; stock days

Details of performance of individual outlets in USA and in the United Kingdom

All figures refer to the calendar year 2000 (£'000 where appropriate)

	UK outlet	USA outlet
Sales	600	750
Cost of materials	200	200
Labour costs	125	125
Rental/lease costs	125	85
Stocks held	30	20
Wasted materials as a % of sales	22	9
Varieties of products available for juicing (actual numbers)	14	25
Marketing costs allocated per unit	60	35
Administration costs allocated per outlet	20	10
Customers per week (actual numbers)	2,000	2,500
Size of store (square metres)	275	250
Numbers of staff	10	15
Number of hours open as a % of total hours available within any given week	40	65
Waiting time (from order to service) in minutes	15	8
Profit	70	295

Required

Mintzberg	
Personal inclination	

(a) It appears that Lionel is a follower of the **emergent** school of strategy formulation as distinct from the rational model (planning) approach. Discuss the **benefits** that such an opportunistic approach may bring Lionel and comment on any **problems** he may experience with such an approach to setting strategy. | Personal | Business | **(15 marks)**

Numbers

(b) **Assess the performance** of the UK outlets compared with their US equivalents, as indicated in Table 1, and identify from your analysis any **critical success factors** which may be currently lacking in Lionel's enterprise. **(15 marks)**

Things that *must* go well

Environment

(c) What **external information** would you recommend that Lionel should have obtained prior to his decision to enter this market? Consider **appropriate academic models** Lionel might have utilised to obtain this information. **(10 marks)**

PEST/SLEPT five forces

(d) Discuss both the advantages and disadvantages of | Not many marks for this |

(i) internal growth;
(ii) acquisition; and | Must combine theory with Lionel's circumstances |
(iii) franchising

as methods whereby Lionel can achieve the expansion which he believes is necessary for his fresh juice outlets. | Lots of marks available – say 7 or 8 for each method | **(20 marks)**

(Total = 60 marks)

46 Question with student answer: Bethesda Heights (6/02)

108 mins

The Management Committee of the Bethesda Heights Memorial Hospital was meeting under crisis conditions. The Hospital had moved into a financial deficit and most of the key participants in the decision making process could not agree on the best way to resolve the crisis.

The Hospital was located in the less affluent part of a North American city. It was a large general purpose hospital which served a stable population. Its revenue came mainly from the central government in the form of a grant, based on the size of population served and the actual surgical and medical work carried out. Central government grants accounted for about 65% of total revenue, and the remainder was almost equally split between two other funding bodies. Firstly, the local city council provided about US$ 20 million of grants and secondly, private medical insurance companies paid a similar amount for treatment of their insurance holders. This gave a total annual revenue of some US$ 115 million but costs had risen to US$ 125 million with all parts of the cost structure, including medicines, salaries and materials, seeing increases above the level of inflation. Unfortunately, the outlook did not look good for the Hospital. Revenue from central government was under pressure as the government sought to reduce public expenditure in order to fund significant tax cuts. Grants from the city council were linked to the level of the central government grant and consequently revenue from this source was not expected to increase. Even more depressing for the Hospital was its failure to attract private healthcare patients. They were choosing to go to a neighbouring hospital with a better reputation for patient care and more attractive facilities. Consequently income from medical insurance was likely to decline further. (The current financial and comparative performance data for the two hospitals can be seen in Table 1.)

The Management Committee estimated that if the situation did not improve the Bethesda Heights Memorial Hospital would have a deficit of US$ 75 million within three years. Action needed to be taken urgently. The Management Committee was made up of a number of coalitions. One was led by Michael Gonzales, the Chief Executive of the Hospital. He was an administrator and an accountant by training. His concern was that Bethesda Heights should be run efficiently. To him, and his fellow administrators on the Management Committee, it was important that the Hospital should be financially viable. However efficiency and effectiveness are not always the same thing. In fact some of the actions taken may also lead to further ineffectiveness or inefficiencies elsewhere. An indication of this dilemma was the administrators. wish to reduce the length of time patients spent in hospital so as to reduce costs. However sending patients home early could result in them requiring home visits from nursing staff for up to four or five extra days and in some circumstances this early release might require a re-admission to the Hospital. Consequently initial savings might be eroded by further unanticipated costs. Furthermore some medical staff suspected that these administrators were more concerned with short-term financial concerns than with medical ones. Certain medicines may be rationed or withheld to reduce costs and patients might be denied treatments such as physiotherapy or occupational therapy in a similar drive for cost savings.

Another group was represented by Stefan Kopechnik, a consultant surgeon. He was in favour of developing 'leading edge' micro-surgery. For Stefan and his fellow surgeons the Bethesda Heights Memorial Hospital was losing out to its rival hospital because it was seen as old-fashioned and out of touch with modern medicine and surgery. This was affecting its ability to attract the affluent private healthcare patient. Unfortunately the Hospital would require substantial capital investment to implement such a high-tech medical strategy.

A third group was influenced by the Mayor of the city, Elizabeth Fuller. This group was made up mainly of councillors (local politicians) who sat on various Hospital committees and were anxious to see the Hospital kept open and effectively serving the city's medical needs. Surprisingly, the city council had recently threatened to cut back its funding as a means of avoiding an increase in local taxes. The local news media had attempted to embarrass the local ruling party about this policy but the councillors involved, led by Mrs Fuller, were in no mood to give in to media pressure. There was a real fear that strategy might now be formulated in response to media headlines rather than rational argument.

Naturally the local population within the catchment area of the Hospital wanted it to continue its function as a viable concern and even invest in more modern facilities. Unfortunately this stakeholder group had little power or influence. The residents were socially disadvantaged and were unable to bring concerted pressure to bear on the Hospital's decision-makers.

There was one other important pressure group who were very vocal in their support of the Hospital. These were the employees, including the nurses and the general medical and support staff (not the high-ranking surgeons). Their interests were not political or financial, or even professional, unlike the surgeons who were looking to expand their power and influence. This employee grouping was primarily concerned with the maintenance of an efficient and effective hospital for the local population who could not afford private medical insurance and who relied mainly on government funded healthcare provision.

As one might have expected with these divisions, the Management Committee found it difficult to agree upon an acceptable strategy to solve the financial crisis. Eventually the one chosen reflected the power wielded by the surgeons. These senior medical staff (the surgeons) had threatened to resign if the Committee did not agree to a capital investment programme designed to enhance the Hospital's surgical reputation. The Hospital would effectively cease to function without its surgical teams. Unfortunately the trade-off for this investment was to reduce the number of beds within the Hospital. It was argued that this reduced provision reflected the current utilisation patterns. Unfortunately this did not reflect the latent demand within the community. There were a significant number of patients who were not being given the treatment they needed as they did not have private healthcare insurance. Furthermore, waiting times for seeing the appropriate consultant surgeon or for being admitted to the Hospital were lengthening for this disadvantaged group of patients.

Table 1

Comparison of Statistical Data between Bethesda Heights Memorial Hospital and the

Neighbouring Hospital for calendar year 2001 (figures for 2000 in brackets)

(unless otherwise stated figures are in US$'000)

	Bethesda Heights Hospital		Neighbouring Hospital	
Income from central government	76,000	(76,000)	85,000	(85,000)
Income from local government	20,000	(19,000)	22,000	(21,000)
Income from medical insurance	19,000	(23,000)	63,000	(60,000)
Total income	115,000	(118,000)	170,000	(166,000)
Labour costs	55,000	(53,000)	57,000	(55,000)
Medical equipment	20,000	(19,000)	28,000	(25,000)
Drugs	25,000	(22,000)	30,000	(28,000)
Other variable costs: catering, laundry	10,000	(9,000)	13,000	(12,000)
Fixed costs	15,000	(15,000)	17,000	(16,000)
Total costs	125,000	(118,000)	145,000	(136,000)
Surplus/deficit	−10,000	(0)	+25,000	(+30,000)
Further referrals required % (need for re-admittance)	17	(14)	9	(7)
Mortality % (% of patients dying in hospital)	0·05	(0·03)	0·007	(0·003)
Number of staff (actual)	1,000	(970)	1,100	(1,150)
Number of beds (actual)	350	(350)	450	(450)
Waiting time (days)*	95	(90)	35	(40)
Post-operation time in hospital (days)**	7	(8)	10	(10)
Day surgery operations*** (actual numbers)	1,500	(1,150)	7,000	(1,500)
Number of patients treated annually residentially	10,650	(10,900)	12,700	(12,500)
Ratio outpatients to those committed to hospital****	3:1	(3:1)	5:1	(4:1)

*   from seeing doctor to hospital admittance

**   number of days kept in hospital after an operation

***   minor operations which require no overnight stay

****   number of patients dealt with as external patients (excluding day surgery) compared with those committed to hospital for one night or longer

Required

(a)   It is apparent that the goals and objectives of the senior medical staff have profoundly influenced the chosen strategy. Discuss the factors which have enabled this group to dominate the other stakeholders. What are the main arguments which the other groups might have used to promote their objectives?   **(15 marks)**

(b)   Using the quantitative data provided, identify the major problems facing the Bethesda Heights Memorial Hospital. Examine the extent to which the proposed high-tech strategy will address these problems.

(20 marks)

(c)   Assess the other strategic options open to the Management Committee.   **(15 marks)**

(d)   When dealing with issues concerning health care, financial outcomes are not the only criteria to be considered. Ethical factors must also be taken into account. Discuss the role that social responsibility might play in this context.   **(10 marks)**

(Total = 60 marks)

47 World-Wide Agricultural (12/02)   108 mins

Kenneth Murphy is the Managing Director of the World-Wide Agricultural Machinery Company plc (WAMC). The company was founded almost 100 years ago in 1904 and with its approaching centenary Murphy is worried that the company may be about to lose its independence. The company came into existence with the industrialization of the United Kingdom agricultural sector. It manufactured tractors (power units) and an array of associated agricultural machinery such as rakes, balers, ploughs and grass cutting equipment. The company grew at a rapid rate in the early part of the twentieth century. The successful demand within the domestic market led the company into a false sense of security. It neglected both product and market development, despite its ambitious company name. It was unaware of the growth of competitors, mainly from mainland Europe and the USA. In recent years the company has attempted to improve its situation by exporting to the major countries within the European Union but again its marketing knowledge is poor. Agricultural policies in many European countries favour smaller farming units. Generally the size of these units is too small to necessitate the degree of mechanisation which WAMC caters for. Furthermore the lack of innovation within the company means that the products are old-fashioned, often costly to repair and lack the flexibility and adaptability of competitive machines. Furthermore as many farms are becoming more specialist in their output the need to purchase a wide range of equipment is less prevalent.

By the beginning of the 1990s the company had been experiencing a financial crisis. Profits had been low for a number of years but now small losses were occurring. Management consultants were brought in and suggested that the range of products should be drastically reduced so as to control a seemingly inexorable rise in costs. In 1993 Kenneth was appointed to oversee this strategy. He decided that one of the first areas to be axed should be the production of the power units – the tractors (referred to henceforth as tractor units). Research demonstrated that these products required the largest amount of investment. Unfortunately for the company total sales were insufficient to provide the economies of scale necessary for it to be successful in this area. In addition the large auto producers, particularly the American ones, were now dominating this market. The strategy seemed a sensible one. Unfortunately it had disastrous results for WAMC. It became apparent that the remaining range of agricultural products (those towed behind a tractor unit) were seen as an ancillary to the tractors. Farmers, who now could no longer buy WAMC-produced tractor units, now decided not to buy WAMC's ploughs, rakes and balers etc. The farmers were looking for a single supplier for their mechanised equipment. This enabled them to have easier access to finance and it also gave the customer a more comprehensive and easily co-ordinated service facility. Sales by WAMC fell dramatically and by early 2002 the company was making unacceptable losses. The company did attempt to impose some cost saving strategies. The number of factories, located throughout the country, was cut from seven to three, and redundancies reduced the work force to 700 from a total exceeding 2,500 in 1993 when Murphy had become MD. Most of the employees had been with the firm for all their working lives and were devastated by the savage cut-backs in employment. As a unionised organisation there had been some resistance to the redundancies, but after a costly strike the workers realised that there was no hope of keeping the organization at the size it was and they reluctantly accepted the new structure.

The factories are now organised so that each of the three produce a narrow range of products, enabling specialisation to take place. This replaces the previously inefficient system whereby each of the seven factories produced the whole range of products, the theory being that they served local geographic markets, necessitating little transportation and enabling demand to be met quickly. The reality was that the costs of production were higher and stock-holding was expensive even though regional demand was being more conveniently serviced. Traditionally WAMC has owned and controlled its distribution outlets. There are 10 of these outlets spread regionally throughout the United Kingdom. Murphy is contemplating selling these off, to raise additional working capital. It is estimated that the sale could realise about £15 million, mainly because the company owned the freeholds of the land on which these outlets are built, and they could be profitably sold for development. Murphy is also contemplating re-entering the tractor-unit production business but in a less committed fashion. He is planning to sub-contract the manufacturing to an established tractor manufacturing company and having the WAMC brand placed on these products. This, he believes, will provide the company with the required flexibility but at minimum cost.

Murphy is also contemplating a strategy of product development to provide increased work for his factories. As the main business is now really in metal fabrication, not tractor units, he is looking to produce equipment for the road building and road repair industry, now expected to be more growth oriented given the central government's recent commitment to spend more on transport improvements. Such equipment could include portable traffic lights, metal signs and road barriers for improving motorway safety.

WAMC has also begun talks with a large financial institution with the intention of borrowing funds so that it (WAMC) can provide loans to farmers so that they can purchase the farm equipment at favourable terms of credit. Currently it is believed that WAMC is losing business because it is not able to offer potential customers sufficient financial support.

Whilst these negotiations are taking place the company has been approached by a rival producer from France. The French company, Agricole Mecanique (AM), is suggesting a defensive merger so as to better combat threats from competing US producers. The French company is slightly smaller than WAMC, with only 500 employees and two factories. However it is a relatively young company, only being established for ten years with a limited product range and a largely unknown brand name but it does have up-to-date manufacturing facilities, and it does produce its own tractor units. In the process of consolidation the French company is suggesting that much of the production should be transferred to the French factories and that most of the senior management positions in the new company should be French. Murphy has been offered a significant number of shares and a future management position in the newly merged company if he is able to successfully conclude such a 'merger', at a price acceptable to the French company. As the merger will be achieved by a share exchange between the two companies it is in the interests of Agricole Mecanique for the share price of WAMC to be low on the date of inception – a possibly illegal inducement to Murphy.

Murphy is fully aware of the precarious position of WAMC and he is not convinced of the wisdom of the so-called 'merger'. He feels that he is too involved in the situation to take a dispassionate view, so he has called in a management consultant, experienced in strategy formulation and in mergers and acquisitions, to advise him on the current situation.

Table 1: Financial Data for World-Wide Agricultural Machinery Company and Agricole Mecanique

	WAMC 2000 £'000	WAMC 2001 £'000	AM 2000 £'000	AM 2001 £'000
Sales Revenue	30,000	28,000	25,000	24,500
Cost of Sales	18,000	18,200	13,000	12,900
Gross Margin	12,000	9,800	12,000	11,600
Expenses	9,000	9,200	8,000	8,100
Marketing	4,000	4,000	1,500	2,000
R & D	3,000	3,000	4,500	4,100
Overheads	2,000	2,200	2,000	2,000
Operating Profit	3,000	600	4,000	3,500
Interest Paid	1,000	1,200	2,000	2,200
Profit/(Loss) after Interest	2,000	(600)	2,000	1,300
Fixed Assets	24,000	24,000	19,000	19,500
Current Assets	8,000	7,500	7,000	8,000
Current Liabilities	6,500	6,300	5,000	6,000
Equity	27,000	27,000	14,000	14,500
Debt	12,000	14,000	12,000	15,000
Return on Sales	10·0%	2·1%	16·0%	14·3%
P/E ratio	11	10	16	17
Gearing Ratio	0·444	0·519	0·857	1·034

Required

Acting in the role as management consultant:

(a)   Critically review the current position of the World-Wide Agricultural Machinery Company. Present your review in a report format and use academic models, wherever practical, to support your arguments. How does WAMC's performance compare with that of Agricole Mecanique?   **(20 marks)**

(b)   Evaluate the strategies being proposed by Kenneth Murphy. To what extent would they help to rectify the underlying problems?   **(20 marks)**

(c)   Identify the main factors which need to be considered if a merger is to be successful. (The answer must relate to the above case scenario.)   **(12 marks)**

(d)   What ethical problems might Murphy face in considering the incentive offered to him by Agricole Mecanique to facilitate the merger?   **(8 marks)**

(Total = 60 marks)

48 Hair Care (6/03)   108 mins

Sam and Annabelle Burns own and manage the firm Hair Care Ltd, based in the United Kingdom. The firm was formed in 1998 when Sam and his wife re-mortgaged their house and borrowed heavily from the bank to buy out the company from a conglomerate organization who were disposing of non-core businesses. Sam had been a senior salesman with the hair-care subsidiary of the conglomerate. This subsidiary bought hair care products, mainly small value items and consumables – scissors, brushes, combs, hair nets, curlers and hair driers, from manufacturers and resold them to wholesalers and large retail chemist chains within the United Kingdom, mainly for use in hairdressing salons. The new business has continued in this direction. The manufacturers are almost entirely non-UK suppliers, many based in Hong Kong but with manufacturing facilities in mainland China, Taiwan and Malaysia. However about 30% of the products are sourced in Europe – Italy and Germany predominantly.

The company has met with success very quickly and the initial loans have already been repaid ahead of schedule. The company now owns the freehold of a large warehouse/distribution centre which is five times the size of the original depot, leased when the company first started trading five years ago. Sales turnover, now in excess of £5 million, has increased by more than 50% each year and shows little sign of slowing down. Despite this apparent rapid growth Hair Care Ltd only accounts for about half of the current market, leaving some potential for growth. The company is run cost effectively, with minimum staffing. Sam, as Managing Director is solely concerned with the marketing side of the business. He spends most of his time in the selling role and in customer care which he rates as a major contributor to the company's success. The only other key manager is his wife who is responsible for managing the warehouse staff, arranging distribution, general administration and financial management. The company started with six employees, in addition to Sam and Annabelle, and now has 15. Staff rarely leave the company. The staff is almost entirely employed in the distribution and packaging function, although there are two other sales people apart from Sam, but they only deal with the smaller buyers. With the continued growth in turnover it is inevitable that the number of employees will have to increase. It is expected that there will have to be a total of about 30 staff, all non managerial, in two years if sales continue to increase at the current rate.

The success of Hair Care Ltd can be accounted for by a number of factors. Sam is a very good salesman who is responsible for looking after all the major accounts. He is popular and much of the business is built on his personal relationship with the key clients. There is a considerable amount of customer loyalty which is mainly attributable to Sam, and both he and his wife are always accessible to customers and they go out of their way to provide a first class service. Even on vacation the two owners are in daily contact with the office. The company has been able to manage its purchases wisely. Most of the products, being purchased abroad, require payment in a foreign currency. Hair Care has been able to benefit from the relative weakness of the euro against sterling for its European supplies. Although most of the products sourced in the Far East are priced in US dollars, the relative strength of that currency has enabled Hair Care Ltd to negotiate lower purchasing prices. However it is questionable as to how long this situation concerning foreign exchange can be held. The situation may change should the United Kingdom join the euro in the near future and much, of course, will depend upon the level at which sterling enters the euro exchange.

Sam has also developed strong links with his suppliers and he has, until recently, attempted to trade with only a few so that his lines of communication and control are kept as simple as possible. Most of his current suppliers have been with him since the start of the company in 1998. This has provided the company with reliable and good quality products. In fact Hair Care Ltd often has exclusive access to certain products. For example it has the sole rights to

distribute an Italian hair-dryer which is generally recognized to be the best on the market. This product strength has enabled the company to build on the customer loyalty. However, it is inevitable that as demand has increased, existing suppliers have not been able to keep up with the necessary volumes and Sam has had to look for, and buy from new manufacturers.

The company has benefited from a period of relatively steady growth in the economy and even in the current economic down-turn Sam has argued that demand for hair care products is usually recession-proof. Furthermore Hair Care Ltd has currently no near competitors. Many of the small competitors in the wholesale market place have chosen to concentrate on other areas of the hair care business – salon furnishings and the supply of cheap, low-value items such as towels, razors etc, leaving much of this basic business (sales of other relatively low-value and mainly disposable products) to Sam's company. Additionally quite a number of the small firms have even left the market. All this has helped to contribute to the overall growth rate of Hair Care Ltd. There are some major international companies who make shampoos, conditioners and other cosmetic type products who also buy-in consumer hairdressing products such as the ones sold by Hair Care Ltd. They then sell these mainly to the retail trade for domestic use by consumers and not directly to the hairdressing salons as does Hair Care Ltd. Furthermore these are large companies and Sam believes that they do not currently see his company as a major threat.

The company has registered a brand name for its main products which it re-packages, rather than using the individual brands of the original manufacturers. This has enabled Hair Care Ltd to generate even greater loyalty from its customers and often to obtain a price premium from these products. Sam believes that part of the company's success stems from the fact that he has an organization with minimal administrative overheads. He outsources all of his products, adding value mainly through branding and the maintenance of customer care. He believes that strategy is not mainly about beating the competition but in serving the real needs of the customer. The company has also been able to develop a strong relationship with the country's leading retail chemist chain, providing it with good quality, low-cost disposable products such as hair nets and brushes to be sold under an own-brand label. Although the margins are inevitably small, the volumes involved more than compensate for this. The company has had to incur increased investment as a result of the large growth in turnover. The building of the warehouse, the increased stock-holding costs, capital expenditure on items such as computing systems, fork-lift trucks and automated stock control and retrieval systems could not be financed out of current earnings, but the company's bank was only too ready to lend the company the necessary money considering that the original loan had been repaid ahead of schedule.

All the success which Hair Care Ltd has achieved has not diminished Sam's appetite for growth. He now seems to be driven more by seeking power and influence than acquiring wealth. He questions the ability of the company to continue its current growth in the prevailing environment and therefore he is looking for ideas which may facilitate corporate expansion. He has asked his accountant to provide some options for him to consider.

Table 1: Details of Performance of Hair Care Ltd: 2000–2003
(unless otherwise stated, figures are in £'000)

	2000	2001	2002	2003 (forecast)
	£'000	£'000	£'000	£'000
Sales	2,300	3,500	5,010	7,500
Cost of Sales	1,450	2,380	3,507	5,250
Marketing Costs	200	250	290	350
Distribution Costs	300	400	430	500
Administration	50	55	80	120
Interest Payments	0	80	220	700
Operating Profit	300	335	483	580
Loans	0	850	2,400	5,000
Number of suppliers (actual)	15	20	30	50
Range of products (actual)	35	85	110	130
Total staff including Sam and Annabelle	12	14	15	23
Stocks	230	400	700	1,400
Fixed assets	500	1,500	2,700	6,300
Return on Sales (%)	13.0	9.6	9.6	7.7

Required

(a) Assuming the role of Sam's accountant, prepare a report for Sam, evaluating the current position of Hair Care Ltd and highlighting any financial and strategic issues concerning future developments which you feel should be brought to his attention. **(20 marks)**

(b) As his accountant, prepare a short report for Sam, identifying and assessing the strategies which he could consider in attempting to further the company's development. **(20 marks)**

(c) Sam seems pre-occupied with growth. Identify reasons for potential corporate decline and suggest ways that Sam could avoid them in the context of the case study scenario. **(10 marks)**

(d) Sam currently appears to have a successful formula for growth. Using the concept of the value chain, demonstrate how he has been able to achieve this success. **(10 marks)**

(Total = 60 marks)

49 Polymat Tapes (12/03)

108 mins

Introduction

Richard Johnson, Managing Director of Polymat Industrial Tapes Limited (PIT), was worried. The global economic slowdown following the events of 11 September 2001, and subsequent Stock Market falls had meant 2002 had been a difficult year for the company. The company manufactured a range of industrial tapes for sale to a wide range of customers, from masking tape used by individual Do-It-Yourself (DIY) enthusiasts through to high performance tapes for the major automotive and aerospace companies. The origins of the company were in the late 1920s when PIT set up as a private company making tapes for use by cable manufacturers who were meeting the growing needs of the National Grid (a Government owned electricity supply network). The technology for making its products was, therefore, reasonably mature though breakthrough products did occasionally occur – as witnessed by the explosive demand for optic fibre cable and PIT's hi-tech cable jointing tapes. The tapes were mainly produced by a process that coats adhesive on to a variety of materials, including PVC, textiles and paper.

Product range and competitive environment PIT had grown up in close proximity to some of its much larger cable manufacturing and automotive customers. There were currently three factories manufacturing its product range. Its original factory concentrates on cable jointing products supplied to the large UK cable manufacturers. These manufacturers are exerting strong pressure for price reductions on their suppliers in order to prevent entry into the market by large US global cable manufacturers. PIT's products need to respond to any significant product developments by the UK cable manufacturers and by its US tape competitors. Johnson is very aware of the global brand recognition of one of its major US competitors, which has a strong consumer products division and a reputation for aggressive product innovation.

At its second factory PIT produces PVC tapes, mainly standardised products with a typical 30-year product life cycle. Distribution is primarily through electrical wholesalers with an extremely wide customer base. PIT's main UK competition is of a similar size and not regarded as being particularly innovative. PIT has also had some success in meeting the particular tape needs of car makers in their new car model programmes. PIT has had to satisfy the demanding quality standards required by each car manufacturer of their suppliers. The main competition comes from low cost base manufacturers from Europe and the Far East.

At its third factory PIT produces paper masking tape. The move into paper masking tape is a more recent move aimed at the apparently ever-increasing market for masking tape with particularly heavy demands by the car industry for use in paint spraying and in the domestic market by DIY customers. The technology to produce the tape was imported from the USA under licence with a very modern factory being built to manufacture these products. Unfortunately, PIT's masking tape capacity became available just as there was a significant slow down in global car sales. Tape manufacturers such as PIT are faced with the dual problem of excess industry capacity and sales of low priced tape in Europe by low cost North American producers. The main competitor is an American company with access to lower cost raw materials and a 35% share of the UK market compared to PIT's 20% share. PIT's difficulties were further exacerbated by its inability to achieve efficient low cost operation, partly due to a high level of fixed overhead cost for the company as a whole. The fixed overhead had been significantly increased by an investment in, and operation of, a centralised warehouse facility. This warehouse and distribution facility had been designed to alleviate major space problems at the factories and improve service to all of the key clients, but in practice has merely added to overhead costs and working capital levels with little added value to the company's activities. Safety stocks of finished products continue to be held at the three factories. Distribution to the customers is through the company's own transport system.

Current situation and financial performance

PIT had been acquired by one of the UK's largest cable manufacturers during the Second World War. However, the recession of the early 1990s had seen the parent company look to concentrate on its core product – cable manufacture – and dispose of non-core activities including PIT's industrial tapes. Thus an opportunity was presented to the three senior directors to buy out the company. The subsequent buyout had, to use Richard Johnson's words, given them 'a company with a mature product range produced by outdated equipment'. Each of the directors has spent the majority of their careers in the industry and recognises the challenge of competing in markets that are dominated by large customers looking to drive prices down and rationalise their supplier base. The directors are committed to securing the future of the business and saving as many jobs as possible.

PIT is very much a product led as opposed to a marketing led company. The nature of its products mean that it employs a significant number of chemistry graduates at its three factories and each factory pursues a separate R & D strategy. Recognition of the changing marketplace had come with the appointment of Paul Wright, an economics graduate, as Marketing Manager. Paul soon recognised that the company lacked key information on its customers, the products they bought and which were profitable. To use Paul's words, there were some 'little gems' where the product was generating good margins from a small number of industrial customers. But identifying them is the problem. Many of its customers are small DIY retailers and information on the profitability of such orders was less than impressive. Equally worrying is the lack of any process through which the ideas for new or improved products brought back by its sales force are effectively considered in terms of PIT's ability to develop, make and then sell them at a profit. The dominance of the company by technologists means that there is a real gap between understanding market opportunities and the products developed in the company. There is also a failure to identify the key decision makers in their larger cable manufacture and automotive customers and little external recognition of the technological advances made by PIT's R & D activity.

Table 1: Information on PIT's current sales and financial performance
(£'000) (where appropriate)

	2001/02 £'000	2002/03 £'000	2003/04 (forecast) £'000
Product group			
Cable Jointing Tapes			
Sales	4,000	4,510	5,100
Cost of sales	2,400	2,593	2,805
Gross profit	1,600	1,917	2,295
Transport costs	120	135	153
R & D	High	High	High
Market share	25%	25%	25%
Sales volume index	100	110	121
Product range	Narrow	Narrow	Medium
PVC Industrial Tapes	£'000	£'000	£'000
Sales	3,000	3,100	3,200
Cost of sales	1,650	1,705	1,760
Gross profit	1,350	1,395	1,440
Transport costs	150	155	160
R & D	Low	Low	Low
Market share	10%	9%	8%
Sales volume index	100	103	106
Product range	Wide	Wide	Wide
Paper Masking Tapes	£'000	£'000	£'000
Sales	2,500	2,400	2,300
Cost of sales	1,625	1,680	1,725
Gross profit	875	720	575
Transport costs	150	192	230
R & D	Moderate	Moderate	Moderate
Market share	20%	20%	20%
Sales volume index	100	106	112
Product range	Narrow	Medium	Medium

Company	£'000	£'000	£'000
Sales	9,500	10,010	10,600
Cost of sales	5,675	5,978	6,290
Gross profit	3,825	4,032	4,310
Transport costs	420	482	543
Other fixed costs	3,080	3,270	3,500
Operating profit	325	280	267
ROS	3.4%	2.8%	2.5%

Retardon

Indicative of the problems PIT faces, is its one and only breakthrough product 'Retardon'. This tape had been developed some five years earlier and offered significant fire resistant properties over the normal tapes supplied to cable manufacturers installing their cables in high risk environments, such as underground railway systems, airports and high rise buildings. Environmental conditions are favourable for a product with the ability to both reduce the risk of fire and the toxic fumes given off should a fire occur. However, despite significant R & D investment, the lack of adequate patent protection, a deficient product design and a failure to stimulate the market means that the threat of competition from more effectively organised competitors is increasingly likely.

Outlook for the future

Richard is sympathetic to Paul's concern over the lack of marketing information and the consequent failure to generate new products. Equally concerning is the speed at which many of its products are becoming commodity products in which price is the key factor influencing supplier choice. Certainly there are opportunities to work with the large automotive companies in their development of new models, but such projects were typically of five years duration and PIT's lack of market presence is not helping it secure these long-term contracts. Richard has now decided to get an external assessment of the company's position.

Required

(a) Assuming the role of an external consultant, prepare a report for Richard evaluating the performance of the three product groups and their contribution to overall company results. Use appropriate models to support your analysis. **(25 marks)**

(b) Assess the main strategic options open to PIT and recommend a preferred strategy. **(15 marks)**

(c) Explain how PIT might change from a technology driven culture to a marketing led one. **(10 marks)**

(d) Examine the steps necessary to create a more effective New Product Development system. **(10 marks)**

(Total = 60 marks)

50 NMS (6/04)

108 mins

Introduction

Network Management Systems (NMS) is a privately owned hi-tech business set up in 1993 and located close to London. NMS was the brainchild of a Canadian computer engineer, Ray Edwards looking to meet the needs of the converging computer and telecommunication industries. Ray, in many ways, is a classic hi-tech entrepreneur, constantly searching for ways to exploit technological opportunities and unafraid to take the risks associated with hitech start-ups. In his words an entrepreneur is 'someone willing to work 18 hours a day for themselves.... to keep from working 8 hours a day for someone else!'.

Structure of the business and key product areas

By 2003 NMS was employing 75 full time staff in a new, purpose built factory and office unit. These staff were a mix of technically qualified engineers working in R&D, staff concerned with the manufacturing and assembly side of the business and a small sales and service support team. Its first product was a digital error detection box able to 'listen' to computer signals and detect faults. The original box designed by Ray, was built on his kitchen table and manufactured in a garage. NMS had developed three distinctive product/service areas. Firstly, data communications components sold to original equipment manufacturers (OEMs) that incorporated NMS components into their hardware. Both the OEMs and their customers were likely to be large, international companies. NMS's had a less than 1% share of the UK market and faced competition from more than twenty suppliers, most of whom competed internationally. One of NMS's main UK customers accounted for 40% of its sales. NMS had established a good reputation for the quality and performance of its components, which were competitively priced. The European market for data communications equipment had increased from some $3·3 billion in 1999 to $6·0 billion in 2003. Forecasts for 2004 and beyond predicted growth as coming from increased sales to currently installed networks rather than from new networks. As the technology was becoming more mature, so the product lifecycles were becoming shorter. Success came from producing large volumes of relatively low priced reliable components. However, all new components had to be approved by the relevant government approval body in each country being supplied. Approval for new data communication equipment was both costly and time consuming.

NMS's second product area was network management systems – hence the name of the company. Once again the customers were typically large companies – but the fault detecting systems were supplied directly to a small number of large end-users such as banks, public utility providers and global manufacturers. NMS's approach recognised that no two companies information systems were the same and therefore NMS needed to customise its products to meet these specific needs. NMS pioneered a 'modular building block' design, which allowed the customer to adapt standard system modules to fit their exact networking requirements. NMS products were focused on solving network management problems and the success of its products was reflected in the award of the prestigious 'Queen's Award for Technological Achievement' in the prevention of computer data communication downtime. This was recognition of the excellence of the R&D project teams who developed the software and related hardware. NMS's reputation had enabled it to become a successful niche player in this low volume market with healthy gross margins in excess of 40%. NMS faced two or three competitors in this specialist market which had the advantage of not requiring new systems to have government approval.

Finally, the complexity of NMS products meant than technical support was a third key business area. This reflected Ray's continuing concern with customer care. NMS again had established a reputation for excellent technical support – the only problem being that the company lacked a national network for service support, with all technical support coming from its London base. This contrasted with the international service structure operated by the large, international competitors.

NMS's growth had made Ray aware of a number of problem areas the company faced compared with its larger competitors. One problem concerned the ability of NMS to read market trends, scan its competitive environment and create marketing strategies and plans. NMS's market and sales planning only covered the year ahead. Larger competitors could invest heavily in sophisticated market research analysis and customer relationship marketing. Accurate sales forecasting was a key input into production planning and scheduling. NMS manufactured some 40%

of its systems and bought in many items, including semiconductors and microchips, from global suppliers, which were then built into its complex products. Serious problems occurred when component shortages occurred, creating significant delays in manufacturing, assembly, and customer deliveries. The growth of NMS had outstripped the largely manual control systems designed to support production and sales.

Emerging problems

Ray was acutely aware of his key role as founder and chairman of the firm. He was finding the skills and attributes necessary for founding and growing the business were no longer as critical to the mature business. Heavily reliant on his extrovert personality and ability to muddle through with informal, flexible systems, the limitations of such an approach were now beginning to show. How could he combine the day-to-day demands of running the business while at the same time planning its future? Functional departments in the shape of Sales and Marketing, Technical (R&D), Manufacturing and Administration were in place but strategic planning, such as there was, was very much Ray's responsibility. Recruitment of high calibre staff was also a problem – NMS's small size and location near London, meant it was struggling to attract key personnel necessary for future growth. Ray felt acutely aware of the pressure on him to either develop the necessary skills himself, or to develop the right people with the right skills. In Ray's words, starting a business was like 'building your own airplane and then teaching yourself how to fly'. One further skill set in short supply was the financial capability necessary to deal with growth. His dealings with his bankers and other financial intermediaries had become increasingly difficult and time consuming. The financial control information required to support growth, and more recently, survival was often inadequate. 2003 had started well with NMS being approached by a major data communications company as a target for a possible acquisition. The opportunity to realise some of the equity in the business had considerable appeal. Unfortunately, while protracted negotiations were taking place, a major downturn in the global economy began and many of Ray's worst fears were confirmed. The order book was drying up and the banks and venture capitalists 'supporting' NMS through overdraft and long-term investment became much less sympathetic. The final insult occurred when Ray had been approached by a venture capitalist with a management buyout proposal put together with NMS's Financial Director and General Manager. The value placed on the business was a derisory £50K. Ray was incensed and hurt by the size of the offer and the disloyalty of his senior staff in trying to buy the business. To make matters worse the uncertainty over the future of the business had led to a number of key members of staff deciding to leave the company.

Ray's future at NMS

Ray seemed to be confronted by so many options including whether he should leave the business. The three main exit options he has identified were, firstly, to personally lead the company out of its current problems, which he largely attributes to the global economic slowdown and float the business on the Stock Exchange as soon as possible. Secondly, to simply walk away and sell the business for a figure which more accurately reflected its real value. Thirdly, to look for acquisition by one of his large customers and to become part of a much larger organisation. By nature a fighter, the recent uncertainties over ownership and the gloomy forecasts for the global economy, have made him seriously reflect on his own priorities. His hands-on approach and involvement with all aspects of the business seems increasingly inappropriate for solving the problems of a hi-tech business such as NMS.

Table 1: Financial data for Network Management Systems

	2001 £'000	2002 £'000	2003 £'000	2004 (forecast) £'000
Sales				
UK sales	4,500	6,300	6,930	6,235
Export sales	300	500	650	520
Total sales	4,800	6,800	7,580	6,755
Cost of sales	2,640	3,770	4,550	4,320
Gross margin	2,160	3,030	3,030	2,435
Expenses				
Admin	500	630	700	665
Distribution	715	940	945	885
Marketing	50	60	70	70
R & D	495	590	870	690
Overheads	200	280	320	325
Operating profit	200	530	125	−200
Interest paid	25	120	150	165
Net profit	175	410	−25	−365
Financing				
Long term debt	160	750	1,000	1,100
Share capital & & reserves	375	605	600	575
Other information				
Employees	50	60	75	60
% of orders late	5	7	10	6
Outstanding orders	4,725	4,150	3,150	2,500

Required

(a) Ray has recently attended a course on strategic planning in hi-tech businesses. He is particularly interested in the contribution of mission statements to the strategic management process. Explain the purpose of a mission statement and evaluate the contribution which a mission statement could make to a company such as NMS. **(10 marks)**

(b) Using appropriate models and financial and quantitative data from the scenario to support your analysis, provide a report on the current position of NMS, highlighting major problem areas. **(25 marks)**

(c) Ray is now seeking to make a planned exit from the business as it currently exists. He has asked you to assess each of the three identified exit options in terms of their ability to solve the problems highlighted in your report. **(15 marks)**

(d) With particular reference to NMS, what are the features that distinguish business-to-business marketing from its consumer goods equivalent? **(10 marks)**

(Total = 60 marks)

51 Elite Plastic Packaging (12/04)

108 mins

Introduction

Jeff Wainwright is Managing Director of Elite Plastic Packaging (EPP), part of the Print and Packaging Division, which, in turn, is part of the Sigma Group plc, a diversified company with other separate product divisions in building materials, flooring products and speciality chemicals. The group had emerged during the 1970s as Sigma, like other companies, tried to compensate for the slowdown in internal growth by moving into different industries mainly through merger and acquisition. The grouping into product divisions was largely one of administrative convenience rather than compelling industrial logic and the Print and Packaging Division contained a number of companies which operated largely independently of one another.

Sigma Group corporate headquarters

The Sigma Group headquarters (HQ) is dominated by accountants who Jeff regards as reacting to, rather than anticipating, rivals. Risk is to be avoided wherever possible and projects only approved if they can demonstrate a three year payback – typically a 'one solution fits all' to the companies in the group. This view of risk was reinforced by the Divisional Chief Executive of the Print and Packaging Division, Tim Sterling, also an accountant by background, with whom Jeff had a working but uneasy relationship. There was little confidence that Tim would champion the cause of the companies within the Print and Packaging Division against the wishes of the Sigma Group's domineering Chairman and Chief Executive, Archie Williams.

Archie is convinced that a decentralised management style is the key to maintaining profitable growth in the future. Under him corporate HQ has two key functions, firstly, an executive role carried out by a small team of four – Archie Williams and three Group Directors, collectively known as the Group Executive. Each of the Group Directors takes a special interest in, but not responsibility for, one or more of the divisions and heads up a central support function. Of prime importance are the monthly meetings reviewing, sanctioning, and monitoring each Division's budgets. The process involves the Group Executive and the Division's senior management team and takes a minimum of one week every month generating the information and holding meetings with each of the divisions. Other Group Executive activities include the approval of divisional capital expenditure proposals, policies towards the appointing and remuneration of the top divisional management and planning and managing relationships with the financial world. The second distinct function carried out by corporate HQ are those support activities that were carried out centrally including treasury, financial reporting, tax planning, personnel and legal activities. Fewer than 100 people work at Group HQ.

The Group Executive has a very distinctive view of the relationship between company headquarters and the operating divisions. Archie Williams had been the architect of a recovery plan in the early 1990s which had cut costs and increased profits by getting rid of a number of earlier attempts to reduce geographic dependency on UK markets by moves into Europe, the Middle East and Asia, partly through acquisition. Focus had been placed on growing product areas with the potential for a quick turnaround in results. This on occasion meant reducing sales but improving profitability. The avoidance of earnings dilution was of central importance.

Sigma Group organisation chart

Strategic planning and budgeting in the Sigma Group

Elite Plastic Packaging (EPP)

EPP's main business is advanced plastic packaging where Jeff sees the greatest potential for growth. It manufactures injection moulded plastic packaging primarily for the food, drinks and confectionery markets. Jeff is encouraged by the support of large supermarket customers who have begun to insist that their major suppliers of both food and non-food goods use EPP's packaging. This means that EPP is now a supplier of plastic packaging to global manufacturers. Even more exciting is the development of 'intelligent' packaging where computer chips are built into the packaging allowing companies to 'track and trace' their products all over the world. Such a product has considerable appeal to manufacturers of expensive consumer luxury products such as perfume, alcohol and music discs where counterfeiting is a growing global problem.

EPP's global opportunities

Jeff's frustration with his Divisional Chief Executive and the Group Executive team at Sigma has been brought to a head by their reaction to a major opportunity to move the packaging business on to a global basis. EPP has had five years of fast and very profitable growth in the European market and now wants to exploit the full global market by expansion into both the USA and Asian markets. EPP's share of the European specialist plastic packaging market has reached 50% generating some £50 million in sales revenue. The latest version of the packaging yields significant operating benefits to the manufacturers using it and as a result is generating a 15% net sales margin for EPP. The total world market is estimated at £300 million a year split evenly between the three major regional markets – Europe, the Americas and Asia. Potential competitor packaging companies exist but these have generally failed to invest sufficiently in the new technology to be effective. The issue is how best to enter the American and Asian markets and to convince the risk averse Sigma Group HQ to provide the necessary investment.

Four market entry strategies are available. Firstly, to license the technology to third parties and obtain a royalty of 5% of sales. Secondly, to set up with new green field sites. Net margins would be greater than 15% as the European region would absorb most of the marketing, development and administration costs. Thirdly, subcontracting the manufacturing to a suitable partner. Profits would need to be shared 60:40 in favour of the subcontractor. Finally, by acquisition which would need to be in a related technology and provide access to the relevant sales channels to achieve growth. Each option has its own advantages and disadvantages and capital investment and budgetary consequences.

The HQ philosophy is to devolve and decentralise to the divisions all activities that affect a division's costs and revenues. They want the Divisional Chief Executives to feel that they have complete control over their division's performance. The division's senior management team and the Group Executive at the monthly board meeting critically review each division's performance. These monthly Divisional Executive Boards, in addition to reviewing the division's on-going performance against budget, also considers opportunities and threats and formal plans and budgets. It is the detailed attention and care given to budgeting and performance monitoring that determines the relationship between the Group Executive and its operating divisions. The bottom-up planning process starts with the individual companies in each division developing their own strategy. The financial consequences of this strategy are then built into a divisional budget that is stretching but achievable. This target is designed to be owned by the division and motivate the management team. Budget procedures are formally laid down and extremely comprehensive. Tim Sterling spends a day with each company's MD working on the budget to be presented to the Group Executive. Agreeing the budget is a stressful time as it is the key to Sigma's performance evaluation. Failure to achieve is unacceptable and a divisional management team unable to deliver its promises is under considerable pressure from the Group Executive.

The Group Executive do not get involved with the strategy planning process and see the budget as the tangible evidence of division's strategic planning and in effect a contract to deliver over the coming year. Budgets are typically agreed at the November or December meeting of the Divisional Executive Board and reviewed at subsequent Board meetings, which can last up to half-a-day. The process ensures that the Group Executive are fully aware of each division's performance, where problems are occurring, and able to share thinking on solutions. The Group Executive firmly resists telling a division what to do.

Agreement to significant capital expenditure will be influenced by the previous track record of the division, the fit with their current business, a potential return above that currently being achieved and above all the commitment of the management team. Avoidance of projects with long lead times and in areas not closely connected to existing activities guides approval. Overall, therefore, the Sigma Group has no centrally determined strategy and its broad objectives are aimed at ensuring profitable growth each and every year. Acquisitions, when approved, are focused on the buying of assets rather than incumbent management. Such acquisitions are then left to the divisions to successfully integrate them. Archie Williams firmly believes that the tight budgetary control operated from the centre provides both the incentive and punishment for divisions to achieve profits today and profitable growth tomorrow.

Table 1: Information on the Sigma Group's current sales and financial performance (£'000) (where appropriate)

Year	20X0	20X1	20X2	20X3	20X4
Sigma Group	£m	£m	£m	£m	£m
Group sales	580.2	419.8	382.6	354.6	350.7
Group operating profit	62.9	34.7	23.6	21.9	20.1
Operating margin (%)	10.8	8.3	6.2	6.2	5.7
Print & Packaging	£m	£m	£m	£m	£m
Sales	107.5	87.6	97.4	111.3	117.9
Operating profit	17.2	13.0	11.8	13.5	12.3
Operating margin (%)	16.0	14.9	12.1	12.1	10.4
Elite Plastic Packaging company (EPP)	£m	£m	£m	£m	£m
Sales	28.1	31.5	35.2	45.1	52.3
Operating profit	9.3	10.9	13.2	17.6	21.1
Operating margin (%)	33.1	34.6	37.5	39.0	40.3

Required

Jeff is keen to evaluate the current strategic position and future options facing Elite Plastic Packaging and has asked you to do the following for him:

(a)   Prepare a short report evaluating the advantages and disadvantages of each market entry strategy taking into account the Group Executive's short-term performance focus.   **(20 marks)**

(b)   Examine the value added by the Group Executive to the strategic management of the divisions and the costs and benefits of this style of involvement.   **(15 marks)**

(c)   Assuming that Jeff is successful in his plan to move EPP into a global operation, discuss which communication, control and co-ordination issues are raised by such a change.   **(15 marks)**

Jeff is sceptical of the contribution that accountants can make to the strategic management process.

(d)   Write a brief report explaining the positive contribution senior accountants within the Sigma Group can make to the strategic management process in their organisation.   **(10 marks)**

(Total = 60 marks)

52 LRP   108 mins

LRP is a division of Stillwell Slim, a large, diversified conglomerate with extensive operations in Europe, North America and the Far East. Originally a UK general engineering business, LRP now operates internationally and specialises in the production of high quality fasteners. Its products range from simple nuts and bolts to complex devices for high stress applications such as submersibles and satellites. The company was sold to Stillwell Slim by its founder, Mr Wingate, when he retired in 1990 and is now managed by Joe Lentaigne, who had joined five years before the sale as Deputy Production Manager.

Stillwell Slim is controlled from a small global headquarters in Lickskillet, Ohio. Its overall strategy may be described as high technology products subject to satisfactory cash flow. Other SBUs include a manufacturer of airliner galleys; an aviation service company whose operations range from engine overhaul to the management of complete airports; a company that builds high capacity trunk telecomms switching nodes; and a design boutique specialising in military standard printed circuits. LRP is a typical Stillwell Slim SBU, having provided a satisfactory return on investment in nine of the past ten years and having funded much of its expansion from its own profits. There is considerable intra-group trade, which is managed by negotiation among the SBUs.

Mr Lentaigne, while essentially a practical engineer, has become accustomed to thinking strategically and globally. LRP has no formal mission statement, but if asked for one, Mr Lentaigne would probably say something along the lines of 'making profit by making very good fasteners'. He feels that the success of the company depends on two main factors: efficiency in production and keeping up with the technology. He has therefore employed Dr Mike Calvert, a recent PhD in metallurgy, to maintain a continuing review of developments in all aspects of the technology. LRP does no research itself, but has developed several new products by applying the research of others, including competitors.

Production efficiency is the responsibility of Jack Masters, the Production Director. His background is in production engineering in the motor components sector. LRP has plants in Ireland, Taiwan and the UK and Mr Masters spends about 180 days a year away from the UK headquarters. He thinks the company has made great progress in both productivity and quality, but does not have the volume of throughput in any of its plants to achieve major purchasing economies. Mr Masters' ambitions for the company include the updating of the machinery in the UK plant, where some machines date back to Mr Wingate's time, and the introduction of computer-based resource scheduling systems to each of the three plants.

Sales and marketing issues are dealt with by Bernard Fergusson, the Sales Director. The market for LRP's more mundane products is very large and competition is tough. Price and delivery are what customers look for, and there is little opportunity to differentiate products. The market is global, but the weight of the products means that airfreight is expensive; on the other hand, intercontinental surface transport inevitably imposes a time penalty on delivery. While the global market is growing at about 4% per annum, historically, the USA has always outstripped the average, and even with the slowdown in the US economy, the lack of a manufacturing facility in North America has always hampered sales.

It has also affected the sale of the more complex, higher value-added products, though not to the same extent, because high and consistent quality is the key to the markets for those products. A more important factor in this market has been the appearance of TIG Products. TIG's production facilities are located in an eastern European country, which combines high technical ability with low costs. Mr Fergusson has recently established that TIG is a joint venture between an established western competitor and a local company, rather than being a wholly owned subsidiary of the competitor. Mr Fergusson made informal contact with the CEO of the eastern European partner company at a recent trade fair and was surprised at a revelation made by him in an unguarded moment late one evening. The CEO stated his belief that the western partner company intends to renege on the joint venture agreement (which was committed to paper but never signed) because it is restructuring its operations. This could lead to major loss for the eastern company. The CEO indicated that he would welcome an approach from LRP to replace the competitor. He went on to explain that such a deal should be very attractive to LRP, since it would enable it to join a price-fixing trade association in a particular regional market that it had never previously been able to penetrate.

Table 1 – Data pertaining to LRP

	1998	1999	2000
Turnover – North America	£7.23m	£7.37m	£7.35m
Turnover – Europe	£27.56m	£28.39m	£29.12m
Turnover – Rest of the world	£14.63m	£15.92m	£17.03m
Profit after capital charges	£4.82m	£6.23m	£6.05m
Market share – basic fasteners	9.76%	9.82%	8.32%
Market share – sophisticated fasteners	4.67%	5.21%	6.83%
Number of employees	147	159	163
Overdraft	£9.78m	£10.24m	£11.02m
WIP*	107%	112%	103%
Finished goods stocks*	98%	115%	121%
Customer returns by value*	57%	87%	124%
Reject rate*	87%	114%	137%
Productivity index*	84%	92%	102%
Average age of machinery	8.6 yrs	9.6 yrs	10.2 yrs

* LRP participates in a confidential benchmarking scheme that includes most major manufacturers of fasteners globally. Industry averages are computed from information provided by member firms; the performance of each member is then assessed against the averages and the results fed back. For example, LRP's productivity index for 2000 means that it achieved 102% of the industry global average productivity.

Required

(a) As a consultant, prepare a report for the CEO of Stillwell Slim assessing the strategic potential of LRP. (You are not required to undertake portfolio analysis of the Stillwell Slim group as a whole.) Mr Fergusson has not revealed his conversation with the eastern European CEO to you. **(25 marks)**

(b) Discuss the usefulness of the diversified conglomerate business model. **(15 marks)**

(c) Neither Stillwell Slim nor LRP has any formal policy on business ethics. Discuss the ethical dimension of the TIG partner CEO's proposal. **(20 marks)**

(Total = 60 marks)

53 Screen Books

108 mins

Jack Benfold Limited is a small independent publisher in London. The management of the business is still dominated by the Benfold family, though several professional managers have been recruited in the last fifteen years. At one time the company specialised in medical text books, but it lost substantial ground in this field during the prolonged illness of the then managing director, George Benfold, the founder's son. The present managing director, Thomas Speight, is George's son-in-law. He brought considerable publishing experience when he joined the company as editorial director twelve years ago and he has succeeded in restoring the company's fortunes by moving into the travel and cookery markets. However, the trend in publishing has been towards the creation of ever-larger companies by amalgamations and takeovers, and independent publishers are tending to become niche operators.

Mr Speight has taken a close interest in the development of Internet commerce as a strategic option for smaller businesses. He formed an alliance with John Rogers Books Limited, a small chain of bookshops in the Midlands. The original plan was to sell books over the Internet, with John Rogers Books providing most of the administrative and logistic facilities and Jack Benfold the capital and Internet technology. A joint venture subsidiary called Screen Books Limited was set up in 1996, with a website called Screenbooks.com.

Screen Books expanded quite successfully and more or less in accordance with its business plan. Its advertising and rapid growth attracted the attention of Rupert Coke, who was at school with Thomas Speight and is now a senior merchant banker. Mr Coke's bank was promoting the dotcom business model heavily in the late 1990's and saw Screen Books as a candidate for heavy capital injection. Mr Speight was enthusiastic about this possibility because he had an idea for a technology-based strategy that would require considerable investment to launch.

Mr Speight proposed the development of a small, portable, liquid crystal display (LCD) screen device dedicated to the presentation of text. The device's memory would be capable of holding the equivalent of up to ten 'blockbuster' novels. It would be inherently Internet-capable, though without a proper browser and it would be programmed to connect automatically to Screenbooks.com. Customers would be able to review Screen Books' catalogue, download books and magazines and pay for them by credit card on line.

Mr Speight felt that such a device would appeal to a wide range of potential customers and suggested that such a device was particularly attractive because it exploited the main characteristic of the Internet: the high-speed transfer of information in electronic form. It would be independent of warehouses and carriers and other aspects of physical order fulfilment, with consequent benefits for efficiency and quality.

Such devices had already been produced but not on a large scale: there was a need for considerable technical development, which would be expensive. The success of the venture would also depend on the size of Screen Books' own catalogue and permission from other publishers to offer their titles in electronic form.

Mr Coke was sufficiently impressed with the proposal to arrange an initial injection of loan capital in early 1998. Contracts were let with research agencies and marketing staff were recruited. Such was the interest in the proposed product that a flotation on the London Stock Exchange was undertaken in late 1998 and the initial issue of 10p shares was heavily oversubscribed. More research was undertaken, with in-house staff being hired, and a major marketing campaign was planned to launch the new product. To fill the gap until the new device was available, the existing Screenbooks.com website was heavily promoted, with a major advertising campaign and generous discounts. CDs and 'lifestyle' accessories were added to the product range and more marketing, sales and administrative staff were recruited at all levels.

Unfortunately, there are now indications that all is not well. The development of the crucial screen-based device has been held up by fundamental technical limitations. It also seems that the demand for LCD screens has grown to such an extent that prices remain higher than forecast, which will have a major effect on selling price when the device is launched. Expenditure on both research and marketing has been higher than forecast and the marketing director has left the company after only ten months in the job.

There is some doubt about the ultimate demand for the product, as well; research seems to indicate that people are very happy with electronic games consoles, since they offer facilities unobtainable elsewhere, but they do not see the point of the electronic book. A recent article in an influential business newspaper discussed this problem in detail, and some investors are getting cold feet.

Table 1 – Summary data

	1996	1997	1998	1999	2000
Turnover £'000	367	635	1026	2176	4309
Operating loss £'000	42	54	728	1032	1097
Marketing costs £'000	5.5	8.2	198	349	422
Loan capital £'000			500	550	1700
Spending on R&D £'000			204	639	721
Headcount - Marketing	2	4	9	18	42
Headcount – R&D	1	1	17	24	28
Head count - Telesales	4	5	7	16	28
Nominal value of capital at year end £'000	200	200	12498	12498	12498
Share price p high/low	–	–	72/46	85/63	67/17

Required

(a)   Assess the strategy adopted by Screen Books to date.   **(25 marks)**

(b)   Acting in the role of consultant, consider how Screen Books' operations could be developed in the future.
                                                                                                               (15 marks)

(c)   Screen Books' plans appear to have been heavily dependent on the new screen-based product. How could it have best managed its technological innovation?   **(20 marks)**

                                                                                                  (Total = 60 marks)

54 Universal Roofing Systems (6/05)   108 mins

Introduction

Universal Roofing Systems is a family owned and managed business specialising in the design, assembly and installation of low maintenance PVC roofing products for domestic housing. These products include PVC fascia boards and rainwater drainage systems. Set up in 1995 by two brothers, Matthew and Simon Black, the firm has grown year on year, achieving almost £1 million sales by the year 2001. Universal's products, or rather services, are primarily for private house owners, though a significant amount of sales are coming from commercial house owners, mainly local government authorities and housing associations, providing cheaper housing for rent. Universal have recently received central government recognition and an award for their contribution to providing employment in deprived inner city areas. In 2002 and 2003, they were the fastest growing inner city firm in their region.

Origins and competitive environment

Matthew and Simon's decision to go into business owed a considerable amount to the experience and skills they had gained working in their father's local cabinet and carpentry business. At their father's insistence, both were skilled cabinet-makers and shared his commitment to quality workmanship and installation. Their decision to start a business using PVC materials as opposed to wood came as an unwelcome shock to their father. However, the opportunity to install PVC roofing boards on the house of a commercial contact provided the stimulus for them to go into business on their own account.

In the UK there are some 25 million houses, of which 17 million are privately owned and 8 million rented. New housing is now usually built with PVC doors and windows installed, so it is the replacement market of rotten wooden doors and windows in existing houses that the manufacturers and installers of PVC windows and doors focus on. PVC offers some significant advantages to the owner/occupier – it is virtually maintenance free and improves the appearance of the house. Consequently, there is a high demand for PVC replacement doors and windows, estimated at £1·5 billion in the year 2000. This has attracted some large-scale manufacturers and installers. They compete aggressively for market share and use equally aggressive direct sales and promotion techniques to attract house owners to their product.

Although the market for PVC windows and doors is reasonably mature, there has been no significant movement of large companies into the installation of roofing products. Their complex design and location at the top of a house mean that these products are much more complex and difficult to install. Economies of scale are harder to achieve and, as a consequence, the installation of PVC roofing systems is largely in the hands of small businesses able to charge high prices and frequently giving a poor quality service to the house owner. In a market with potential sales of £750 million a year, no firm accounts for more than 3%. It was against this fragmented, but significant market that Universal wanted to offer something distinctively different.

Operational processes

Matthew and Simon looked at the whole process of delivering a quality service in replacement PVC roofing systems. The experience of the PVC door and window installers showed the long-term rates of growth possible through actively promoting and selling the service. Supplies of PVC board and fittings were reasonably easy to obtain from the small number of large UK companies extruding PVC boards in large volumes. However, the unequal bargaining power meant that these suppliers dominated and were difficult to involve in any product development. Sales were generated by door-to-door canvassing, followed by a visit from a company sales representative who tried to complete the sale. Advertising in the press, radio and TV now supported this sales activity. In the early days the opportunity was taken to sell the service at Saturday markets and, being so small, Universal could often pleasantly surprise the house owner by offering virtually immediate installation. Matthew and Simon promoted, sold and installed the systems. One of their key early decisions was to use a new Mercedes van with Universal's name and logo prominently displayed, to carry the bulky PVC materials to their customers' houses. In one move they differentiated themselves from their low cost/low quality competitors and got the company's name recognised.

The skills and experience of the brothers meant that they were able to critically examine the installation process being used by their small competitors to deliver a poor standard of service. Their eventual design incorporated innovative roofing design and parts from Europe and a unique installation stand or frame that provided the installer with quick, easy and safe access to the roofs of the houses being worked on. This greatly improved the productivity of Universal's installation team over competitors using traditional methods. The brothers recognised that without the ability to offer a service that could be packaged, given standard prices and procedures and made as 'installer friendly' as possible they too would be limited to small scale operation and poor service. Being able to replicate a process time after time was the key to delivering an improved service and preventing each job being seen as a 'one-off'. In Matthew's words, 'Whenever the customer can have a predictable experience and you can say that this is what we are going to do, this is the way we are going to do it and this is how much it will cost, the product/service usually goes problem free'.

Ultimately, the installers of the roofing systems determined quality. The brothers quickly built up a team of installers, all of whom worked as sub-contractors and were not directly employed by the company. This gave the company the flexibility to vary the number of teams according to the level of customer demand. Installation took place throughout the year, though it could be affected by winter weather. The two man teams were given comprehensive training in installation and customer care. Payment was by results and responsibility for correcting any installation faults rested with the team doing the particular installation.

Sales and marketing

Marketing and promotion were recognised as key to getting the company's name known and its reputation for a quality installation service established. Comprehensive sales support materials were created for use by the canvassers and sales representatives. Sales representative were able to offer significant discounts to house owners willing to make an immediate decision to buy a Universal roofing system. In addition Universal received a significant income stream from a finance house for roofing systems, sold on extended payment terms.

Universal offered a unique 10-year guarantee on its installations and proudly announced that over 30% of new customers were directly recommended from existing satisfied customers. The growth of the company had led to showrooms being set up in six large towns in the region and the business plans for 2005 and 2006 will see a further nine showrooms opening in the region, each of which costs £30K. Brand awareness was reinforced by the continued use of up-to-date Mercedes vans with the company's logo and contact details prominently shown.

Company structure and performance

By 2005, the organisational structure of the company was in place, based on functional responsibilities. Matthew was now Managing Director, Simon was Operations Director with responsibility for the installation teams, and Matthew's wife, Fiona, was Company Secretary and responsible for the administration and scheduling side of the business. Two key appointments had facilitated Universal's rapid growth. In 2002, Mick Hendry was appointed as Sales and Marketing Director. Mick had 20 years of experience with direct sales in a large installer of PVC windows and doors. Through his efforts, Universal achieved a step change in sales growth, with sales increasing from £1 million in 2001 to £3·3 million in 2002. However, the increased costs involved meant the company made a loss of some £250,000. 2003 saw sales increase to £5·4 million and a profit generated. 2004 saw further sales increase to £6·8 million and a net profit of about £400K. Matthew recognised the increasing pressure on his own time and an inability to control the financial side of the business. 2003 saw Harry Potts appointed as Finance Director and put in much needed financial and management information systems.

Future growth and development

By 2005 Universal had seen 10 years of significant growth and was facing some interesting decisions as to how that growth was to be sustained. Firstly, there was the opportunity to move from a largely regional operation into being a national company. Indeed, the company's vision statement expressed the desire to become 'the most respected roofing company in Britain', based on a 'no surprises' philosophy that house owners all around the country could trust. Economic factors encouraging growth looked fairly promising with a growing economy, stable interest rates and house owners finding it fairly easy to raise additional funding necessary to pay for home improvements. Secondly, there was a real opportunity to develop their share of the commercial housing market. The government had committed itself to a significant improvement in the standard of housing provided to people renting from local authorities and housing associations. Despite the appointment of a Commercial Manager to concentrate on sales into this specialist market, Universal had real difficulty in committing sufficient resources into exploiting this opportunity. In 2002 commercial sales represented over 11% of total sales, but currently commercial sales were around 5% of the total sales. Such were the overall growth predictions, however, that to maintain this share of sales would need commercial sales to more than double over the 2005–7 period. Without the necessary commitment of resources, particularly people, this target was unlikely to be realised. Universal's products also need to be improved and this largely depended on its ability to get into partnerships with its large PVC suppliers. There were some encouraging signs in this direction, but Universal's reliance on PVC opened it to future challenges from installers using more environmentally friendly materials.

Above all, however, the rate of projected growth would place considerable pressures on the senior management team's ability to manage the process. The move towards becoming a national installer was already prompting thoughts about creating a regional level of management. Finally, such had been the firm's growth record that its inability to meet the budgeted sales targets in the first quarter of 2005 was causing real concern for Matthew and Simon.

Table 1: Information on Universal's current sales and financial performance (£'000) (where appropriate)

Universal Roofing Systems Financial information

	2001	2002	2003	2004	2005 Budget	2006 Forecast	2007 Forecast
Domestic sales	854	2,914	5,073	6,451	9,600	15,000	20,500
Commercial sales	36	362	269	324	450	750	1,100
Total Sales	890	3,276	5,342	6,775	10,050	15,750	21,600
Materials	169	589	766	925	1,339	2,105	2,890
Direct Labour	329	1,105	1,941	2,290	3,333	5,125	7,019
Gross Margin	392	1,582	2,635	3,560	5,378	8,520	11,691
Sales commission	20	369	627	781	1,171	1,845	2,501
Canvassers' commissions	74	563	764	962	1,420	2,190	2,993
Marketing	32	171	223	398	657	1,020	1,374
Total sales costs	126	1,103	1,614	2,141	3,248	5,055	6,868
Contribution before overhead	266	479	1,021	1,419	2,130	3,465	4,823
Total overheads	272	723	862	1,140	1,536	2,030	2,627
Trading profit before commission	–6	–244	159	279	594	1,435	2,196
Finance income	0	25	65	115	167	262	342
Net profit	–6	–219	224	394	761	1,697	2,538

Required

(a) Using an appropriate model, analyse the ways in which Universal has provided a superior level of service to its customers. **(20 marks)**

(b) Using the information provided in the case scenario, strategically evaluate the performance of the company up to 2004, indicating any areas of particular concern. **(20 marks)**

(c) Matthew Black is well aware that the achievement of the growth targets for the 2005 to 2007 period will depend on successful implementation of the strategy, affecting all parts of the company's activities.

Required

Explain the key issues affecting implementation and the changes necessary to achieve Universal's ambitious growth strategy. **(15 marks)**

(d) What criteria would you use to assess whether Universal is an 'excellent' company? **(5 marks)**

(Total = 60 marks)

55 Datum Paper Products (12/05)　　　108 mins

Introduction and industry background

The current European market for Datum Paper Products (DPP) in 2005 is not encouraging. The company designs and manufactures textile fabrics for use in the paper industry. Its main customers are large European and American paper making companies and while the UK market is fairly stable, over 80% of DPP's products are sold abroad. Its customers use highly expensive capital equipment, with a new paper mill costing £300 million or more. The paper makers supply paper to global newspaper and book publishers who themselves are under pressure to consolidate as a result of the growing competition from alternative information providers, such as TV and the Internet. The industry, therefore, carries many of the signs of a mature industry, the paper manufacturers have considerable overcapacity and are supplying customers who themselves are facing intense competition. Paper makers are looking to reduce the number of suppliers and for these suppliers to meet all their needs. The net result is heavy pressure on suppliers such as DPP to discount prices and improve international service levels, although there is little potential to increase sales volumes to achieve further economies of scale. DPP's response to this more competitive environment has been to attempt to secure higher volumes through increasing their market share and to search for cost reductions in spite of the need to improve customer service levels.

DPP is one of a number of operating companies in the paper and ancillary products division of Park Group Industries plc, a diversified company with other divisions in industrial materials, automotive products and speciality chemicals. The paper and ancillary products division itself is split into the North American Region and the European Region. There are some 30 companies in the division with plants in 13 countries. Within the paper and ancillary products division there is recognition that in order to survive let alone make a profit some industry restructuring is necessary. Currently, DPP has some four UK plants manufacturing different parts of their product range. Any consolidation, including acquisition, is best done on a regional basis and Europe seems a logical place to start.

Strategic options – acquisition or a greenfield site?

Ken Drummond is Managing Director of DPP, and has spent a lifetime in the paper industry but has had little experience in acquiring other companies. The pressures faced by the European industry mean that there are, in reality, two strategic options to achieve the necessary restructuring. Firstly, there are opportunities to buy existing companies available in most European countries. The identification of suitable target companies, the carrying out of due diligence procedures before negotiating a deal and integration of the acquired company typically takes a year to complete. The second option is to move to one of the countries that have entered the European Union in 2004 where operating costs are significantly lower. There are significant government and European Union incentives for firms that move to a new or greenfield site in one of the many economically depressed areas. The greenfield option would take up to three years to get a plant set up and operating.

The acquisition option

Ken is able to draw on the expertise of corporate headquarters that has had some experience with growth by both organic expansion and by acquisition. The initial search for possible acquisition candidates has revealed a French family owned and managed firm, 'Papier Presse', based in the southwest of France, some 800 kilometres from DPP's main plant in the UK. Papier Presse has three manufacturing plants in France, each heavily unionised and controlled by the owner Philippe Truffaud. Papier Presse's markets are exclusively with European paper makers and it has no significant international business outside of the EU. The technology used is more dated than DPP's and manning levels are significantly higher. Papier Presse's product range has some significant overlap with DPP's but there are also some distinctive products. Philippe's son, Francois, is Sales and Marketing Director and his son-in-law, Henri, is Operations Manager. Philippe himself is the third generation of Truffauds to run the firm. Ken recognises the considerable differences between DPP and its potential French partner – language being only the most obvious one.

The sales, service and distribution systems of the two firms are totally distinct but their customers include the same European paper makers. Reconciling the two information systems would be difficult, with customers looking for much higher service levels. Historically, DPP, with its own research and development function, has a better record of product improvement and innovation. However, Papier Presse is better regarded by its customers for its flexibility in meeting their changing demands. In terms of strategic planning DPP contributes to the strategic plans drawn up at divisional level, while the family dominance at Papier Presse means that planning is much more opportunistic and largely focused on the year ahead. Each company has to operate within a climate of heightened environmental concern over toxic by-products of the manufacturing process. There are other similarities in that both companies have felt that product superiority is the route to success but whereas DPP's is through product innovation; Papier Presse's is through customer service. Clearly integrating the two companies will present some interesting challenges and the family ownership of Papier Presse means that a significant premium may have to be paid over the current book value of the company.

The greenfield option

Ken, however, also recognises that the apparent benefits of moving onto a new greenfield site in one of the countries recently admitted into the European Union will itself bring difficulties. One obvious difficulty is the lack of a modern support infrastructure in terms of suppliers, distributors and logistical support. There is also a strong tradition of government intervention in company growth and development. Although there are government agencies looking to attract new companies to set up in these countries, there are considerable bureaucratic and time consuming procedures to overcome. Above all there is continuing government financial support for small inefficient, formerly state-owned, companies making the products for the national paper makers, who themselves are small and inefficient compared to the customers being supplied by DPP and Papier Presse.

BPP
LEARNING MEDIA

Table 1: Financial information on DPP and Papier Presse (£'000,000) for 2005

	Datum Paper Products	Papier Presse
Sales	195.5	90.0
Cost of sales	122.2	67.5
Gross margin	73.3	22.5
Sales and administration	27.4	9.0
Marketing	9.5	1.4
R&D	4.5	0.5
Depreciation	10.0	1.0
Operating profit	21.9	10.6
Net assets	275.0	148.0
Debt	100.0	68.0
Equity	175.0	80.0
Earnings per share	12·5p	13·3p
Dividend per share	5·6p	10·0p
Return on sales	11·2%	11·8%
Employees	1,250	750
Absenteeism (days p.a.)	8	16
Patents – 2004	5	0
Manufacturing facilities	4	3
Sales from products less than 5 years old	20%	5%
Share of major European markets:		
UK	45%	14%
France	10%	60%
Italy	8%	20%
Germany	15%	15%
Spain	10%	25%
Sales outside Europe	50%	5%
North America region	40%	3%
Rest of World	10%	2%

Required

(a) Using the data provided and models where appropriate, assess the strategic fit between Datum Paper Products and Papier Presse, indicating areas where positive or negative synergies are likely to exist.

(20 marks)

(b) Assuming that the acquisition proceeds, what steps will Datum Paper Products need to take to build a shared culture in the two companies? **(10 marks)**

(c) Assess the advantages and disadvantages to Datum Paper Products taking the greenfield option as opposed to the acquisition of Papier Presse. **(15 marks)**

(d) There is considerable evidence to suggest that as a result of implementation problems less than 50% of all acquisitions achieve their objectives and actually end up reducing shareholder value.

Required

Provide Ken with a brief report on the most likely sources of integration problems and describe the key performance indicators he should use to measure progress towards acquisition objectives. **(15 marks)**

(Total = 60 marks)

56 Churchill Ice Cream (6/06)   108 mins

Origins and ownership

Churchill Ice Cream is a medium-sized family owned company, making and selling a range of premium ice cream products. Its origins were in the middle years of the twentieth century, when John Churchill saw an opportunity to supply a growing consumer demand for luxury products. John has been followed into the business by his two sons and the Churchill family has dominated the ownership and management of the company. In 2001 there was recognition of the need to bring in outside management expertise and John reluctantly accepted the need to relinquish his position as chairman and chief executive of the company. Richard Smith, formerly a senior executive with one of the major supermarket chains, was appointed as chief executive. Within one year of Richard's appointment he had recruited Churchill's first sales and marketing director. Richard was consciously looking to reduce the dominance by the Churchill family and make the company a more marketing orientated business able to meet the increased competitive challenges of the 21st century.

Churchill's distinctive strategy

Churchill Ice Cream is in many ways an unusual company, choosing to both manufacture its premium ice cream and sell its products through its own stores. Specialist ice cream stores or parlours had started in the US and soon spread to the UK. Customers can both buy and eat ice cream in the store. John Churchill saw the growing demand for such specialist ice cream stores and created a unique store format, which quickly established the Churchill brand. Most of these stores are owned by the company, but there are also some smaller franchised outlets. By 2005 it had 40 ice cream stores owned by the company and a further 18 owned by franchise holders. Franchise stores typically are in less attractive locations than their company-owned equivalents. All stores are located in and around the London area.

The logic for manufacturing its own ice cream is a strongly held belief that through sourcing its ingredients from local farmers and suppliers it gains a significant competitive advantage. Making its own ice cream also has enabled it to retain control over the unique recipes used in its premium ice cream product range. John Churchill summed up the policy saying 'We are no more expensive than the market leader but we are much better. We use real chocolate and it's real dairy ice cream. Half our expenditure goes on our ingredients and packaging. It's by far our highest cost.' Dairy ice cream, as opposed to cheaper ice cream, uses milk, butter and cream instead of vegetable oils to blend with sugar and flavourings. These ingredients are blended to produce a wide range of products. Churchill has also developed a product range with no artificial additives hoping to differentiate itself from the competition.

Product innovation is a key capability in the ice cream market and 40% of industry sales are made from products less than three years old. Churchill's products are made at a new purpose built factory and supplied quickly and directly to its own ice cream stores and other retail outlets. Unfortunately, detailed and timely information about product and store performance has suffered through a delay in introducing a management information system. Consequently its stores often faced product shortages during the peak summer months.

In 2003 Churchill became the sponsor and sole supplier to a number of high profile summer sporting events held in London. Churchill also supplies eight million tubs of ice cream each year to London based cinemas and theatres. As a consequence, Churchill is now an established regional brand with 90% customer recognition in the London area. It also has major ambitions to become a national and eventually an international brand though facing significant competition from two global chains of US owned premium ice cream stores. Their high profile moves into the UK market was backed with expensive advertising and succeeded in expanding the demand for all premium ice creams.

The UK retail ice cream market

Ice cream is bought in two main ways: either from retail outlets such as supermarkets for later consumption at home or on impulse for immediate consumption from a range of outlets, including ice cream stores such as Churchill's. Impulse sales are much more dependent on the weather and in 2003 sales of take home ice cream and impulse ice cream were roughly equal. Total sales of ice cream in the UK reached £1·3 billion in 2003. Premium ice cream in 2005 accounted for 19% of the UK's take home market, up from 15% in 2002.

Churchill itself does not use advertising. In John Churchill's words, 'There is no point in advertising your product if consumers are unable to buy the product.' Churchill has yet to achieve significant sales into the take home market. Two major barriers exist. Firstly, global manufacturers with significant global brands dominate the industry. Secondly, four major UK supermarket chains dominate the take home market. These supermarket chains account for over 80% of food spending in the UK and have the power to demand that suppliers manufacture their products under the supermarket's own label brand. Supermarkets currently account for 41% of the sales of ice cream in the UK.

However, it is proving difficult to get the Churchill product range into the ice cream cabinets of the supermarket chains. In John Churchill's opinion 'If you want to buy a tub of premium ice cream and you go to a supermarket you have a choice of two American brands or its own label. I think there should be a British brand in there. Our prices are competitive, at least £1 cheaper than our rivals and our aim is to get Churchill ice cream into every major supermarket.' Some limited success has been achieved with two of the smaller supermarket chains with premium ice cream supplied under their own label brands. However, margins are very slim on these sales.

Churchill's international strategy

Churchill, in seeking to increase its sales, has had no success in moving into foreign markets. In the 1990s it tried both setting up its own ice cream stores abroad and acquiring specialist ice cream makers with their own ice cream outlets. Its attempted entry into the US market was by using the established Churchill ice cream store format. Two stores were opened in New York, but the hopes that the emphasis on classic English quality and style and the slogan 'tradition with taste', would prove successful did not materialise and the stores were closed with significant losses – each store took upwards of £100K to fit out.

Acquisition of two established ice cream makers, one in Germany and one in Italy also proved failures. Access to their retail outlets and to complementary product ranges did not overcome differences in taste and customer buying behaviour. Despite attempts to change some of the German and Italian outlets to the Churchill store format the results were less than impressive and the two companies were eventually sold at a combined loss of £5 million.

Table 1 Financial information on Churchill Ice Cream (£'000)

	2002	2003	2004	2005	2006 forecast
Sales	14,100	15,300	16,000	16,400	16,700
Cost of sales	12,790	14,250	14,990	15,360	15,760
Operating profit	1,310	1,050	1,010	1,040	940
Product development	340	530	560	310	500
Net profit	970	520	450	730	440
Fixed assets	10,910	10,400	9,670	8,880	8,320
Net assets	4,810	4,910	4,000	4,300	4,300
Gearing (%)	105	130	111	86	67
Number of UK outlets					
Own stores	39	41	40	40	39
Franchised stores	11	13	16	18	20
Index of UK ice cream sales	106	109	107	104	109

Table 2 Typical product cost breakdown of a Churchill half-litre tub of premium ice cream

	£
Labour	0·63
Ingredients	1·00
Packaging	0·25
Overheads	0·28
Distribution	0·09
Total cost	2·25
Sales price	2·50
Net profit	0·25

Table 3 Sales breakdown for Churchill's premium ice cream

Sales to own stores	60%
Sales to franchise stores	10%
Sales to leisure outlets	25%
Sales to supermarkets	5%
Sales to London region	90%
Sales outside London region	10%

Summary

Overall, Churchill has a distinctive strategy linking the manufacturing of premium ice cream with its distribution through the company's own ice cream stores. This has secured them a regional reputation for a quality product. It has had little success to date in penetrating the major supermarket chains with the Churchill brand and in moving its distinctive ice cream store format into foreign markets. Finally, to complicate both the manufacturing and retail sides of the Churchill business, seasonality is a real issue. Ice cream is still heavily dominated by sales in the summer months. In fact the peak demand in summer is typically five times the demand in the middle of winter. Equally serious is the impact of a cold summer on impulse ice cream sales. This has a number of consequences, which affect the costs of the product and capacity usage at both manufacturing and retail levels.

Despite this, Richard Smith has set three clear strategic goals to be achieved over the next five years. Firstly, to become the leading premium ice cream brand in the UK, secondly, to increase sales to £25 million and finally, to penetrate the supermarket sector with the Churchill product range.

Required

Richard Smith has set three clear strategic goals for Churchill's growth and development over the next five years.

(a)   Using models where appropriate, assess the advantages and disadvantages of the current strategy being pursued by Churchill Ice Cream and its impact on performance up to 2005.   **(20 marks)**

(b)   Using relevant evaluation criteria, assess how achievable and compatible these three strategic goals are over the next five years.   **(20 marks)**

(c)   What changes to Churchill's existing marketing mix will be needed to achieve the three strategic goals?

(15 marks)

Churchill Ice Cream has to date made two unsuccessful attempts to become an international company.

(d)   What reasons would you suggest to explain this failure of Churchill Ice Cream to become an international company?   **(5 marks)**

(Total = 60 marks)

Answers

1 Question with analysis: Bartok Fuel

Text reference. The topics mentioned in this answer are discussed in Chapters 1 and 13 of your BPP Study Text.

Top tips. This is quite a simple question that offers a gentle introduction to the style of the examination. Part (c) is typical of the sort of question that usually forms one of the requirements of a 60 mark case study, being essentially a critical discussion of possible specific strategies. It is usually pretty clear what the overall worth of the proposals is, but not always. Discuss this sort of thing as rationally as you can, using simple models and pointing out any implications you can discern.

Easy marks. As we have already remarked, this is quite a simple question: only part (c) could be considered at all challenging. Part (a) simply requires that you recognise the emergent and incrementalist aspects of the way the Bartok brothers have gone about running their business in the past, while in part (b) there will be up to four marks for brief introductions to the stages of the rational model.

Part (a)

There would appear to be no real evidence of any formal strategic planning in the past. There is no mention of any mission statement or objectives for the company. The company seems to have moved from a garage and workshop into fuel distribution and glass manufacture almost by accident. These developments might have **emerged from patterns of behaviour** rather than any planning process and it could be argued that the company illustrates the emergent strategy model. However, there is also an element of **logical incrementalism** as the business has not strayed far from its origins but has taken small steps into new areas where it already has some knowledge and expertise.

It could also be argued that only a small number of strategic options were ever considered and the options that have been taken in the past have perhaps simply been accepted as satisfactory rather than embraced as ideal. This approach has been termed **bounded rationality** by *Herbert Simon*.

Part (b)

Given the lack of formal strategic planning in the past and the quite fundamental suggestions being made at the recent board meeting, it may be time for Bartok Fuel to consider a more formal approach to strategic planning, such as the traditional **rational model**. On the other hand, this model is complex and difficult to follow without experience or guidance. The rational model has three main stages: **strategic analysis, strategic choice** and **implementation.**

The starting point is **strategic analysis**. This in turn begins with a consideration of the organisation's **mission**: where it is going and where it intends to be in the future. The mission statement can then be converted into goals and objectives that satisfy the various stakeholders in the company and can be quantified. Sean and David would have to be in clear agreement at this stage.

The next stage in strategic analysis is **environmental analysis**, perhaps utilising such models as PEST and Porter's five forces in order to identify opportunities and threats in the business environment. Bartok Fuel must also identify its own strengths and weaknesses through a **position audit** that considers the resources and competences of the company, how it creates value and its systems and structure. Finally, an overall **corporate appraisal** brings together the internal strengths and weaknesses and the external opportunities and threats in a SWOT analysis. This process is difficult and complex: many factors do not fall neatly into a single category of strength, weakness, opportunity or threat; also, it is necessary to assess the relative importance of the various factors identified and this is not simple.

The next phase in the rational model process is that of **strategic choice**. Here David and Sean must consider how to compete, where to compete and how the company can grow. Models that can help in this area are *Porter's* generic strategic choices analysis, value chain analysis, *Ansoff's* growth vector model and considerations of acquisition or organic growth. Each strategic option that is identified must then be considered in terms of **acceptability** to stakeholders; **suitability** in terms of the mission and overall strategic posture; and **feasibility** in terms of the resources of Bartok Fuel.

This process is in itself rather simpler than the analysis stage and can be undertaken using simple **scoring and ranking** techniques. However, proper use of the models mentioned is likely to show that David's two suggestions are not the only possibilities and this might lead to dissension between the brothers.

It would also be advisable to prepare some **numerical forecasts** of the probable outcomes of each course of action: this might be beyond the capability of the brothers and their staff. However, it is only by having a reasonable idea of what to expect from each option that reasonable decisions can be taken and proper control applied to eventual performance.

Finally, having determined their strategy, the brothers must **implement and control** it. Both of David's suggestions could involve significant work and change. In particular, closing down an element of the business would require major **human resources planning** and a move into another country may involve fundamental changes in functions such as marketing and personnel.

All things being considered, the rational model might be to difficult for the brothers to use and distract them from making the best use of their experience, judgement and business flair.

Part (c)

Each of the two strategies being considered requires very different considerations from the board.

If the Woking site is sold for its development potential, this will clearly be a boost to the company's cash flow. However, as we have no information about the company's current financial position, we cannot comment as to whether this is an element of the decision to sell. Nevertheless, the board must consider what use can be made of the funds received. It may be that the two options are related in David's mind and the funds from the sale of the Woking site are to be earmarked for investment in the Far East. In any case, the sale should only be considered further if it seems likely that the income can be invested in a way that will **generate a higher return** than the garage business currently achieves.

If the Woking site is to be shut down there are also considerable **human resource issues** to be addressed. The division employs 50 people who must either be made redundant or be re-employed in other areas of the business. In either case, the cost of redundancy payments or of retraining must be taken into account. The car dealership appears to be a fairly stand-alone element of the business but it must also be considered whether its closure will have any **knock-on effects** on the other parts of the company.

The proposed expansion into the Far East is fraught with potential problems. Bartok Fuel has always been a UK based business and therefore expansion abroad is a major issue. The results of a **PEST analysis** would be daunting. The company has no experience of doing business in any country in the Far East. It knows nothing of local business conditions or regulations. Language and culture are likely to present major difficulties.

All this is partially countered by the existence of a partner who knows the market and the culture of the Far East, but Bartok Fuel will still be making something of a leap in the dark. In fact, they would be **wholly dependent** on the probity, efficiency and goodwill of their partner. It would appear that the company's only real contribution will be to provide risk capital and the brothers must ask themselves if they really see that as their area of expertise – they are not running a bank, after all.

2 Aurora Lighting plc

Text reference. The topics mentioned in this answer are discussed in Chapters 1, 2 and 3 of your BPP Study Text.

Top tips. This is another simple question and should not present too much difficulty. Use it to practice your essay skills as well as to revise your basic knowledge. Notice the way we make frequent reference to the detail of the scenario. This is a particularly important aspect of exams at this level. They are intended to be as relevant as possible to real-world business situations, so you should always think in terms of using theory to arrive at practical analysis, comment and proposal.

Easy marks. Requirement (b) makes reference to 'appropriate models'. Such a requirement is like money in the bank for even the moderately prepared student. You will not score 50% of the available marks for simply displaying knowledge of theory, but 40% might be possible in a requirement like this.

Part (a)

Aurora Lighting plc's strategic planning system

Aurora plc has a formal strategic planning system, but it is **dormant** and **incomplete.**

(a) Aurora has a **mission statement** – but how relevant is it to the company's **actual** business? Does it conceal rather than enlighten? Does it allow managers to deceive themselves as to what the business is about?

(b) Aurora has **objectives**, both for profit and for market share, which is a good balance.

(c) There is **no** evidence, however, of any **environmental monitoring** activities, nor indeed any regular **position audit** or **SWOT analysis**.

(d) **Age.** Perhaps most damning is that the strategy devised in 1989 is now too old. Helmut still refers to it, yet ignores the changes in the environment. Arguably, there is a **failure of double loop feedback**: the plan itself has to be questioned. In this respect the comments in the Financial News are fair and apt. The company has survived more through luck than judgement.

Part (b)

There are three models of the strategic management process that we can examine to shed some light, as it were, on Aurora Lighting plc's condition.

(a) The **rational model** suggests there are three stages to strategic management: strategic analysis, strategic choice and strategy implementation. Clearly this is **not relevant to Aurora Lighting plc**. Little analysis is carried out, and the various choices made by the business, such as entry to Germany or the developing bespoke product business, are made reactively.

(b) **Logical incrementalism.** In this case, strategy is made by minor adjustments to existing behaviour, as part of a political negotiation process. This **does not apply** in this case: Aurora Lighting plc is a company, and it appears that the lines of authority are very straight: Helmut and Dawn are both in charge.

(c) Mintzberg's **crafting strategy** model. An **emergent strategy** develops out of a pattern of behaviour, or out of responses to the particular circumstances in which the business finds itself. Examples in this case would be:

  (i) Aurora's **export drive**; and (more importantly)

  (ii) the continued development and growth of the **bespoke manufacturing business** as opposed to the Borealis range which appears to be absorbing most management attention.

The art of the strategic management of emergent strategies is not simply to let them develop and take over but to **select** those which are most desirable and to **shape them** in the right direction.

The **crafting strategy model** is probably most **appropriate** to Aurora's process of strategic management, but it in no way describes what Aurora **actually** does.

(a)   **Manage stability**. Managers should spend more time implementing than planning.

(b)   **Detect discontinuity**. Environments neither change all the time, nor are they all turbulent. In Aurora's case, the company has exploited the opportunities of the environment, but had obviously not considered the collapse of the commercial property market in London.

(c)   **Know the business**. Helmut and Dawn are fairly aware of what goes on. They know the needs of the bespoke business as well as Borealis. However, concentration on Borealis means that not enough attention is being paid to the area of the business that perhaps holds out most hope for the future.

(d)   **Manage patterns**. This means that emerging patterns of business behaviour, such as the bespoke business, must be nurtured and others uprooted.

(e)   **Reconcile change and continuity**.

Helmut and Dawn are **failing to craft strategy effectively**. Even the *Financial News* recognises that it is the **bespoke business**, not Borealis, which is crucial to the firm's long term success. Instead they are operating hand-to-mouth, taking advantage of such opportunities as they arise, but not developing them. Perhaps the export business could be expanded. In short, Helmut and Dawn need to ask the basic question: 'What business are we in?'

Part (c)

Goals and objectives

(a)   The **mission statement** does not describe mission: it is more of an operational goal, which can be turned into objectives, than a mission as such. It is only partly relevant as it deals only with Borealis rather than the bespoke aspect of the business. It **confuses** rather than enlightens.

(b)   There are a number of **formal goals**, not least the goal of achieving market share and the required profit. The profitability goals are those demanded by shareholders. In this case, Aurora is exceeding expectations.

(c)   **System goals**. Survival is obviously one, as is growth. There is nothing wrong with these as such, but there are times when they tend to subvert mission. As the business's stated mission is at variance with reality, these system goals have in fact, paradoxically, acted to the shareholders' benefit. After all, the company has prospered through its export and bespoke production business.

(d)   **Personal goals**

        (i)   Dawn and Helmut have invested much money and effort in Borealis. Their commitment to the range reflects this past investment rather than an objective assessment of the range's future prospects.

        (ii)   The **production director** of the Borealis range might have been empire building to enhance his importance as the company invests more money in the Borealis range.

3 Preparation question: Planning components

Part (a)

The three levels of strategic planning are considered individually below.

Corporate

Strategic analysis

(a)   The analysis will deal with **internal factors** (skills available, the organisation's resources and so on) and **external factors** which can be seen in the operating environment (competition, PEST factors).

(b)   Variables of direct relevance to the organisation's plans will be the subject of very **specific** forecasts, frequently of an annual duration. These will include market share, demand and similar factors.

It is on the basis of this analysis that the organisation will make the necessary choices.

(a)   The company **mission** is a broad statement of the organisation's purpose, serving to orientate it within its environment and to inform more specific decisions as to its objectives and mode of operation.

(b)   Goals and **objectives** define the targets towards which the organisation will work in the light of the mission.

(c)   **Strategies** give effect to objectives. Taken as a whole, they are the overall means by which the organisation intends to progress towards its strategic goals.

Tactical. This concerns the measures used to follow the strategy and how resources are deployed.

(a)   **Policy making** occurs at this level, so that the organisation has a standardised response to particular sets of circumstances. Consistency is thus assured.

(b)   Many control measures such as variances are picked up at this level.

Operational. Planning at this level is very detailed. It includes the setting of **rules**, so that discretion in response is removed in certain circumstances, **procedures** (which are usually a bundle of rules), and **programmes** (which can be viewed as a collection of procedures). **Budgetary planning** allows for feedback, review and therefore control.

Corporate and operational planning are sometimes connected. In a service industry, for example, service quality is achieved at operational level, but must be considered in its minutiae higher up.

Planning can be both top down and bottom up. In practice, both are necessary. Strategists may be unaware of the operational difficulties or pitfalls. At operational level, staff may know more about how the company actually works than the planners.

Part (b)

Mintzberg defines goals as '**the intentions behind decisions or actions**, the states of mind that drive individuals or collectives of individuals called organisations to do what they do.'

(a)   **Operational goals** can be expressed as **objectives**. Mintzberg says that an objective is a goal expressed in a form by which its attainment can be measured. Here is an example.

   (i)   An operational goal: 'Cut costs'

   (ii)   The objective: 'Reduce budget by 5%'

(b)   **Non-operational goals** (or **aims**) on the other hand do not express themselves as objectives. Mintzberg quotes the example of a university, whose goal might be to 'seek truth'. This cannot really be expressed as an **objective**. To 'increase truth by 5% this year' does not make a great deal of sense.

Part (c)

The **environment of a business**

(a)   Politico-legal factors include political changes (eg change in government, operation of the executive, openness of political institutions to business influence) and legal developments (eg health and safety legislation, developments in company law).

(b)   Economic factors include overall economic growth levels, interest and exchange rate and the effects of government fiscal and monetary policies.

(c)   Social and cultural factors include the country's demographic profile (eg age structure), the class system, and trends in consumer tastes and wants.

(d)   Technological factors include new product technologies, new materials, and new techniques in production.

4 Introducing strategic management

Text reference. The topics mentioned in this answer are discussed in Chapters 1, 2 and 3 of your BPP Study Text.

Top tips. Operational management is generally short-term and internally focused when compared with wider strategic considerations. Strategic management can be undertaken in a number of ways. This answer follows the standard rational approach. You could possibly argue that N Ltd has followed, albeit unconsciously, an incrementalist approach, by small scale change when necessary. Strategic management extends beyond the rational model – Mintzberg's crafting strategies approach might also be worth a mention, especially in part (b), to reduce the shock of the new approach – but the tone of the question suggests that the rational model was what the examiner was mainly interested in. You need to focus on the specific organisational and cultural issues required by the question.

Easy marks. This is not a difficult question at all and you should be able to score well with basic knowledge. The eight marks for part (a) are probably the easiest of all since the explanation called for amounts to little more than contrasting the fairly obvious differences between the two kinds of management.

Part (a)

Strategic management

Strategic management is an integrated management approach drawing together all the elements involved in planning, integrating and controlling a business strategy. The concerns of **corporate strategic decisions** are these.

(a)   The **scope** of the organisation's activities, in other words the product and markets the organisation deals with

(b)   The organisation's **fit with the environment** and the relationships it has with stakeholder groups

(c)   Matching its **resource capability** with the environment

(d)   **Resource allocation** between divisions or functions of the business, and direction towards different product-market areas

(e)   The organisation's **long term direction**

(f)   **Change**

(g)   **Value systems**

The implementation of a strategic management approach, according to the **rational model**, involves a three-stage process of **strategic analysis** of the organisation's current situation and the environment, **strategic choice** (the generation and evaluation of alternative strategic options) and **implementation** of the chosen strategy. Many strategic decisions are one-off, non-programmable decisions.

Operational management

The concerns of **operational management** are quite different.

(a)   Its **scope is restricted** to the particular task in hand

(b)   **Internal.** Operational management is generally more **internally focused** – although day to day relationships with customers are an operational concern.

(c)   **Implementation.** Operations managers have to work with the resource allocation decisions set by the strategy. Their concern is the most **efficient** use of these resources.

(d)   **Time scale.** Operations management is generally **shorter-term** than strategic management

(e)   **Routine.** Operational decisions are often more **routine** than strategic decisions and are more likely to be programmed.

There are some cases when short-term decisions are of strategic importance, for example if the survival of the organisation is at stake. Moreover, poor performance at operational level can make or break a strategy.

Part (b)

Cultural and organisational changes at N Ltd

There are a variety of different approaches to strategic management. The extent of organisational and cultural change required will depend on the type of strategic management style adopted.

The current strategic management style is incrementalist.

There is little strategic review, and the underlying assumption of managers is that things will continue more or less as they are, any changes being coped with by incremental adjustment at an operational level. The lack of market information is particularly worrying. The company appears to be **reactive rather than proactive**.

Introducing the rational model: organisational changes

(a)   **Resources** must be diverted to strategic management.

   (i)   The strategic management system must be **designed for future use**.

   (ii)   The initial stages of strategic analysis need to be done, and the directors will need some **guidance,** so management consultants may be employed.

(b)   **Intelligence.** Strategic management requires suitable **information systems**. This also requires resources. The scope of the strategic intelligence systems will almost certainly include **marketing research data**.

(c)   **People.** Changes to the **job descriptions** of existing personnel might be needed so that their new responsibilities, especially for information gathering, are outlined.

(d)   **The management accounting system,** if any, must be configured to provide information related **to product profitability**, so the firm can identify life cycle and portfolio issues.

(e)   **Objectives and indicators.** Strategic management involves the **setting of objectives**, and so new performance indicators will be needed to ensure that the strategies chosen are implemented successfully.

The **balanced scorecard** approach could probably be adopted – given falling profitability, it is likely that financial indicators assume a great deal of importance. However other operational performance indicators need to be used so that managers do not become too short-termist in their outlook. A technique using some of the insights of management by objectives might be employed.

To summarise, the organisational changes involve new information systems, changes to job descriptions and new performance indicators to encourage a strategic perspective and a more strategic approach to marketing.

Clearly, this involves a **change in the management style** of the company.

(a)   **New approach to strategy**. There will have to be a cultural change at board level. Directors will have to consider strategic issues in an active way. This may involve challenging some of their assumptions as to how the business is run.

(b)   **Professional approach, not family management.** The company certainly needs professional management. Hopefully, the decline in profits and turnover provides a sense of urgency, but the family may still find it hard to accept the dilution of its power.

(c)   **A new approach to risk** is needed, especially with regard to products and markets.

(d)   Operational decision-makers who were used to doing more or less what they pleased will be faced with **objectives set by their managers higher up**. This is a resumption of **control**, and operations managers may feel that they are losing power and authority. It may be **demotivating**.

ANSWERS

(e)   **Innovation** will have to be addressed, both in products and in processes. The existing managers are probably technically aware in their own fields, but the firm needs a **marketing orientation** to ensure its continued success via a proper focus on the needs of its customers.

(f)   A programme of **education** will be needed to convince managers that it is necessary.

Arguably, strategic decisions have **emerged** from patterns of operational behaviour, but this mode of making strategy is obviously insufficient at the moment. Accepting some **bottom-up input** into the strategic decision making process will mean:

- The new system is accepted more **readily**
- The **expertise** of operational decision makers is exploited

5 Gould & King

Part (a)

> **Top tips**. We consider this to be an unfair question. We have not been able to find any reference to the preparation of business plans in either the syllabus or the teaching guide for this exam. Such preparation is a specialised technical process and no more an aspect of general strategic management than the preparation of a marketing plan, for instance. If you work in accountancy practice or in banking, you may be lucky enough to have some knowledge of the sort of thing that is commonly included in such a document, but for many candidates this will have been a baffling requirement: the most detailed and conscientious preparation would not have equipped them to answer this question.
>
> If you are reduced to tackling a question of this sort in the exam you can only use your common sense and hope for the best.
>
> Our answer reflects the Examiner's marking scheme. His suggested solution states that 'You should regard the business plan as a management tool and not simply a sales document.' We disagree. A business plan presented to a bank is exclusively a sales tool designed to raise finance in exactly the same way as a prospectus for a stock market offer. Obviously, it should be based on carefully prepared plans, budgets and estimates, but it is those underlying documents that are management tools, not the business plan itself.
>
> **Easy marks**. There are no easy marks here unless you have a good knowledge of what is normally found in a business plan.
>
> **Examiner's comments**. Not surprisingly, the Examiner commented that 'many candidates confused a business plan with a strategic plan'.

124
BPP
LEARNING MEDIA

Marks

(a) Key features of a business plan — up to 2 per feature
Executive summary
Purpose, philosophy and objectives
Financial targets
Target market and forecasts
Product/service range
Marketing strategy
Resource availability and funding needed
People and organisation
Performance measurement and milestones
Summary of financial information

Maximum 12 marks

(b) Advantages of strategic plans — up to 5
Speedier decision making
Change management capability enhanced
Better performance
Longer term focus
Surfaces assumptions

Disadvantages of strategic plans:
Time involved
Flexibility reduced
Planning skills not available
Tools and techniques not known
Information disclosure

Maximum 8 marks
Total 20 marks

To: David Gould
From: Accountant

Preparing a Business Plan

The presentation of a comprehensive business plan to your bank is an important step towards **obtaining the finance** you need to launch and expand your new enterprise. Banks make use of a **range of criteria** in making lending decisions and a sound business plan will provide information relevant to many of them. Your business plan should be authoritative, comprehensive and logical. It should, therefore, be based on **reasonable assumptions**, **careful estimation** and **rational thought**. You must present a very clear view of your **business goals** and the **strategy** you intend to use in order to achieve them.

As your proposed partnership is based on two existing businesses, you should give a brief account of the history and performance of each. Many of your forecasts for the combined business will be based on extrapolation from past experience, so you must establish the credibility of this foundation. An important input into credit decisions is the **personal history of the owners of the business**, so this section could include a summary of your personal details, qualifications and experience.

The main part of your business plan should start with a **statement of the nature and commercial purpose** of your business. You should also mention any special features that differentiate it from similar enterprises. This would be the place in which to introduce, briefly and in general terms, your views on improved customer service and use of the Internet.

You might then go on to give a more detailed account of your strategy, giving details of your **products**, your **target markets** (such as the property development market) and your **marketing plan**. This could be based on the service marketing mix, product, price, promotion, place, people, processes and physical evidence. The bank will expect to see

You should give a full, though not over-detailed, statement of your **financial targets**. A series of **budgeted accounts** for the first three years would be a good start. You should be realistic in your forecasts, building on your current experience and making reasonable assumptions. Associated with these purely financial details could be other quantitative measures, such as anticipated client numbers and **growth**. If you are able to provide extensive data it is probably a good idea to put most of the information into an appendix and present a summary in the main part of your plan.

An essential feature of your submission to the bank will be a detailed statement of **requirements for finance**. The bank will expect you to have a very clear forecast of how much cash you will need, when you will need it and where it is to come from. The whole purpose of the document is to help you to obtain funds from the bank, so you must be **realistic and specific** about your need for finance. Bear in mind that your ability to pay interest and repay principal will be a major consideration for the bank in deciding whether to finance you: the amounts you ask for must be reasonable in the light of your forecasts for your business, both in terms of what they will enable you to do and what you will be able to repay.

Finally, when you are happy with your overall business plan, you should prepare an **executive summary**. This will precede the main body of the document and summarize its most important elements, such as the nature and main features of the business; and leading indicators of growth and profitability.

Part (b)

> **Text reference.** The topics mentioned in this answer are discussed in Chapter 1 of your BPP Study Text.
>
> **Top tips.** It is very easy to see phrases such as 'strategic plan' and start to think in terms of the rational model of strategy. Don't forget that there are lots of other ideas about the nature of business strategy and planning. A further important consideration here is that you are asked to talk about strategic planning in the context of Gould and King Associates, which is a very small enterprise indeed.
>
> **Examiner's comments.** Some candidates produced very good answers to this requirement.

Advantages of having a strategic plan

Business plan

We have defined Gould and King Associates' business plan as essentially a sales document. However, the preparation of such a document would require the principals to carry out much activity that could only be called strategic planning. Thus, the preparation of a true strategic plan for the business, as well as being of great value itself, would make the creation of the 'business plan' a relatively simple and undemanding process, since much of its content could simply be copied across from one document to the other.

SWOT

To some extent, business strategy consists of the exploitation of strengths, the nurturing of weaknesses, the seizing of opportunities and the neutralisation of threats. Even the most rudimentary strategy-making process that includes some consideration of these factors will improve the entity's chances of dealing with them in a satisfactory way; or, at least, in a non-disastrous way. Basic **assumptions** will be articulated and considered and a range of **options** will become apparent.

Implementation

The managers of small businesses are often overloaded with the detail of daily survival. Growth and profit will often require **innovation** and **change**. The possession of at least a rough idea of where they want to take their organisations should make it easier for such managers to steer them in the right direction. The **speed** and **consistency** of decision-making are likely to be enhanced

Perceived disadvantages of having a strategic plan

Resources

Any planning process, however brief or informal, will **consume resources**, even if only to the extent of the planner's time. Most small businesses are under-resourced, so this will be a seductive consideration. Less apparent to many small business managers will be that they are themselves lacking in many of the **skills** and knowledge of the **techniques** needed to undertake any degree of worthwhile strategic planning.

Confidentiality

Owner managers are often very anxious to conceal their ideas about their businesses, believing that their competitors are only too anxious to steal and exploit them. They are thus likely to regard any **consultative** aspect of strategic planning with suspicion.

Flexibility

Managers may feel that a firm plan would constrain their freedom of action, not appreciating that plans can be written flexibly and, indeed, amended if necessary.

6 Question with analysis: Fancy Packaging

Text reference. The topics mentioned in this answer are discussed in Chapter 5 of your BPP Study Text.

Top tips. Marketing is very important in this exam. It is no longer an ancillary topic worth only a few marks – there are questions based entirely on marketing activities. You need an understanding of marketing as an integrated business function so that you can answer a question such as this.

Easy marks. Do not be led into thinking that part (a) is about the details of overseas market research: stick to the simple ideas you have learned about the general environment (using PEST) and the five forces. Remember to relate these general ideas to the special circumstances of The Fancy Packaging Company where you can.

Examiner's comments. Some candidates provided a simple list when answering part (a). This is never a satisfactory technique and should only be resorted to when very short of time. Part (a) also illustrated some inappropriate use of models, such as Porter's diamond and Ohmae's Cs model. In part (b), the use of the word 'methodology' confused some candidates: at this level vocabulary wide enough to deal with such a word is expected.

ANSWERS

		Marks
(a)	Customer profile	up to 5
	External environment research	up to 5
	Competitive framework	up to 4
		Maximum for section (a) 12 marks
(b)	Desk research	up to 3
	Primary research	up to 3
	Sources of data	up to 2
	Methods for carrying out survey	up to 2
		Maximum for section (b) 8 marks
		Total 20 marks

Part (a)

REPORT

To: Eddie Lomax, Marketing Director, The Fancy Packaging Company
From: Market research consultant
Date: December 200X
Subject: Overseas market research

1   I understand that your company is considering expansion into a non-European market sector for your decorative packaging. As you have no experience in non-European markets it is essential that full information is found about potential markets before any decision is made as to which, if any, markets to enter. There are three key areas that you will require information about.

The general environment
Competitors
Customers

2   **The general environment**

The general environment may be analysed using the **PEST analysis model**, which breaks the environment down into four main parts: political/legal factors, economic factors, social and cultural factors and technological factors.

2.1 *Political/legal factors*

One of the key issues in this area is the **attitude of the local government** to foreign imports. If a government wishes to protect indigenous businesses, then trade barriers may be an obstacle to entry into the market concerned. These barriers can take more subtle forms than simple tariffs and quotas yet be just as effective at discouraging imports. It is also important to be aware of the nature and extent of legal regulation and how it differs from what you are used to. For example, there may be legal restraints on relationships with agents and distributors; on the amount or type of packaging used; and on the remittance of funds out of the country.

2.2 *Economic factors*

The **general economy of the proposed new market** will be of prime importance. The **general economic condition** of the country is likely to have a direct effect on demand for your products. You should consider general structural economic factors such as the trend rate of growth, degree of economic stability and current stage of the economic cycle. The current state and prospects for **specific indicators** such as levels of inflation, unemployment and interest rates will be relevant for judging whether the time is ripe for an entry.

2.3 *Social and cultural factors*

One of the problems you have encountered in the European market has been **environmentally concerned customers'** preference for reductions in conspicuous wastage. You need to be confident that this will not be a major problem in the markets you are considering.

2.4 *Technological factors*

You will need to consider the technological infrastructure of the proposed markets in terms of **transport** and **communications facilities**, the degree of technical sophistication of the population and whether e-commerce is relevant in these markets.

3 **Competitors and customers**

Once the general economic climate of the countries you are interested in has been investigated you will require detailed knowledge of conditions in your specific potential markets that you will face. **Customers** and **competitors** will be two of the more important factors: they can be analysed together with other important influences using *Porter's* five competitive forces model.

3.1 *Threat of new entrants*

You will be the new entrant, presenting a threat to existing suppliers. You need to know the extent to which **effective barriers to entry** exist and the likely response of existing players to the entry of a new supplier.

3.2 *Threat of substitute products*

The new markets are perhaps unlikely to present any substitute products that you are not already aware of, but it is possible and you should attempt to become familiar with likely local developments.

3.3 *Bargaining power of customers*

Customers' bargaining power is enhanced when suppliers are plentiful and products are commoditised. You need **detailed knowledge of the state of the local packaging industry** and you must be sure that you know how you will impress your customers with the extra value provided by your products. You must obtain quantitative data, such as the number of potential customers, their size, location, buying patterns and purchasing policies. You should also consider qualitative factors, key amongst which is the answer to the questions 'why do these customers buy?' and 'how do they choose who they buy from?' Other relevant concerns will be the quantity in which the customer buys, the number of potential customers, the importance of the product to the customer and the potential customers' own profitability.

3.4 *Bargaining power of suppliers*

The **balance of power** in your relationship with your own suppliers in the potential market will depend upon a number of factors such as their overall number, the threat of new entrants or substitute products, the importance of your purchases to your suppliers' businesses and any differentiation of their products.

3.5 *Rivalry amongst current competitors*

This is an important area for you as it is likely to affect your profitability directly. The more intense the current competitive rivalry, is the **less potentially profitable** the market is.

4 **Conclusion**

The decision to enter a new geographical is an important and difficult one and it must not be undertaken lightly. Any failure could not only be financially damaging but damaging also to the reputation of the business elsewhere in the world. Before such a decision is taken, therefore, every effort must be taken to ensure that you have as much information as possible about the general environment in which you would be trading as well as detailed information about your competitors and the customers for your particular product.

Part (b)

Methodology for obtaining the required information

The marketing research required for a successful move into a new geographical area is enormous and should not be undertaken lightly. In general terms there should be five stages in the approach to collecting the necessary information.

Definition of the problem

The research problem here is to gather the type of wide-ranging information that is required and has been set out in detail above. Any research must have in mind the *purpose* for which it is being carried out, which is, specifically, to make a decision about market entry.

Design of the research

Primary data is information collected specifically for a particular purpose whereas **secondary data** is data that already exists in an organised and accessible form.

In this situation it is probably cost-effective to **start with secondary data and desk research** using tools such as newspapers, trade journals, trade association publications, government and embassy reports and the Internet.

This process will be a useful filter exercise: if the desk research indicates that the general economic environment is not suitable for a profitable expansion then the research need go no further. However, if secondary data indicate that the general and market environment appear promising, then further research is indicated, possibly including the collection of primary data.

Collection of primary data

It is probably best to make use of a **research agency**, since the collection of primary data is a specialised skill. The first stage will be ensure that the agency selected is suitable for the task. A local agency could be expected to have detailed knowledge of the market being investigated. However, in some less developed countries, such agencies may not exist or have the necessary expertise and, therefore, an **international agency** will be required, with the caveat that their local knowledge may be limited.

The agency would proceed to data collection, possibly using personal or telephone interviews or postal questionnaires. The design of surveys is a very technical process.

Analysis of the data

When the details of the desk research and the primary research data are known then this must be collated and analysed, possibly using statistical techniques.

Report

Finally, you could expect your agency to prepare a **detailed report**, bringing together all of the market research carried out, with a conclusion and recommendations for action.

7 Lawson Engineering

Part (a)

Text reference. The topics mentioned in this answer are discussed in Chapter 2 of your BPP Study Text.

Top tips. This is a puzzling question. The Examiner asks us for a 'resource analysis' but we lack much of the basic information that we would need to carry out such an exercise, even supposing we confined ourselves to generalities and made no attempt at quantification.

The Ms model might be useful though see the examiner's comments below for a caution. At best, we could list the following: reputation for engineering excellence; good relationships with customers and suppliers; significant number of patents; skilled staff; innovative design; and 'can do' philosophy. We have no information on markets, specific product features, manufacturing techniques, knowledge management or particular staff aptitudes, let alone details of financial resources, brands, marketing practices and fixed assets.

How then, are we to approach this question? In essence, it would seem that what the Examiner really wants is a discussion of the importance of intangible assets in the context of Lawson Engineering. The requirement is worth twelve marks, so we are going to have to make three or four good, well-explained points. The idea of resource-based strategy is obviously relevant.

One important point we should make is that no matter how excellent Lawson Engineering's endowment of intangible assets may be, they will be of little importance if the company is not able to use them to generate superior financial results. Making clever, innovative and high performance products is, no doubt, a very good thing, but if it does not produce profits, it is more akin to a hobby than to a business.

Be prepared to interpret the Examiner's requirements in the light of what is feasible – but stay as relevant as you can, and **apply** theoretical knowledge to the details of the scenario to the greatest extent possible.

Easy marks. Given the curious wording of the question requirement, we would hesitate to suggest that there are any easy marks here at all.

Examiner's comments. The Ms resource listing was used by many candidates as the basis of their answers. The problem with this is that it tends to lead to a simple listing, without any focus on the key elements.

Marking scheme

		Marks
(a)	Identification of intangible assets and capabilities up to 2 per point	up to 2 per point
	Use of model(s) up to 3	up to 3
		up to 4
	Maximum for section (a) 12 marks	
(b)	Advantages and disadvantages of the balanced scorecard up to 2 per point	up to 2 per point
	Maximum for section (b) 8 marks	
	Total 20 marks	

The importance of intangible assets

The rational model of strategy is based on the idea of creating value by managing the business so as to best respond to the environment. This is often called the **positioning** view of strategy. This positioning view has been criticised for two main reasons.

(a)   Many business environments are too complex and dynamic to permit timely and effective analysis and response.

(b)   Once a market offering has been made, it is very easy for competitors to make similar offerings, thus rapidly eroding competitive advantage.

These problems lead to the development of a resource-based theory of strategy: this suggests that competitive advantage comes not from the achievement of a close fit with the environment but from the possession of **unique resources**. These resources may be physical in nature, as in the case of *De Beers* monopoly of diamonds, or, more typically in today's advanced service economies, they may be unique **competences**.

Johnson and Scholes divide competences into two types. An organisation must achieve at least a **threshold level** of competence in everything it does. Its **core competences** are those that are both **unique** and in which it **outperform competitors**. *Hamel and Prahalad* suggest that an important aspect of strategic management is the determination of the competences the company will require in the future in order to provide new benefits to customers. They say a core competence will have three benefits.

(a)   It will make a **disproportionate contribution to the value** the customer perceives.

(b)   It must be '**competitively unique**', which means one of three things: actually unique; superior to competitors; or capable of dramatic improvement.

(c)   It must be **extendable**, in that it must allow for the development of an array of new products and services.

Lawson Engineering seems to be well placed to build a resource-based strategy. It has **important intangible assets** in the form of its reputation for engineering excellence; its (presumably good) long-term relationships with its customers and suppliers; and its 'can do' philosophy. It has a number of patents for innovative products, indicating that its research and development effort is effective. Perhaps most significantly of all, it has made a practice of recruiting and developing **highly skilled engineers**.

However, the company has a serious problem: despite continuing growth, its 'performance against traditional financial measures has been relatively modest'. From this statement we may suspect that Lawson Engineering has fallen into the error committed by so many British engineering-based companies. Engineering excellence is not sufficient. Innovative products must be marketed in a way that generates **satisfactory profit**, or the work is wasted. We are told that the company's products command premium prices, so, unless its cost accounting practices are inadequate, we must suspect that its costs themselves are **not under control** and are swallowing up too much of the gross margin.

The classic culprit would be the **cost of research and development**. Overspending on the development of the RB211 engine led the original Rolls-Royce aero engine company into insolvency, for example. It may be that Lawson Engineering's R&D, while **effective**, as pointed out above, is not sufficiently **economical** in its use of resources. This is a failure of management to which Joe Lawson should pay close attention in the future.

A further possibility is that the products themselves are **over-engineered** and **over-specified**. This is another undesirable tradition in British engineering, known colloquially as 'brass plating'. **Value engineering** offers a solution here: products should be analysed to determine how cost could be reduced without affecting performance.

In summary, we might say that it is perfectly reasonable for Lawson Engineering's bankers to be wary of heavy investment in the company. It has a great deal of potential but if it continues to be run in its present fashion it will find itself more and more unable to pay its way.

Part (b)

Kaplan and Norton proposed their balanced scorecard approach to performance monitoring and control in order that **proper emphasis** should be laid on **business functions** that build **future performance**: they felt that reliance on a single financial measure such as return on investment was akin to flying an aircraft in cloud using only one instrument. If the four perspectives of the balanced scorecard are all monitored and attention paid to achieving equally good performance in all of them, the business should be well placed for continuing success.

This is not to say that financial performance is in some way discountable against performance in the other perspectives: a **vertical vector** can be seen to link the four perspectives together.

Perspective		*Measures*
Financial		ROCE
Customer		Relationships and loyalty
Internal business		Quality, efficiency and timeliness
Innovation and learning		Skills and processes

The **skills learned** and **processes developed** as a result of attention to the innovation and learning perspective support and enable **high standards of quality**, **efficiency** and **timeliness**, which are measured by the internal business process. These features help to develop the **good relationships** and **loyalty** that are in turn essential if financial performance is to be satisfactory.

Referring back to our discussion of the way things seem to be done at Lawson engineering, we might suspect that not enough attention has been paid to the **efficiency** aspect of the internal business perspective: a balanced scorecard approach, properly implemented might make that clear to Joe Lawson.

A further aspect of the balanced scorecard is the way it sees the organisation in terms of **outcomes** rather than **inputs**. Objectives are set and performance measured not in departmental or functional terms but in ways that **integrate important activities** that cut across traditional boundaries. The customer service perspective at Lawson Engineering ought to be just as relevant to the R&D activity as to the sales office, especially, for example, where customers look to the company to solve technical problems with innovative products. This orientation to outcomes means that there is a potential link between **activity based costing** and the use of a balanced scorecard.

This aspect can be seen as something of a disadvantage, since it can be very challenging for a **traditionally run organisation** to adjust its ideas about hierarchy and responsibility sufficiently to be able to use a balanced scorecard. However, this is not so much a disadvantage of the technique as a disadvantage of running organisations in that kind of way. It does, however, mean that much work can be required in order to implement a balanced scorecard approach. Simply designing the measures to be used can be very difficult and assigning responsibility for the performance they measure even more so.

A further problem can arise when an organisation has a **complex mission**, as is likely to be the case, for example, in a not-for-profit organisation. In such an organisation there may be **several important stakeholder groups**, each with its own interests to promote and defend. The vertical vector described above may be absent and the financial perspective something to be satisfied only.

8 Five forces

> **Text reference.** The topics mentioned in this answer are discussed in Chapter 5 of your BPP Study Text.
>
> **Top tips.** Explain the model and, as always, apply each element in detail to the question scenario and E's market. This will enable you to establish the relative importance of each force, and indicate and justify appropriate performance indicators, such as customer satisfaction (not just in the current situation, but in the business environment in the future. Customer expectations may be satisfied now, but their needs may change). You must make a conclusion as to whether or not you agree with the Marketing Director.
>
> **Easy marks.** The question mentions each of the five forces but does not really explain them: a brief explanation is necessary for each one if your recommendations are to make sense. Here are some easy marks.

REPORT

To: Marketing Director
From: Management accountant
Date: May 200X
Subject: Performance indicators – competitive forces

Introduction

CIMA defines the **five competitive forces** as 'external influences upon the extent of actual and potential competition within any industry which in aggregate determine the ability of firms within that industry to earn a profit'. Porter argues that a firm must adopt a strategy that combats these forces better than its rivals' strategies if it is to enhance shareholder value.

If some of these forces are weak, it is easier to be profitable. How can they be applied to E, and their relative strength measured? We shall look at each force in turn and consider some appropriate indicators.

The threat of new entrants (and barriers to entry to keep them out)

A new entrant into an industry will bring extra capacity and more competition. The strength of this threat is likely to vary from industry to industry, depending on the strength of the barriers to entry, and the likely **response of existing competitors** to the new entrant. The **emergence of new competitors** can be easily monitored.

Existing firms in an industry, such as E, may have built up a good brand image and strong customer loyalty over a long period of time. A few firms may promote a large number of brands to crowd out the competition, especially in the cosmetics market. Perhaps for this reason, it could be concluded that this particular competitive force is a low risk, but the situation should be monitored.

The threat from substitute products

A **substitute product** is a good/service which satisfies the same customer needs. There are many companies producing cosmetics, and they invest heavily in research and development. E's own **spend on research and development** is a likely indication of the activity of competitors of a similar size in producing substitute products , such as the use of different ingredients (as in the case of the Body Shop, promoting ethical products) or the possible promotion of a cosmetic-free way of life by other industries. This could be more of a threat than is currently being recognised.

The bargaining power of customers

Customers want better quality products and services at a lower price. Satisfying this might force down the profitability of suppliers in the industry. Just how strong the position of customers is dependent on several factors.

How much the **customer buys**, and the relative importance of each customer in each market served (possibly segmented by location), can be easily measured by **analysis of sales and profit** per product.

There is more to consider than product profitability. Customers have a wide **choice** available to them, and their tastes and fashions will change all the time. This range of choice means the power of customers is a very important one for E's competitiveness.

Variations in customer taste and attitude can be measured using **marketing research**. **Product quality** will be an important consideration and measurement, and its careful control may lead E to conclude that investment in product quality will help to grow sales.

The bargaining power of suppliers

Suppliers can sometimes exert pressure for higher prices. If E had just **one or two dominant suppliers**, able to charge high prices, simple cost analysis will make this clear. However, it is more likely that E is being be served by a multitude of suppliers. The **range of prices charged** by different suppliers can be compared to assess whether E is at the mercy of its suppliers (unlikely, given E's global presence and the fact that most suppliers operate on a small scale) or if it is able to negotiate better terms to ensure consistency and quality of supply.

If some suppliers also supply E's **competitors**, and do not rely heavily on E for the majority of their sales, this will indicate a relative strength. However, the size of E is likely to mean that this competitive force is of less significance. It is more likely to be able to dictate to suppliers what it wants and when it wants it.

The rivalry amongst current competitors in the industry

It is clear that the **intensity of competitive rivalry** within an industry will affect the profitability of the industry as a whole. This is an important force for E. **Competitive actions** to influence customer opinion and increase **market share** can be tracked and might take the form of **price competition, advertising battles, sales promotion campaigns**, introducing **new products** for the market, improving **after sales service** or providing **guarantees or warranties**.

All of these marketing activities can be measured in terms of **cost** and perceived **benefit** (although the relationship between initiatives such as advertising campaigns and subsequent sales levels may be difficult to pin down).

E could employ **market share analysis** to assess whether its cosmetic products are holding their position against competitors, or if new and attractive competitor products can come to the market quickly and establish competitive advantage over E. Products can be assessed using the BCG matrix.

Conclusion

This brief analysis shows that the intensity of competitive rivalry is the most potent force affecting the profitability of E. While it is not strictly necessary to rank the forces in order of influence, it could be concluded that the buying power of customers is also strong (given that they can change their minds, particularly in a fashion-driven industry) and allied to this is the threat from substitute products, which is likely to be stronger than is currently being allowed. Because of E's size, the power of suppliers and the threat of new entrants could rightly be interpreted as lesser threats.

It should be noted that Porter's five forces model has come in for criticism. Perhaps most importantly, it overemphasises the importance of the **wider environment** and therefore ignores the significance of the **individual advantages held by E** with regard to **resources, capabilities** and **competence**.

9 Classics on the cheap

Text reference. The topics mentioned in this answer are discussed in Chapter 6 of your BPP Study Text.

Top tips. This question basically deals with the ideas of Michael Porter on value chain analysis. The question asks you to conduct an analysis to assess what features in the company's operations, as indicated by its value chain, support its recent success. You should also note the industry structure: the vast majority of publishers subcontract their printing to outside firms.

Easy marks. You should find it easy to analyse Wordsworth's operation in value chain terms. Note for future reference that it is not at all unusual for some activities to be minimal or missing altogether.

Part (a)

Classics for under £1: exploiting cost leadership or possibly a cost-focus strategy

The strategy depends on **high volume** sales of low priced books, out of copyright, and a willingness to use **novel distribution channels**, such as supermarkets etc, where suitable. The books themselves are competing with other publishers' editions such as Penguin, Everyman and Oxford University Press. Wordsworth offers a different packaging of the same text, but **claims** to be pursuing a **focus** strategy, as its editions are not produced for schools and universities, but for the price-conscious general reader. In practice, the campaign can have two consequences.

(a)   **Competitors.** Wordsworth's competitors (Penguin etc) do **not** consider themselves restricted to the school and university market and so Wordsworth's claim not to be competing directly with them looks rather extraordinary.

(b)   The **market for the classics may grow**, so that people who would not consider buying classic literature, for whatever reason, now can do so, as it is so much cheaper than before.

Wordsworth is thus competing in the market for classic titles. **Cost leadership** is the most appropriate description of the strategy: the directors say as much by stating that they cannot be undercut. At the moment no-one can produce books more cheaply.

Wordsworth's **price strategy** used to have another function. It enabled Wordsworth to differentiate its offer to booksellers and other retailers; they were given the freedom to price as they wish; they were not subject to the Net Book Agreement. This flexibility on pricing was probably necessary to attract retailers new to bookselling. The Net Book Agreement has now been abolished.

Part (b)

The **value chain** is a sort of model of how firms create value for their customers. The value chain describes a number of activities carried out in a firm.

Primary activities are directly related to the processes of production and sales.

(a)   **Inbound logistics** are those activities involved with receiving, handling and storing inputs to the production system.

(b)   **Operations** convert the resource input into the end product.

(c)   **Outbound logistics** relate to storage and distribution.

(d)   **Marketing and sales** inform customers about the product, and include advertising and promotion.

(e)   **After sales service** – this rarely applies to publishing companies.

Support activities obtain purchased inputs, human resources, technology and infrastructure to support the primary activities.

Competitive advantage is obtained by configuring the value chain in certain ways.

Primary activities

(a) There is little in the way of **inbound logistics**. Like most publishers, it subcontracts other firms to do its printing, so it would not need to warehouse stocks of paper. There is little effort required to find books out of copyright.

(b) **Operations**: editorial work is done in house, but the conversion of paper and ink into books for sale is done by outsiders.

(c) Outbound logistics and distribution, on the other hand, are very important indeed to reach the right markets at the right time, especially as the firm eschews advertising and promotion.

Of the **support activities**, the size of the firm (ten staff) means that these might be the responsibility of a few people. **Technology development**, for example, would mean reviewing the latest word processing technology, if appropriate; **procurement** is simply a matter of researching back catalogues for old editions. The firm perhaps does not have to bother with market research; the books are so cheap (the price of a Sunday Newspaper) that they are easy to sell.

What Wordsworth does is to **manage the linkages in the value chain**, even though many of the activities in the value chain are contracted to outsiders, **to squeeze out costs**. Wordsworth has combined a number of elements in a normal publisher's value chain and **configured them in its own unique way**. This is why it has been successful.

10 Question with answer plan: Grow or buy?

Top tips. You may have learned most of what you know about outsourcing when considering the strategic management of ICT. It is quite important to adapt ideas learned in one context if you use them in another. As the Examiner pointed out, preserving the confidentiality of data is not really an aspect of outsourcing that is relevant to this setting! As always, answer the question that was set, not the one you wish had been set.

Easy marks. The cost and price advantages of the proposed strategy are clear and discussing them would be worth three to five marks. The rest of the question revolves around the idea of competences and resource-based strategy. If you are happy with this, the marks are easy to get; if not, not.

Examiner's comments. Generally, a well answered question, though the phrase 'buy instead of grow' led some candidates to discuss the merits of internally generated growth and growth by acquisition, while part (b) was sometimes answered entirely in terms of outsourcing IT, with irrelevant matters such as data confidentiality being dragged in.

Marking scheme

		Marks
(a)	Reasons to buy in	
	Increase margins	up to 2 marks
	Lower costs	up to 2 marks
	Access to expertise	up to 2 marks
	Access to wider range	up to 2 marks
		Maximum 7 marks
	Reasons to grow	
	Control of quality	up to 2 marks
	Control of delivery	up to 2 marks
	Maintain expertise	up to 2 marks
	Maintain presence within the industry	up to 2 marks
		Maximum 6 marks

(b) Reporting structure   up to 2 marks
     Chain of command broken   up to 2 marks
     Managing and monitoring contract   up to 2 marks
     Dispute procedure   up to 2 marks
     Maximum 7 marks
     Total 20 marks

Answer plan

Part (a)

	3D	Investment needed
	2A	Increased profit margin
	1A	Site limits of growth – growth market
	C	Range of suppliers – not dependent on any
	3A	Wider product range
	2D	Capital cost
Poss D1	C	Selling skills – core competences
Conclusion	C	Return to growing

A = advantage D = disadvantage C = wider consideration

Note. This is a typical brainstorming list, supplemented by consideration of how to structure the answer by distinguishing advantages from disadvantages and putting them in a suitable order.

Part (b)

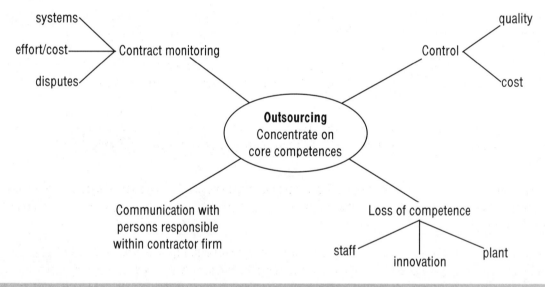

Part (a)

Greenfield Nurseries is currently profitable and growing. However, the **opportunities for additional growth are limited on the current site**. The options are either to acquire new land or to switch from the current strategy of growing in order to sell to distributors to one of buying plants from other suppliers to sell direct to the public. There are arguments both for and against this proposed new strategy.

Arguments for buying instead of growing

Probably the main argument for the proposed switch in strategy would be the **higher profit margins** that are normally available to retailers selling directly to the public. This is particularly true in a growth market such as the garden centre horticultural market.

The proposition would involve buying from a number of specialist nurseries. This would enable Greenfield to offer a **wider range of products** and to benefit from their suppliers' economies of scale, in buying at a cost lower than their own production cost.

Arguments against buying instead of growing

Perhaps the most persuasive argument against this strategy is that of **core competences**. Mark Roberts and Greenfield Nurseries have expertise in growing plants rather than in selling to the general public. Not only would **working practices** have to change, but there may also be a **requirement for new staff** with selling rather than horticultural skills.

There is also the capital investment cost required to convert the glasshouses into a suitable garden centre.

By buying plants from other suppliers rather than growing them, Greenfield risks losing a degree of control over the **quality** of the products that it sells. If poor quality products are sold to the public, this will reflect on Greenfield Nurseries rather than on the ultimate supplier.

It could be argued that Greenfield Nurseries risks **disruption to its supplies** if it moves away from growing its own plants. However, as the intention is to buy from a number of suppliers, this is probably not a major problem. There might also be the fear that if Greenfield is not successful in this new retail operation it may not be able to re-enter the production market. However as the expertise, technology and capital cost requirements of production are fairly low, it should not be too difficult a task to re-enter the production market if required.

Part (b)

Outsourcing

Outsourcing has become a popular strategy for many companies; it enables them to concentrate resources on their **value-adding core activities**. Despite the popularity of this strategy, however, there are a number of problems that management may face when outsourcing.

One of the main problems is that of **lack of direct control**. If a function of a business is outsourced, its management lose direct managerial control over it. This may result in a poor quality of service, which may require expense and time to remedy.

If outsourcing is to be used successfully, then management must negotiate carefully and set up **systems for review and monitoring** of the contract and the services provided under it. There must also be a system set up for **dealing with disputes** over quality or service.

A further potential problem related to lack of direct control is that of **responsibility**. If an activity is dealt with in-house, then there will be an individual who is directly responsible for that activity who will report to management on it. If there are problems, the individual responsible is clearly identifiable. However, if the activity is outsourced it may be harder to determine who is responsible in the outsourcing agency and therefore **disputes may be harder to settle**.

A further problem is the **loss of internal competences** that accompanies outsourcing. Staff may leave or be transferred, and those who remain will lose their skills. Plant and equipment also will be sold or transferred. Finally, this surrender of competence prevents further immoration in the outsourced function.

11 Question with student answer: McGeorge Holdings

Student answer

Marking scheme

		Marks
(a)	Use of product life cycle	up to 4 marks
	Use of BCG matrix	up to 6 marks
		Maximum 10 marks
(b)	Methods of benchmarking up to 2 marks for each	
	Internal	
	Competitive	
	Customer	
	Generic	
	Process	**Maximum 6 marks**
	Problems of benchmarking	
	Data availability	up to 1·5 marks each
	Difficulties in making comparisons	
	Does it add value?	
	Historical tendency	**Maximum 4 marks**
		Maximum for section 10 marks
		Total 20 marks

> The student makes a reasonable start to their answer by briefly describing an appropriate model – the BCG matrix.

> Ensure that you are clear about the main models on the syllabus and can describe them clearly. This is a poor description of the axis of the BCG model.

(a) Portfolio analysis

To discover and select the products that can be removed from the portfolio of McGeorge Adrian could have the BGG matrix.

The BCG matrix examines the interrelationships between products. It is broken into four sections two cash using and two cash generating.

It examines how strong a product is in its market and the growth of the market it's self.

Question mark

This would be an new entry to the market or a product still in research and development stage. It uses more funds than generates and it is unclear how the product will achieve.

Rising stars

Products that are through the research and development stage but are not known to the market yet. They are still using company funds rather than generating, however they could be getting closer to the next stage in the cycle of being a cash cow.

Cash Cow

This is the ideal section in the matrix for a product to be. It will have a high market share and is the stage of the product that generates the highest income.

Adrian should retain all products in this section.

Dog

A product generally becomes a dog when the market is flooded and there are not many growth opportunities. Timing is eventual in this area as products can still be income generating

However its knowing when to pull out because your product is no longer required by the market and could easily turn to loss making.

I would recommend that Adrian researches products that are in the dog and question mark stage of the matrix to start with.

Those in the question mark stage could well be draining funds and never amount to turning into rising stars or cash cows.

Large savings could be made

For those products in the dog stage are they still profitable. If not they should be discontinued or in possible developed to bring them back to being an income generating unit.

> These are good relevant points but are a little brief and under explained. This is the value adding part of the answer as explanations score more marks than regurgitation of facts learnt before entering the exam hall.

To enable Adrian to place products correctly he should also look at the value chain and how each product meets the objectives of McGeorge Plc.

> This final point is tagged on at the end of the question as an after thought. Plan your answer briefly before you start writing and this way appropriate models could have been introduced at the start and then developed later if you have time.

> Overall this part of the question is fair and would have scored a borderline pass.

(b) _Benchmarking_

Adrian needs to compare McGeorge against its competitors in the same industries.

McGeorge is an international company Adrian needs to find a similar international company to compare profit margins and costs. Costs should be broken down into the different areas, production, sales, marketing, distribution etc.

Adrian could also break McGeorge down into areas such as countries, products or global regions eg Europe SE Asia etc Adrian would then need to compare each of these areas to similar companies.

> Again the marker would want to know why or how does this help the company.

A limitation of benchmarking is finding a suitable company to benchmark against.

> A series of subheadings to break the answer in to its relevant parts helps out the marker and gives the answer a clear structure.

If a company is benchmarking it's self against a competitor it is safe to say they are not going to be market leaders.

There could also be problems in obtaining information on other companies be bench mark against and Adrian will be looking at historical information.

There are other forms of bench marking that using competitor information.

> The candidate has written very little for 10 marks and this may be due to poor timing and spending too long on part a of the question. Ensure you split your time carefully over each part of the question before you start writing.

Side annotations:

This long description of each quadrant would have been greatly improved and would have scored more marks if it had been related to the scenario and demonstrated for example using washing powders to make the answer more specific to the situation in the company. When you are answering the questions imagine you are a consultant who has been asked to help this particular company with its issues.

This is a fair point but lacks explanation ie why should the cost be broken down and how will this help the company. At this level in your studies the examiner will be looking for a brief explanation of each of the points made.

This point is unclear and unexplained.

Overall the answer to part (b) is not strong and would score a marginal fail.

BPP answer

Part (a)

> **Text reference.** The topics mentioned in this answer are discussed in Chapter 6 of your BPP Study Text.
>
> **Top tips.** Do not overlook the product life cycle model when thinking about product portfolios. It is very simple but can give very useful clues about managing a portfolio.
>
> **Easy marks.** This is a very easy question. Product portfolio analysis matrix models abound and the BCG classification is as good as any.

McGeorge Holdings has a diverse range of products that has grown in a rather opportunistic fashion, without a clear vision to guide its structure. Two key models can be used to analyse the product portfolio in order to decide which to remove.

The Product Life Cycle

A **balanced portfolio** is likely to include products at different stages of their lifecycles. Today's mature products will generate the cash needed to launch and build the innovations that will become tomorrow's cash generators. Then, inevitably, one by one, mature products will eventually go into decline.

At the **introduction stage**, a product will need considerable resources to be invested in research, development and marketing and is therefore a loss maker. Such products will however generate profits in the future and are unlikely to be candidates for divestment.

In the growth stage, the product has gained market acceptance, unit costs are falling and the product should be providing profits.

It is in the **later stages of maturity and decline** that particular attention needs to be focused. Most products on the market will be at the mature stage of their life and profits should be good. It can be hard to determine when decline will start, but it will be signalled by **falling profits**. Some products may go straight from growth to decline. At this point, the company needs to decide whether or not to leave the market. The consequences of such action need to be analysed carefully. The product may be popular with customers whose displeasure at its withdrawal could have a negative impact on linked products and may lead to them switch to competitors. Furthermore, if costs such as marketing and distribution have been **apportioned** over a range of products, withdrawal of some of them may result in a higher allocation of costs to the remainder, making them potentially uncompetitive.

The BCG Matrix

The BCG matrix assesses a company's products according to their relative market share (which is, effectively, a proxy for the extent of economies of scale they enjoy), and the rate of growth of their market. Their position in the matrix has general implications for potential cash generation and cash expenditure requirements.

Stars require capital expenditure in excess of the cash they generate, in order to maintain their market position, but promise high returns in the future. The strategy for stars is therefore to **build** them and they would not usually be candidates for divestment.

Cash cows have low market growth but high relative market share and generate high levels of cash income whilst needing very little capital expenditure. They are therefore often used to finance other products' development and would not, therefore, be recommended for divestment.

Problem children (or **question marks**) are the opposite of cash cows: they have a low share of a growing market. They would require considerable capital expenditure in order to increase their market share, as, effectively, they are being squeezed out of the market by rival products. A decision needs to be made whether it is worthwhile continuing with these products.

LEARNING MEDIA

Dogs have a low share of a low-growth market. They may be cash cows that have fallen on hard times. They tie up funds, provide a poor return on investment and are, therefore, candidates for withdrawal. Alternatively, they may still have a useful role in completing a product range or keeping competitors out. There are also many smaller **niche businesses** in markets that are **difficult to consolidate** that would count as dogs but which are quite successful.

Adrian Reed needs to look carefully at all of the products in the range, obtain full information about each one and categorise them accordingly. A fully informed, sensible decision can then be made about which products to remove from the portfolio.

Part (b)

Top tips. This question calls for a simple account of the theory of benchmarking, which is, in principle, not a terribly complex idea.

Examiner's comments. Candidates' accounts of the disadvantages of benchmarking were rather rudimentary.

Benchmarking is the establishment, through data gathering, of targets and comparators, through whose use relative levels of performance can be identified. By the adoption of identified best practices it is hoped that performance will improve.

Benchmarking can be carried out in a number of different ways:

Internal benchmarking would compare one operating unit or function with another one within McGeorge Holdings plc. A unit that is particularly effective in one area could be used as an example of best practice and their knowledge and skills transferred to other units within the group.

Competitive benchmarking **would involve gathering information about direct competitors in order to compare products, processes and results and attempt to copy best practice. The obvious problem is the difficulty in obtaining such information.**

Functional benchmarking would compare functions within McGeorge Holdings with similar functions in the best external practitioners, regardless of their industry. Financial indicators such as gearing and liquidity may be easier to obtain than detailed operational information.

Disadvantages of benchmarking

There is an increased flow of information that must be monitored, summarised and assessed. These processes are not cost-free and they can lead to management overload. In a charity, the work involved in benchmarking can be discouraging for volunteer staff.

Overload can also occur when a successful benchmarking exercise produces a large volume of requests to participate from organisations that have themselves little to offer in potential improvements.

Benchmarking usually involves the exchange of information with other organisations. There is a threat to confidentiality, both commercial and personal.

Poor results from a benchmarking exercise can be disproportionately discouraging and demotivating, particularly to managers.

The benchmarking process itself can distract managers' attention from their primary responsibilities. Even when this does not happen, managers may put too much emphasis on improving the efficiency with which they do the things they have always done and fail to ask if new ways of doing things would be better overall.

12 KPG Systems

Text reference. The topics mentioned in this answer are discussed in Chapter 3 of your BPP Study Text.

Top tips. Mission statements are often rightly regarded with some cynicism as being mere public relations exercises. However, they can be extremely useful devices to focus attention on what is really important. They are probably most useful when they are kept short.

In Part (b), we enumerate a number of models that could be used. You will often find in the field of general strategic analysis that any one of several models could be used. If this happens, it is simplest to confine your answer to one model only; however, there may be valid extra points that can be made using another model as well. If you want to do this, try to keep the models separate and your reasoning clear.

Easy marks. This question is a good example of a common type, in that it has a very specific and fairly simple task in part (a) and a more open-ended one in part (b). Part (a) is therefore easier, since it requires little more than knowledge, while part (b) requires thought and the careful application of theory to the scenario.

Part (a)

A mission statement expounds an organisation's purpose in society. It might appear in the annual report, on the organisation's publicity material or on the notice board in the office. There is no set format for a mission statement but it should be **brief**, **flexible** and **distinctive**. The mission statement should also be of relevance to all of the stakeholders in the business. The mission statement will define the **reasons why the organisation exists**, what it aims to achieve, how it aims to achieve them and who it is in business for.

A mission statement will cover the **products or services** that it offers and the **competences** by which it aims to compete and be successful. It will also specify the policies and standards of behaviour expected of its staff and the organisation's overall values and culture. The mission statement should include the organisation's commitment to staff, suppliers and customers, and give all of those involved in the business a common sense of purpose.

A good mission statement can act as a **powerful motivating force** for individual employees and the organisation as a whole; in strategic terms it can clarify the markets the organisation intends to serve, the products and services provided in those markets and how they are to be served. It may specify the technologies to be used and the competences the organisation will use in order to compete in the chosen markets.

It is generally thought that production of a mission statement should take place at the start of the planning process, but it can also be argued that as a business progresses it will **discover** its proper mission rather than the mission being artificially invented. Therefore, in the case of KPG this may well be the right time to consider the business and its mission. Andy may now be able to reflect in a mission statement the origins of the business, his own personal preferences as owner, the environmental issues influencing the organisation and the resources, competencies and capabilities available to the company as well as the values that pervade the business.

The production of an effective, meaningful mission statement for KPG may help in the process of determining where the business is going and provide a framework for consistent planning and goal setting. The mission statement can also be used to communicate with all stakeholders in the business about what the firm stands for.

Part (b)

There is a variety of models that could be used to assess the current position of KPG Systems, including PEST, gap and SWOT analysis, and Porter's five forces model. In this answer we will use a **SWOT analysis**.

A SWOT analysis is a critical assessment of the strengths, weaknesses, opportunities and threats facing the organisation in relation to the internal and environmental factors affecting it, carried out in order to establish its condition prior to the preparation of a long-term plan. Strengths and weaknesses are discovered by internal analysis, whereas opportunities and threats are diagnosed by environmental analysis. The internal analysis should determine strengths that can be exploited and weaknesses that should be improved upon. Opportunities are areas that can be exploited, while threats need to be recognised and assessed for their potential effect on the organisation itself and its competitors.

Strengths

One of the main strengths of the business is the **commitment, enthusiasm and technical ability of the owner**, Andy Rowe. **Customer care** is also a major strength in that products are designed to the requirements of individual customers, which gives KPG a competitive edge. Allied to this is the importance of the **technical support** provided by the company. As technology becomes more complex, it is likely that companies will rely more on specialist technical support rather than on in-house abilities.

Weaknesses

One of the major weaknesses of the firm, and one that Andy has recognised, is that it may have **lost its direction**. There is also a **lack of creative marketing strategies** and allied to this a **failure of business forecasting**. Although the technical support activities of KPG are a strength, there is also a problem with **providing support throughout the UK**. Finally, there would appear to be an **over-dependence upon Andy Rowe**, which may mean that there will be senior management problems as the firm grows further.

Opportunities

In this age of high-technology, there is little doubt that KPG's market will continue to grow and expand. The opportunity here is for KPG to increase its share of this market. In this area there are likely to be many **innovations and advances** that KPG could adapt and embody in its products.

Threats

One major threat to KPG is that it is only a small player in this market with a **small and vulnerable market share**. Many of its competitors are larger companies with heavy investment in market, product and competitor research, which may give them a competitive edge over KPG. A further threat to all participants in this market is the **global economic downturn**, which may affect potential customers' investment plans and will almost certainly make customers more price-conscious. **Changes in technology** are considered as an opportunity if KPG has the technical expertise to capitalise on them; however, if KPG cannot keep abreast of changes in technology, the company may fall behind its competitors.

13 Airtite

Part (a)

Text reference. The topics mentioned in this answer are discussed in Chapter 5 of your BPP Study Text.

Top tips. The marking scheme for this question emphasises PESTEL, apparently offering full marks for proper consideration of each of the six factors listed in the mnemonic. This would seem reasonable, given that nearly all of the information in the scenario relates to the general environment. However, the Examiner's suggested solution is largely concerned with a discussion the **nature and process** of environmental scanning and offers little in the way of actual analysis of the data given in the setting.

The message to take away from all this is that this question is not quite as simple as it looks. While you could score quite well with a simple discussion of the PESTEL factors in the scenario, you should also consider **environmental uncertainty**, its implications for **risk** and the potential **impact** of the various environmental factors on Airtite and its operations.

On a different topic, you may find some aspects of the environmental influences given in the scenario rather debatable. A good example would be the potential effects of the demographic changes mentioned in the third paragraph. The way to deal with such a problem is to ignore it: deal with the circumstances as they are given in the scenario.

Of course, if the setting includes unrealistic or one-sided opinions *expressed by a character* within it, it is appropriate to talk about them. This is a fairly common device used by examiners to encourage you to give balanced consideration to a topic. But when the setting is essentially a simple narrative of prevailing conditions, as this one is (despite the identification of John Sykes as a character within it), you should think of it as an **alternative reality with its own rules** and play within them.

Don't forget that all versions of the PEST model are fairly arbitrary in the way they analyse the general environment into sectors. It doesn't really matter whether you cover the demographic issues in the setting under the economic heading or the society one, for instance, so long as you cover it.

Easy marks. As mentioned above, a reasonably competent discussion of the relevant PESTEL items should score well.

Examiner's comments. The important factors in the setting included the key drivers of change.

Marking scheme

		Marks
(a)	PESTEL analysis including:	up to 2 per variable
	Political – increasing government control	up to 5
	Economic – trends in disposable income	
	Social – ageing population	
	Technological – more efficient aircraft	
	Environmental – tighter emission control	
	Legal – global agreement on emissions	up to 3
	Assessing impact and uncertainty	**Maximum for section (a) 12 marks**
(b)	Key features in using a scenario:	up to 5
	Identifying high impact/high uncertainty factors in environment	
	Identifying different possible futures by factor	
	Building scenarios of plausible configurations of factors	
	Links to Airtite's strategy	up to 5
		Maximum for section (b) 8 marks
		Total 20 marks

Airtite – the general environment

Political and legal factors

Generally, European governments are sympathetic to the idea of low cost air travel, since it has the potential to increase the effective **wealth** of the less affluent. However, the influential green lobby objects to the **environmental effects** of increased air travel. In any event, there is a continuing possibility of **increased taxation** or **direct controls** on the growth of air travel.

Economic factors

Fuel is becoming more expensive and this trend is unlikely to change very much because of the increasing demand from China and India as they develop their economies. **Growth** in the European economies varies from country to country. New entrants to the EU tend to have a relatively low GNP per head, while some of the more prosperous countries are finding their growth constrained by their failure to **reform their labour markets**. Nevertheless, Europe remains a generally wealthy region and the market for air travel is likely to continue to grow, though perhaps at a reduced rate.

Socio-cultural factors

The incidence of **terrorist activity** aimed air transport seems to be increasing, bringing with it a major increase in security-related costs and, on occasion, a reluctance to travel by air.

Demographic change in Europe may constrain growth in demand for air travel. Aging populations and growth in the number of one parent families are likely to increase the **burden of welfare costs**, leading to increased levels of taxation and reduced disposable income.

Technological factors

The technology of all aspects of air travel continues to develop, with consequent **increases in safety** and **reductions in cost and emissions**. The spread of broadband access to the Internet increases the size of Airtite's potential market, relying, as it does, on on-line bookings.

Environmental uncertainty

As the analysis above shows, within Europe the general environment for the air travel industry is both **complex** and **dynamic**, with a large number of major factors interacting in complex ways. The effect of this is to create a high level of **uncertainty**. The implication of this for Airtite is that John Sykes and his fellow senior managers must remain alert for developments that might affect them and be innovative and flexible in their policies and plans. **Experience in the industry** is likely to be of great value in assessing the importance of future environmental developments.

Part (b)

Top tips. We all know what scenarios are, more or less, but many of us are unsure about both when it would be a good idea to prepare one and how to go about doing it.

The clue to the first problem – when scenarios are a good idea – lies in **environmental uncertainty**. A high degree of uncertainty limits to usefulness of techniques based on extrapolation: the possibility of a transformational change must be considered.

The scenario-writing process then requires a consideration of potential **impact** on the organisation and what it does.

A scenario is an internally consistent view of how the future might turn out to be. Scenarios are useful when there is **high environmental uncertainty** as a result of complexity or rapid change, or both and thus difficulty in forecasting how a range of important influences might affect the future.

Scenario building is not an attempt to foretell the future. It is rather an attempt to **identify critical outcomes or branching points** that may arise at some future time and to work out how to deal with the various possible future states that they imply.

A very large number of factors may influence the way future events develop. *Johnson, Scholes and Whittington* suggest that only a few of them should be considered so as to reduce the complexity that is likely to arise from a large number of assumptions and uncertainties. This can be done by basing scenario development on those factors that display both **high uncertainty** and the **potential for major impact** on the industry in question. Such an approach would concentrate John's mind on the most important environmental features.

The chosen factors, or **drivers of change** are assessed for the ways in which they might interact and a small number of different but equally logically consistent scenarios are created. A **time horizon** of perhaps ten years is used, partly to enhance the usefulness of the scenarios that are developed and partly to discourage simple extrapolation from the present. No attempt is made to allocate probabilities to the various future states envisioned: this would lend them a spurious accuracy and would detract from their utility.

The process of writing scenarios depends on an ability to discern patterns and a general awareness of the potential significance of widely disparate data. It can be taken in stages, with the initial production of up to a dozen mini scenarios, each dealing with a restricted set of factors and interactions. These can then be combined into, say, three larger scenarios dealing with all of the drivers.

The preparation and discussion of scenarios would contributes to **organisational learning** in Airtite by developing its senior managers' awareness of the environmental factors influencing the airline's development. This awareness should lead to **more informed environmental monitoring** and prompt the development of appropriate **contingency plans**.

14 Pharmia plc

Top tips. We include this question for completeness. It is really very unlikely that you will be asked to construct a decision tree in the examination, but you do need to be aware of how the technique works and what it can do to assist strategic decision-making. The requirement in part (c) is by far the most important part of this question.

Easy marks. The decision tree is simple and should not present you with any problems. Similarly, the discussion in part (b) is fairly obvious.

Part (a)

A decision tree is provided below. The outcomes are multiplied by the probabilities which are then aggregated. Before the initial investment of £5m is taken into account, the expected value (EV) of each option is as follows.

EV of Tyrix   = $0.03 \times £150m = £4.5m$
EV of Medvac = $(£48m \times 1/6) + (£27m \times 1/3) + (-£10m \times 1/2) = £12m$
EV of Sonprex =   £14m

The net payoff, after the investment cost, is as follows.

Tyrix £4.5m – £5m   =   £(0.5m) (ie a loss of £500,000)
Medvac £12m – £5m =   £7m profit
Sonprex £14m – £5m =   £9m profit

Part (b)

The appropriateness of expected values and subjective probabilities

Any strategic decision is taken in a state of partial ignorance as to the future: this is why strategies are necessary. You cannot be sure that a quantitative exercise necessarily gives the right result without questioning the **assumptions** on which it is based and the **context** in which it is made. The probabilities in this example are merely **subjective** quantifications of uncertainty. In the cases of the options suggested we can note the following.

(a) **Possible overconfidence about Sonprex.** Can we really be 100% certain about Sonprex's success? The answer has to be **no**, as this would imply that the company's forecasters had an absolute knowledge of the future. However, this does indicate that the project is low risk, but that is all it indicates.

(b) **Sensitivity to the 'risky' Tyrix.** The decision is sensitive to the low (3%) probability of Tyrix's success. Tyrix offers a huge reward. Were the success of Tyrix to have a 5% probability, the EV before investment would be £150m × 5% = £7.5m. A 10% probability of success, still very low, would give it an EV before investment costs of £15m, which would make it, on the basis of EVs alone, an attractive option even though a high risk. The decision is thus sensitive to changes in probability estimates. As these are subjective anyway, they need to be taken with a pinch of salt.

(c) **Bizarre profit/market share figures for Medvac.** How realistic are the market share projections for Medvac?

    (i)   It is hard to see how an **increase in market share**, even if only 10%, could lead to a loss of £10m, especially after £5m had been invested in advertising, and the loss did not take this advertising into account.

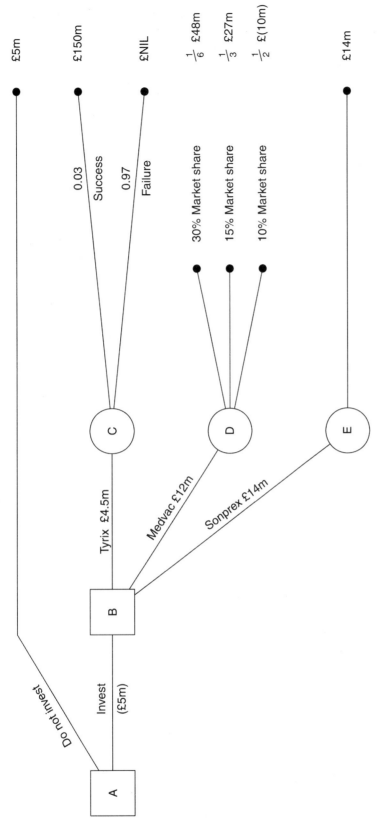

Expected value of different products

(ii) The difference in payoff between a 10% market share and a 15% market share is extraordinary (£37m). This needs to be looked into. It is unlikely that there would be a sudden jump in market share. When would the outcome be positive? at 11%? or 12%?

To summarise, the decision cannot be taken in isolation from the firm's commercial strategy of innovation, its need to maintain a balanced portfolio of projects in the present, and its need to invest in future successful projects. Furthermore, especially in the case of Medvac, more information is needed.

Part (c)

The relative merits of each drug. This decision should not be taken without considering other products in the portfolio, about which we know little. Nor can we ignore the circumstances of the decision: the £5m is 'unexpected', additional to the existing allocation of resources. The company's policy is to take a **scattergun approach**, investing large sums in R & D in many projects in the hope of producing a sure fire winner.

(a)   **Tyrix** is an innovative investment.

   (i)   **Cheap.** The actual investment (£5m) is small in comparison to the potential reward (£150m) even though the probability of achieving the reward is very low.

   (ii)   **Safe.** The investment of £5m is hardly critical to the firm's success: otherwise it would not have been conjured out of a hat and made unexpectedly available. The risk is perhaps less important than it would be normally.

   (iii)   **Strategic conformity.** The firm's overall approach to the market is product **innovation**. Tyrix conforms to this strategy. Sonprex does not.

(b)   **Medvac**

   (i)   It has already been successfully introduced. The chances of the advertising campaign being successful is about 50%.

   (ii)   Despite the competition, and the rather bizarre negative payoff resulting from an increase in market share, there are substantial benefits to be had from supporting it. Again, this will depend on the firm's attitude to risk. Risk is spread through a number of different products in the portfolio, and so Medvac may be worth it in the light of the rest of the portfolio.

(c)   Sonprex gives the **highest** payoff compared to the other two, but that is the **only** thing in its favour.

   (i)   Investing in Sonprex will be an investment in a product which would shortly be superseded: a **harvesting strategy**.

   (ii)   If this means that the firm's portfolio is too heavily weighted towards mature products, the firm's **long term future is in danger.**

(d)   **Remaining uncertainties. We do not know much about the timing of the cash flows.**

   (i)   If Sonprex brings in £14m in the year **after** the investment, this might be used to subsidise investment in the other two. Nor do we know if Medvac's condition will get much worse if the money is not invested.

   (ii)   If the price of investing in Sonprex is the failure, say, of Medvac, then this must be taken into account when devising expected values. Tyrix is an opportunity: it does not need the investment, whereas Medvac's competitive position may be undermined if it is not supported.

The EVs provide some useful information to make a decision, but because we do not know the state of the **entire product portfolio**; and the firm's attitude to **risk**, a comparison of EVs **cannot** be used as the determining factor in this case.

15 Qualispecs

Part (a)

Text reference. The topics mentioned in this answer are discussed in Chapters 5 and 6 of your BPP Study Text.

Top tips. In answering this question, you should use a SWOT analysis approach rather than one based on environmental scanning and internal appraisal. How were you to know this? Note first that there are twelve marks for this part, which allows three marks for each quadrant of the SWOT diagram. Second, be aware that there is not really enough data available for you to be able to carry out a thorough external and internal review. The material given is in a significantly summarised form: this is ideal for the SWOT analysis approach.

Take great care in answering part (a) not to leave yourself with nothing to say in part (b). A useful approach would be to confine yourself to more general comments in part (a) and be more specific in part (b).

Qualispecs corporate appraisal

Strengths

- New CEO with good track record in the industry, intimate knowledge of a major competitor and willingness to take vigorous steps
- Reputation for quality products
- Celebrity endorsement
- Strong financial position including large cash reserves

Weaknesses

- Failure to utilise new technology
- High production costs
- Failure to use reward system for motivation
- Over-centralisation

Opportunities

- Fashion 'eye-wear', including designer frames and sunglasses
- Availability of new production technology
- Increased spending among 18-30 year old customers

Threats

- Economic slowdown
- Decline in customer loyalty/increasing competition from innovative rivals

Key strategic challenges

Qualispecs is in danger of being left behind by its competitors. The erosion of its customer base shows that it can no longer allow its product to 'speak for itself'. Unless it takes vigorous steps, its rivals will draw further ahead and its decline will accelerate.

The company has been reluctant to make use of **improved technology**; this is probably linked to its high production costs. Improved technology would almost certainly reduce cost and improve quality simultaneously. There would be important implications for cashflow, production management and training, but these will not be reduced by putting improvements off even longer.

Qualispecs has a rather unimaginative **reward policy** and this is probably having an effect on the productivity of its staff. While *Herzberg* tells us that pay is not a motivating factor, we should be aware that it can be used to enhance the effect of motivational factors. Taking the example of innovation, there are probably people working for Qualispecs who have good ideas that could enhance the company's success. If their ideas were taken up and proved successful, they would probably be disappointed if their reward were confined to praise and a certificate. Something more materially convertible would emphasise the company's appreciation.

The **profitability** of Qualispecs' shops varies enormously. This must be investigated. We know that fixed costs are high in shopping malls; there may be other factors at work, not least the performance of shop managers and staff. This is an area where analysis of performance figures will be useful, if only in highlighting areas for further investigation.

Part (b)

> **Top tips.** This part of the question requires you to recommend specific strategies. A solution might be based on converting threats to opportunities and weaknesses to strengths; matching strengths with opportunities and remedying weaknesses. It would probably also be possible to base an answer on Porter's generic strategies. The product/market vector matrix is perhaps less useful.
>
> **Easy marks.** We have used what the Examiner calls a 'freeform' approach, simply identifying areas that are reasonably obviously in need of improvement, based on our discussion of strategic challenges.
>
> Of these, perhaps the most obvious are:
>
> - Computer aided production to cut costs
> - Wide variation in site profitability

Qualispecs is fortunate in that its finances are sound and it has large cash reserves. It would be appropriate to use some of that financial strength to make investments that will improve the company's competitive position. Qualispecs should seek improvements in three main areas of its operations.

- **Innovation**
- **Performance management**
- **Distribution**

Innovation

Two areas are ripe for innovation: products and production methods. In both areas, Qualispecs has to catch up with its competitors. The economic downturn means that growth will be most easily achieved in the 18-30 year old market. Fashion-consciousness is important here, so the design and variety of prescription spectacles and sunglasses must be improved. At the same time, suitable promotion must be undertaken, perhaps making use of sports star endorsement.

Production methods must be examined for opportunities to reduce cost and improve efficiency. The one hour laboratory approach should be considered, as discussed below.

In addition to these two matters, it would be appropriate for Qualispecs to begin to foster a culture of innovation. Given its existing stagnation, there are almost certainly several other aspects of its operation that would benefit from new ideas. Such cultural change is linked to our next area of consideration.

Performance management

We mentioned performance management in our earlier discussion of key strategic challenges. The principle could also be applied in the form of management bonuses based on the overall performance individual shops and regions and individual pay increases and bonuses related to sales and profit performance. Such a change would require greater autonomy for managers at shop level in particular if it were to have significant effect, so there would have to be some delegation of control over such matters as working conditions, job roles and pay rates.

Distribution

Qualispecs must do something about the wide variation in its shops' performance. A careful examination of costs and revenues is needed. There is also a need to look at the shops estate from a marketing point of view. The estate may be in need of renovation or even complete redesign. The company should aim to make its shops pleasant and interesting places to visit. Fastglass has entered into partnership with a high-street shopping group. This may be an innovation that Qualispecs could imitate as part of its attention to product development. A fashion retailer would be a good choice of partner for a new group of in-store shops concentrating on the new designer styles, for example. A partnership approach to costs and revenues may be possible and appropriate.

Qualispecs must also examine the Fastglass mini-lab approach with an open mind. This method may be worth adopting, assuming the technology is not protected, but caution should be employed: a full examination of costs and market prospects should be carried out and implications fully explored.

16 Question with answer plan: Digwell

Text reference. The topics mentioned in this answer are discussed in Chapter 4 of your BPP Study Text.

Top tips. Ethics is the study of concepts of right and wrong. Business ethics is the application of ethical ideas to business. It is doubtful whether this question is actually about *ethics* at all. Looked at objectively, the question is about conflicts of interest rather than notions of right and wrong.

Nevertheless, some pressure groups will always attempt to occupy the moral high ground – and public opinion tends to allow them to do so, often in defiance of rational analysis. Environmental pressure groups are among the worst offenders here, and it is well to be aware of the threat they constitute to some legitimate business operations.

All that being said, you are unlikely to be given any marks for discussing the failings of the question. Proceed as though it made perfect sense.

Easy marks. There are two important areas to consider: environmental protection and the right of communities affected by business externalities to be heard and to have their views considered. However, to obtain a pass mark, you should have to explore the implications of the various points of view in some detail, rather than just asserting a particular opinion.

Answer plan

Part (a)

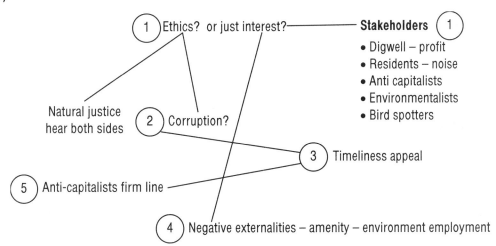

Part (b)

1　Explain Mendelow's map and uses
2　Classify groups and suggest response

A	B Eastborough Alliance Wildlife Anti capitalists Residents Greens
C	D Government

Part (a)

> **Top tips.** Bearing in mind our introductory comments above, it is probably best to avoid too much use of the word 'ethics' here. Think, rather, in terms of 'stakeholder interest'.

This scenario may be summed up as a fairly routine conflict of **environmental amenity against economic activity**. This is a continuing thorn in the side of governments: they are expected both to increase prosperity and to promote environmental improvement. The two goals are not incompatible, but they are difficult to reconcile.

On the one hand we have Digwell proposing to make profit, provide opportunity for the unemployed and generally invigorate the local economy. On the other, we have a loose grouping of interests: local residents afraid of noise, dirt and congestion; wildlife protectors concerned about the effect of the proposed scheme on the rare birds; a vaguer group of presumably all-purpose 'environmentalists' and the lunatic fringe of anti-capitalist activists.

We are not told what matters the government considered when granting permission for mining, nor what representations it heard from those opposed to the mining proposal, but we might hope that it has proceeded in a **transparent** and **even-handed** way.

First and most important, there should be no question that the decision was the result of **corruption**. Some companies and some governments are known to collaborate in a corrupt fashion: money changes hands, favours are done, invoices are adjusted and so on. If there has been any of that sort of thing here, it can be dismissed out of hand as not only unethical but also illegal in all modern jurisdictions.

When considering a decision of this type, a government should apply the basic rules of natural justice and, in particular, **hear both sides**. Extensive opportunities should be given to objectors to state their cases and there should be a right of appeal against the initial decision.

In the UK, the laws relating to planning would cover this matter only too well: the appeals and public hearings could continue indefinitely. We might propose as a matter of principle that the whole process should be not merely impartial and transparent but **timely** as well.

The case for Digwell is that the Eastborough region is suffering from a long-standing **deficit of investment**. Unemployment is high, the infrastructure is poor and there is a general lack of amenity that is hampering the development of tourism. Digwell's scheme will provide jobs and boost tax receipts, making regional improvements easier to finance. Digwell may even undertake to fund some local improvements directly as an incentive to acceptance of its scheme.

The case against Digwell is less clear-cut.

Some local residents are concerned about traffic and noise. These are presumably the ones who have jobs already and can afford to worry about amenity. We might imagine the local long-term unemployed to be less concerned. Nevertheless, the concerned residents have a valid point and one that should be considered. Digwell should be expected to proceed in a way that would **minimise the negative externalities** of their operations.

Wildlife protection representatives are concerned about the rare birds. Their interest is legitimate and can be accommodated in the same way.

The all-purpose 'environmentalists' are a dubious quantity. Such groups tend to object to any development **on principle** and to **manipulate public opinion** unscrupulously. The fact that their position is usually untenable on rational analysis does not deter them. The environmentally undesirable outcome of their interference in the *Brent Spar* problem is a case in point. Such groups can have an impact out of all proportion to their numbers: the validity of their case must be assessed realistically and they must be dealt with firmly.

The views of the anti-capitalist groups may be dismissed without further ado and the advice of London's police sought if they attempt to cause trouble.

Part (b)

> **Text reference.** The topics mentioned in this answer are discussed in Chapter 8 of your BPP Study Text.
>
> **Top tips.** The obvious model here is *Mendelow's* matrix. This is a very simple analysis, but the Examiner remarked that a common error was to fail to relate it to the scenario, with stakeholders being placed in the wrong quadrant. A further common error was to fail to identify how Digwell might respond to the various groups,
>
> We have taken a firm line on this last point, as we did in part (a). Be aware that it would be quite in order to argue for a softer line, but a good answer to this sort of question really requires that you take a position and do not rely on generalities and vague possibilities.

Mendelow classifies stakeholders on a matrix whose axes are **power held** and **likelihood of showing an interest** in the organisation's activities. These factors will help define the type of relationship the organisation should seek with its stakeholders.

Level of interest

	Low	High
Low	A	B
Power		
High	C	D

(a) **Key players** are found in segment D: strategy must be *acceptable* to them, at least. An example would be a major customer.

(b) Stakeholders in **segment C** must be treated with care. While often passive, they are capable of moving to segment D. They should, therefore be **kept satisfied.** Large institutional shareholders might fall into segment C.

(c) Stakeholders in **segment B** do not have great ability to influence strategy, but their views can be important in influencing more powerful stakeholders, perhaps by lobbying. They should therefore be **kept informed**. Community representatives and charities might fall into segment B.

(d) Minimal effort is expended on **segment A**.

Stakeholder mapping is used to assess the significance of stakeholder groups. This in turn has implications for the organisation.

(a)   The framework of **corporate governance** should recognise stakeholders' levels of interest and power.

(b)   It may be appropriate to seek to **reposition** certain stakeholders and discourage others from repositioning themselves, depending on their attitudes.

(c)   Key **blockers** and **facilitators** of change must be identified.

Stakeholder mapping can also be used to establish political priorities. A map of the current position can be compared with a map of a desired future state. This will indicate critical shifts that must be pursued.

A matrix of this type could be useful to Digwell in analysing its relationships with the various groups concerned with its Eastborough operations.

Shareholders as a body probably have low interest in the Eastborough project. They can probably be kept satisfied by careful public relations effort.

The **government** is a particularly important stakeholder as far as *Digwell's* project is concerned. Permission for mining has been granted, but governments are quite capable of betraying trusts of this type if the environmental alarm is sounded. The UK government's change of heart over the dismantling of US Navy freighters in 2003 is a case in point. The government has almost absolute power and can be provoked into deep interest by bad publicity. It belongs in quadrant D. Digwell must manage its relations with government carefully, paying particular attention to how its project is presented in the mass media: modern governments are unhealthily concerned with short-term image and opinion.

The **Eastborough Protection Alliance** is a classic quadrant B player. Its level of interest is high but it has little power of its own. However, it may exert considerable influence upon government, as outlined above. Digwell's obvious tactic for dealing with this group is to **divide and rule**. If one or more of the member factions can be neutralised, the arguments against Digwell will become less coherent and convincing.

(a)   The **economic benefits** of the project should be emphasised to local residents, perhaps sweetened with the offer of some desirable local facility, such as a general clean up of the beaches and older mine workings. At the same time, a spokesperson might be found to put the case for the improved prospects for the local unemployed and decry the selfishness of those who oppose the project.

(b)   The **wildlife groups** should be treated with respect: Digwell should be prepared to make any modifications to its plans necessary to **protect** the rare birds. This will be rewarded with further public approval.

(c)   The approach to the **environmentalists** will depend on the strength, if any, of their case. If they are the usual doom-mongers, an impartial environmental impact assessment may limit their opposition to nuisance value only. If there are genuine reasons for environmental concern, Digwell should proceed as for the wildlife groups. However, a robust approach is needed to ensure that a kind of creeping veto does not develop.

(d)   Taken by themselves, the anti-capitalists are at the lowest end of the power spectrum. If the local community and wildlife groups can be separated from them, they too will have nuisance value only.

17 MegaMart

Part (a)

Text reference. The topics mentioned in this answer are discussed in Chapter 4 of your BPP Study Text.

Top tips. The term 'management style' might put you in mind of models of management behaviour such as those developed by *Blake and Mouton*, *Rensis Likert* or *Tannenbaum and Schmidt*. This was not what the Examiner had in mind. This question is entirely about corporate governance, but it would have been clearer if the words 'management style' had been replaced by the single word 'conduct'.

That said, the scenario gives a pretty clear account of several very significant failures of corporate governance and it should be easy for you to write them up.

Make sure you do not leave yourself with nothing to say about non-executive directors in part (b).

Easy marks. Rex Lord's transgressions are pretty blatant, so you should have no difficulty in securing one or two marks at least for each of the main issues we deal with in our answer.

Examiner's comments. This was a popular question. Candidates from outside the UK gave particularly good accounts of the issues involved.

Marking scheme

		Marks
(a)	Identification of main issues:	up to 3 marks each
	Chairman and Chief Executive roles combined	
	Remuneration packages	
	Monitoring and control	
	Role and independence of auditors	
	Communication	
		Maximum 12 marks
(b)	Strategic v scrutiny role	up to 3 marks each
	Source of independent thinking	
	Role on executive remuneration	
	Involvement in audit committee	
	'Corporate conscience' on corporate social responsibility	
		Maximum 8 marks
		Total 20 marks

Rex Lord has been using MegaMart plc as a vehicle to **pursue his own ends**, thus depriving the shareholders and other stakeholders of their legitimate expectations. In order to do this he has contravened several well-established **rules of corporate governance** that are incorporated in, for example, the London Stock Exchange Combined Code.

Leading management roles

There are **two leading management roles**: running the Board and running the company. There should be a clear division of responsibilities so that there is a balance of power and no single person has unfettered powers of decision-making. Rex Lord's clear **exploitation of his power** illustrates why this is a good rule.

Non-executive directors

Non-executive directors (NEDs) are dealt with more fully in Part (b). Here it suffices to say that there should be a **strong and independent** body of NEDs with a recognised senior member other than the Chairman. MegaMart does not have this.

Directors' remuneration

Remuneration levels should be sufficient to attract directors of sufficient calibre, but companies should not pay more than is necessary. Directors should not be involved in setting their own remuneration. A **remuneration committee**, staffed by independent NEDs, should determine specific remuneration packages.

Quite clearly, MegaMart has failed to conform with these requirements as far as Rex Lord's remuneration is concerned.

Communication with shareholders

Rex Lord has appears to have failed to abide by the rule that companies should be prepared to communicate directly with **institutional shareholders** and to use the AGM as a means of communication with **private investors**.

Auditors

There are two significant threats to the **independence of the auditors** that should be reviewed both by them and by MegaMart's audit committee (which should be made up of NEDs). The first is that having been in post for 20 years, there is a danger that the auditors have become **complacent and even acquiescent** in their relationship with Rex Lord. In any event, it is necessary that the partner in charge of the audit is changed after a maximum of five years.

The second threat is associated with the provision of services other than audit. This is called **management risk** and is the risk that the auditors effectively act in a management role, doing things that should be reserved to the directors and managers of the company.

Compliance with the Stock Exchange Combined Code

As a quoted company, MegaMart should include in its financial statements a narrative report of how it applied the **principles** of the Combined Code and a statement as to whether it complied with its **specific provisions**. We are not told whether or not this was done, but it was, it must have made interesting reading.

Part (b)

> **Text reference.** The topics mentioned in this answer are discussed in Chapter 4 of your BPP Study Text.
>
> **Top tips.** The Examiner intended you to talk in general terms about the wider role of NEDs in your answer to this part of the question, basing his own suggested solution on an article that had recently appeared in the ACCA magazine.
>
> **Examiner's comments.** It is easy to find yourself repeating points you have already made in your answer to part (a).

Quoted companies such as MegaMart should have a body of NEDs: the **Hampel report** suggested that they should make up at least one third of the board. As already mentioned, these directors should form both the **audit** and **remuneration committees**. All members of the remuneration committee and a majority of the audit committee should be independent NEDs.

NEDs have much to offer the company in addition to these prescribed roles.

They should bring to their role **wide experience of business** and possibly of organisations in other spheres. This should enable them to give **good strategic advice** to the board as a whole and to individual directors, possibly in a mentoring role.

They should be alert for the emergence of problems with an **ethical dimension** or issues of **corporate social responsibility**. Independent NEDs, in particular, should be able to act as a kind of **conscience** for the board as a whole.

NEDs may have a valuable role to play in the **selection and appointment of new board members**, particularly in the case of the Chairman and the Chief Executive.

Recent improvements in corporate governance have led to the emergence of a significant body of NEDs in UK business. There is a common perception that this is something of a **charmed circle** and that many supposedly independent NEDs are in fact nothing of the sort, since they are drawn from the **same pool of senior managers** as their executive director colleagues. There is thus an imperative to widen the bounds of the portion of society from which NEDs are drawn.

18 Salt and Soap

Text reference. The topics mentioned in this answer are discussed in Chapter 7 of your BPP Study Text.

Top tips. This is not a difficult question, though there are two aspects to the requirement in part (a), which complicates it a little. Also, discussing the importance of marketing is complicated by the fact that the term has several different meanings and a range of connotations. For the purpose of this question, it will be best to stick to a simple concept of marketing that emphasises the marketing mix and the importance of the customer.

In part (b), do not be put off by the term 'niche player': it simply means the use, in *Porter's* terms, of a focus strategy. This is an aspect of Porter's model of generic strategy that is easy to gloss over in study: really all it means is doing things on a small scale, most commonly in terms of product range or market served.

Easy marks. The marking scheme for part (a) indicates that there were easy marks for introducing and using very simple models such as the product life cycle and *Ansoff's* matrix.

Examiner's comments. This was a popular and generally well-answered question, though a common problem in part (a) was to fail to assess the relevance of marketing to the company.

Marking scheme

		Marks
(a)	Identification of relevant models:	up to 2 marks each
	Macro-environmental/SLEPT	
	Ansoff's growth matrix	
	Porter's models	
	Product positioning	
	Product life cycle	
	Marketing mix	
		Maximum 12 marks
(b)	Advantages of a niche strategy	up to 2 marks each
	Benefits of specialisation	
	Identifying segment(s) too small to interest major competitors	
	Opportunity to move into emerging markets	
	Create customer goodwill and barriers to entry	
	Ability to charge prices that give better margins	
	Positive approach to market opportunities	
		Maximum 8 marks
		Total 20 marks

Part (a)

To: Sales and Marketing Director
            Salt and Soap Ltd

From: Marketing Consultant

Date: 1 July 200X

Report

1   Salt and Soap – current position.

1.1   As a supplier of own brand goods to supermarkets, the company is under intense pressure to cut prices, thus eroding its margins. There is really only one way to make a reasonable margin on this basis and that is to achieve scale economies by supplying in extremely large quantities. Salt and Soap, as a medium-sized business would find this difficult to do.

1.2   The ability of the supermarket majors to dictate prices arises from a marked imbalance in what *Porter* calls **the bargaining power of the customers and suppliers** in the industry. The customers really have all the power, for several reasons.

- They take 70% of the Company's output so the Company relies heavily on their business.

- Even so, these purchases represent an insignificant part of their total sales of cleansers: they could manage quite well without stocking them at all.

- The products themselves are entirely generic. This means that the Company can really only add value by breaking bulk and that it would be very easy for other companies to enter the industry.

1.3   The basic products of salt, soap and soda are very mature and may even be regarded as approaching the decline stage of their **product life cycles**: many people are consciously reducing the salt intake in their diet and plain soda crystals and soap flakes have been largely replaced by modern detergents.

All this supports your desire to reshape your business with new products and outlets.

Your principal concern must be to **add value**, because that translates directly into **improved margins**. Porter's **value chain** analysis indicates that value can be added by both **primary activities**, such as, in your case, efficient packaging and delivery, and by **supporting activities**, such as the management of human resources. Salt and Soap will probably find it easiest to pursue the creation of value in its primary operational areas.

The future for Salt and Soap must lie in **product and market development**, as defined by *Ansoff.*

The first step would be to pursue **market development** by selling existing cleaning products through the specialist wholesalers already identified. Following on, it may be possible to develop new products to exploit this market even further.

2   The role of marketing

2.1   Marketing is important to Salt and Soap, both as a concept of the way business should be done and as a group of defined business functions.

Marketing as a concept or model of the way business should work emphasises the **primary importance of the customer**. Business activity can be defined as providing customer satisfaction profitably. The implication is that all members of the business organisation and all of its activities should have as their principal purpose making some contribution to providing customer satisfaction.

Marketing as a function encompasses a range of important activities:

Marketing research will identify potential customers and their needs.

Brand management will build and exploit the company's own brand to enhance both sales and margins.

Marketing communications activities will inform, persuade, reassure and remind both existing and potential customers of the Company.

Customer relationship management will retain existing customers and exploit information about them to expand sales.

Part (b)

If Salt and Soap decides that it wishes to move away from the business of supplying supermarkets, its medium size will still make it necessary for the company to continue with a **focus** generic strategy. That is, it must concentrate its efforts on a fairly small part of the total market, at least to begin with, perhaps defining its chosen segment in terms of geography or type of customer. The current strategy is one of attempting to achieve **cost focus**: this emphasis on price is what makes it vulnerable to the large supermarkets. It may be that the company should aim to move as fast as possible towards a strategy of **differentiation focus**, since that may be the way to improve its margins.

Such a **niche** strategy can have significant advantages.

(a)   A small, specialised manufacturer may not attract the attention of **larger competitors** with lower costs and greater resources.

(b)   It may be possible to create **high customer loyalty** by building personal relationships and providing good service. This might act as an effective barrier to entry. Also, **word of mouth** is a good form of marketing communication.

(c)   **Smaller customers can be targeted**. Such customers may be too small for larger suppliers to take much care over, so healthy margins may be available on sales to them.

The catering and gardening markets that David Kirk has identified are very large overall and may contain some very large wholesalers: such organisations may be potential customers or competitors, or even both. However, both markets also include **numerous small and medium-sized potential customers**, such as garden centres, and small chains of caterers and hardware stores.

Because it will not be constantly seeking the highest possible volumes, Salt and Soap will be able to **develop its product range** for these markets so as to meet a variety of customer needs. Simple additions would include an expanded range of pack sizes, while more complex developments might include convenient, throwaway dispensers and applicators.

There is also great potential for **brand development** as part of the marketing mix, since much more output will be sold under the company's own brand.

19 Environmental strategy

Part (a)

> **Text reference.** The topics mentioned in this answer are discussed in Chapters 4 and 10 of your BPP Study Text.
>
> **Top tips.** You might think that project management is a rather peripheral topic for this exam; combining it with corporate social responsibility makes for a very unusual question indeed.
>
> Note that the question asks about **skills required to achieve commitment**. You might think that the emphasis here should be on such inter-personal skills as **communication** and **negotiation**. It is clear from the suggested solution and the marking scheme that the Examiner did not wish to be quite so restrictive: marks were available for a wider discussion of project management **activities,** such as planning and post-completion review.
>
> The suggested solution also emphasised the need for a **strategic approach** to such an important development.
>
> **Easy marks.** In general terms, project manager duties are neither complex nor a great deal different from ordinary management duties: it is the context that provides the contrast. If you could remember what you have learned about project management, this should have been a fairly easy question.
>
> **Examiner's comments.** It seems that not many candidates were, in fact, able to remember very much at all about project management.

Marking scheme

		Marks
(a)	Project management skills: defining the project	up to 3 marks per skill
	Creating the strategy	
	Project planning	
	Implementation and control	
	Review and learning	
	Project leadership	**Maximum 15 marks**
(b)	Assessment of environmental strategy as a means to:	
	Competitive advantage	up to 3 marks
	Social responsibility	up to 3 marks
		Maximum 5 marks
		Total 20 marks

Graham Smith is promoting the CFS 'environmentally aware' project for strategic reasons to do with pressure from government and customers. The project manager would ideally have an appreciation of the strategic impact of the project, therefore.

A project is 'an undertaking that has a beginning and an end and is carried out to meet established goals within cost, schedule and quality objectives' (Haynes, *Project Management*). Every project therefore has a finite life and it is possible to identify life-cycle stages through which all projects pass. The activities that project managers undertake and many of the skills they must deploy are related to the different life-cycle stages.

Conception and definition is the first stage and includes problem analysis, assessment of possible solutions and definition of the objectives and scope of the project. This may be the most difficult phase for Graham Smith's project manager to undertake, since we know that several senior people in the organisation are not convinced that a problem exists at all. It is really Graham's role as **project sponsor** or '**project champion**' to gain commitment from his peers within the organisation at this stage. The project manager will be able to support him in this activity by providing details of the advantages the proposed accreditation will bring and the work that will have to be done to achieve it; these facts may be used to oppose to the many vague and imprecise arguments that are likely to be raised against the scheme. The project manager will also undertake an important **communication** and **negotiation role** with his or her own organisational peers.

The second stage of the project life cycle is **planning**. Here the project manager will deploy very specific project management skills, such as work breakdown structure and network analysis. The **project team** will start to form at this stage and the project manager will be responsible for leading and co-ordinating its efforts. An important aspect of this phase is **obtaining and scheduling resources**, so once again, negotiation is likely to be an important part of the project manager's job.

The third stage is **implementation**. Here the project manager must deploy normal managerial skills such as delegating and controlling, and continue to display both **leadership** and **team–building skills**. However, projects always involve dealing with the unexpected, so problem-solving skills will be very important. Also during this phase rescheduling and reassessment of priorities may become necessary, so the ability to **negotiate and balance the interests of the various project stakeholders** comes into play.

The final stage of the project includes the administrative work needed to complete it and to close down the project organisation. This stage should also include an audit or **post-completion review** of methods and achievement so that the organisation can learn from the experience gained and improve its future project management performance.

Part (b)

Corporate social responsibility (CSR) is often regarded simply as a drag on business efficiency, something that imposes cost but brings no tangible benefits in return. However, while costs must always be carefully controlled, CSR spending can be beneficial.

Like much other CSR spending, the CFS 'environmentally aware' project has a great deal of potential to provide competitive advantage in two principal ways. First, it may be a very effective way to **differentiate the company** from its competitors: larger customers are already beginning to show an interest in environmental concerns. Second, it is likely that at some time in the future further government regulation may be imposed. If CFS were already performing to the highest standards, the **impact of such regulation would be minimised**.

A further potential benefit to environmental awareness is the **avoidance of waste**. Policies designed to reduce energy consumption, for example, have an obvious impact on costs. These can include investment in insulation and efficient heating and the use of diesel rather than petrol engine vehicles.

Pressure to meet environmental standards can drive **innovation**, with the introduction of new technology and methods of working. Recycled materials of all kinds can offer cheaper alternatives to traditional options. Similar ideas may be applied to the use of other types of resource so that efficiency and productivity are enhanced.

In order to achieve these benefits, it is necessary that managers embrace the challenge of environmental responsibility, treating it as an opportunity and a challenge rather than as a dead weight loss.

20 Question with analysis: Apex culture

Text reference. The topics mentioned in this answer are discussed in Chapter 11 of your BPP Study Text.

Top tips. This question proved to be particularly difficult, with many candidates misunderstanding the requirement in part (b). The question was intended to be about change management in unpromising circumstances, not what might have been done at an earlier stage to avoid the problems described in the setting.

You should be aware of two things: first, the overriding need to read the question very carefully and answer it as set; and, second, if you do misunderstand the question, the Examiner *may* do what he did here and give you some credit for your efforts. Note, however, that this is **not** an invitation to answer the question you wish had been set!

Easy marks. As is so often the case, part (a) of this question is easier than part (b). This is because the effects of a clash of corporate cultures of the type envisaged are reasonably easy to predict, revolving, as they do, around the stress caused by new ways of doing things.

Examiner's comments. This question was found to be difficult by many candidates. In part (a) a very restricted view of problems was taken, with few candidates mentioning potential effects on customers or the administrative infrastructure. The confusion was worse in part (b), with many candidates explaining how greater care before the acquisition could have avoided problems, rather than discussing ways of managing the problems that would be likely to arise after the acquisition.

Marking scheme

		Marks
(a)	Problems with the acquisition	
	Demotivated staff	up to 2
	Confused culture	up to 2
	Effect on clients	up to 2
	Conflict	up to 2
	Increased labour turnover	up to 2
	Expensive administrative infrastructure	up to 2
		Maximum for section (a) 10 marks
(b)	Factors to be considered	
	Communication	up to 3
	Participation	up to 3
	Training	up to 3
	Pace of change	up to 3
	Manner of change	up to 3
	Scope of change	up to 3
		Maximum for section (b) 10 marks
		Total 20 marks

Part (a)

The clear problem with this acquisition, if it is not managed carefully, is the potential for a **clash of corporate cultures** and the effect this may have on each of the two sets of employees.

The corporate culture of Apex Finance Ltd is one of **centralisation** and **standardisation** of working practices and work outputs, with procedures and policies being imposed from a central management function. If this culture were to be imposed upon the new acquisition group of companies, then their staff, who are used to managing and motivating themselves and using their initiative, would find the atmosphere stultifying and demotivating, which must inevitably generate resentment and opposition.

LEARNING MEDIA

Alternatively, if the **more relaxed style of management** were introduced throughout the group, it is likely that the original Apex employees would feel that there was a lack of direction and leadership, they may not be able to operate effectively without the centralised management structure that they have been used to.

An alternative might be to try to keep the two cultures separate and to allow each part of the entity to continue with its own management style. However, this is not likely to be successful, as there is likely to be a **degree of leakage**, which may lead to **discontent**. The original Apex employees may desire a degree of independence whereas those who were used to freedom may not always use their initiative and may desire more dependence upon others to give them direction.

If it is decided to impose one culture upon the other part of the organisation, there is likely to be a degree of discontent, probably leading to an **increase in labour turnover**. There may also be an effect on the **clients** of the new amalgamated company who may feel a degree of uncertainty about their relationship with their supplier. Clients will need to know whether they approach individual staff or a centralised management function.

A further problem if the centralised management system is to be continued, is that by its very nature, due to the acquisition, it must become **larger** and **more expensive**. Increased infrastructure will almost certainly add to the overheads of the joint operations. Other considerations are whether there is any possibility of sharing resources and skills between the two entities and the viability of integration of the necessary IT systems.

Part (b)

Carol Brindle is looking at a major **change management** exercise. There are bound to be wide-ranging changes in policy and practice in both halves of the merged company, and the acquisition will only succeed if these changes are undertaken in a proper fashion.

The **scope**, or extent, of any programme of change must be carefully considered. Staff will inevitably be apprehensive about **job security** and also for less specific reasons. Many people are naturally very conservative and dislike change. In extreme cases, severe depression can result. Reaction to change can include passive and active opposition and irrational behaviour: an increase in **conflict** between people and departments is likely. There is a case for keeping change to the minimum in order to, in turn, minimise its undesirable effects; this idea must not be used to justify the avoidance of difficult decisions and adjustments.

A **plan of integration** must be prepared, dealing with such matters as new responsibilities, procedures, structure, appointments and, very critically, the implications for job losses if any. At the same time, the process of **communication** must commence in order to allay the natural sense of apprehension, upset and disturbance that is likely to be present.

The **manner** in which change is introduced is very important. Staff participation in the decision-making process may be useful and provide both an element of motivation and a sense of ownership. However, staff will rapidly detect any tendency to *pseudo-participation*, and its effect will be less desirable than no participation at all. Staff participation in planning the implementation of necessary change is likely to be both less contentious and very useful.

Communication of decisions and developments must be prompt and honest. Resistance must be confronted and any necessary re-training undertaken.

Ms Brindle should also consider the **pace** of the change that is to take place. Slower change is perhaps easier to assimilate and less disturbing for staff. It also allows for review and adjustment of the new ways of doing things. However, there are usually operational imperatives that dictate a minimum acceptable speed and there is something to be said for a brisk approach that gets the upheaval over as soon as possible.

21 Supaserve

Part (a)

Marking scheme

		Marks
(a)	Bases for segmentation	up to 2 per point
	Significance of segment	up to 4
		Maximum for section (a) 10 marks
(b)	Assessment of impact of new system on internal operations	up to 6
	Assessment of Supaserve's ability to differentiate itself	up to 6
		Maximum for section (b) 10 marks
		Total 20 marks

The practice of market segmentation is based on the idea of creating value by adjusting the marketing mix so as to **satisfy more precisely** the needs and wants of customers. It is part of the move away from a one-size-fits-all mass marketing approach and toward a more targeted system that focuses on smaller market groups without sacrificing the scale economies of the mass market approach. A market segment is only valid if it is worth designing a **unique marketing mix** for it.

In broader terms, Chris Jones seems to have already largely defined his new marketing mix, in the form of his proposed online shopping service. He thus seems to be approaching the segmentation problem from the wrong direction, unless it is his intention to somehow adjust the functionality of his website to provide different service to separately identified different customer segments. This seems unlikely, given that getting just one online shopping website to work well is a major challenge.

Working at a more detailed scale, we might say that probably the only adjustment Supaserve can make to its existing marketing mix lies in the range of products it offers. The company's core products are food and drink. It would be useful to know whether the potential online market would buy the same products in the same proportions as the existing store customers, since this would have immediate implications for buying and stockholding. **Behavioural segmentation** would be the obvious approach here: survey techniques could find existing users of online grocery services and establish their existing preferences. Note that it is a principle of the scientific approach to market research that it is only data about existing behaviour that are worth having. Asking customers about possible future intentions is of little value: it is well-known that interview subjects' responses are affected by their perceptions of what constitutes the 'correct' answer, for example.

Socio-demographic segmentation would not really be useful, since it is linked only loosely to buying practices, and neither would **psychographic** or lifestyle segmentation, since that is really of use only in the development of new products. A basic **geographic** segmentation would presumably be automatically imposed by the imperative of delivery cost: Chris Jones would have to set a maximum radius from Supasave premises that he was prepared to service.

LEARNING MEDIA

The validity or viability of a segment is determined by asking four questions.

(a)   Can the segment be measured? It may be possible to conceive of a segment that cannot actually be measured sufficiently easily.

(b)   Is the segment large enough to bother with?

(c)   Can the segment be reached, in terms of both promotion and distribution?

(d)   Is the segment actually different from existing ones, in terms of requiring a separate marketing mix?

In the case of Supaserve's potential online market, it would be necessary to seek answers to these questions using the survey techniques already mentioned.

Part (b)

Text reference. The topics mentioned in this answer are discussed in Chapter 6 of your BPP Study Text.

Top tips. It is clear from the Examiner's answer that you will understand his intention for this requirement better if you mentally insert the word 'internal' between 'Supaserve's' and 'activities' and then think in terms of the value chain. Also, do not be deceived by the reference to 'the new customer delivery system': the Examiner wants you to consider all aspects of the new strategy, not just the delivery of goods to the customer.

The spectacular failure of *Webvan's* attempt to rebuild the grocery business model from the ground up compared with the success of *Tesco's* incremental approach should be enough to convince Chris Jones to proceed by emulating the latter. Supaserve is only a medium-sized operator, so this will mean running the **fulfilment** operation from Supsaserve's existing store premises, probably by having a **dedicated team of in-store shoppers** filling orders from normal display shelf stock. The alternative, of running it from central warehouses, will require breaking bulk at those locations; this would make any unpicked items unusable for normal store deliveries, simply because of the inefficiencies involved in handling small quantities.

We may thus envisage, at best, a website that automatically forwards picking lists to the stores nearest to the customers concerned and produces optimised route delivery lists for the delivery vehicles. Within this basic model we might expect a range of effects on Supaserve's value activities.

Procurement and **inbound logistics** will simply adjust to a slightly different mix and, it is to be hoped, increased volume of purchases.

Operations will be extended to include the order picking activity outlined above and, more dramatically, the maintenance and development of the **sales website**. The quality of this will be critical to success. It must be secure, simple to use and offer access to the full range of Supaserve's stocks. There are likely to be thousands of separate items to be dealt with, so the hardware used will have to be extremely capable.

Outbound logistics will complete the home shopping loop by delivering the orders. Close attention will have to be paid to **requested delivery time slots** if customers are to be satisfied with the online shopping service. It may be possible to outsource this aspect of the operation, but this could only be done with very great care, since it puts the only opportunity for direct personal contact with the customer into the hands of outsiders. It would almost certainly be best to make deliveries in Supasave liveried vans driven by uniformed Supasave employees.

Marketing and sales may be able to obtain important customer information from the details of orders delivered. However, this will not be different in degree or in kind from the information collected by a good loyalty card scheme: the experience of Tesco, the acknowledged UK leader in this field, is that it is difficult to exploit this detailed information simply because of its sheer volume.

Supasave is suffering under intense competition from larger competitors. The scenario does not tell us which country it operates in, but if it is anywhere in the developed world, it seems unlikely that online shopping will provide any degree of differentiation at all. All the large supermarkets in the UK, for example, offer this service.

If Supasave is, in fact, operating in a market where none of its competitors has an online operation, then its new venture would provide a very marked point of differentiation. This is so much the case that we might question the wisdom of a medium size company's implementing such a radical idea. It would probably make better use of its resources if it sought to expand its conventional operation through promotion and opening newer, larger stores in prime locations.

22 Global Imaging

Text reference. The topics mentioned in this answer are discussed in Chapter 13 of your BPP Study Text.

Top tips. The problem with the setting to this question is that it assumes you agree with Paul Simpson's view of the place of HRM in the organisation. It is possible to argue strongly that HRM, like marketing, is too important to be left to a functional department and should be an element of general strategic management. Under this model, HR policy would be set by the board and a restricted personnel management function might well be outsourced to an external supplier.

Fortunately, the Examiner does not ask you to make a case for Paul Simpson's personal security of employment: you are actually asked to describe how a properly considered and constructed human resource plan would contribute to Global Imaging's strategy.

Easy marks. Unless you have made the mistake of regarding HRM as not really relevant to an accountant and skipped the topic completely, you should have no difficulty in at least outlining the process of HR planning.

Examiner's comments. Many answers failed to consider the strategic important of HRM and merely described recruitment procedures.

Marking scheme

		Marks
(a)	Identification of key stages in HR plan:	up to 3 per activity
	Audit of current HR resources	
	Forecast of future needs	
	Planning to fill identified 'gap'	
	Measuring performance against goals set	
	Linkages with growth strategy	up to 4
		maximum 12 marks
(b)	Advantages of outsourcing HR:	up to 5
	Freedom to contribute to strategy	
	Reduced HR administration costs	
	Focus on critical HR competences for growth strategy	
	Improved service levels	
	Disadvantages of outsourcing HR:	up to 5
	Loss of control	
	Confidentiality issue	
	Long term dependence on outside provider	
	Adverse workforce reaction	
		maximum 8 marks
		Total 20 marks

Part (a)

DRAFT

From: HR Manager
To: Board of Directors
Date: 6 June 200X

Human resource planning and strategy

Global Imaging's strategy calls for the company to double in size over the next three years. This will require the employment of extra staff, particularly in marketing, sales and manufacturing. The ambitious planned rate of growth and the high technology base of Global Imaging's business mean that these extra staff must be of very high quality. Human resource (HR) management is thus an **essential component** of the company's business strategy and so should be **integrated with its development**. The alternative is increased potential for serious shortages of staff and mismatches between job requirements and staff availability. The establishment of a foreign manufacturing plant will complicate all HR issues significantly and will demand very careful consideration.

Human resource planning follows a logical sequence, echoing the rational model of strategy. This is not necessarily linear and some of the activities involved in establishing a satisfactory plan can overlap chronologically. There will also be occasions where the various activities influence one another, as, for example, when the persistence of staff shortages in important areas leads to a change in reward policy.

An **audit of existing staff** should reveal those with potential for promotion or employability in new specialisations. It would also indicate where shortages already exist.

Concurrently, an analysis of **likely future staff requirements** could be carried out. We anticipate the need to employ more staff in the areas already mentioned, but we do not really know how many will be required, whether other functions will need to be increased in size or if more support and administrative staff will be needed. There are also the related and sensitive issues of **management succession** and **internal promotion** to consider. In particular, we must consider the eventual replacement of our existing joint Managing Directors, who are likely to leave once the current growth objective has been achieved.

These two studies should enable us to identify the gaps that we need to fill if we are to have the staff required for our overall strategy.

Recruitment, in the sense of attracting applicants, and **selection** from within the pool of applicants are the logical next steps. This work is often **outsourced** and it will be necessary to decide whether the **expertise** and **economies of scale** offered by outsourcing outweigh the need for deep familiarity with our operations on the part of the recruiters.

Reward policy must be considered. At the moment, Global Imaging's staff profile is heavily biased towards people with a background in research and development. Different types of people will be required in the future and their expectations must be expected to show some differences. A doubling in size to, say, 200 employees is likely to take the company into an area of HR complexity in which a formal reward policy and structure is required. Informal decisions about pay and benefits will not be satisfactory. It may be necessary to establish a more formal scheme of **employee relations**, possibly along the lines of a works council.

Increasing size is also likely to require the establishment of a policy on **appraisal and performance management**. This should be linked to a programme of **training and development**. No doubt Global Imaging will continue to hire well-qualified technical staff, but there will be a need for development of staff in other functions and for management development in particular.

Part (b)

> **Easy marks**. This is a fairly simple question: the usual arguments about outsourcing any activity apply, including cost reduction, degree of control and loss of internal competence.

Advantages of outsourcing HR activities

Cost

Outsourcing can be a good way to **reduce costs** since the external supplier should be able to achieve **economies of scale and scope** and achieve higher levels of productivity through **specialisation**. In a properly negotiated outsourcing relationship, some of these cost savings should be passed on to the purchaser.

Expertise

An external agency specialising in HR work should be able to employ a range of full-time HR specialists. This would be prohibitively expensive for a small company such as Global Imaging, which is probably likely to employ only Paul Simpson and one or two assistants. Outsourcing can thus give access to a more **comprehensive range of expertise**. This can be useful for both routine but vital matters such as advice on payroll technicalities and also for more demanding specialist work, such as assessment and selection of candidates.

Focus

Devolvement of generic HR work to an external agency would reduce the demands of routine work on Paul Simpson's time. This would enable him to give greater attention to developing those aspects of HR policy that will make the **greatest contribution to Global Imaging's strategy**.

Disadvantages of outsourcing HR activities

Control

Outsourcing brings the possibility of **loss of control**. This can affect such matters as quality of service and response time. The outsourcing contract must be written carefully to ensure that the potential for loss of control is minimised.

Confidentiality

HR data is particularly sensitive because of the **need to maintain individual privacy**. It is also subject to **data protection legislation** in most Western jurisdictions. An organisation contemplating outsourcing HR services must therefore ensure that it chooses a contractor capable of providing the necessary data security. However, because of the loss of control mentioned above, the ability of the principal to maintain the confidentiality of its data is reduced.

Workforce reaction

Associated with confidentiality is workforce reaction. Employees may object to then release of their data to an outside agency and may be uncomfortable in making use of personal services aspects of HRM such as counselling. On the other hand, some staff may appreciate the extra element of impartiality potentially available from outsourced services.

Loss of expertise

Outsourcing brings with it the possibility of **loss of expertise**. This is particularly apparent in activities that that require regular practice for proficiency or regular updates on current information and practice. HRM is not a core competence for Global Imaging, but, bearing in mind the company's reliance on highly skilled staff, it might well be regarded as an area in which a threshold competence is required.

A problem associated with loss of expertise is that the company may become **over-dependent** on its outside provider, losing its autonomy of action. This is probably not too much of a problem for Global Imaging, since there is no shortage of external HR service providers that would be happy to bid for its work.

23 IT Project

Text reference. The topics mentioned in this answer are discussed in Chapters 10 and 15 of your BPP Study Text.

Top tips. Do not be put off by the superfluous word *and* in the third line of the second paragraph of the scenario; minor typos can occur in exam papers; the meaning is clear. Serious errors are rare, but if you have the misfortune to encounter one, report it to the examination staff and ask for guidance.

Easy marks. Many candidates will struggle with questions like this, as they do not fit into a neat category. A little lateral thinking is required. If you feel you have to tackle a question like this, remember that relevance to the scenario is *always* important and use key words like *strategy, organisation structure, competitive advantage, value chain, marketing* and *HRM* to guide your thinking.

Part (a)

The project is to be assessed against 'competing IT project proposals'. Such a comparison should **focus on costs and benefits** and would have two main aspects: matters which could be quantified with some precision, such as capital cost, and more **qualitative factors** such as efficiency of working.

Standard investment appraisal techniques such as NPV should be applied to any **quantifiable costs and benefits**. These should include the capital cost of hardware and software, including physical security measures and any structural work such as enhanced fire precautions and installation of ducts and cables; maintenance costs, including an allowance for contingencies; increased insurance cost; the cost of training; extra telephone costs arising from internet access; and any savings which might arise from staff reductions.

These aspects are probably quite simple to determine and assess. However, it is probable that **such an appraisal will produce a negative NPV** for any project, as costs are fairly easy to establish, but **benefits are likely to be largely unquantifiable.** Nevertheless, a successful IT project can offer benefits which are of major significance for an organisation and they must be taken into account.

It would be normal to attempt to deal with this by **ranking competing projects** by scoring them against **objective criteria**. The scoring could be done by a committee or by several individuals separately, with a moderator combining their scores. This would bring a kind of collective judgement to the process, but would be subject to personal bias, which might break out into acrimony in the later stages of selection.

Projects should be assessed against criteria such as those below.

- Expected improvement in quality of **management information** in such matters as speed of provision and completeness

- **Compatibility** with the existing organisation in terms of structure, responsibilities, personalities, culture and skill levels

- Fit with the current **strategic posture** of the organisation, and, if a commercial organisation, contribution to competitive advantage

- **Risk** associated with the technology: is it proven or groundbreaking? How big is the installed base?
- Extent to which **existing equipment** can be reused

When the financial and qualitative assessments are complete, it will be necessary to integrate them. This should only present a problem if they produce radically different solutions; if that is the case, **rational decision rules** such as minimising the maximum possible loss may help.

Part (b)

The broad objectives of project management are as follows.

Quality. The end result should conform to the project specification. In other words, the result should achieve what the project was supposed to do.

Budget. The project should be completed without exceeding authorised expenditure.

Timescale. The installation should be ready for use by the agreed date.

A typical project has a **project life cycle** and is likely to progress through **four stages**:

- **conception and project definition;**
- **planning;**
- **implementation;**
- **completion and evaluation.**

The first stage may be based on the work already done and described in part (a) above. It will be necessary to define the final objectives and agree fundamental and desirable success criteria.

Project planning breaks the project down into manageable units, estimates the resources required for each and establishes the necessary work schedules. Tools such as critical path analysis and Gantt charts may be used where there are time and sequence constraints.

Implementation must be controlled and progress monitored to ensure that, for instance, quality and financial requirements are being achieved. It is often suggested with IT projects that there should be an extended period of parallel running; it must be remembered, however, that this implies a great deal of extra work by the staff involved and may be impractical for all but the most important elements.

When the installation is complete it should be **appraised for success** in meeting user expectations. With internally managed projects, this provides invaluable opportunities to learn from mistakes.

24 Westport University

> **Text reference.** The topics mentioned in this answer are discussed in Chapters 5 and 7 of your BPP Study Text.
>
> **Top tips.** The question asks you to 'present a report'. Do not waste time on elaborate presentation or layout. Write a business letter, but avoid being too formal.
>
> **Easy marks.** This is effectively a question about marketing, a subject of which even well prepared candidates may feel they know little. This should not lead you to reject the question out of hand. The examiner does not expect you to be an expert and it is possible to score quite well by applying basic knowledge and some common sense.

Part (a)

Head of Faculty

Business and Finance Faculty   1 April 200X

PROFESSIONAL ACCOUNTANCY TRAINING – MARKET RESEARCH

1   We discussed briefly the possibility of the Faculty's using some of its spare capacity to provide professional training in accountancy. I undertook to report on the market research implications of this idea.

2   **Information requirements**

2.1   **Market size.** We need some estimate of the number of students we might reasonably expect to attract to our courses. The total numbers of students registered with each of the main accountancy bodies should be easily ascertained, but we need more than this. The geographical distribution of students will be important, as will their chosen method of study. Our market will probably lie among those who both live close enough to travel to us each day and are able fund their study.

2.2   **Student preferences.** Students' study preferences should be established in detail.

- What size are the markets for full-time and part-time courses respectively?
- How should the cycle of training relate to the professional bodies' exams?
- How would students be funded and at what target cost should we aim?
- Should we provide printed teaching notes or teach from an established text?
- How much tutorial input would students expect and how would it be funded?
- Should we provide generic courses or classes specific to one or more of the professional accountancy bodies.

2.3   **Competition.** It would be important to assess the local competition before committing ourselves to providing training. We need to know the extent to which it is feasible for us to contest the local market.

3   **Methods of research**

3.1   **Desk research.** It will be feasible to obtain much of the information we need from the accountancy bodies. They will almost certainly have well-organised databases that will reveal numbers of students in our area, probably analysed by post code; the stage of their studies; and, possibly, how they study. Potential competitors in both the public and private sector can be assessed on the basis of their prospectuses and other publicity material.

3.2   **Primary research.** Primary research is a highly specialised professional field and is expensive if it is reliable. It is not something that I would recommend we do in house, unless there are members of the academic staff who can claim more than a theoretical acquaintance with the processes involved. It is probably inappropriate for a project of this type. However, if undertaken, it could amplify our knowledge of the potential market generally and of student preferences specifically. A telephone survey would probably be most effective. A postal survey would be cheaper, but this method suffers both from a low response rate and the fact that the respondents self-select.

4   **Conclusion.** A successful entry into the professional accountancy training market will depend on our acquiring greater knowledge about that market than we possess now. Much of the information we need may be obtained by desk research. Greater detail and certainty could be obtained by primary research in the form of a survey, but this is probably too expensive to be practical.

Bill Loftus

Commercial Manager

Part (b)

Text reference. The topics mentioned in this answer are discussed in Chapter 7 of your BPP Study Text.

Top tips. You may wonder, on examining this part of the question, just what marketing strategy is and how it differs from ordinary strategy. Well, clearly, for 10 marks you don't have to be too abstruse. Nor does the scenario give you enough information to build up an answer in terms of *Porter's* generic strategies, for instance, or *Ansoff's* product market vector. The examiner's suggested solution simply considers the Faculty's proposed project in terms of the 4 Ps of the basic marketing mix. This solution could have been improved by including the other 3 Ps of the extended marketing mix, as we do, since they are relevant to **services** and that is what the Faculty provides, after all.

Don't forget that the elements of the marketing mix must be consistent with one another.

Marketing strategies

Product. Unfortunately, the examining bodies have different syllabuses and, though there is great similarity in total coverage, there is wide variation between individual examinations. We shall thus have to decide whether or not to provide courses for more than one set of examinations to begin with. This will depend in part on the size of the potential markets involved.

Our greatest opportunity to add value probably comes from the provision of lectures, since that is what we are best equipped to do. However, we must carefully consider course design, in the light of our market research. Part time courses, including day release and evening classes, may be most appropriate at first. Commercial providers tend to have two types of short course: teaching and revision. We should aim to do the same.

Place. The location of our courses must also be decided. It would be cheapest to use our own premises, but part-time courses may prove more popular if we can take them to the student by establishing local venues.

Price. We probably need to be competitive in our pricing. Many students fund themselves and employers who pay for training are likely to be equally price-conscious. If we are convinced of our excellence we may be able to justify a price premium, but we will be judged by results. At the moment we do not have much experience of the demands of the examinations.

Promotion. This would be a new venture for us and we would need effective promotion to get it off the ground. We must apply the same standards of decorum and academic appropriateness to this project as to any other of our activities. To be effective, our promotion and the media we use must be carefully targeted. Advertisements in the journals aimed at accountancy students will be a good starting point, supplemented by information on the University website and, possibly, direct mail.

People. People are fundamental to marketing services. The members of our target market are older than our undergraduates and likely to be more demanding of lecturers. If they are not satisfied they will vote with their feet.

Process. Similar considerations apply to processes and particularly to administration. Our existing enrolment system, for example, is used to dealing with a bulge of work before the commencement of the academic year. If we are to run short courses, enrolment queries must be dealt with throughout the year.

Physical evidence. Since education is so very intangible, it may be worth considering the provision of physical evidence. An obvious example would be the provision of course notes. A standard textbook written by a member of our staff would be almost too good to be true.

Conclusion. It is important that decisions about these matters are not taken in isolation. If we are to go ahead with this project, I suggest that a marketing committee be formed and charged with responsibility for ensuring that our plans form a coherent whole.

25 Ashkol Furniture

Part (a)

Text reference. The topics mentioned in this answer are discussed in Chapter 7 of your BPP Study Text.

Top tips. This is an important question simply because it deals with marketing, a topic that is becoming more and more important both in the exam and in the real world. Students often discount the importance of marketing, possibly because they do not understand how it fits into the wider field of business strategy. Make sure you have read the appropriate sections in your BPP Study Text.

Easy marks. That very simple model, the marketing mix, would form the basis of a good answer to this requirement.

Examiner's comments. Many candidates were unable to answer in terms of marketing practice at all.

		Marks
(a)	Marketing mix	up to 3 marks each
	Product	
	Place	
	Price	
	Promotion	**Maximum 12 marks**
(b)	Maintain low costs	up to 2 marks
	Maintain distinctiveness	up to 2 marks
	Impose switching costs	up to 2 marks
	Develop brand loyalty	up to 2 marks
	Patents	up to 2 marks
	Trademarks	up to 2 marks
		Maximum 8 marks
		Total 20 marks

Salim needs to develop a marketing strategy for entry into the domestic market in Europe. This can be achieved by looking at the factors that make up the **marketing mix**: product, price, place and promotion. The design of the marketing mix should be decided on the basis of management intuition and judgement, together with information provided by market research. Elements in the marketing mix partly act as substitutes for each other and they must be **integrated**. The product needs to be positioned to appeal to the target customer. For example, Ashkol would struggle to develop a luxury brand image if they set price at a low, penetration level.

The physical **product** needs to be appropriate for the private household market. Office furniture may have a very different style to household furniture, so a different approach may need to be taken to the design of the product in order to make it appealing for the domestic buyer. For example, it may need to be smaller and made of better quality material.

Place deals with how the product is distributed, and how it reaches its customers. The products will be manufactured in India, so serious consideration will need to be given to how customers will be able to view, order and receive delivery of the products. Furniture showrooms are necessarily large areas and need to be in areas where customers will be attracted. The **logistics** of the distribution system are also important: customers will not be impressed with delays in delivery, so reliable transport, storage and delivery arrangements must be made. This has major cost implications, perhaps offsetting the cost savings from cheaper labour.

Promotion involves arousing attention, generating interest, inspiring desire and initiating action. Marketing communication involved in this could be advertising, public relations, direct selling or sales promotion. A furniture showroom would be part of this but a wider approach will be needed. The target market is people working from home and the promotional methods used should be appropriate to this market. Direct promotion *via* mailing lists may be appropriate; there are numerous home style magazines in which adverts could be placed; the Internet is a vital part of the life of people working from home and its potential for promotion should be fully utilised, perhaps by setting up a dedicated website.

Price is the final element of the marketing mix and is an important signal to customers about the product. It is important that the price should be competitive but also synonymous with the quality of the product. Discounts and payment terms need to be considered as a potential way of attracting customers.

Part (b)

Competitive advantage is anything that gives one organisation an edge over its rivals. *Porter* argues that a firm should adopt a competitive strategy intended to achieve competitive advantage for the firm. This can be achieved via three generic strategies.

Cost leadership

The organisation seeks to achieve the position of lowest cost producer in the industry as a whole. In order to create and sustain this position, it will need to maximise economies of scale; invest in and use innovative technology to reduce costs and/or enhance productivity; exploit the learning curve effect; minimise overhead costs; get favourable access to sources of supply; and ensure low distribution costs.

Differentiation

Competitive advantage is gained through particular characteristics of a firm's products. This can be achieved through the creation of a **brand** or giving the product special features. The value chain may be used to differentiate in terms of quality or service. Sustaining competitive advantage through differentiation will involve spending on market research to ensure the firm is still supplying what the customer wants; research into new or improved products; and promotion to build a strong corporate identity. Patents and trademark legislation can be used to protect the unique identity of a product, but imitation is always a danger and will narrow the advantage of differentiation.

Focus

A firm concentrates its attention on one or more segments of the market and does not try to serve the entire market with a single product. Cost-focus or differentiation-focus can be used within the segment and the firm can insulate itself from competition within its niche. However, it will not benefit from economies of scale and competitors may still move in. In order to sustain competitive advantage, the firm will still need to remain in touch with its market and innovate as necessary.

26 Smalltown

Part (a)

REPORT

To: Smalltown Horticultural Society

From: XXXX

Date: 1/6/20X2

The Society's Annual Show

1   Background

There is considerable public interest in horticulture and gardening generally, as witnessed by the variety of television programmes on the subject, and the success of flower shows generally. The Society should be able to flourish in such a setting, as there appears to be no dearth of public interest.

Although the Society should be flourishing, it has not succeeded in tapping the wealth of public interest. This is shown in the slow decline of people attending the annual flower show.

This decline has prevented the Society from pursuing some of its traditional activities in the local community, such as providing seeds for the elderly. The club is not paying its way.

2   Possible causes of decline

There have been significant social changes since the Society was founded. One significant change, identified by the Chairman's plea to the ladies of the town, is the changing role of women. Perhaps women are just not available to carry out the Society's functions any more. Reasons for this might include the increase in female employment.

Another significant change is the overall increase in car ownership. This has meant it is a easier than before for people to travel the distance to the next town with its competing flower show. This means that the catchment area of any show has grown larger, and people's activities may not be restricted to the strictly local environment.

3   The marketing concept

The marketing concept puts customers at the centre of what the organisation tries to do. It accepts that people have a right to choose and will not simply accept what they are given. The route to success with customers is to **establish their needs and wants and then to satisfy them**.

This is obviously a **commercial orientation** and the Smalltown Horticulture Society is a **not-for-profit organisation**. Nevertheless, the basic principle is applicable, since the society needs to attract the general public to its shows.

Although the Society is not a business seeking to make a profit, the marketing concept is still relevant to the past and future of the society. There has been no decline in public interest in horticulture, but it is clear that the Society is failing to tap the interest that does exist in the subject.

It is clear that the marketing concept has not applied to any significant degrees.

(a)   The Chairman believes the Society is of benefit to the local townsfolk, but the declining interests and attendances would indicate that this is definitely not the case. Fewer people are attending the shows, and this implies that people are being put off.

(b)   The Chairman is simply trying to carry on with the existing practices. This is at best a sales or a production orientation.

[Report continued in part (b) of this question]

Part (b)

> **Text reference.** The topics mentioned in this answer are discussed in Chapter 5 of your BPP Study Text.
>
> **Top tips.** Part (b), which can be viewed as a continuation of the report or completely separate, requires you to consider how a marketing strategy could be devised and applied with specific emphasis placed on the role of researching the market.

Suggested strategies

In order to address the slow decline in public interest, first of all an analysis should be carried out as to why there is a decline in interest.

(a)   Existing members of the society should be asked for their views, as those who are not on the committee of the society may have their own views.

(b)   The society should conduct a survey to identify the following.

- The population profile of Smalltown, to see how this relates to the Association's traditional membership

- The general interest in horticulture amongst residents

- How well known the Society is

- How many people knew about the show last year

- For those that attended the show, what they liked and disliked about it.

- For those that did not, reasons for non-attendance

- What they would expect to see at a show

- What they liked about the show 60 miles away

- The best date for a show

- Any other activities they would like to see the Society perform

- Their image of the society and whether they think it is relevant and friendly

The research is quite important. It may suggest that the society is simply not publicising itself or the show properly; perhaps it needs to arrange advance coverage in the local news media or local BBC or commercial radio station.

On the other hand, the society may have a poor but unjustified image; perhaps people perceive it as being run by a clique, who are out of touch with current demand. Certainly the Chairman's plea to the ladies of the town to perform their traditional duties suggests he is out of touch.

The study might reveal other activities that the society could carry out.

(a)   It does some charitable work and this could be publicised.

(b)   It could run evening classes for those residents who might be interested, but who work during the day. This might enable the society to attract a new audience.

(c)   Society members could run a column in the local paper giving useful advice.

(d)   The society might get involved with local schools, promote competitions etc.

The cost of the survey would not be prohibitive, and the Society's reserves of £12,000 would suggest that it could be afforded.

The Society should also consider how to promote the annual flower show more effectively, as this is its main source of funds.

(a)   Ensure that the show does not clash with larger ones held elsewhere.

(b)   Give proper notice in local papers, or indeed by leafleting local people, or buy advertising at local garden centres, DIY stores.

(c)   Try and obtain sponsorship from local businesses. Such funds might be used for advertising.

(d)   Most importantly, address the identified deficiencies in the show, so that people are not disappointed

27 Helen's Cakes

Part (a)

Text reference. The topics mentioned in this answer are discussed in Chapter 8 of your BPP Study Text.

Top tips. It is a general principle of Paper 3.5 that you do not need any industry-specific technical knowledge to be able to answer any examination question that might be set. However, you do need an **understanding of the way a modern economy works** and an intelligent **awareness of the main characteristics of its more visible industries**. You can achieve this awareness and understanding from your own economic interactions and from the **business pages of the quality press**.

It should not be difficult for you to make sensible remarks about the **consumer interface** with most industries, in particular, and so in a question like this, you should be aware, for example, of how supermarkets operate and the way they use their purchasing power to dominate their suppliers.

The question asks for a short report. There is unlikely to be more than one mark available for report format (if that) so do not waste time on an ornate layout for your answer.

Easy marks. Your basic knowledge about batch sizes, branding and costs should enable you to say something relevant about each of the options.

Examiner's comments. Do not end a report with your own real name! Your exam script must be anonymous.

Marking scheme

		Marks
(a)	Market entry strategy: advantages and disadvantages	
	Premium cake shop market	up to 5 marks
	Supermarkets	up to 5 marks
	Catering wholesalers	up to 5 marks
		Maximum 12 marks
(b)	Marketing mix: premium market	up to 3 marks
	Supermarkets	up to 3 marks
	Catering wholesalers	up to 3 marks
		Maximum 8 marks
		Total 20 marks

Sharpe and Keene
Business consultants

Report: 'Helen's Cakes'

Dear Ms Bradshaw

You have been considering starting to supply cakes to three different types of customer: supermarkets, catering wholesalers and cake shops. You asked us to advise you on the advantages and disadvantages of each potential market from the point of view of your new business.

Supermarkets

In general terms, supermarkets like to sell goods in high volumes. Hygiene and freshness in food products are very important, but long shelf life, uniform attractive appearance and reliability of supply are probably more important than excellence of flavour.

Supplying a supermarket could give excellent visibility to your brand. You would probably be required to deliver to a central depot, which would minimise your distribution costs. However, the supermarket route is probably impractical for a number of reasons.

Generally speaking, supermarkets require supply of branded goods in large volumes: this would offer economies of scale to a large producer, but you do not have the productive capacity necessary to supply on the required scale, even if you severely restrict the range you offer.

Supermarkets are very aggressive on price and aim to cut their suppliers' margins to the absolute minimum. They are also likely to demand extended periods of credit. As a start-up, your business is unlikely to achieve the production efficiencies necessary for survival under such conditions.

The early development of an own-brand range of cakes would put downward pressure on your margins, since the supermarket would aim to sell these cakes at a lower price than your own brand. This would also undermine sales of your own brand cakes. A likely outcome of this scenario is that you would be reduced to being one supplier among many, since the supermarket would demand ownership of the intellectual property rights in their own-brand cakes.

Catering wholesalers

Catering wholesalers will supply both shops and catering establishments such as hotels and tearooms: the former could give **good exposure to your brand**, since they would sell your cakes in their branded packaging, but the latter would not.

Wholesalers are likely to want **large batches of a small number of products**. This may reduce your production costs, though this effect would be limited if your premises and equipment placed a limit on the maximum batch size you could achieve. As with the supermarkets, your **distribution effort** would be limited, but, equally, you may not be able to **produce in the quantities** the wholesalers require.

Also, wholesalers seeking volume sales may not be interested in your **aspirations for a quality brand**: they will be unwilling to pay the necessary price premium and may sell your products into sales outlets that you might not wish them to be seen in. Like the supermarkets, they may be more interested in a long shelf life than in freshness. You may find yourself **trapped into producing an inferior, mass-market product** rather than the distinctive, quality cakes you wish to offer.

Premium cake shops

The premium cake shop market offers you the opportunity to build your brand and add value by combining **differentiation through quality** with **distinctive packaging**. This should enable you to charge higher prices.

You will be able to build up your business in a managed way, operating on a **scale that suits your resources** without pressure to produce in large quantities; this will also assist you in maintaining the high standards you wish to set. However, you may find that your customers require a **wide variety of cakes in small numbers**, which may be challenging in terms of scheduling and the most effective use of your equipment, as well as having the potential to reduce your overall margin if you cannot achieve **economical batch sizes**. You may have to insist on minimum order quantities for some products.

Your **distribution costs** will be higher because you will have to deliver to each shop individually; perhaps the most important aspect of this would be the cost in terms of your own time (assuming you do not employ an assistant, which would, of course be an extra variable cost for your business).

Part (b)

Text reference. The topics mentioned in this answer are discussed in Chapter 7 of your BPP Study Text.

Top tips. This part of the question is only worth eight marks: it is not very challenging and we need to deal with it briskly. However, using the four elements of the basic marketing mix and considering the three possible market options, we have the potential for **twelve separate small discussions**, some of which may well be more or less identical.

A possible way to proceed here would be to use a **tabulation**, which is, in part, what the Examiner's own suggested solution does. However, you would have to exercise some caution with this approach: if you are to produce a neat and legible table you need to have a good idea of how much writing is going to go into each cell, which might be difficult without trying it out first. This would be unacceptably time consuming, so a simple narrative broken up by headings is probably the best way to present your answer.

For eight marks, an **introduction** is unnecessary: plunge straight in.

Supermarket

Product: hygiene and product integrity are paramount, followed closely by shelf life and consistency and attractiveness of appearance; quality must be good. Volumes required will be large.

Price: is likely to be settled in very unequal bargaining with purchaser.

Promotion for the 'Helen's cakes' brand is likely to be limited to packaging; the supermarket's own brand will benefit from the company's generic promotions.

Place: distribution is likely to be to the purchaser's own depot with their own logistics taking over thereafter.

Wholesalers

Product: as for supermarket, though generally lower quality may be preferred and volumes may be lower.

Price: probably a little less disadvantageous than with supermarkets, especially if 'pull' from catering establishments can be created by promotion.

Promotion: there will probably be opportunities to promote the 'Helen's cakes' brand through packaging and personal selling, but the main sales effort will probably be to the wholesalers' buyers.

Place: as for supermarket.

Premium outlets

Product: all aspects of quality will be of great importance. A wide and innovative range will be an advantage and volumes both overall and for each product are likely to be manageable.

Price: to some extent price can reflect quality, bearing in mind the priorities of the ultimate consumers. Premium cake shops will be pleased to stock expensive products with high margins if they can sell them. If cakes are sold under the Helen's cakes brand, it will be necessary to guard against undermining of brand values by discounting: recommended retail prices should be established.

Promotion: word of mouth may be enough initially, perhaps combined with providing cakes for free trials in the shops. Eventually, a co-operative approach to promotion involving the shops may be appropriate, with the use of discreet point of sale material.

Place: it will be necessary to make individual deliveries to multiple outlets; accuracy of order-taking and delivery will be important if good relations are to be maintained with the shops concerned.

28 Lakeside Business School

Part (a)

Text reference. The topics mentioned in this answer are discussed in Chapter 8 of your BPP Study Text.

Top tips. A satisfactory answer to this question will have two main elements. The first thing to do is to identify the various stakeholder groups whose opinions are relevant to the e-learning problem. The second is to discuss the techniques that would be useful in dealing with the various groups identified.

Easy marks. Whenever you encounter a question on stakeholders, see if it is useful to make use of *Mendelow's* mapping approach. It is certainly appropriate here, since slightly different approaches are probably appropriate to different groups. When using Mendelow's matrix remember that the classification of stakeholder groups will vary according to the specific problem under consideration.

Examiner's comments. The Examiner makes two very good points in his model answer about the possible inconsistency of stakeholder motivation. The first is that individual stakeholders, being human, are capable of holding more than one point of view at the same time; the second is that identified stakeholder groups may not be united in their views and may contain factions with divergent or even opposing objectives. This heterogeneity of motivation, operative at both individual and group levels, may make the job of dealing with stakeholders even more complex; alternatively, it may offer good opportunities to proceed by promoting a course of action that has the potential for wide, if less than whole-hearted, acceptability.

Marking scheme

		Marks
(a)	Stakeholder mapping	up to 4
	Change management processes	up to 4
	Education, participation, coercion, manipulation, negotiation	up to 4
		Maximum 10 marks
(b)	Areas of concern: financial and customer perspectives	up to 4
	Internal processes and learning and growth perspectives	up to 4
	Advantages and disadvantages of balanced scorecard	up to 4
		Maximum 10 marks
		Total 20 marks

Mendelow suggests that, in relation to any given issue that might affect them, stakeholders may usefully be classified into four groups according to the extent of their **influence or power** and the extent of their **interest** in the issue.

Stakeholders with high levels of both interest and power are **key players** and must be dealt with carefully. Those with little power but a high level of interest are able to influence more powerful groups and should be **kept informed**. Those with power but little interest are capable of becoming interested and so should be **kept satisfied**. **Minimal effort** is expended on stakeholders with neither interest nor power.

Several stakeholder groups have significance for the e-learning issue at Lakeside Business School (LBS).

Central government is the most powerful stakeholder and its position is clear: student numbers are to be increased while funding is cut. The threat of further cuts in the future if student number targets are not met means that productivity improvements such as an expansion of e-learning cannot be avoided. There may be some small possibility of softening the government's stance through normal processes of consultation, PR and lobbying, but LBS should not count on this.

We are not told very much about the nature of the power relationship between LBS and the **central University authority**, but we know the latter has a strong interest in having their e-learning system taken up by the former. **Negotiation and compromise** are probably the way forward here.

By contrast, we know quite a lot about the attitudes of the **students** and the **staff** of LBS.

Collectively, **the staff of LBS** have a considerable degree of both power and interest in the future of e-learning. However, they are **not a cohesive group**: some are computer-literate and have adopted the new techniques, while others have dragged their feet and are likely to continue to do so. The problem for LBS lies with the latter. Because of their status and significance for the work of LBS, the best approach may be one of **integration and collaboration**. This technique emphasises the importance of the overall mission and the need for individuals to support the overall efforts of the group. This might be combined with a programme of internal co-operation under which the more computer-literate members of each section or discipline might undertake to assist their colleagues with the preparation of e-learning materials.

Like the staff, **the students at LBS** have a significant level of interest in the development of e-learning since it seems to be the only real possibility for maintaining study opportunities under budget pressure. However, like the staff, they seem to vary in their inclination and ability to use the new techniques. This may reflect their varying degree of motivation to work towards their degrees or, indeed, at all. University students can be outspoken and the more activist among them may attempt to agitate on the issue. A programme of **communication and consultation** with student representatives is probably required to handle this tendency. There may also be a need for LBS to provide extra **training** in the use of e-learning materials for students whose computer literacy may leave something to be desired.

Part (b)

> **Text reference.** The topics mentioned in this answer are discussed in Chapter 16 of your BPP Study Text.
>
> **Easy marks.** When the Examiner asks you about a particular model, as he has done in this question, you really have no alternative to discussing it in some detail. However, you may be able to score up to, say, 30% of the available marks for sensible supplementary suggestions involving other relevant models or methods.
>
> In this case we feel that the balanced scorecard is of limited applicability, so we say why and propose a different approach.

The balanced scorecard is much promoted as a robust approach to the measurement of business performance. It is based on four **perspectives**, or views of performance from different standpoints. The **financial** perspective uses traditional financial indicators; the **customer** perspective uses measures that reflect the degree of success in providing customer satisfactions; the **internal** perspective considers the efficiency of business systems and procedures; and the **innovation and learning** perspective looks at the extent to which the business is keeping up with changing circumstances.

The balanced scorecard was devised as an improved way of monitoring continuing, all-round business performance. As such, it can have only **limited relevance** to the e-learning issue at LBS. That issue and the measures appropriate to its resolution have more in common with **project management** than they do with routine business operations: it would be reasonable to think in terms of reaching a satisfactory solution to a problem in a finite period of time rather than of monitoring a continuing process of business activity.

It would therefore be appropriate to use **project management techniques** on the e-learning problem. In very simple terms this would involve the agreement of specific objectives, or 'deliverables'; the creation and monitoring of a project plan and budget; the provision of resources and accounting for them; leadership and management of a project team; management of stakeholder expectations and disputes; an acknowledged formal completion of the project; and a proper post-completion audit of the whole process so that it could be refined for future reference.

That being said, there is no reason why the **perspectives of the balanced scorecard** should not be used to structure thinking about the problem and its resolution. This might be particularly useful in the establishment of **objectives** and the consideration of **resources** and **constraints**.

Thinking about the **financial perspective** would remind the planners of the constraints imposed by the University's financial position and would encourage the creative use of staff time and other existing resources. While the project is intended to improve the productivity of these factors, it is likely to markedly increase the demands made on the time of the staff concerned; indeed, extra temporary staff may have to be provided.

The relevance of the **innovation and learning** perspective is so obvious as to need little further comment: the project is one of learning development and has implications for both staff and students.

The **customer** perspective is an interesting one, in that both students and government might be regarded as customers. This is not a dilemma, however: thinking of them in stakeholder terms would be a proper approach.

Finally, consideration of the **internal** perspective underlines the need to manage the project in an efficient manner.

29 Connie Head

Text reference. The topics mentioned in this answer are discussed in Chapter 13 of your BPP Study Text.

Top tips. This is a quite difficult question, which requires consideration of both performance management and the process of appraisal, together with its potential to assist with strategic management.

Easy marks. The only easy marks were available in part (a), for discussing the uses to which appraisal is put: that is to say, basically, assessment of performance, potential and training needs. To score well, you would also need to discuss how effective implementation of an appraisal scheme can be achieved.

Examiner's comments. This was not a very popular question: part (b), in particular, was not well done overall, a lack of understanding of performance management being very clear.

Marking scheme

		Marks
(a)	Objectives and purpose model of the appraisal process	Up to 4 marks each
	Characteristics of the process	
	Results v activities	
	Frequency of appraisal	**Maximum 12 marks**
(b)	Individual and organisational objectives Up to 3 marks each	
	Place in the strategy process	
	Feedback and control	
	Implementation issues	**Maximum 8 marks**
		Total 20 marks

Part (a)

The Senior Partner and Connie emphasise the aspects of appraisal schemes that **support their own favoured policies**. Such schemes should support the organisation's overall objectives without incurring excessive administrative and management costs.

In an organisation such as an accounting practice, the professional staff should indeed be highly **self-motivated**, able to judge the effectiveness of their own performance and bring to their work a commitment to high professional standards. On the other hand, it is inevitable that their **talents and performance will vary** and they will need **guidance and help with their future development**. Dealing with these issues would be the role of an appraisal scheme.

The overall aim of such a scheme would be to **support progress toward the achievement of corporate objectives** and it would do this in three ways: performance review, potential review and training needs review.

Performance review. Performance review should provide employees with an **impartial and authoritative assessment of the quality and effect of their work**. Individuals should have personal objectives that support corporate goals via intermediate objectives relevant to the roles of their work groups. A reasoned assessment of performance can have a **positive motivating effect**, simply as a kind of positive, reinforcing feedback. It can also provide an opportunity for analysing and addressing the **reasons for sub-optimal performance.**

Potential review. Any organisation needs to make the best use it can of its people; an accountancy practice is typical of many modern organisations in that its people are its greatest asset and its future success depends on managing them in a way that makes the best use of their skills and aptitudes. An important aspect of this is **assessing potential for promotion and moves into other positions of greater challenge and responsibility.**

Training needs review. A further aspect of the desirable practice of enabling staff to achieve their potential is the provision of training and development activities. The appraisal system is one means by which **training needs can be assessed** and training provision initiated.

The appraisal system

An appraisal system must be properly administered and operated if it is make a proper contribution to the organisation's progress.

The appraisal cycle. Formal appraisal, with interviews and written assessments, is typically undertaken on an **annual cycle**. This interval is commonly regarded as too long to be effective because of the speed with which individual roles can evolve and their holders can develop, so the annual appraisal is often supplemented with a less detailed review after six months. Sometimes the procedure is sufficiently simplified that the whole thing can be done at six monthly intervals. Much modern thinking on this topic is now suggesting that any frequency of periodic appraisal is unsatisfactory and that it should be replaced by a **continuous process of coaching and assessment**.

Objectivity and reliability. Appraisal involves an element of direct personal criticism that can be stressful for all parties involved. If the system is to be credible its outputs must be seen to be objective and reliable. This requires proper **training for appraisers**, the establishment of appropriate **performance standards** and, preferably, input into each appraisal from **more than one person**. Having reports reviewed by the appraiser's own manager is one approach to the last point; 360 degree appraisal is another.

Setting targets. Past performance should be reviewed against **objective standards** and this raises the question of the type of objective that should be set. Objectives set in terms of **results** or outcomes to be achieved can encourage **creativity** and **innovation** but may also lead to **unscrupulous, unethical** and even **illegal choice of method**. On the other hand, objectives designed to maintain and improve the quality of output by **encouraging conformity** with approved procedure and method may stifle the creativity and innovation widely regarded as a vital source of continuing competitive advantage.

Part (b)

Performance management involves the establishment of clear, agreed individual **goals and performance standards**; continuous leadership action to both **motivate and appraise subordinates**; and a **periodic review** of performance at which the goals and performance standards for the next cycle are set.

Performance management is an application of the **rational model** of strategic management, in that individual goals are intended to form the lowest echelon of a **hierarchy of objectives** that builds up to support the **overall mission** of the organisation. It is an essential aspect of the system that individual goals should be **agreed and internalised** so that true **goal congruence** is achieved.

This overall approach was first described (as is so often the case) by *Peter Drucker*, in 1954, and is seen most clearly in the system of **management by objectives** (MbO). MbO as a management system has fallen somewhat from favour with the rise of quality management methods that emphasise processual and procedural conformance rather than the attainment of overall performance goals. Nevertheless, it has much to offer.

Under a formal MbO system, the process of setting goals is part of the **implementation phase** of strategic management and follows consideration of resources, overall objectives and SWOT analysis. Top level subordinate goals are agreed for heads of departments, divisions or functions: these goals should be specific, measurable, attainable, relevant and time-bounded (SMART). It is particularly important that the achievement of a goal can be established by objective **measurement**. There may be different timescales for different objectives, with short-term goals supporting longer-term ones.

Departmental heads then agree SMART goals for their subordinates in discussion with them, that support their own personal goals, and so on down the hierarchy to the level of the individual employee. All members of the organisation thus know what they are expected to achieve and how it fits into the wider fabric of the organisation's mission.

Periodic **performance review** is based on the objective appraisal of success against agreed goals, the agreement of goals for the next period and an assessment of the resources, including training, that the reviewee may require to reach those goals. The MbO system thus closes the **feedback loop** in the corporate control system.

30 Isabella Correlli

Text reference. The topics mentioned in this answer are discussed in Chapter 13 of your BPP Study Text.

Top tips. This question is worthy of a little further consideration than just preparing an answer. Whether or not to outsource is an important strategic decision for other functions besides HR. Many of the salient points covered in the context of HR, such as technical expertise and company experience will be relevant in other areas.

Of course, the whole problem of outsourcing also has wider strategic implications when examined from the standpoint of resource-based strategic theory. If an organisation's strategy is built around core competences, as many are, there is a strong case for outsourcing non-core activities simply to allow for maximum managerial attention to the critical ones.

Easy marks. This is a challenging question but there are some clear symptoms of what is wrong in the organisation, such as the poorly structured interviews. Careful reading of the question is essential to avoid skipping over these obvious points.

Part (a)

REPORT

To: Line Manager
From: Isabella Correlli, Personnel Manager
Date: December 2000
Subject: In-house Recruitment

1   **Introduction**

Over the last three years the company has suffered from unusually high staff turnover rates. In addition, many new employees are leaving the company within two years of joining. As the cost of recruiting and training these employees is high, their short time with the firm is not allowing us to benefit in full from the costs incurred in employing them.

2   **Reasons for leaving**

Unfortunately, due to the **lack of structure in exit interviews and annual appraisals** there is no clear picture as to why so many staff are leaving after such a short time with the firm. However one factor that does appear to be clear is that the reasons for leaving are not financial. The company's **salary structure appears to be competitive** and many employees are leaving for employment that pays no more than is paid here.

Therefore, it would appear that the reasons for the high staff turnover are more complex and I believe that this stems from the **type of individual that we are recruiting**.

3   **External agency**

Our current policy is to use a specialist external recruitment agency with knowledge of the business for recruitment and selection. The agency obviously has detailed knowledge of the type of business that we are in and has the technical skills and resources appropriate for recruitment and selection. However they do not have detailed knowledge of our particular company and environment and therefore are perhaps **not recruiting the type of person that is right for our organisation**.

I believe that we should carry out the process of selection and recruitment of staff in-house.

4   **Job specification**

If we start with the important area of **job specification** it can be argued that the existing managers in the business have a more detailed knowledge of the actual requirements of the role being recruited for. They have experience of the difficulties and requirements of the job and are better placed than an outside agency to provide an accurate job description. It can be argued that these managers are too close to the situation and may include some bias in their job description, but their detailed knowledge in the area should outweigh this. If the external agency is recruiting staff on the basis of a spurious job description, then it is not surprising that these staff are leaving after such a short period of time.

5   **Internal candidates**

The use of an external agency to recruit staff will often limit the possibility of **filling a post internally**. Existing staff and management will have a better idea of any internal candidates that are suitable for the appointment or promotion without having to recruit externally.

6   **In-house interviews**

The arguments for using an external agency for the interviewing are that it saves management time and that the agency has technical expertise in interviewing that is not available internally. However, there are also a number of arguments that can be put forward for interviews being carried out by existing managers.

Although external agency staff will be able to assess the technical competence of a candidate they will not have the **detailed knowledge** of the intricacies and difficulties of the role that existing managers will have. A large part of the recruitment process will not necessarily be dependent upon the technical skills of the recruit but rather on the way in which they will **fit in with those with whom they must work**. Such an assessment cannot be made by an external agency: the managers actively involved in the working environment will be **better placed to judge** whether a recruit will fit in, thereby reducing the chance of conflict at a later date.

If managers are involved in the recruitment process, then they may be **more committed** to making the appointment work in the future. At the moment, managers perceive that they are having new employees imposed on them by outsiders.

If managers are involved in the interviewing process, they should be able to make an early assessment of the **development requirements** of the person appointed, rather than this only becoming apparent once the employee has started work.

7   **Employment contract agreement**

Once the candidate has been chosen, the process of agreeing salary levels and other elements of the remuneration package can be dealt with **much more rapidly** in-house than when dealing through an intermediary.

8   **Conclusion on recruitment staffing**

It is quite clear from our experiences with staff recruited by the agency that in many cases they are not getting it right. If the process is brought in-house, although our managers do not necessarily have the interviewing expertise of the external agency, they can bring their detailed knowledge of the job, the team and the environment to the process. Obviously recruitment of staff should not be left entirely in the hands of line managers because of potential individual biases. However, if a panel of recruiters is used then assessment of a candidate can be made from both the departmental and the corporate perspective.

9   **Criteria for selection of candidates**

The most important criterion for selection of candidates is that they have the ability to **fulfil the job description**. However, as we have seen from our recent experiences this is not always enough for the placing to be a success. Although it can be argued that a detailed list of selection criteria is not appropriate, as it removes the personal subjectivity involved in the recruitment process, I feel that some guidelines on selection criteria are necessary.

The **Munro-Fraser Five Point Plan** provides an outline of non-specific criteria that can be useful when assessing candidates and I propose that this is used as our basis for assessment.

10   **Qualifications**

Obviously candidates must have the appropriate qualifications otherwise they may not be allowed to carry out their role or will not be capable of carrying it out.

11   **Brains and abilities**

We must be able to assess whether a candidate who has the correct qualifications also has the ability to apply technical knowledge and to innovate and improvise where necessary.

12   **Impact on others**

The candidate will be expected to work as part of a team and to be able to communicate and operate both with internal and external customers. Therefore the ability to get on with the current team and to be able to integrate into that team will be a vital element of the selection process.

13   **Motivation**

Candidates must be sufficiently well-motivated to be able to fulfil their duties without constant supervision and to be able to deal effectively with periodic heavy workloads.

14   **Adjustment**

Candidates must show an ability to be able to deal with change in such areas as technology, work practices, the work environment or customer needs.

These five general headings can be useful pointers to the more specific selection criteria that we may wish to set.

Part (b)

The firm needs to reduce the number of staff that are leaving so soon after having joined the firm. There is no clear reason for the high level of staff turnover. Ways of reducing this turnover and consequently improving morale within the company will be considered under five headings: salary, appraisals, training, career progression and the social framework.

Salary

Although it would appear that the reasons for the staff turnover levels are not predominantly financial, the business should consider its remuneration package as a whole. Is the **entire package** seen as competitive, not just the actual salary level? It may be that competitors in this market pay similar levels of salary but provide a better all round remuneration package, such as pensions, company cars, bonus schemes and so on.

In the company's environment of selling financial services it is likely that the sales staff will be set **annual targets** to meet. Are these targets viewed as attainable? If staff are given a role in the setting of such sales targets or their views are taken into consideration then this involvement will normally increase their motivation to meet the targets and reduce any irritation regarding what are perceived as unattainable targets.

Appraisal

It would appear that the annual appraisal system needs to be assessed as the **appraisals do not appear to be well structured**. Appraisals are a two way process and are not just about management assessing the performance of individuals. Employees need to know how management assess their strengths and weaknesses and what can be done to address any problem areas. Managers must also be aware that the appraisal process must allow the employees **a chance to communicate** with them and to express any problems that they have in the working environment.

Training

In the environment of financial services selling the staff will often have to **pass exams** in order to be allowed to operate. The firm should ensure that it provides **appropriate technical support** in this area. Individuals may also require technical updating or more general training such as in the area of sales techniques. Any support of this kind will normally be well received by employees and viewed as a benefit of working for the organisation. Training courses that encompass the **philosophy of the organisation** can also serve to improve the **commitment and loyalty** of the staff.

Career progression

Most employees find it beneficial and motivating to have a **clear career structure** in place. If an employee knows that there is potential career progression within the organisation then this can serve as a motivating factor.

Social framework

The sales staff in a financial services firm are likely to spend much of their time away from the office, working alone with customers. They may feel **isolated** and not part of the team which will undoubtedly be supporting them in the head office. A **social framework** such as regular social events or a sports and social club can bring employees together and can be a very motivating factor. Often friendships made at work can increase an employees loyalty to the organisation as well.

31 Question with analysis: Fashion retailer

Text reference. The topics mentioned in this answer are discussed in Chapter 6 of your BPP Study Text.

Top tips. Fashion retailing is a fairly specialised job. However, we all have some experience of it from the customer's side of the counter. Don't be afraid to make some educated deductions about, for instance, the need for careful stock control when a wide range of goods is moving rather quickly.

Part (a)

Paul's business is in the fashion clothing industry with 20 retail stores but little integration between the stores. This part of the fashion industry operates with very slim margins and with profitability not keeping pace with the increase in turnover, Paul realises that he must operate in a more cost-conscious manner. The computer system is currently underused and is operating in a passive manner or in the 'support' quadrant of the *McFarlan and McKenney* grid.

Top tips. An organisation's value-creating activities must be mutually supporting.

In order to consider how the IT function can be used to provide Paul with a competitive edge in his business we can use Porter's value chain model to illustrate how this could be done. The firm will be as strong as the weakest link in the chain. The value chain consists of five primary activities and four support activities. The IT investment will be worthwhile if it can be used to reduce costs or to differentiate Paul's business from the others in the industry sector.

Primary activities

Inbound logistics

This relates to the purchasing function and the storage of stock and distribution to the stores. An IT system can help with stock control levels, economic ordering and efficient distribution routings.

Operations

IT can be used to monitor the performance of each store with details being provided about profitability, stock levels, stock turnover, expense levels, staff absences and so on. IT could also be used to analyse the different consumer demand profile in different locations in order to help each store ensure that it has sufficient stocks of the type of sales made in its store.

Outbound logistics

This element of the chain concerns distribution to customers and is more relevant in a manufacturing industry. In Paul's business there will not be much distribution to customers but the system may be able to produce a customer database to assist with marketing and promotions.

Marketing and sales

Paul could use IT to indicate customer purchasing patterns for different stores and to develop databases for promotions. Internet retailing is a possibility, though it would create a fulfilment problem.

Service

This area of the chain is to do with the provision of service to the customers and it is not likely that IT can be of much use here although it could be used to monitor, control and facilitate transfers between stores.

Support activities

Firm's infrastructure

In this area IT can be used to help with the budgeting, finance and management information in order to improve the Paul's company's performance compared to that of his competitors.

Human resources management

As Paul's organisation is quite small and consists largely of retail sales staff, there will not be many very useful applications of IT in this area however it may be used to make recruitment and appraisals more efficient.

Technology development

It is unlikely that the IT function would move from McFarlan and McKenney's support quadrant to the strategic quadrant.

Procurement

This area of support activity is concerned with linking the purchasing system to the sales system. This could be used to automatically update stock records and indicate when new orders should be placed and could also help to minimise times when excessive stock is held in a store. It could also consolidate orders to achieve bulk purchase discounts.

Part (b)

> **Text reference.** The topics mentioned in this answer are discussed in Chapter 15 of your BPP Study Text.
>
> **Top tips.** Outsourcing is a very important business trend and IT has been a good example of the sort of function that has commonly been outsourced in the past. However, it is becoming very common for companies to view IT systems as fundamental to their operations and as a major source of added value. Under these circumstances, a decision to outsource would probably be unwise.

To:	Paul Singh
From:	A Consultant
Date:	December 200X
Subject:	Outsourcing of the IT function

1   Introduction

Outsourcing of specialist functions such as the IT function can in many cases be a cost effective method of gaining benefits from the specialism. Given the lack of in-house IT expertise, outsourcing could be of great value to your business, although I fully understand your concerns about loss of control. In the paragraphs below I will summarise the potential advantages and disadvantages of outsourcing the IT function.

2   Advantages

2.1   By outsourcing the IT function your business will be gaining access to knowledge and expertise that would be expensive to recruit and employ internally

2.2   The cost of a sophisticated IT function can be considerable and will only pay for itself if fully utilised. If you operate in-house there are likely to be certain peak periods of operation and you may have to recruit for this period or have idle time in non-peak periods. An external specialist can spread the costs of the function by working at full capacity by serving the needs of different clients at different times. Therefore despite the costs of the outsourcing it may well be cheaper than attempting to run a similar function in house with large amounts of idle time

2.3   Your experience and expertise are in the fashion industry not the IT industry. By outsourcing the IT function you can concentrate on the core functions of your business whilst this area is dealt with by experts in their own field

2.4   It has been found that some businesses may become excessively influenced, in terms of strategy, by the personnel in the IT function. They may pursue strategies that are in their own interests whereas the only interest that an external supplier would have would be to provide a satisfactory service so that the contract will be renewed.

3 **Disadvantages**

3.1 Your concern about losing control may be due to a fear that the external IT supplier may only provide you with limited information. Therefore it would be essential that you are quite clear about the functions that you require in your business from the outsourcing. This can be difficult if you have no detailed knowledge of IT and the possibilities of what it can achieve for you. However any reputable IT provider should be able to brief you fully on all of the possibilities so that you can choose what information will be of competitive advantage to your company

3.2 There might be a concern that the IT company, although having specialist IT expertise, may not have full knowledge of the fashion industry sector in which you operate

3.3 An outside agency will tend to provide a fairly standard service to all clients and any special needs may not be met or the provision of the information may be slow in coming. An in-house system may provide such bespoke services more promptly

3.4 If the external supplier deals with other businesses which are your competitors there may be some concerns about confidentiality.

I hope that this brief has been useful and I would be happy to discuss the matter further if you wish to.

32 Auto Direct

Part (a)

Text reference. The topics mentioned in this answer are discussed in Chapter 11 of your BPP Study Text.

Top tips. You must think hard about the wording of this question. Superficially, it asks you for a summary of change management strategies in a particular context, which would be a large job to do properly, but offers only twelve marks. The implication is that you must not descend into too much detail about any particular model or approach.

The Examiner's suggested solution includes a very brief skim across the better-known models but concentrates on **advice on the implementation phase** of change management and the various methods (or 'strategies') that might be used to 'create a positive staff response'.

Easy marks. When you find yourself committed to a question like this for want of anything better, you can probably assume that a fairly wide range of answers will be catered for in the marking scheme and that markers will be a generous as they can.

Examiner's comments. Many candidates answered this part of the question very well.

Marking scheme

		Marks
(a)	Strategies for managing change	up to 2 marks per strategy
	Alternative models for managing change	up to 5 marks
		Maximum 12 marks
(b)	Marketing research process	up to 2 marks per stage
		Maximum 8 marks
		Total 20 marks

Report: Change management strategies and methods

Several researchers and writers have proposed models of the change process and strategies for change management. We might mention Gemini 4Rs, Systems Intervention Strategy and the Lewin/Schein unfreeze-change-refreeze approach. All these approaches are essentially **rational** in their methodology, emphasising the need for **reasoned analysis of the problems** that make change necessary; effective communication of the need and programme for change; and the use of a variety of methods to put the plan into action. The potential change has for upsetting people's lives (and even their health) is recognised and recommendations are made that change should be introduced as humanely as possible under the prevailing economic circumstances.

While good **project management** of a programme of change is very important, it is the **human aspects of the change management process** that are crucial. This is because change will not happen unless people make it happen. A number of strategies are proposed for dealing with this aspect of change management.

Participation in decision-making is sometimes recommended as a way of improving motivation generally and may be useful in the context of change. It is probably advantageous to involve staff in decisions affecting them, their conditions and their work processes and at least hear what they have to say. However, participation is not a universal panacea and can be very **time consuming**. Also, the normal **management style and culture** of the organisation must be considered. It is probably inappropriate to promote participation exclusively in the context of change if staff are not used to it: their main reaction may be one of suspicious cynicism.

An **autocratic** approach, imposing change by means of **coercion** can work reasonably well in some circumstances, especially where the staff expect nothing else. It has the benefit of saving time and is probably the **best approach in times of crisis**. However, it does have the weakness of ignoring the experience and knowledge that staff may be able to offer.

In any event, **communication** with staff about the proposed change is commonly regarded as an essential process. Ideally, information will be provided as early as possible, explaining why change is necessary and the course that will be followed. Anxiety, particularly over job security, is common during change and a programme of communication and education can go a long way to allay it.

Sometimes neither participation nor coercion can resolve all problems and **negotiation** may be required. This is often the case when the labour force is strongly organised and when there is disagreement between management factions as to the best course to follow.

This has been a brief overview of some approaches to change management. You will no doubt be in a position to decide which are most appropriate to the circumstances of Auto Direct.

Part (b)

Top tips. This question probes the boundaries of the syllabus envelope. There is a loose link with market research; the Examiner may feel this justifies the question, since he has stated an intention to make marketing issues an important feature of the exam. Indeed, the suggested solutions to both parts of this question make reference to 'internal marketing'. This again, is not a mainstream topic for this paper and is a phrase used in a variety of different ways by marketing people and others. The significance of all this is that you must be prepared for questions on any aspect of the syllabus at all; there are not really any areas that you can afford to neglect.

Easy marks. In any event, **there are no marks for despair**, so, when faced with a question like this, you just have to do your best and try to think of intelligent comments.

Examiner's comments. Answers to this part were often less good than those to part (a), with evidence of confusion and lack of understanding.

Attempts are commonly made to **assess consumer and voter attitudes** for purposes of political and market research. Common techniques include postal questionnaires and questionnaire-based telephone and in-person interviews; open-ended interviews and focus groups are more expensive, but may produce more accurate results. Covert surveillance can be used to observe shopper behaviour and overt surveillance is used to measure TV audience size.

In an ordinary business HRM context, such as that of Auto Direct, it may be possible to obtain much useful information through the **normal informal communication network** that permeates any organisation. There are two caveats, however: a manager who is not already in touch with the informal organisation through ordinary social links with colleagues and staff will find it difficult to establish such links at short notice; and information relayed through such links is very likely to be coloured and distorted by the opinions and priorities of the people involved in the relaying.

A **programme of research conducted by consultants** may be an appropriate technique to use here. Anxiety about the implications of the anticipated change would probably make it easier for outsiders to win the confidence of the Auto Direct staff than it would be for managers if they attempted to research this topic. Also, outsiders would bring the required interviewing skills and objectivity necessary to such an exercise.

Consultants would establish the aims and scope of the research in discussion with Mark Howe and advise on the best techniques to use. They would also be able to analyse, summarise and present the data obtained in the most appropriate way and even to advise on its best use.

33 Focus Bank

Text reference. The topics mentioned in this answer are discussed in Chapters 2 and 6 of your BPP Study Text.

Top tips. Outsourcing and core competences are so closely linked conceptually that it is very difficult to answer the two parts of this question separately. This illustrates the importance of reading all the requirements of a question before starting to answer it. Only in this way can you ensure that you make your points in the correct place.

It is necessary to read the scenario for this question quite carefully. Note that it is Focus Bank's *own* call centres that have been more efficient and given better customer service, while the (presumably not yet complete) process of *off-shoring* call-centre activity has led to complaints of reduced customer service.

Easy marks. In your answer to part (a) it is not necessary to distinguish too carefully between the strategic and operational levels. The Examiner is not over-precise in his use of language and here the phrase 'strategic and operational' merely indicates that there will be marks for advantages and disadvantages of any kind or significance.

In part (b) the Examiner seems to have been looking for evidence of understanding of what core competences are and an appreciation of the resource-based theory of competitive advantage.

Examiner's comments. Candidates found that part (b) of the question was more difficult than part (a).

		Marks
(a)	Advantages of outsourcing customer services:	up to 2 per point
	Cost savings	
	Improved productivity	
	Focus on core competences	
	Service quality improvements	
	Disadvantages of customer services outsourcing:	up to 2 per point
	Loss of control	
	Loss of core competence	
	Bargaining power reduced	
	Reversal of policy difficult	
	Staff morale	
		Maximum 14 marks
(b)	Differentiated customer service	up to 4
	Value chain/process improvement	up to 4
		Maximum 6 marks
		Total 20 marks

Part (a)

Outsourcing has always been a feature of business life. It is the natural way to fit a business into the **upstream supply chain**, for both goods and services. 'Make or buy' is a classic cost accounting problem. Also, it has long been used by businesses too small to be able to establish in-house sources of **highly specialised or expensive goods and services** such as legal services and safety equipment

More recently, in an increasingly competitive and globalised business environment, outsourcing has become popular largely because it holds out the promise of **reduced costs**. Cost reductions become possible for two main reasons. First, the provider may be able to achieve **economies of scale** by concentrating some aspect of the production or service process. Second, particularly in work employing low-skilled labour, a major employer is better placed to exert **downward pressure on wage rates** than are a large number of businesses employing a few staff each, especially when casual, part-time or temporary work patterns predominate.

A further potential advantage is the **increased effectiveness** that can arise from **greater specialisation**. This can be achieved both by the supplier, who concentrates on a particular type of work, and by the purchaser, whose executives are liberated from the management of peripheral activities.

Focus Bank seems to be in the middle of outsourcing its call-centre operation and is wondering how far to take it. It could certainly expect to achieve the **cost reductions** mentioned above. It is now quite common for call centre work to be outsourced to countries with lower labour costs, such as India. However, there have been complaints from customers about **poor service**, so the potential for improved efficiency has not yet been achieved. This may illustrate an important disadvantage of outsourcing, which is the potential for **loss of control** of the work involved.

The significance of this loss extends beyond concerns about quality. There is also a loss of managerial expertise relating to the outsourced function or activity. This means that when changes occur in the market or the environment, it may be much more difficult to plan a suitable response. It will be necessary to consult with the service providers concerned and, naturally enough, they will have their own priorities that affect their stance.

The customer dissatisfaction and staff union resistance illustrate a further disadvantage to outsourcing, which is its potential for generating **stakeholder concern**. It is natural enough that staff union organisers should be opposed to anything that threatens their members' livelihood and their own status. Managing this opposition would be difficult enough; when customers find a reason to be sympathetic to the unions' stand, the Bank is likely to find itself having to adjust its policy.

Stakeholder concern about outsourcing was of particular importance to *British Airways* in 2005, when a dispute arose at *Gate Gourmet*, its Heathrow in-flight catering supplier. Gate Gourmet had, in fact, been spun off from BA some years previously. The dispute caused extensive delays to BA flights out of Heathrow, not merely because of disruption to catering supplies, but because BA's baggage handlers, many of whom were related to Gate Gourmet staff, stopped work in sympathy.

Part (b)

A modern approach to strategic management called **resource based theory** has been widely accepted. Its basic premise is at odd with more traditional theories, collectively known as **positioning theory**, which see strategy as a process of **adaptation to the environment**.

Resource based theory argues that such adaptation is available to all businesses and **cannot, therefore, create a unique competitive advantage**: that is only made possible by the possession of **unique resources**. Such resources include, for example, protected intellectual property or exclusive access to a raw material. More probably in today's complex developed economies, such a unique resource may reside in the **skills and experience** of the people working in the business. *Enron*, in its early days, for example, developed a particular competence in energy trading. Such collective skills and abilities constitute the business's **core competences.**

Hamel and Prahalad suggest that a **core competence** must have three qualities.

- It must make a **disproportionate** contribution to the **value** the customer perceives.

- It must be '**competitively unique**', which means one of three things: actually unique; superior to competitors; or capable of dramatic improvement.

- It must be **extendable**, in that it must allow for the development of an array of new products and services.

A core competence is not a strategy in itself. However, it can form a basis for a strategy. Here it is important to reiterate that a core competence must be difficult to imitate if it is to confer lasting competitive advantage. In particular, skills that can be bought in are unlikely to form the basis of core competences, since competitors would be able to buy them in just as easily.

Focus Bank might therefore benefit from a clear understanding of its own core competences when considering its overall strategy. A particularly fundamental and fairly obvious application of the concept is that no attempt should be made to outsource activities that constitute core competences; that is an obvious way to lose the advantage they confer, both through loss of control and as a result of atrophy of the competence within the organisation.

34 Smith Norman

Text reference. The topics mentioned in this answer are discussed in Chapter 5 and 7 of your BPP Study Text.

Top tips. Many financial services firms have real difficulty in differentiating themselves from their competitors. The ability to understand the needs of the customer, and how those needs can be met, lies at the heart of marketing, and this should be your starting point, but place it firmly in the overall context of the entire business strategy developed by Smith Norman. Do not be confined to a discussion of the marketing mix – this is really just the way of implementing a chosen marketing strategy, which in turn reflects key understanding of customers and competitors. Make sure that you can distinguish between these various 'layers'.

Marking scheme

		Marks
(a)	Marketing's relevance in a financial services business: Sensing/scanning changes to customer needs Sensing/scanning changes in competitive environment Strategic choices of markets and segments served Choosing the company's competitive position Selecting the means of differentiation Communicating the corporate/service brand Implementing the marketing mix	Up to 2 per point **Maximum 12 marks**
(b)	Measuring marketing's impact: Customer/potential customer awareness surveys Share of key client's business Benchmarking/market share Customer retention/recruitment Sales growth and profitability Press & PR coverage Evidence of customers acting as advocates/customer referrals	Up to 2 per point **Maximum 8 marks** **Total 20 marks**

Part (a)

The recognition of the need for marketing in financial services is a relatively recent business phenomenon. Although Smith Norman has, to date, relied on one-to-one close relationships with customer contacts, this approach will be increasingly outdated as financial service firms seek to **differentiate themselves from competitors**. These competitors will, in many cases, be offering very similar products that are viewed as commodities by many, purchasers whose buying decisions will therefore be driven by price considerations alone.

It is well recognised that **the competitive environment has changed dramatically**: markets have become international and global, technological change has increased competition dramatically and customers are much more aware of their ability to shop around, especially via the Internet.

Marketing plays a critical role in understanding this new customer environment, by helping to **identify new customer needs** and specify new competitor offerings. Furthermore, a market is not a mass, homogeneous group of customers, each wanting an identical product. Every market consists of potential buyers with different needs and different buying behaviour. A different marketing approach should be taken by Smith Norman for each **market segment**. As a result the targeting of particular groups, the understanding of their needs, and the opportunities this gives for differentiation and positioning of the company's services, are key parts of the overall firm's strategy. This should involve service superiority, better understanding of customer needs and the successful launch of new services. Within the overall marketing strategy, marketing mix decisions will need to be made that will focus upon exactly how the marketing strategy is to be planned, implemented and made successful.

Branding is an important part of this, as a brand can identify the financial services provided by Smith Norman, and will distinguish them from competitors. Large companies such as the major FMCG multinationals may produce a number of different brands to cover only a few basic products, but this approach would not be appropriate for a company the size of Smith Norman. An overall corporate brand would be sufficient, especially if teamed with a slogan. Successful brands build reputation and customer confidence, and in so doing may provide the best means of differentiation.

Part (b)

Julia faces one of the biggest problems in marketing – how to justify the amount spent on promoting the company. The marketing budget is often the **first to be cut** if a company is undertaking a cost reduction exercise, largely because marketing spend is so **difficult to evaluate** in terms of its effectiveness. If marketing expenditure is to be protected, its benefits need to be sold to senior management. Measures of success can be both qualitative and quantitative, but they should always be taken with reference to Smith Norman's **goals and objectives**. There are some measures that can be pointed out.

(a)   **Customer awareness. Surveys** can be taken before and after a marketing campaign to show whether or not customers are more likely to recognise the Smith Norman brand, or a service offered, and whether or not the recollection is positive. A higher profile for the company is always desirable. **Public relations** and **press coverage** are a key part of marketing communication, and Julia may have a planned series of events to raise client awareness. Sponsorship (maybe of the arts or a sporting event) may be a useful means of developing the brand.

(b)   **Market share** is an important measure of company success. Market share compared with the market share of the largest competitor (known as relative market share) is a refinement of this measure and should be readily available from industry statistics. Assessing the **rate of market growth** is less useful as a measure of marketing success, since new markets may grow explosively while mature ones grow hardly at all. **Customer retention** is similarly important. Industrial and commercial clients in the financial services sector may be more willing to change their service provider in search of either better or cheaper services.

(c)   **Sales** (and particularly **growth of sales**) are another key indicator of marketing success and will be easy to extract from the company's internal data. It is, however, difficult to prove a direct link between marketing activity and sales levels: who can say whether or not any sales increase would have occurred anyway?

(d)   **Benchmarking** against close industry rivals to indicate where customer preferences lie can also provide useful information.

(e)   A **balanced scorecard** could offer Julia a mix of internal and external performance measures against which to assess the contribution of marketing initiatives. It extends beyond traditional financial accounting measures to provide information about customer perspectives, financial performance, internal processes and the level of innovation in the company.

35 La Familia Amable

Part (a)

Marking scheme

		Marks
(a)	Areas of value chain delivering customer comfort, convenience, price/performance etc	up to 3 per point
	Use of appropriate models	up to 4
		Maximum 12 marks
(b)	Advantages and disadvantages of franchising	up to 2 per point
		Maximum 8 marks
		Total 20 marks

To:	Ramon Silva
From:	Accountant
Date:	December 2005
Subject:	**Proposed new venture**

Creation of value

Your proposed new venture is based on the identification of a gap in the hotel market for an inexpensive but good quality product. You propose to create value by innovative bedroom design and efficient use of a minimal staff. The main source of value would therefore lie in what *Porter* calls **operations**.

I would question your belief that little **marketing** (another of Porter's primary value activities) would be required. You intend that your market offering should be recognised by potential customers as innovative: the launch of a new product of this type should include informative advertising simply to let potential customers know what is available and where. Later, promotion aimed at building the brand would be appropriate. This would be based on the **brand values** of comfort, convenience and moderate cost.

Intensity of competition and new entrants

At the moment, available hotel accommodation is of two general types that are, respectively, cheaper and of lower quality than your concept, or more expensive, but offering extra features that add little extra value. You believe that there is **little direct competition** in your chosen segment. Since much of your ability to combine good quality with low cost depends on room design and construction, building costs should create a **barrier to entry** against potential new entrants seeking to imitate your strategy. However, I would sound a note of caution here.

Currently, the hotel industry in the Spanish holiday areas is somewhat depressed, with overcapacity. While there may be no direct competitors for your new venture, if it is a success, it will attract the attention of the established two star hotel operators and they may start to compete directly by **discounting their own product**. They may do this outside the highest season in the first place, but if they need to do so, they will be able to cut their costs by offering fewer facilities and extend their revised offer into busier periods.

Substitute products

You have identified a gap in the currently available product range provided by hotels. However, there is a **substitute product** that may represent an immediate threat to your proposed operation. This is **self-catering holiday accommodation**, a well-established alternative to the more expensive type of hotel. There is probably a segment of the market for which this option is not particularly practical, which is the aspiring holiday home purchaser making a short visit of one or two days, for whom the normal booking period of one week would be excessive. However, whether it would be possible to base a business on this presumably rather small segment would remain to be seen.

Part (b)

Text reference. The topics mentioned in this answer are discussed in Chapter 7 of your BPP Study Text.

Easy marks. This is almost an opportunity to write down all you know about franchising, but even so, you must bias your remarks towards the hotel industry.

Examiner's comments. There were some exceptionally good answers to this part of the question.

Advantages of franchising

Ramon Silva's plan to franchise his operation would have **financial benefits** in that he could charge franchisees a substantial initial **premium** and **service fees** subsequently. This would provide a useful positive cash flow that would enable him to expand the business faster than might otherwise be the case.

An important potential advantage of franchising is the **motivation and commitment** that comes from capital participation. A good franchising structure will be fair to both parties and will allow franchisees to benefit in proportion to their input to their businesses.

Franchising should be attractive to franchisees because it should allow them to benefit from a **strong brand** and to run their own businesses with **less risk** then a completely independent venture. However, these aspects are only present when the business model is proven and the brand established: this is not yet the case with 'La Familia Aimable' project. Ramon Silva should set up at least his first hotel and to run it himself for a few years to **prove the concept** and **establish** the brand before seeking franchisees for further expansion.

Disadvantages of franchising

An important potential disadvantage of franchising is the **division of control** between franchiser and franchisee. The franchiser relies on the efforts of the franchisee for the attainment of crucial outcomes such as quality of service, while the franchisee will normally be constrained many operational matters, such as the nature of the services offered and almost any aspect of promotion. The **franchise contract** must be drawn up very carefully, so that both parties to the franchise know what their rights and responsibilities are and, in particular, **how disputes are to be resolved**.

Recruitment and selection of suitable franchisees can be a significant burden for the franchiser, both in terms of **cost incurred** and also as a **distraction** from the overall management of the business. Franchisees can make or break the operation and must be selected with great care. Ramon Silva is considering a chain of hotels, which will probably not grow in the medium term to more than, say, a dozen franchises, if only because of the capital costs involved. The rate at which he needs to recruit is therefore fairly low, but, conversely, the importance of each selection is very high. He will have to spend a lot of time and effort on it.

Training the new franchisees will be as important as selection and for the same reasons. The franchisees will form the organisation's principal point of contact with the customers: they will judge the whole operation by the treatment and quality of service they receive. Ramon Silva will have to provide initial training and motivate the franchisees to work to high standards. He will also have to install a monitoring system to ensure that those standards are maintained.

36 Rameses International

Top tips. Fairly obviously, not all businesses are equally successful and some of this difference can be traced to strategic failure. It is important to realise that strategy is not a machine that you put money and models into and get growth and profit out of: things can go wrong. An acquaintance with the real world of business will help you to answer questions like this, so make sure you spend a little while reading the business press each week.

Easy marks. Note the use of the word 'might' in the part (a) requirement. This means you are free to speculate on the basis of the brief information given, so apply all your general background knowledge of how things should be done.

Examiner's comments. The Examiner's original intention for part (a) of this question was that it should be about the failure of strategy in general terms, rather than the failure of the specific strategies tried by Rameses International. Quite properly, better candidates based their answer on the scenario and the Examiner rapidly adjusted the marking scheme to give them proper credit. Always try to relate your answer to the scenario!

However, part (b) was often badly answered: candidates produced answers about strategy selection rather than the factors that affect successful implementation. Read the question carefully!

Marking scheme

		Marks
(a)	Too many strategies	up to 2 marks
	Poor planning	up to 2 marks
	Inappropriate structure	up to 2 marks
	Information inadequacy	up to 2 marks
	Competitive actions	up to 2 marks
	Inadequate understanding of purpose of strategy	up to 2 marks
	Competitive activity	up to 2 marks
	Resistance to change	up to 2 marks
		Maximum 12 marks
(b)	Maintain existing business	up to 2 marks
	Use of milestones and controls	up to 2 marks
	Explain strategy	up to 2 marks
	Allocate responsibilities and accountability	up to 2 marks
	Be prepared for every eventuality	up to 2 marks
	Involvement of senior management	up to 2 marks
		Maximum 8 marks
		Total 20 marks

Part (a)

REPORT

To: Board of Directors
From: Jeannette Singh, Strategic Policy Director
Date: December 200X
Subject: Corporate strategy

Introduction

In recent years, Rameses International has faced strong opposition from other companies providing a similar service and in particular from manufacturing companies who resent our re-selling their products at a profit. Over the last year, we have tried a **number of different strategies** to try to minimise these problems, including seeking a wider range of products from a wider supplier base, entering collaborative agreements with suppliers and attempting to operate in additional markets. None of these strategies have worked and the purpose of this brief report is to outline the major reasons for these strategies not being successful.

One major reason for the lack of success of our chosen strategies has been their **number and variety**. This has led to extensive change within the company in a very short period of time and, in consequence, confusion about priorities and inattention to our core business.

In attempting to carry out so many changes at once, it is likely that we may have **alienated many of our stakeholders**, including employees and suppliers. For a change of strategy to be successful, it is important that the stakeholders concerned are committed to the change and that they understand the reasons and justifications for them.

The array of changes indicates a **lack of prioritisation and planning** and has been overly reactive to perceived problems. We appear to be trying to change everything in the hope of getting it right without carrying out appropriate planning and ensuring appropriate resource utilisation. This may be as a result of an **over-rigid organisational structure**; we need to ask ourselves whether a more flexible structure would enable us to respond more appropriately to market changes.

My final point is that we **failed to anticipate our competitors' reaction** to the strategic changes we made; we have made it easier for them to react effectively by our own **confused execution of our chosen strategies**.

Conclusion

In order to improve our market position and our long-term profitability, it is important that there is **strong, committed and professional leadership** and a more effective implementation of any chosen strategic changes.

Part (b)

Issues for successful strategy implementation

In order to ensure that a strategy is successfully implemented a number of issues have to be considered.

Firstly, as mentioned earlier, it is vital that affected **stakeholders** are involved, informed and committed to the strategy. Staff must be aware of their responsibilities and the parts that they must play in the implementation of the strategy. It is also extremely important that management do not lose sight or control of core business operations.

Leadership must come from the top of the business and it is vital that the senior management are involved in any strategy implementation. Senior management are primarily concerned with the identification, evaluation and selection of strategies, but their involvement must not end there.

There must also be **constant monitoring** of progress and implementation to ensure that the new strategy continues to meet the objectives of the organisation, that it is not too costly and that any remedial action required is taken. Management must be aware that strategic change is unlikely to proceed smoothly and must be prepared to implement contingency plans if necessary.

37 John Hudson

Text reference. The topics mentioned in this answer are discussed in Chapter 9 of your BPP Study Text.

Top tips. A common problem for candidates in the Paper 3.5 examination is the **application** of their theoretical knowledge to question scenarios. In this answer we show in *italics* those parts that constitute application of theory to the specific problems represented by the scenario.

Marking scheme

		Marks
(a)	Definition of project team/matrix structure	up to 2
	Benefits of such a structure	up to 1½ for each point made
	Increased integration	
	More responsive and flexible teams	
	No dominance of a functional area	
	Staff more involved and motivated	
	Good general management training	
	Problems with the structure	up to 1½ for each point made
	Dilution of priorities	
	Conflict and confusion in reporting	
	Complexity of administration	
	Slower decision making	
	Difficult allocation of responsibility	
		Maximum 10 marks
(b)	Influencing factors in organisational design	up to 2 for each point made
	Internal	
	Past performance	
	Type of employee	
	Change in objectives	
	Change in strategies	
	Change in ownership (organisation culture)	
	External	
	Ideology	
	Change in knowledge	
	Change in economic circumstances	
	Change in socio-demographic factors	
		Maximum 10 marks
		Total 20 marks

Part (a)

Easy marks. The setting for this question points you fairly clearly towards the matrix and project team approaches. When you get a question that gives you this kind of steer, accept it gratefully and don't waste time trying to think of something different, even if you think you can. However, relevant comment on suitability and potential problems is clearly called for.

ALG Technology might consider a **matrix** *form of organisation structure.* This provides control of activities that overlap functional boundaries, while at the same time maintaining functional departmentation. Senior managers are appointed to oversee activities that span functional boundaries. Lateral lines of communication and authority are thus superimposed on the functional departmental structure. A common example is the appointment of marketing managers with responsibility for all aspects of the marketing of a particular product group. *In ALG, for instance, a manager might be appointed to draw together all the design, manufacturing, financial and promotion efforts relating to the fighter avionics business.*

A related approach is **project team** organisation. This is very similar to matrix management, but is based on *ad hoc* cross-functional teams with responsibility for a defined project. *This might be more appropriate for ALG, since the company is effectively working on specific projects with a defined life cycle rather than steady-state production.* Project team organisation allows for the co-ordination of interdisciplinary effort, with experts in different functions appointed to the team while retaining membership and status within their own functional department.

Advantages of a cross-disciplinary structure

(a) It offers greater **flexibility**. This applies both to **people,** as employees adapt more quickly to a new challenge or new task, and develop an attitude which is geared to accepting change; and to **task and structure**, as the matrix may be short-term (as with project teams) or readily amended (eg a new product manager can be introduced by superimposing his tasks on those of the existing functional managers). *Flexibility should facilitate efficient operations at ALG by helping it to cope with the complexity of the technology it is deploying and the dynamism of the markets in which it operates.*

(b) It provides for **inter-disciplinary co-operation** and a mixing of skills and expertise. This should improve **communication** within the organisation and give ALG the **multiple orientation** it needs to integrate its key activities and keep functional specialists from becoming wrapped up in their own concerns.

(c) It provides a **structure for allocating responsibility to managers for end-results**. A product manager is responsible for product profitability, and a project leader is responsible for ensuring that the task is completed. *This also will promote the integration of effort that ALG needs.*

Disadvantages of a cross-disciplinary structure

(a) Dual authority threatens a **conflict** between managers. It is important that the authority of superiors should not overlap and areas of responsibility must be clearly defined. *John Hudson must ensure that subordinates know to which of their superiors they are responsible for each aspect of their duties.*

(b) One individual with two or more bosses is more likely to suffer **role stress** at work. *This is another problem for senior management at ALG to monitor.*

(c) It is likely to be more **costly**, since additional managers are appointed that would not be required in a simple structure of functional departmentation. *ALG is already quite lean, so it may be able to absorb these costs without great difficulty.*

(d) It may be difficult for managers **to accept**. It is possible that managers will feel that their authority is being eroded. Similarly, it requires consensus and agreement which may **slow down** decision-making. *John Hudson must monitor managerial attitudes to ensure that managerial conservatism does not seize opportunities to make any new approach fail.*

Part (b)

> **Top tips**. The Examiner's model answer was based on an analysis of factors affecting structure into two categories: internal and external. In our answer, we have followed the analysis we use in the BPP Study Manual. This is a good example of how there is likely to be more than one possible approach to answering many questions in Paper 3.5.

Organisational structure determines to how work is co-ordinated, how decisions are taken, how work and information flow through the organisation. It is thus a fundamental aspect of management. We can identify a range of possible influences on organisation structure.

Age. The older the organisation, the more formalised its behaviour is likely to be. When work is repeated it is easily formalised and standardised. In a similar way, structure is likely to reflects the age of the **industry's** foundation.

Size and growth. The larger the organisation, the **more elaborate** its structure is likely to be, the larger the average size of the units within it and the more formalised its behaviour (for consistency).

Tasks and technology. The complexity of the task and the technology in use tends to be reflected in the structure of the organisation. In particular, the more sophisticated the technology in use, the more elaborate and professional the support staff will be. **Information technology** has a profound effect on organisation structure, especially with regard to delayering. *This point is clearly very relevant to ALG, working as it does in advanced electronics. No doubt it has significant numbers of staff whose work relates to the maintenance of complex design and production equipment. ALG's products also incorporate very high technology and this will have a similar effect.*

Co-ordination. Mutual adjustment, direct supervision and standardisation all have consequences for structure. It is certain that. Any requirement for close supervision has an immediate effect on structure, usually leading to the establishment of an element of technostructure. Similarly, the more an organisation is subject to **external control**, for example, by government or a holding company, the more centralised and formalised its structure is likely to be. *It is certain that ALG employs highly skilled workers, so there is likely to be a large element of mutual adjustment in the co-ordination of their work. This may reduce the role of the technostructure*

Geographic dispersion. An organisation with several sites will have a different organisation structure from one located in one place.

Fashion. Bureaucracies are deeply unfashionable, but they are often the best at doing of work repetitive work where there is a high need for exactness of execution.

Strategy. *Chandler* found that a strategy of diversification is likely to lead to a decentralised structure. His detailed historical study of four major US corporations*: Du Pont, General Motors, Standard Oil of New Jersey* and *Sears Roebuck* found that all four had evolved a decentralised structure based on operating divisions, though by different routes. The creation of the multi-unit structures was a logical managerial response to the problems associated with strategies that create very large organisations. These tend to revolve around the need for control that does not inhibit creativity and the need for rational allocation of resources. *ALG has not yet reached the scale of operation that makes a multi-unit structure desirable, though John Hudson has contemplated such an approach. The advantage it would offer is the motivating effect of autonomy on the division heads.*

38 Pamper Products

Text reference. The topics mentioned in this answer are discussed in Chapter 16 of your BPP Study Text.

Top tips. As a general rule, it is necessary to address the question scenario in an answer, However, sometimes this is not possible, as is the case in Part (a) of this question. This is unusual, but it can happen. You must take care with your reading and understanding of questions to be sure that you do not assume this is the case when it is not. A good principle would be to assume that the scenario will feature in every answer and to be very dubious if it seems to you in a particular case that it does not.

Part (a)

There have been many attempts to find a methodology to predict corporate decline, or companies at risk of decline, including **Z scores** and *Argenti's* **A score**. This interest in the subject means that the main reasons for corporate decline are heavily documented. There are many reasons why companies fail and in most cases it will be due to a combination of such reasons.

Sales and profitability

Declining profitability is a clear reason for the eventual failure of a company. A decline in profits is not always accompanied by a decrease in sales volume, but this is often the case. As sales fall, the same level of fixed costs must be paid from reduced revenue, inevitably reducing profits. Also, if a company expects increases in sales volume that do not materialize, this will also cut profits if the company has invested further, in staff, plant and stocks, for example. An important implication of this for Pamper products is that a close eye must be kept on costs of all kinds. The need to seek out low cost suppliers may be of particular relevance, considering the past policy of only dealing with a few of those available.

Gearing and liquidity

As a company's borrowing increases, so do the costs of servicing loans. This can significantly increase the risk of the company and in extreme cases if the loans or debentures are not serviced they could be called in and the company put into liquidation. The Sample brothers have borrowed extensively, so they should take great care over this. Allied to this problem is that of a decrease in liquidity. A company can still be profitable but if it cannot pay its debts as they fall due then eventually it will fail. One particular problem here is where seemingly growing companies fall foul of overtrading. This occurs when sales are increasing and therefore so are stock holding costs and payments to suppliers but these costs are not being matched in cash terms by money received from debtors. Pamper products has expanded rapidly and has avoided this problem so far, but the brothers must continue to take care of their cashflow.

Suppliers and customers

A company can appear to be successful, but if it is over-reliant on a few suppliers or customers then the failure of one of these parties can have a disastrous knock-on effect. If a principal supplier fails, this will have a major effect on the ability of the company to supply its own customers. The loss of a major customer means a significant fall in turnover and cashflow. This calls for close management attention.

Management

So far we have considered largely financial reasons for company failure; however, Argenti argues that many causes of corporate failure are due to poor management. For example, an autocratic Chief Executive, a passive board of directors and a weak Finance Director is a common scenario of corporate failure. Finally, there is always the issue of complacence. If a company is seemingly successful, then senior management may become complacent about performance, growth and innovation, which will eventually lead to a loss of market share and declining revenues. The implications for Pamper Products are obvious.

Part (b)

> **Text reference.** The topics mentioned in this answer are discussed in Chapter 16 of your BPP Study Text.
>
> **Top tips.** The balanced scorecard is a useful and popular model, both in the exam and in the real world. Make sure you have learned and understood the nature of the four perspectives and expect to have to suggest relevant possible measures for each one.
>
> **Easy marks.** The balanced score card should be one of those models you know by heart. Simply identifying and briefly explaining the four perspectives should score you two marks.

A **balanced scorecard** considers performance indicators for a business within four **perspectives**:

- The financial perspective
- The customer perspective
- The internal business perspective
- The innovation and learning perspective

While these four categories may be regarded as widely applicable, it is important to understand that **different organizations will require different measures** for each if the approach is to be useful. For example, a woodworking business would almost certainly be very concerned about the safe use of its machinery: this would hardly be a topic of concern for most financial service businesses, however.

Product safety is likely to be an important concern for Pamper Products, dealing as it does in cosmetics.

As David is quite happy with the financial performance measures we will concentrate on the other three perspectives.

Customer perspective

Performance measures in this are should measure how satisfied the customers are with the **quality of product** and **level of service** provided by the company. Possible performance measures might include:

- Sales returns levels
- Percentage of customers who do not return for repeat business
- Levels of customer complaints

Internal business perspective

This perspective is concerned with the efficiency of the company's internal systems. Possible performance measures might include:

- Percentage of products returned to suppliers
- Percentage of sales of products exclusive to Pamper Products
- Labour turnover levels
- Total number of suppliers

Innovation and learning perspective

This perspective is concerned with how the business is developing and moving forward, both in its products and in its methods. Possible performance measures might include:

- Time taken to introduce a new product
- Percentage of sales revenue generated by products introduced within the last year
- Extent of management training undertaken

39 Sykes Engineering

Marking scheme

		Marks
(a)	Separation of functions of MD and Chairman	up to 3 marks
	Role of non executive directors	up to 2 marks
	Management culture with reference to harassment, bribery	up to 3 marks
	Role of auditors	up to 2 marks
	Role of financial institutions	up to 2 marks
		Maximum 10 marks
(b)	Need for use of	up to 1 mark each
	Participation	
	Education	
	Communication	
	Negotiation	
	Need for good leadership	up to 2 marks
	Use of appropriate change model – ie Lewin	up to 6 marks
		Maximum 10 marks
		Total 20 marks

Part (a)

> **Text reference.** The topics mentioned in this answer are discussed in Chapter 4 of your BPP Study Text.
>
> **Top tips.** Take a very high moral stance on any matters of corporate governance and business ethics and do not hesitate to condemn dubious practices. Note, however, that you do not have to endorse the stakeholder view of the corporation if you do not want to: that is not an ethical matter.
>
> **Examiner's comments.** This requirement was disappointingly answered, with too many candidates putting their trust in a mission statement as an ethical cure-all.

The situation at Sykes Engineering Group is extremely worrying and action should have been taken much earlier to prevent its arising.

Corporate governance

Too much power is **concentrated in one person**, Jerome Sykes. Corporate governance reports have recommended that the roles of Chairman and Managing Director should be held by two different people: this is now a requirement of the London Stock Exchange Combined Code. Also, there should be a strong and independent body of non-executive directors on the board. The role of these non-executive directors should have been to question any dubious policies or actions at an early stage. They would also take charge of executive directors' pay and benefits packages and auditor liaison.

Organisational culture

The autocratic behaviour of Jerome Sykes has influenced the culture of the whole organisation and resulted in sexual and racial harassment. His involvement at all levels of decision-making should have been prevented by a strong organisational hierarchy and control system, with a key role for supervisory management. The non-executive directors would have played an important role here.

Corruption

Bribery is a more difficult issue since it is difficult to define and standards vary from country to country. Nevertheless, a reputation for corrupt practices will seriously harm the reputation of the company. Control procedures and clear guidelines should be in place to prevent corruption and immoral business practice.

Role of the auditors and institutional shareholders

It is surprising that a publicly quoted company has been allowed by the auditors and the institutional shareholders to deteriorate to this extent without intervention. They have a duty to monitor the activities of the company and take action if unacceptable activities are taking place. The auditors, in particular, should have been aware of what was happening and should have taken proper steps.

Part (b)

> **Text reference.** The topics mentioned in this answer are discussed in Chapter 11 of your BPP Study Text.
>
> **Top tips.** This requirement places a heavy reliance on knowledge of models of the change process, but you must not answer in a vacuum – try to refer back to Sykes Engineering whenever you can.
>
> **Examiner's comments.** This part of the question was popular and produced good answers.

The culture changes that are needed at Sykes Engineering are so extensive as to amount to **transformation**. People within the organisation are likely to resist change, so it will not be achieved immediately. Resistance to change arises when behaviour has become embedded: people will be uncertain, fearful, lacking in confidence and suffer a sense of dissonance between the old certainties and the new requirements. However, a range of strategies can be used to facilitate acceptance of necessary changes.

A common-sense approach suggests that participation, education, communication and negotiation will be needed. Involving employees in the decision-making process will increase motivation and help to reduce resistance, whilst education and communication will help them to understand why change is needed. It will also be important to involve management at all levels and have a clear, defined process for change.

Several change process models could be used.

Systems intervention strategy involves the three stages of diagnosis, design and implementation. It is a logical approach and is iterative in nature, reflecting the complexity of human behaviour.

Gemini 4Rs framework involves reframing, restructuring, revitalising and renewal and aims to cover all the important components of the organisation's identity.

Lewin/Schein three stage approach

The three phases are unfreeze, change and refreeze. **Unfreeze** is the most difficult stage of the process, since it is during this phase that all of the reluctance and fear outlined above has to be broken down. It concerned mainly with selling the change by giving people appropriate motives to accept change. The **change** phase is mainly concerned with identifying what the new, desirable behaviour should be, communicating it and encouraging individuals and groups to accept it. The **refreeze** phase consolidates the new behaviour by means of positive and negative reinforcement: praise, reward and sanctions are used here.

The key aspect of implementation of change in Sykes Engineering Group will be a **change in leadership**. It seems inevitable that a new managing director will have to be appointed in order to drive through the necessary changes and provide a new image and direction for the company.

40 Question with analysis: Service performance

Text reference. The topics mentioned in this answer are discussed in Chapter 16 of your BPP Study Text.

Top tips. This question deals with core syllabus ideas. Questions like this tend to tempt candidates to concentrate on explaining the theory at the expense of applying it to the given scenario. You must always relate your answer to the circumstances described in the question if you are to score well – theory alone is not enough. Here, all that was needed was some reasonably scenario-related examples.

Easy marks. Any question on performance management is likely to be amenable to an answer using the balanced score card and explaining the framework should be worth a couple of marks.

Examiner's comments. While most candidates were able to discuss the balanced scorecard adequately in part (a) far too many failed to apply the theory to the facts of the scenario. In part (b), many candidates seemed not to understand the nature of a critical success factor. Few answers were relevant to the circumstances of a holiday company.

ANSWERS

		Marks
(a)	Performance indicators – consideration of Kaplan's balanced scorecard	up to 2
	Customer perspectives	up to 5
	Internal business perspectives	up to 4
	Innovative perspectives	up to 2
	Maximum for section (a) 10 marks	
(b)	Critical success factors	
	Brand name	up to 2
	Financial controls	up to 2
	Administrative infrastructure	up to 3
	Product portfolio	up to 2
	Good brochure	up to 2
	Retail coverage	up to 2
	Maximum for section (b) 10 marks	
	Total 20 marks	

Part (a)

Performance indicators

It is clear from the information provided that Sun and Sand Travel Ltd has **sacrificed quality and customer service** in order to **compete exclusively on price**. The current unwelcome media comment and fall in bookings show that this is not a good strategy, even in the short term. The continuing longer-term fall in profitability points to the same conclusion. Customers clearly require higher standards from the company, even if it continues to make low prices its main value proposition.

Relying on a single measure of performance, such as profit or ROI, is now widely considered inadvisable, since it tends to produce just the effect Sun and Sand Travel Limited (SSTL) is now experiencing. A widely used technique is *Kaplan and Norton's* **balanced scorecard** approach. This uses four 'perspectives' from which the performance of an organisation should be measured:

- The financial perspective
- The customer perspective
- The internal business perspective
- The innovation and learning perspective

Past practice at SSTL has been to concentrate on the financial perspective, but even this has been confined to a single measure. Other financial measures that are likely to be relevant to a service business are those relating to gearing, cash flow, overheads and product costs.

Customer perspective

In a service industry such as travel, **customer satisfaction** is vital and it is this aspect that must be considered. In particular the three problem areas in the scenario must be addressed – poor accommodation, flight delays, changes in travel time. Possible performance indicators include the following:

- Number of complaints from customers
- Percentage of flights delayed
- Average flight delay time
- Number of schedule changes as a percentage of total holidays
- Number of repeat purchases of holidays
- Number of referrals from satisfied customers

210

LEARNING MEDIA

Internal business perspective

This perspective deals with the efficiency of important internal systems and operations. The question to be answered is: what processes must the business perform well in order to deliver customer satisfaction? Potential performance indicators include:

- Time taken to deal with complaints
- Time taken to process a holiday order
- Number of errors in booking procedures
- Number of queries satisfactorily resolved

Innovation and learning perspective

This perspective measures the rate and success of innovation in the organisation. This is likely to be particularly important for a holiday business. The products are high value shopping goods; purchase decisions are subject to detailed consideration and influenced by fashion; and there is likely to be considerable competitive advantage to be gained from offering new destinations and holiday activities. Possible performance indicators include:

- Rate of introduction of new destinations
- Percentage of sales from new destinations compared to standard destinations
- Availability of new or improved accommodation and activities

Adoption of a multi-perspective approach is probably the key to improving SSLT's overall performance and moving it towards a position of improved long-term viability.

Part (b)

Critical success factors

In this market segment there are a number of factors that might be viewed as critical to business success.

People

In a service industry such as this, good relations with customers are vital: this appears to have been an area where the company has not been succeeding well in the past. The quality and effectiveness of the **holiday representatives** in the resorts is extremely important in this area. In most cases if a problem can be sorted out on the spot and at the time by the holiday that they establish and maintain good relationships with chosen suppliers they feel they can trust, since they must **hand over responsibility** for satisfying their customers to them. Good **negotiating skills** will contribute to building a proper relationship and ensure that they get the best deals for their customers.

Administrative skills

The successful administration of thousands of holidays in dozens of resorts using a variety of suppliers must present complex administrative problems. The staff involved must have both the skills required and the dedication to use them effectively: what seems like a minor problem when viewed from an office in the home country may make **the difference between a successful holiday and a disaster**, from the customer's point of view.

Product portfolio

Although many customers may wish to return to the same resort each year, an increasing number of customers wish to try **new, exciting adventures**. Therefore, the company must ensure that as well as old favourites it is constantly updating its portfolio with new holidays.

Financial controls

The holiday business has **low profit margins** because of intense competition; these must be protected by sound internal financial controls.

41 Excalibur Sportswear

Top tips. A common problem for candidates in the Paper 3.5 examination is the **application** of their theoretical knowledge to question scenarios. In this answer we show in *italics* those parts that constitute application of theory to the specific problems represented by the scenario.

		Marks
(a)	Reasons for going international and possibly global and applied to Excalibur Customer Company Competitor Currency Country	up to 3 for each point
		Maximum 12 marks
(b)	Recognition of increasing risk and commitment linked with control examples to relate to Excalibur	
		Maximum 8 marks **Total 20 marks**

Part (a)

Text reference. The topics mentioned in this answer are discussed in Chapter 17 of your BPP Study Text.

Easy marks. This first part of this question is best answered using *Ohmae's* **5Cs** model; indeed, the Examiner's own suggested solution is based on this model. Unfortunately, this is a fairly complex theory: the 5Cs themselves do not really give much clue as to what the model is about. On the other hand, if you learn this important theory and a suitable question comes up, you should find it easy to score well. The essence of the theory is given in our answer.

Ohmae suggests that companies *such as Excalibur Sportswear* move towards overseas marketing and eventually to globalisation for five reasons.

(a) **Customers**. Some market segments exhibit a degree of **convergence** across regions and even across the planet. This is particularly noticeable among the young and fashion-conscious and others who are easily persuaded of the importance of major brand names to their personal fulfilment and happiness. *Excalibur Sportswear is operating in such a market segment: its products are well known throughout the world because of its endorsement by those who have achieved fame by being good at games.* Where such transnational market segments exist, it is easy to sell to with a standardised product and brand.

(b) **Company**. Selling globally is likely to bring significant **economies of scale**. In particular, Simon Smith will find that his necessarily heavy spending on promotion can be spread across a higher volume of sales, allowing him to increase his profitability or reduce his prices, whichever seems most appropriate. Similarly, when he increases the size of the orders he places with his suppliers, he will be able obtain lower prices, since increased manufacturing economies of scale are likely to arise.

(c) **Competition**. The effect of the first 2 factors above is that Excalibur Sportswear's competitors have higher turnover and probably higher revenue. Excalibur is driven by competitive pressure to follow them into the global market place. If it fails to do this, it's high costs will erode its ability to compete and may threaten its survival. Ohmae suggests that a further likely result of global competitive pressure is a degree of **strategic co-operation** between competitors. This is seen, for example, in the air travel industry, where co-operate to provide an increased number of travel options to their customers. Excalibur Sportswear may find it appropriate to share distribution systems with one or more competitors, for example.

(d) **Currency**. A company that is essentially based in one country and exports but exports to others has to deal with the problem of **varying exchange rates**. When costs arise mostly in the home country's currency but significant revenues arise in one or more foreign currencies, unfavourable shifts in exchange rates can be extremely damaging. A simple solution to this problem is to manufacture in the countries where sales are made. Costs and revenues are then to some extent matched in currency terms and exchange rate risk is reduced. *Excalibur Sportswear, may find this difficult to achieve, since its products are likely to be sourced in low wage economies but sold in richer countries whose customers will pay the high prices typical of this market.*

(e) **Country**. The company that manufactures and sells in countries across the globe is able to export both **absolute and comparative advantage**. Low wages, mentioned above, are one example of such advantage: cheap and readily available raw materials are another. *If Excalibur sets up its own overseas manufacturing and distribution facilities, it may also find that* local manufacturing status can confer important benefits of an essentially political or social nature. The governments of developing countries may place obstacles in the way of importers in order to defend their balances of payments and, equally, may assist foreign companies prepared to invest in local manufacture. Similarly, locally manufactured goods may be particularly attractive to customers in some markets and confer important selling advantages.

Part (b)

> **Text reference.** The topics mentioned in this answer are discussed in Chapter 8 of your BPP Study Text.
>
> **Top tips.** The Examiner makes the point in his suggested solution that generally, 'risk and resource commitment are positively correlated with control.' This is a very neat encapsulation of what can seem a rather paradoxical situation.

Simon Smith is concerned that expanding his operations by the use of further contract manufacturers and distributors might compromise both his ability to control his operations and the quality of his products. He has to face a dilemma: to achieve greater control of critical inputs into his operations he is contemplating setting up his own manufacturing and distributions operations. Inevitably, this will demand greater investment: greater control implies greater risk.

Generally speaking, any expansion of operations is likely to involve the commitment of extra resources and there fore the acceptance of greater risk. Exploitation of underused indivisible resources to their maximum capacity can limit capital expenditures, but it is almost inevitable that labour and consumable costs will rise.

In the case of Excalibur Sportswear, considerable capital will be required to set up manufacturing facilities. Premises and plant must be acquired, labour hired and raw materials and components purchased. All this must be done before production commences. Part of the labour requirement will be for managers with relevant manufacturing expertise.

The creation of distribution networks is likely to be even more demanding. Vehicles, storage facilities and retail outlets will be needed and all will have to be of a high standard if the current brand image is to be maintained. Skilled management will be just as essential as in manufacturing.

Simon Smith himself and any core associates he has will also find that they have to commit much of their time to the management of these new ventures. We are not told whether the strategic apex of Excalibur Sportswear currently has any skill or experience in these matters: if they do not, they will have to acquire some very able senior managers.

Increased risk is likely to go hand with increased commitment of resources. Risk can be analysed into a number of categories.

- **Environmental risk**. In this category we may include risks inherent in the physical environment, such as earthquake and flooding; political risk, such as the risk of government expropriation; and economic risk arising from the nature of the business cycle. At the moment, Simon Smith holds much of this risk at arm's length, since it is largely absorbed by his manufacturing and distribution contractors. He would be much more exposed if he had extensive operations in a range of foreign countries.

- **Financial risk**. Simon Smith is contemplating using bank finance for his expansion. In the UK, this means an increase in gearing with all that implies for cash flow when times are hard. It also means an effective surrender of some autonomy through the acceptance of restrictive loan covenants.

- **Business risk**. It is not possible for Simon Smith to form a perfectly accurate forecast of the effect his contemplated expansion will have on business risk. There is much he does not know: how his competitors will react; how much of his time will be devoted to overseeing the management of his new facilities; whether he is expanding dangerously beyond his core competences; how his customers will react; and how his costs and revenues will develop.

It is clear, therefore, that the expansion Simon Smith is contemplating is likely to produce significant changes in both the risk profile of his business and the resources it requires. The drive to achieve greater control by doing more may prove impracticable for these reasons.

42 Question with analysis: Global marketing

Text reference. The topics mentioned in this answer are discussed in Chapter 17 of your BPP Study Text.

Top tips. The key to the standardisation/customisation problem is market conditions. We have built our answer to part (b) on the PEST framework. It might be worth considering the extent to which the five forces give some insight as well. For example, in an extremely competitive market, a standardised product simply might not work at all.

Easy marks. Global strategy is a topic that students often neglect. This is actually a very easy question, part (a) dealing with a very basic piece of theory and part (b) looking in a little more detail at its implications. However, you cannot write about even a simple matter if you have never heard of it. The part of the syllabus dealing with global strategy is important and should not be ignored.

Examiner's comments. This was the least popular of the questions in the exam. Part (a) was reasonably well done, but part (b) was generally disappointing.

Marking scheme

		Marks
(a)	Description of a polycentricity with cost implications of customisation	up to 6 marks
	Description of geocentricity balancing local with global needs	up to 6 marks
		Maximum 12 marks
(b)	Ability to see difference and benefits of standardisation versus customisation	up to 2 marks
	Application of SLEPT analysis (for each variable)	up to 2 marks
		Maximum 8 marks
		Total 20 marks

Part (a)

REPORT

To:	Board of Directors
From:	Adrian Green, Marketing Department
Date:	December 200X
Subject:	International business orientation

Introduction

Perlmutter, identified four different approaches, or **orientations**, in the management of international business: ethnocentrism, polycentrism, geocentrism and regiocentrism.

Ethnocentrism

Ethnocentrism is a **home country orientation**; the company focuses on its domestic market and views exporting as a secondary activity. Differences between countries are ignored and the same marketing mix is used both at home and abroad. There is no local market research or local customisation; opportunities in overseas markets may not be fully exploited as a result.

Polycentrism

The principle of the polycentric approach is that it is necessary to **adapt the marketing mix to each local environment**. Each country is viewed as having unique conditions and requirements and, as a result, the product and marketing effort are totally customised. This can lead to increases in turnover, but the process of customisation precludes economies of scale and profits are unlikely to increase in proportion.

Geocentrism

A geocentric approach is based upon the assumption that there are **both similarities and differences between various countries' markets**. It accepts that there are areas where customisation is required but also areas where standardisation does not affect customer satisfaction and can be employed in order to reduce costs. Typical areas suitable for standardisation are research and development, hidden parts of products, such as internal mechanisms and the development of a global brand. This approach **'thinks globally, but acts locally'**. Regiocentrism is very similar to geocentrism, but applied to regions rather than to the whole world.

Conclusion

The key difference between the orientations of polycentric companies and geocentric companies is in the **balance** of their approach to standardisation. A polycentric approach sees localisation and customisation as paramount, whereas a geocentric orientation recognises the need for a balance between customisation and standardisation.

Part (b)

As the experience of Kirkbride Weston Inc has shown, although customisation has its benefits in terms of increased volume of sales, it will tend to reduce profits as additional costs are incurred. Therefore, careful consideration should be given to whether customisation is actually necessary in a given export market. This is really an aspect of **environmental analysis**.

Political factors

Political or legal factors can make customisation necessary. Many regimes have made essentially political demands, such as the requirement in some Arab countries that no mention is made of Israel. Product safety regulations also vary from country to country and can require product modification. Some countries use regulation as a form of barrier to imports.

Economic factors

The economic condition of the country must be considered. In wealthy, advanced countries, a luxury version of a product may be required whereas in less wealthy countries only a basic version of the product would be purchased. Indigenous products also have an effect: if they are very specific to the market, importers may have to customise their own products.

Social factors

Differentiation may be required in order to satisfy local taste and social or cultural needs. Demographic factors may also be important here, such matters as family size and integration and the role of women being very important in some countries.

Technological factors

The technological infrastructure of the country may also need to be taken into consideration. If this infrastructure is basic then products may be required to be longer lasting and more durable as there is less opportunity for servicing or repair. Products may have to be customised to deal with issues such as climatic conditions and the impact of the transportation infrastructure.

43 Prestige Packaging

Text reference. The topics mentioned in this answer are discussed in Chapter 18 of your BPP Study Text.

Top tips. Do not ignore the explicit reference in both the scenario and the question to organic options. The firm has ruled out global expansion using either merger and acquisition or joint venture. In the actual exam, many candidates set out to describe the advantages and disadvantages of merger/acquisition and joint ventures – and did not gain any marks. For part (b), there is a distinction between the sort of information that is relevant, and the process by which the information is gained. The question is looking for good sources of information both inside and outside the company.

Examiner's comments. Part (a) was attempted well by most candidates, who showed a real ability to engage with the three organic options facing the firm in its desire to become a more global company. Advantages and disadvantages were clearly and succinctly described.

Part (b) asked for the information which would help in making a choice between the options. Often the information suggested by candidates was derived from a SLEPT analysis, rather than the information to enable a choice to be made. Good candidates were able relate the information needed to the options being considered, and again showed the ability to link their answer to the scenario

Marking scheme

		Marks
(a)	**Advantages/disadvantages of foreign sales office:**	up to 5

       Under Prestige Packaging's control
       Relatively low risk strategy
       Uses European learning and experience
       but
       Slower means of accessing desired markets
       Staffing issues
       Possible resistance by host government – little job creation
       Starting from scratch – getting company name known

Advantages/disadvantages of using agents/distributors   up to 5

Low cost strategy – agent's commission, distributor's profit

Uses networks reputation of local partner – gets over political barriers

Quicker entry

but

Higher dependency on partner performance

Possible divided loyalties

Advantages/disadvantages of wholly owned manufacturing operation   up to 5

May access low cost labour

Politically may be preferred – more job creation and inward investment

Quality under company's control

but

Slower and riskier option

Quality standards may take time to achieve

Transfer pricing issue

Repatriation of profits

Staffing issues – local v expatriate management   **Maximum 12 marks**

(b)   **Sources of information**   up to 2 per point

Internal information – European experience

Primary v secondary sources of information – including commissioned research and Government data

Costs v benefits of information

Learning from others – including potential agents and distributors

Competitor information

Maximum 8 marks

Total 20 marks

Part (a)

Companies can grow **organically** (via internal development), building up their own products and developing their own market. This is the primary method of growth for many companies. Some form of organic growth needs to be chosen by Prestige Packaging: the choice will depend upon the prevailing attitude to **risk**, the **timescale** available and the **opportunities** for growth that each option creates. The preferred strategy should reflect the **long-term goals** of the company. Furthermore, each option will affect the structure and processes within the company, and will have its own implications for staffing and management control.

Overseas sales office

Setting up a sales office in an international location probably involves the **least risk**. The company already has operations in Europe, and this learning may be transferable. Prestige Packaging will need to consider whether it sells to its customers directly, or through a local distributor, after developing its brand sufficiently. Suitable local staff will need to be recruited: but what level of expatriate management and control from head office will be needed?

Manufacturing operation

A manufacturing plant may be the only option in some countries, where governments might be looking for **inward investment and job creation**. Governments may impose **prohibitive tariffs** on imported products to protect local products and jobs.

A manufacturing facility involves **more commitment of finance and other resources**, and a significant alteration to the **value chain**. The required investment may in some cases be prohibitively expensive, and it may be difficult to find enough suitable local staff if there is no local partner in the operation. In Prestige Packaging's case, the **logistics** of getting the semi-finished product to the overseas manufacturing base will also need some thought. The plant may actually end up acting independently, which will affect the **level of control** that can be exercised by Prestige, and may end up increasing the **business risk**.

Quality control will be of importance. Involving another plant may add considerably to quality risks.

Agents and distributors

A major problem here is gaining the **motivation** and **full commitment** of local agents and distributors. They might be carrying the products of several firms, and will be tempted to commit themselves to those products that earn the best return. The question of exclusivity therefore becomes important, and this may be able to be negotiated by Prestige Packaging. **Agents** should be chosen for the **effectiveness of their business networks** and their access to major customers. Regular personal contact with the agent will enable both parties to set out their expectations and any problems that may arise. The provision of attractive commission and other financial incentives will only help the relationship.

A **distributor** typically is used where the company has a large number of small customers that it is trying to service. The distributor buys the product from the supplier and has a greater degree of freedom in deciding price and promotion. Controlling agents and distributors can be difficult, so it is important for Prestige Packaging to set out realistic performance expectations, and contracts should be clear to all parties involved.

Part (b)

The most important requirement of effective international operations is thorough analysis of the market in order to maintain continuous awareness of opportunities, threats and trends. Information can be gathered by Prestige Packaging on:

- Attractive new markets
- General packaging market trends
- Customer needs and preferences
- Competitor plans and strategies
- New product opportunities
- Political, legal, economic, social and technological trends

David should be particularly advised to gather information on the **political** risk associated with operations in different countries. As indicated in the list above, such information could be obtained via a PEST macro-environmental analysis. An industry analysis (such as Porter's Five Forces) would be an important tool in assessing the existing competition, suppliers and key customers. A key issue will be the availability of reliable secondary data, and its ability to generate specific information, but there is always the need to balance the **benefits** of information acquisition against the **costs** (time and money) involved.

44 Asia Invest

Part (a)

> **Text reference.** The topics mentioned in this answer are discussed in Chapter 17 of your BPP Study Text.
>
> **Top tips.** It is quite obvious that you do not have anything like enough information in the scenario to enable you to carry out an environmental analysis. What, then, does the Examiner mean by this curiously worded question?
>
> Judging by the suggested solution, we must conclude that we are required to explain our chosen analysis model in some detail and, using it, indicate the environmental factors that might make a country attractive to a motor manufacturer seeking to invest in new plant.
>
> Be prepared to interpret the Examiner's requirements in the light of what is feasible – but stay as relevant as you can, and **apply** theoretical knowledge to the details of the scenario to the greatest extent possible.
>
> The suggested solution uses *Porter's* **diamond** model as its basis, but the marking scheme also suggests that **PEST** might be used. The diamond is easier to link to a specific industry than is PEST, which is a much more general model of the macro-environment. However, the diamond is really a way to explain how, in the past, some nations have achieved competitive advantage in some industries: it offers few prescriptions for a less developed country wishing to attract investment in the future. It would be useful, therefore, to take a wider view of the environment and mention the possible benefits of government economic and industrial policies and their limitations.
>
> **Easy marks.** The wording of this question makes it difficult to find easy marks, but once you have chosen your model, explaining the basics should be worth a couple.

Marking scheme

		Marks
(a)	Porter's Diamond Model and/or a Macro-environmental/PEST analysis	up to 12
		Maximum 12 marks
(b)	Quality management, control and assurance	up to 6
	Japanese quality techniques	up to 4
		Maximum 8 marks
		Total 20 marks

Porter suggests that the degree of competitive advantage enjoyed by any given one a of nation's industries is determined by four groups of influences or conditions. Porter calls this the 'diamond'. This model can provide useful ideas for Salem Malik in his promotion of an attractive environment for investment.

Factor conditions

Factor conditions are a country's endowment of inputs to production and the efficiency with which they are deployed.

Porter distinguishes between **basic** and **advanced** factors.

(a) **Basic factors** are natural resources such as climate and semiskilled and unskilled labour. They are **unsustainable** as a source of national competitive advantage, since they are widely available.

(b) **Advanced factors** are associated with a well-developed scientific and technological infrastructure and include modern digital communications, highly educated people, university research laboratories and so on. Such factors are far more relevant to the creation of sustainable advantage and **government can encourage their development** through its economic and educational policies.

Demand conditions in the home market

Firms benefit from sophisticated and demanding buyers in a home market that puts pressure on them to **innovate** and provide goods and services of **high quality**. This influence is unlikely to be useful to Salem Malik since it really only applies to home-grown industries.

Nevertheless, in general environmental terms, a **high level of potential domestic demand** in a large developing country would be an important factor in attracting manufacturers, as is seen in the case of China.

Related and supporting industries

Competitive success in one industry is linked to success in related industries. Domestic suppliers are preferable to foreign suppliers, as they offer continuing close co-operation and co-ordination. The process of innovation is also enhanced when suppliers are of high quality, since information is transmitted rapidly and problems are solved by joint effort.

Modern motor assembly plants lie at the centre of a web of highly responsive and cost-conscious sub-contractors supplying a wide range of components and sub-assemblies. This means that a project to create a motor industry would have to proceed on a broad front. The arrival of a major manufacturer would not in itself be sufficient: all the supporting suppliers would have to be set up as well

Firm strategy, structure and rivalry

There are several important factors here.

Management style, industrial structure and basic strategy must not clash with local culture, expectations, financial practices and so on. Industries in different countries have different time horizons and funding needs while national capital markets may set different goals for performance. National attitudes to wealth are important. National culture affects industrial priorities through the relative prestige it allots to various industries and their leaders.

It may be appropriate for Salem Malik to recommend that the government work towards supporting local attitudes that go well with a modern economy and towards discouraging those that do not. On the other hand, it may feel that the price is too high. The King of Bhutan has said that his policies are aimed at improving gross national happiness, not gross national product.

Domestic rivalry is important for several reasons.

- There can be no special pleading about unfair foreign competition.
- With little domestic rivalry, firms are happy to rely on the home market.
- Tough domestic rivals teach a firm about competitive success.
- Domestic rivalry forces firms to compete on grounds other than basic factors.
- Each rival can try a different strategic approach.

Generally, the promotion of one or two **national champions** who can reap major economies of scale in the domestic market is likely to be undermined by vigorous domestic competition among high-performing companies.

Influencing the diamond

Governments cannot compete, only firms can do that. Governments can influence the context in which an industry operates and can create opportunities and pressures for innovation. Government policy should support the development of clusters of producers and suppliers and promote high standards of education, research and commercially relevant technologies.

Salem Malik must remember that the creation of competitive advantage can take many years.

Part (b)

In modern management theory, the word 'quality' when applied to a product or a service means **fitness for purpose**. However, in common parlance it means something closer to **excellence**: a 'quality' product is one that impresses rather than one that merely does what is expected of it.

Both of these aspects of quality are relevant to achieving competitive advantage in the motor industry.

Quality as fitness for purpose

Toyota is probably the world's most successful motor manufacturer. This is largely the result of the famous **Toyota manufacturing system**. This approach to manufacturing is commonly thought of in terms of **just in time**, but its main driving force is the **elimination of waste**. This has, for example, driven the modern approach to quality management: inspection, rectification and scrap do not create value, they consume it. Getting things right, first time, on purpose reduces costs and therefore allows a higher value market offering. The satisfactions the customer receives at the time of purchase are underlined by the subsequent reliability of the car. This was in considerable contrast to other manufacturers' products at the time Toyota were making their name.

A similar concern lies behind **value engineering**. It is just as wasteful to over-engineer a product as it to use a sub-standard one: the sub-standard component gives rise to warranty claims while the over-engineered one costs more than it need.

Another aspect of quality as fitness for purpose is **motor vehicle safety**. *Volvo* has succeeded in differentiating its products by emphasising their safety. This can only be done if the products are, in fact, as safe as they are claimed to be. Extensive independent testing would rapidly reveal any exaggerated claims. To achieve a high level of product safety requires the manufacturer to pursue appropriate quality standards continuously in all aspects of the business, from design through manufacturing to service operations.

Quality as excellence

Excellence itself provides **consumer satisfaction** beyond that provided by fitness for purpose. Furthermore, once a reputation for excellence is created it can be leveraged by appropriate marketing communications to provide even greater satisfaction in a variety of subtle ways involving status and self-image. In brief, this explains then success of *BMW*. Looked at objectively, there is little to choose in *actual* quality between a high specification Ford and a mid specification BMW. However, the BMW is far easier to sell. The problem for the manufacturer is to provide the correct degree of excellence at an appropriate cost.

45 Question with analysis: Lionel Cartwright

> **Top tips.** A common problem for candidates in the Paper 3.5 examination is the **application** of their theoretical knowledge to question scenarios. In this answer we show in *italics* those parts that constitute application of theory to the specific problems represented by the scenario.

Marking scheme

		Marks
(a)	Distinction between rational and emergent strategies	up to 3
	Reasons for emergent strategy:	
	Size of Lionel's company	up to 2
	Lionel's philosophical approach	up to 2
	Need to be flexible	up to 2
	Danger of being over-confident in planning process	up to 2
	Problems with emergent strategy:	
	No sense of corporate direction	up to 2
	No consistency in action	up to 2
	Less support from financial institutions	up to 2
	Reduced opportunity for control	up to 2
	Fails to give employees sense of purpose	up to 2
		Maximum 15 marks
(b)	Current situation and analysis of data	up to 8
	Critical success factors:	
	Need for good promotion/strong reputation	up to 3
	Access to prime sites	up to 3
	Access to raw materials	up to 2
	Acquisition of operational efficiencies	up to 2
		Maximum 15 marks
(c)	SLEPT factors and marketing research	up to 3
	Customer knowledge	
	Traffic patterns	
	Food labelling legislation	
	Economic conditions	
	Technical/operational techniques	
	SWOT analysis	up to 3
	Competitive framework	up to 4
	Porter's five force model and/or Strategic Group Analysis	
		Maximum 10 marks
(d)	Advantages/problems of internal growth	up to 7
	Gain and safeguard knowledge	
	Maintain control	
	Less dependent upon others	
	No problems of confused management style	
	But	
	Slower to achieve results	
	No guarantees	
	Can be expensive if trying to cover all areas	

Advantages/problems of acquisition	up to 7
Rapid growth	
Access to markets and products (retail sites)	
Pre-emptive strike on competition	
But	
Expensive	
Risk of poor cultural fit	
Advantages/problems of franchise operations	up to 6
Quick	
Use other people's resources	
Increased motivation from franchisees	
But	
Conflict of interests	
Poor competence of franchisees	

Maximum 20 marks
Total 60 marks

Part (a)

Text reference. The topics mentioned in this answer are discussed in Chapters 1 and 2 of your BPP Study Text.

Top tips. It would be possible to take issue with the presumption that Lionel makes use of emergent strategies. Such strategies develop out of patterns of behaviour and *ad hoc* choices, perhaps made elsewhere in the organisation than at the strategic apex. Lionel's approach is more a kind of **freewheeling opportunism**. He spots an opportunity and then exploits it as best he can. No one else is involved and the process is as deliberate as he can make it within the limitations of his knowledge and experience.

Do not be tempted to take this approach! No matter how knowledgeable and relevant to the setting your answer may be, and despite the Examiner's clear statement that 'scope is given to markers to award marks for alternative approaches to a scenario', this would be a very dangerous thing to do, simply because it would be so **difficult to mark**. Indeed, a marker who is less clever than you might feel that you had failed to address the question requirements at all and award *nul points*.

This is a subtle but important point. At this level you are expected to be able to use good judgement; one of the areas where this is required lies in understanding the question requirements. It should be clear to you here that the Examiner wants you to talk about what Lionel does in contrast to what the rational model suggests. He does not want you to quibble about terminology.

In fact, in his own suggested solution, the Examiner talks about 'emergent or opportunistic strategy formulation' as though the two terms were interchangeable.

The rational approach to formulating strategy attempts to take into account all the factors that might bear on a business's strategic position by working through a series of linked processes. These commence with the definition of overall objectives and include consideration of the various aspects of the environment; assessment of the business's strengths, weaknesses and other characteristics; the generation and assessment of possible courses of action; and the establishment and operation of appropriate control mechanisms.

While exhaustive and logical, this approach is rather cumbersome and lacking in flexibility. As a result, it can become a recipe for rigidity, inhibiting the flow of strategic ideas. Typically, this occurs when too much faith is placed in the inevitability of the model's arriving at the only correct answer to the strategic problem. The assumption that there is a single acceptable route to a successful strategy tends to stifle invention and ignores the potential of hunch, expedient and opportunism.

A more flexible approach will exploit the potential of these factors, allowing strategy to develop or emerge in a less rigid fashion. *Such an approach is clearly more in Lionel's style. He has made a series of successful strategic decisions, largely, it would seem, without entering into any extensive planning procedure.*

It is fairly easy to discern why Lionel has adopted this approach to strategy. First, it is consistent with his self-image as an entrepreneur, quick to spot and seize profitable opportunities. His record of success in building up his capital must be a great satisfaction to him.

Connected with this is his apparent dislike of working in close co-operation with others. Lionel prefers to be sole master of his destiny, rather than one of a team; he has chosen to rely on his instincts.

He has not provided himself with the specialist advisers whose input would be necessary for a more considered approach. Indeed, he is probably the sort of person who would be rather bad at leading such a group.

So far Lionel has enjoyed success with his opportunistic approach but he should be aware that it has its disadvantages.

Any venture involving more than a few people in face-to-face contact with one another requires a degree of planning if it is to run smoothly. *Lionel's plans for expansion beyond his current 4 outlets will require the acquisition and integration of significant resources. Quite apart from the potential need to raise further finance, which will be difficult without a clear business plan, Lionel may find his* ad hoc *approach hampering his ability to expand smoothly.*

Another very important practical advantage of a planned, cohesive approach is that control becomes easier and more definite. *If Lionel is unsure of just what he can realistically expect to achieve, he will have little ability to assess success or failure, since he will have no objective yardstick.*

An allied problem over the longer term is that a clear vision of where he is going would allow Lionel to develop a depth and breadth of relevant knowledge and expertise. At the moment, he has no potential to develop his operations by learning from experience, except in the very widest sense. His experience in road haulage is unlikely to be very useful in sourcing high-quality fruits and vegetables, for example.

A final problem for Lionel to ponder is this: if he wishes to expand significantly, he will inevitably have to increase the number of his employees and eventually to hire at least a few with significant professional skills. His ability to attract, retain and work through these people is likely to depend in part on their having a clear idea of what they are supposed to be doing and where the organisation is going. So long as he is able to take all the decisions himself, the absence of a clear corporate plan will not matter so much; when significant delegation can no longer be avoided, it may seriously hamper his progress.

Part (b)

Text reference. The topics mentioned in this answer are discussed in Chapter 6 of your BPP Study Text.

Easy marks. Do be aware that there are really two linked requirements in this part of the question: to **analyse the data** and to consider **critical success factors**. An important aspect of examination technique arises here. The marking scheme for a question of this type is likely to offer a similar number of marks for the first, easier, part of the question as for the second, more difficult part. And this is what the marking scheme for this question actually does.

Therefore, even if you think you will have some difficulty talking convincingly about CSFs, you can still score important marks for the analysis, perhaps enough to achieve a 'pass' in this part of the question.

The message, as is so often the case, is do not be put off: get the easier marks first and, if necessary, press on to the easier marks in the next part of the question. You can either leave a decent space in your answer book so that you can come back to part (b), or you can continue it on a different page later. If you take this second course, you **must** label the gap at both ends! For example, 'Answer continued later' at the end of the first bit and 'Q1 part (b) continued' at the beginning of the second bit. Failure to do this will annoy the hard-pressed marker and reduce your chances of scoring well.

There is another, more subtle point about this part of the question. It asks you to identify missing critical success factors **from your analysis of the table**. In fact, the Examiner's suggested solution gives only one CSF that is identifiable from the table: operational efficiency. The others can only be obtained from reading the narrative information given above the table. This is another example of the Examiner's lack of precision in his use of English, similar to the one identified in part (a). You should not, therefore, hesitate to probe the boundaries of relevance when planning your answers in this exam. Do not rely on tenuous links, obviously, but do not omit material because a strict reading of the question would seem to rule it out. If it is reasonably relevant, put it in.

You will notice that all of our answer to this part is in italics: it is all application. This is inevitable with such a question; everything is specific to the scenario

Lionel's operation is much less profitable than similar enterprises in the USA. There are several reasons why this should be so.

To begin with, the typical US outlet has a much higher turnover than Lionel's four stores are achieving, though the cost of materials is identical. The gross profit margin must therefore be much higher; this is always a good point to start from.

The higher turnover per store in the US is presumably associated with the 25% higher number of customers served each week. It is noteworthy that this higher number of customers served is achieved despite much lower marketing costs.

The US stores also have the advantage of much lower rents, though the stores are only slightly smaller. Lionel has chosen expensive Central London sites, but the higher rents payable there do not seem to have been rewarded with higher throughput of customers.

It seems likely that the US outlets are more efficiently run that Lionel's stores. Service is much faster, they have almost twice the variety of product and they are open for much longer. Their stocks are 50% lower and their wastage is less than half that of Lionel's. These figures may be related to efficiencies of scale, as may the much lower allocation of general administrative overhead, which is only half that attributed to Lionel's stores.

The US stores are slightly smaller than the UK ones but employ half as many staff again, though total labour costs are the same. This may be attributable to the use of part-time workers in the US. In any event, it no doubt enhances the quality of the service provided to customers in the US, as shown by the extended opening hours and the much lower average waiting time.

We might suggest several critical success factors for Lionel's venture.

The first is the issue of **operational efficiency** *identified above. Lionel needs to both increase his gross profit and reduce his expenses. An increase in turnover may be available simply by staying open for longer, but this should not be undertaken if it would lead to an increase in total labour cost. Lionel should also look carefully at the speed with which his customers are served.*

The level of stocks and the wastage of materials should also be examined . Wastage may be associated with operator skill, or the lack of it. In any event, it is too high, especially as Lionel is finding it difficult to source high quality materials.

Lionel is aware that one of his main problems stems **from lack of scale***: his ability to secure reliable, high quality supplies of raw material is limited. We are told that it would be difficult for the existing outlets to increase turnover: expansion of the chain would bring its own problems, but it looks as though Lionel must go down this route if his venture is to prosper. A core competence must therefore be the ability to identify and obtain* **suitable sites** *for expansion.*

*A further problem relates to the limited scale of operations. Lionel has chosen to appeal to a youthful, affluent, status conscious market. This strategy must depend upon **effective promotion** of his products as fashionable lifestyle accessories. The current level of promotion seems high when compared with the US stores, but it may not, in fact, be high enough. If Lionel is to succeed, he must be prepared to spend heavily on creating an appropriate brand image in the minds of his target market, so that they are inclined to visit his outlets more frequently and in greater numbers.*

*We may make a final comment of Lionel's prospects. Despite his motivation and commercial agility, it does not seem that he deploys a high level of **commercial ability**. He has not planned this venture carefully enough, as is shown by his parlous supply position and failure to create a large enough initial market. Also, his ability to manage his operations efficiently seems limited. It may be that he would be better off cutting his losses and trying something else.*

Part (c)

> **Text reference.** The topics mentioned in this answer are discussed in Chapter 5 of your BPP Study Text.
>
> **Top tips**. This is an unusual question in that it invites you to talk about academic models. Do not fail to include proper application in your answer. Make your discussion of the models relevant to Lionel's situation.
>
> In addition to the models we mention below, it would also be possible to use a portfolio analysis approach, such as the GE Business Screen and, possibly, the value chain.
>
> Our answer to this part is also highly italicised, since the question demands a highly scenario-specific answer.

Lionel's planning for his new venture should really have started with a consideration of general environmental factors. He could then have focussed on the immediate competitive environment affecting his planned juice bars.

The **SLEPT** model is a good approach to the general environment.

Social aspects of the environment would be very important, because Lionel thinks he has identified a market segment whose motivation to buy is very lifestyle-driven. It would be important to establish the existence and extent of this market so that the outlets could be opened in the right places, an appropriate range of products offered and the difficult matter of pricing settled. Some secondary market research may have helped here. This could have been aimed at discovering the size of the potential market and its buying habits.

Legal matters have not proven to be a problem for Lionel so far, but there is no doubt that retailing a fresh food product has legal complications in the area of labelling and food hygiene. Lionel needs to have the rules on such matters at his fingertips.

Economic aspects of the project are related to its lifestyle nature. The prices charged for freshly prepared natural juice drinks sold in city centre outlets will inevitably be high. Lionel should consider the potential effect of an economic downturn on his target market in order to estimate his business's chances of surviving such an event.

Politics is unlikely to affect Lionel's venture except through any economic effect it may have.

Technology is likely to be very important to Lionel. The high level of wastage evident in his current operations may be connected with his arrangements for the storage and packaging of his raw materials and finished products. Also, he is likely to benefit from the installation of advanced point of-sale technology, both for accounting purposes and for sales analysis. It would therefore be appropriate for him to have a detailed knowledge of the state of the art of such systems.

*The output of the SLEPT analysis would have formed the input into a consideration of **opportunities and threats** (strengths and weaknesses) would be less important for a start up, though still relevant).*

Two other approaches are Porter's **five force** analysis and **strategic group** analysis.

Five force analysis

*It might have been difficult for Lionel to obtain any information about **potential new entrants** to his industry. However, a consideration of the remaining forces would have highlighted several areas worthy of research.*

*As mentioned above, Lionel's product is one of fashion or lifestyle and therefore subject to whims of taste. It will compete to some extent with other, different lifestyle products such as expensive sandwich bars, coffee shops and even miniaturised electronic gadgets. **Rivalry among existing firms** and **threat from substitute products** are thus factors to be reckoned with.*

*Connected with this is the attitude of Lionel's **customers**. They are affluent, sophisticated and, probably, fickle. Lionel already appreciates the need for subtlety in any promotion he undertakes; he must also be prepared for a swing in demand away from healthy juices and must keep his ear close to the ground in order to detect any such development as soon as it gets under way.*

***Bargaining power of suppliers** is obviously important to Lionel's business. He should have been able to foresee his present difficulty in obtaining reliable, high quality sources of supply: the growth in supermarket demand and the attitude of suppliers to volume are not problems that have sprung up overnight. That being the case, he should really have had a plan for his route to achieving his critical mass of 30 stores before setting up his business.*

Strategic group analysis

Strategic group analysis refines the broad, industry-wide perspective of the five forces model by considering groups of close competitors. Such groups may be expected to follow more-or-less similar strategies but there is often competitive advantage to be gained by establishing the gaps in coverage of such elements as product diversity, geographical coverage, distribution methods and market segment targeted. An important technique is the construction of two axis maps showing the relationships between these elements. *In Lionel's case we might anticipate that geography, price structure, products and target segment would be of particular interest.*

Part (d)

Text reference. The topics mentioned in this answer are discussed in Chapter 7 of your BPP Study Text.

Easy marks. Not surprisingly, the marking scheme for this part of the question allocates almost equal marks for the three parts. You must therefore apply the normal rule of examination technique and make sure that you divide your time more or less equally between them. No matter how wonderfully you write about internal growth and acquisition, if you say nothing about franchising you are only shooting for two thirds of the available marks.

Expansion is not merely desirable for Lionel's business, it is essential to its success and even its survival. He must achieve sufficient buying power to guarantee regular supplies of high quality raw materials. However, his options are constrained by his limited financial resources and his personal need to retain control.

Internal growth

*The great advantage of internal growth from Lionel's point of view would be that he would be able to retain **absolute personal control** over his company and maintain his freedom to act at his own discretion, subject only to the externally imposed demands of commercial survival. This would automatically preclude any possibility of **goal conflict** in the management of the venture and retain the opportunistic agility Lionel prizes.*

Another advantage of internal expansion is development and control of internally generated knowledge-based competitive advantage. *Lionel is not making use of any particularly advanced or rare technology, but he may develop **valuable market knowledge** over time.*

However, generating growth from retained profits is normally a slow process *and likely to be particularly so for Lionel, whose business is not particularly successful at the moment.* Also, there are limits to what the single entrepreneur can achieve. Many initially successful businesses **stagnate** when they reach the limit of size and complexity that one person can control.

Acquisition

Growth by acquisition is a very common strategy. It can be financed with loans since the assets to be obtained will keep the balance sheet healthy. It can provide a route to **very rapid expansion**, *which would be a major advantage for Lionel, considering his current problems with the supply of raw materials.*

The acquisition of a competing chain would give Lionel an **enhanced market presence**, *which would in itself provide a form of promotion, via the existence and style of the increased number of outlets. The potential enhanced positive cash flow would allow him to spend more on promotion generally. Also, he could spread his* **overheads** *over more outlets and possibly reduce his stocks while maintaining or increasing his* **purchase quantities**.

A final advantage of acquisition is that it can be a very satisfactory way of **eliminating a competitor**.

On the other hand, acquisition demands important cash resources. *Lionel would almost certainly have to borrow in order to make a significant acquisition and he may well find the terms of a large loan more restrictive than he would like. The* **financial** *risk of gearing up his business in this way might be more than he would care to undertake.*

Also, he would have to decide what to do about the management of his enlarged chain. If the expansion were significant, it might create a business that was larger than he could run alone. Would he wish to retain any of the existing managers in the acquired business, or would he wish to recruit his own people? We cannot know, but it is likely that it would take Lionel a little while at least to create systems and a culture that satisfied him.

Franchising

The essence of franchising is a **sharing** of responsibilities and assets *and this may be the main disadvantage from Lionel's point of view.*

If Lionel were to franchise further outlets, his franchisees would be expected to provide much of the **capital** *for fairly rapid expansion. It would be normal for the franchisees to be* **highly motivated**, *because of their personal financial stake in the success of the venture. They would also be likely to bring some local market knowledge to the venture and even experience of similar retail catering operations.*

However, the rate at which the expansion could take place would be entirely dependent upon Lionel's ability to find **suitable franchisees**. *Even the fairly simple operation of preparing and retailing fruit drinks would require skill and commitment. Potential problems loom in the area of* **corporate image** *in particular, this being so important to Lionel's market offering. Franchisees would have to be totally reliable in matters such as food hygiene, speed of service, opening hours and the appearance of staff and premises.*

Another potential problem with franchising is that, *as Lionel knows from his own experience*, the interests of franchisee and franchiser are not entirely identical. There is **scope for dispute** about such matters as pricing, the cost of supplies, the opening of new branches that might compete with established ones and payment for promotional campaigns.

46 Question with student answer: Bethesda Heights

Text reference. The topics mentioned in this answer are discussed in Chapter 4 of your BPP Study Text.

Top tips. Part (a) of this question is noteworthy for the way it combines ethical ideas with strategic analysis. As the Examiner has himself said, ethics is not going to go away: expect it to be integrated into the question this way, rather than being examined as a separate topic.

The key to answering this question is to identify the various stakeholder groups. Once you have done this you can identify their interests.

Examiner's comments. Parts (a) and (b) were answered competently, but parts (c) and (d) were not.

		Marks
(a)	Factors giving surgeons a powerful negotiating position	
	Scarcity of labour	up to 2
	Status	up to 2
	Single-mindedness and unity of purpose	up to 2
	Power and influence	up to 2
		Maximum 7 marks
	Arguments from other stakeholder groups	
	Patients	up to 3
	Local government	up to 3
	General medical and other staff	up to 3
	Local community	up to 3
		Maximum 8 marks
		Total for section (a) 15 marks
(b)	Problems being experienced by Bethesda	
	Reduced income	up to 3
	Increased costs	up to 3
	Low income from medical insurance	up to 3
	Poor operational efficiencies	
	Lower bed capacity usage	up to 2
	Higher mortality rates	up to 2
	Staff numbers higher	up to 2
	Re-admission rates higher	up to 2
	Less use of day surgery	up to 2
	Poorer ratio of out-patients to residential care	up to 2
		Maximum 14 marks
	Unlikely to solve the problems of Bethesda	
	Fewer beds	up to 3
	Increased costs of investment (scarce resource)	up to 3
	Does not address the real problems – falling revenue etc	up to 3
		Maximum 6 marks
		Total for section (b) 20 marks
(c)	Other strategies including evaluation	
	Improve internal efficiencies	up to 5
	Collaborative strategies	up to 5
	Use of generic strategies – focus differentiation etc	up to 7
		Maximum for section (c) 15 marks
(d)	Definition of social responsibility and its application to a hospital environment	up to 4
	Use of social responsibility in academic models	up to 5
	Stakeholders' objectives linked with social responsibility	up to 3
		Maximum for section (d) 10 marks
		Total 60 marks

Student answer

(a) Based on the Mendelow's matrix, a company should treat stakeholders according to their power & interests. Key players, those with high interest in the company & high power, are the most important & so their opinions prevail.

Senior medical staff is a key player for the Hospital, as the Hospital could not function without then, whereas this staff has no burdens to leave the Hospital if their needs are not met/opinion accepted. Their interest in the Hospital is significant as they longed to expand their power & influence.

However, investment in modern surgery could be a competitive advantage for the Hospital & enhance the Hospital's surgical reputation. Better representation could attract private healthcare patients & thus increase the Hospital's revenues. This would be viewed in a positive way by some other stakeholders including CEO of the Hospital, Mayor of the Coty going to cut back its funding & government not able to increase its funding

Better reputation itself would also be welcomed by the Mayor. Further, modern surgery centre would be appreciated by well off patients.

> The student fairly clearly states the surgeons' position in the matrix and therefore their level of influence as the question requires.

On the other hand, the Mayor group, government and CEO were against this investment as the Hospital is currently in a deficit and should stay in a deficit within next 3 years. Neither government nor Mayor is willing to cover increase of the Hospital costs (-) operational costs or capital investments. However, although power of both government & local council is high its interest in the Hospital is low. Therefore, the hospital preferred fulfilment of senior surgeons' staff.

> This paragraph has some good ideas but makes sweeping unexplained statements in terms of the level of power and interest of the government saying that the government and local council has low interest in the hospital with out explaining why the candidates thinks this is the case.

Local population is really interested in the Hospital but it has little power. Therefore, the Hospital just needs to keep them informed but may not have to follow their requirements. This group is even not likely to achieve more power in future even if not satisfied.

Employees of the Hospital have little power. This lask power results from he fact that they represent only general staff that is easy to replace & they are not supported by unions (if there is any) so far. Therefore the Hospital could afford to overlook their requirements although they showed interest in the efficient & effective hospital treatment of population that could not afford private insurance. This group can increase its influence in future if unions become involved or if high ranking doctors enters this group demanding not only for modern medical centre but also for modern & effective run of the whole Hospital.

> This is a good clear well explained paragraph which would score two marks. The points could have been made slightly more briefly to leave time for more points later.

The student starts well by identifying a key theorist to help provide ideas to answer the question. Many people make the mistake of overlong introductions which simply précis the scenario and therefore score few points. This has been avoided here

A series of subheading for each major stakeholder would have improved the ease of marking of the question and may have earned the candidate more marks.

The other groups could have stated that trade-off for these investment in surgical reputation is too low. Reduced number of beds will result in additional home visits & re-admission to the Hospital, i.e. in additional costs & potential problems with available beds. Longer waiting times can hurt the Hospital's general reputation & as well as insufficient treatment of the disadvantaged group.

The local government could argue that it could not finance the capital investment into surgical centre.

> The structure of the answer is reasonable as it works through the major stakeholders mentioned in the question stating the objectives and arguments of each.
> Overall this part of the answer would score a strong pass.

(b) Compared to neighbouring hospital, the BH Hospital has lower income from central & local government due to less population served & less work carried out. However, the most significant difference is in income from medical insurance. This is a result of bad reputation of the BH Hospital. The new surgical centre will attract more private-insured patients & increase BH Hospital's reputation. Thus it should help increase income from medical insurance.

The most important problem is mortality of the BH Hospital's patient. This should be decreased by the new surgical centre.

> This question is in two clear parts i.e. what is the problem and how will the high tech approach overcome this. In this paragraph the student is attempting to answer the parts of the question but does so with little explanation and therefore would score a maximum of one mark for this point.

Due to lower number of beds, the BH Hospital should concentrate on day surgery operations especially based on the number of these operations being approximately 5 times higher on the neighbouring hospital. This would also decrease costs related to tome patients spent in hospital. This is also supported by ratio outpatients to those committed the hospital that is managed but the neighbouring hospital as 5:2 compared to 5:51 in the BH hospital.

Another problem of BH Hospital is long waiting time. This is nearly, 3 times longer then in the neighbouring hospital and is a fact that discourages patients to visit BH Hospital. The new surgical centre could improve the significantly in respect to patients that are admitted to hospital for surgery and not other long-term healthcare treatment.

Although fixed as well as variable costs are lower in the BH Hospital, this indicates a problem with level of healthcare offered by the BH Hospital which is one of its main weaknesses. The new surgical centre would result in an increase of BH Hospitals costs, but, on the other hand, also in more attractive facility & more patients.

Overall, the key problem in the BH hospital is worse healthcare service. Improving it, the BH Hospital needs to increase the costs but, thanks to increased number of patients due to better reputation, it would increase the BH Hospitals income from grants & private medical insurance companies.

> Overall the volume of ideas here is too low for 20 marks and so this part of the question would be a borderline pass.

Again the candidate gets straight to the point of answering the question and avoids time wasting. A good point for this part of the question will pick out a clear difference in the numbers and then discuss why it is a problem to Bathesda hospital.

This point is quite well explained but only answers part of the requirement.

This is a good well explained point which answers the question set and so would score two marks.

ANSWERS

> This part of the answer gives a good volume of specific ideas but the overall answer lacks theoretical content and structure.

(c) Management assess committee could have concentrated on improval of the Hospital's efficiency & effectiveness via investing in modern facility overall, not specifically, to the surgical centre. This should improve the Hospital's reputation and attract more patients, including private healthcare patients. Such an investment could have been finances by a bank loan of local community loan/bonds.

Alternatively it could fiancé investment in new technology using leasing/ hire-purchase agreements.

> Many of these points are too brief and lack explanation.

Further, it could introduce special treatment programs that patients could partially cover themselves. This may include some alternative medicine programs, examination not covered by the insurance company or only covered over certain time or no/minimal waiting time (if it was not against the local medical legislation) or physiotherapy/occupational therapy that CEO wishes to withheld.

> The student has chosen not to use a theoretical approach to this question. This may mean that the volume of ideas generated may not be sufficient. However the points are well related to the scenario and specific to the situation.

To support treatments of the disadvantaged group of patients, it could (possibly together with the local government) set up a public collection or a foundation voluntary financed by the local community.

Alternatively, it could share some modern healthcare instrument/surgery rooms with other hospital. In such cases no one-one big investment would be required, waiting time & expenses & reputation of the Hospital may be improved. Although this could result in higher operational costs, these would arise only during the time then the hired technology was effectively used by the Hospital's patients.

> Overall this part of the answer would be a borderline pass.

(d) Hospitals, as not-for-profit-making organisations, should not only follow financial goals (such as cost reductions) but also, and primarily, the goals they were established for.

> This answer would have benefited from an introductory paragraph explaining the idea of social as opposed to corporate or individual responsibility. Look out for key terms in the requirement you can define at the start of an answer.

Therefore, they should try to provide public as well as private healthcare effectively & efficiently to as many patients as possible. They cannot afford to trade off decreased operational costs for incomplete treatment for patients (eg in case of reduced length time of patients in hospital) and further re-incurrence of illness of even worse stage. It cannot allow for complications of the illness to arise due to late admission to the Hospital or old-fashioned treatment in case of insufficient investment into modern technology.

> The above points are true but not explained and therefore miss out on valuable marks.

Hospital should not provide treatment exclusively (as is the case of a profit making organisation) to people who are able to pay for it & so is also social responsible for disadvantaged groups of patients.

As it is responsible to general, or at least local, population, it should be able to explain why its decisions introduced a disadvantage to socially disadvantaged people and if it was really unavoidable.

It should treat fairly both private as well as public healthcare patients as they deserve the same treatments regardless of the financial outcome. Otherwise it should be subjected to public criticism which should be reflected by government at all levels.

> This answer to part d is too short and lacks structure. It does not really answer the question set but makes a series of broad statements. Overall it would score a fail. This question is a fairly reasonable attempt by the student which due to a strong part a would have achieved a pass overall.

BPP answer

Part (a)

As in most organizations, within Bethesda Heights Hospital there are several **stakeholder groups**, each with different objectives, varying levels of power and differing degrees of willingness to involve themselves in the future strategy of the hospital. The senior medical staff stand out as having both power and the willingness to use it. Using the *Mendelow* matrix, which classifies stakeholders according to the extent of their power and their willingness to become involved, the senior medical staff are 'key players'. However, their use of their power is ethically questionable as they have threatened to withdraw their services to patients if their demands are not met.

The power of the senior medical group comes from both their status and their importance to the hospital. Consultant surgeons have been respected both for their high degree of professional skill and their dedication to their patients' interest. This respect gives them a degree of **referent power** and extends to their opinions generally, even in areas outside their professional expertise.

The senior medical staff have also exercised **resource power** in their threat to resign; the hospital cannot function without them. Their main power lies in their importance to the hospital which stems from the **scarcity of their skills**. In economic terms, the supply of senior medical staff is inelastic. Some of the staff in a hospital are more easily replaced than others. The administrative staff, cleaners, caterers and so on could easily be recruited from other sectors. Skilled staff, such as nurses, are more problematic but there is likely to be a steady supply of such staff if required. However, skilled specialist surgeons are in short supply and would be extremely difficult to replace. Without their skills the hospital could not operate at all. The surgeons have relied on this fact to put pressure on the Management Committee to agree to their strategy.

There are a number of other stakeholder groups in Bethesda: the administrators, the local politicians, the local population and the general medical staff. Each of these groups has its own potential strategies and arguments that they could have used to promote their objectives.

As far as the **administrators** are concerned, their aim is an efficiently run hospital with cuts in costs. The efficiency drive might not be in the best interests of patients as it is pointed out in the scenario that efficiency is not the same thing as effectiveness. However the **administrators'** strongest argument would be the **financial consequences of the surgeons' strategy**. The requirements of the surgeons' strategy are twofold. First, **substantial capital investment** would be required and as a consequential trade-off, there would be a **reduction in the number of beds** within the hospital. The hospital is currently forecasting a deficit of $75 million dollars in three years' time; if this deficit is not substantially improved, then the survival of the hospital must be in doubt. Not only would the capital investment further increase the deficit, but the reduction in the number of beds (and therefore treatments) will inevitably lead to less government funding and a further increase in the deficit. Many stakeholders in the hospital will be unwilling to acknowledge the primacy of financial considerations but with a reduction in revenue from funding it would seem unlikely that the hospital could survive.

The local **politicians** appear to have two **conflicting objectives**. They are anxious that the hospital should be kept open to service the medical needs of the city, but they also wish to cut back the hospital's funding in order to avoid increasing local taxes. They cannot have it both ways: **they must choose** between a properly funded hospital and tax cuts. As the objectives of this group are confused, it would be difficult for them to prepare any coherent arguments If the local politicians accept that it is necessary politically to keep the hospital open, then they can use the media to illustrate the dangers of the surgeons' approach, which will inevitably lead to fewer beds and less treatment for the local population.

The **local population** themselves are the current and potential patients of the hospital and it is in their interest that there should be no curtailment of the hospital's activities. However, even though they are a large group, they are unorganised and it is unlikely that they will be able to exert any significant influence.

The **general medical staff** have possibly the strongest argument on their side: the **ethical argument**. They are primarily concerned with the maintenance of an efficient and effective hospital for the local population who could not afford private medical insurance. This is a strong argument as it is clear that those with medical insurance have the neighbouring hospital to go to but those without would be severely disadvantaged without the Bethesda Hospital in something like its current form.

Part (b)

Problem areas

It is clear from the quantitative data provided that Bethesda is not run as well as its neighbour institution.

In terms of **income**, the main difference between the two hospitals, other than size (and therefore the amount of government income) is the **income from the medical insurance** sector. Not only is the neighbouring hospital medical insurance income over **three times** that of Bethesda, but it also increased by 5% over the last year, whereas that of Bethesda decreased by 17%. Funding from central and local government would appear to be higher per bed at Bethesda at $274, compared to $238 for the neighbouring hospital. This may be because the medical and surgical work carried out at Bethesda is more complex than at its neighbour, but we have no information to support this supposition.

There are some **areas of cost** that would appear to be beyond the power of the hospital to cut. The costs of labour, medical equipment, drugs and other variable inputs have increased at approximately the same rate in each hospital, indicating that the changes are due to market forces and **must be lived with**. However, the efficiency of the two hospitals does appear to be very different. In particular, the cost per bed at Bethesda is $357 compared to $322 at the neighbouring hospital.

Labour costs are obviously a significant cost in the hospital service; however, Bethesda would appear to be **over-staffed** compared to the other hospital. Not only is the number of staff per bed higher in Bethesda, but its staff numbers have increased since last year, while in the neighbouring hospital staff, numbers were cut.

There are a number of factors that will significantly affect patients' view of Bethesda. Seventeen percent of patients require re-admission, compared to just 9% in the other hospital; this could be caused in part by the **false economies** suggested by the administrative faction on the Management Committee. It could also be related to the time spent in hospital after an operation, which is only 7 days at Bethesda compared to 10 at the other hospital. More concerning are **waiting times** at Bethesda, which is **three times** as long as at the neighbouring hospital, and the **mortality rate** which is over **seven times** higher at Bethesda and increasing. It is, of course, entirely possible that the mortality figures are affected by the type of ailments dealt with at Bethesda, which may be of a more terminal nature than at the other hospital, but we do not have enough information to assess this.

There is obviously a **clear difference in strategy** between the medical treatment in the two hospitals, which may also have adversely affected the efficiency and profitability of Bethesda. The neighbouring hospital has increased the number of **operations that require no overnight stay** by 467%: the equivalent increase at Bethesda has been only 30%. Clearly, an operation that does not require a bed and an overnight stay will be less costly for the hospital than in-patient procedures; such an approach is likely to appeal to the medical insurers as it will be a cheaper option for them.

Similarly, the ratio of the number of patients dealt with as **outpatients** compared to those staying in hospital for one night or more has increased at the neighbouring hospital to 5:1 compared to a constant figure of just 3:1 at Bethesda. Treating outpatients is likely to be a less costly strategy, which although not ignored by Bethesda, does not appear to have been capitalised upon.

The **utilisation of capacity** at each hospital can also be considered from the data provided. For Bethesda with 350 beds, the potential number of bed nights each year is 127,750 (350 x 365 days). With an average stay of 7 nights per patient, this means that potentially 18,250 patients (127,750/7) could be treated in a year. In fact only 10,650 in-patients were treated, which is only 58% of full capacity. The similar figures for the neighbouring hospital indicate that this is operating at 76% capacity. Whereas it is impractical to consider 100% capacity within a hospital system, clearly Bethesda is lagging behind its competitor in this respect.

How the proposed strategy will address these problems

One of the main aims of the surgeons' strategy was to **attract private healthcare patients**. Although the neighbouring hospital is clearly working towards this aim, with substantially more medical insurance income than Bethesda, it must be noted that even at the neighbouring hospital the income from this sector is still only 37% of total income. At Bethesda, such income is significantly lower, currently standing at 16%; it would appear that government payments will remain the most significant element of income despite the surgeons' strategy.

Possibly even more significant in terms of income is the **trade off** for the surgeons' strategy in that the number of beds must be reduced. This will **reduce income** from both central and local government. It would appear unlikely that the move into the medical insurance sector could provide enough income to cover the lost government income and turn the hospital into a profitable venture, particularly considering the natural competition from the established neighbouring hospital. The strategy will also **further increase waiting time** for the non-privately funded patients. It is difficult to see how this will help the hospital.

This strategy will not obviously improve the efficiency of Bethesda or reduce costs. However, it could be argued that with a reduction in beds there could be a drive towards greater efficiency and certainly a reduction in staff numbers, which could serve to improve productivity.

Part (c)

> **Top tips**. This is where you review what you know about strategic options and see how they would fit at Bethesda. You must be logical here and not make irrelevant or impractical suggestions, such as turning the hospital into a hotel. Models are useful here: you will see that we have taken ideas from both *Porter* and *Ansoff*, as well as some simpler thoughts.

Other strategic options

When considering other strategic options open to the Management Committee, we must consider the pressing need in the short term at least to reduce the forecast deficit and improve both effectiveness and productivity. There are a number of strategies that could be considered.

Internal efficiency improvements

From analysis of the quantitative data provided, it is clear that Bethesda does not operate as efficiently as it might. A scheme to improve efficiency might start with a review of staffing requirements in order to improve the staff to bed ratios and costs per bed.

Product development

Analysis of the internal data has also indicated that the neighbouring hospital has made far greater progress with **day surgery**. This could be an area in which Bethesda could concentrate, as it is likely to be less costly and hence more attractive to the medical insurance market.

Similarly, Bethesda could move to increase its **outpatient treatments**: these which have remained static over the past two years in order to improve profitability.

Political pressure

One of the key issues for Bethesda is that its income is largely provided by central and local government. There are both moral and political issues here. The hospital could campaign for greater funding from local government, particularly as it is a hospital that clearly caters largely for individuals who cannot afford private medical insurance.

Focus strategies

A **focus strategy** could might be used by Bethesda, by concentrating on particular areas of healthcare. Such an approach might make better use of the scarce resources available and build up a strong reputation in the chosen specialist areas. This in turn might effectively increase the hospital's catchment area and thus its government and insurance revenue.

Differentiation strategy

Another of *Porter's* generic strategies that could be suitable here is **differentiation.** Bethesda could offer services distinct from those offered by other local hospitals in order to enhance its reputation. Possibilities are improved after care or home support facilities.

Collaborative strategies

In an area such as healthcare it is not necessarily beneficial to society for there to be direct competition between providers. There are a number of areas where collaboration between the two hospitals might be investigated. It could be possible to share key facilities, such as an Accident and Emergency department or maternity ward. The two hospitals could enter into a common purchasing policy in order to try to influence the cost of the drugs and equipment required. The two hospitals could possibly agree to concentrate on separate areas of specialisation.

Part (d)

> **Top tips.** This part of the question is demanding. You must think carefully and do three things.
>
> - Take a high moral stance.
> - Stay relevant to the scenario and its problems.
> - Be consistent and practical in your recommendations.
>
> **Examiner's comments.** There were very few competent answers to this part of the question.

Role of social responsibility

From the information provided in the scenario, it would appear that the major problem for the Management Committee is that they have been **held to ransom by the surgeons**. It also seems that the motivation of the senior surgeons for their strategy of developing leading edge micro-surgery is less than altruistic, as it will serve to increase their own personal power, influence and reputation. The **ethical standards** of the surgeons in particular, and possibly of the medical staff in general, might be questioned.

There is little doubt that the government would be unwilling to leave the provision of medical care entirely to the market, though market forces may be **utilised to ensure efficiency** within the organisation.

Organisations need to promote and enforce a code of behaviour to ensure that acceptable ethical standards are observed by the entire workforce ; this is particularly true in a field such as healthcare. *Campbell and Yeung* suggest that a mission statement should include values and behaviour standards as well as purpose and strategy, while *Peters and Waterman* developed the idea of **superordinate goals**; that is ethical or value driven goals that are more perceived to be of over-arching importance. *Mintzberg* describes the **missionary organisation**, in which the various parts of the organisation unite around a particular belief.

Many of the lower paid staff of Bethesda, such as nurses, general medical staff and support staff, have embraced the altruistic aim of maintaining a hospital for local people who cannot afford private medical insurance and must rely on government funded health care. Social responsibility exists at Bethesda at this level, but is not sufficiently widespread. Bethesda would appear to need to **develop an ethical stance** that embraces all stakeholders in the hospital, including the senior surgeons, in order for the differing groups to unite around an ethical set of objectives and strategies.

This does not mean that the hospital should be run without commercial sense and it is vital that the hospital is financially viable in order for it to be able to continue. This may mean that unpleasant decisions have to be made about such things as redundancies in order to achieve the long-term survival of the hospital. However, for ethical and socially responsible decisions on strategy to be made there would appear to be a need at Bethesda for a central ethical culture espoused by all stakeholders within the hospital.

47 World-Wide Agricultural

Easy marks. This is a difficult case study in that all four requirements are open-ended: only part (b) gives you a firm framework to build on. There are obvious things to say, of course, but a pass mark would require careful analysis and considerations.

Examiner's comments. The Examiner reported that this question was quite well answered overall. His strongest criticism was reserved for answers to part (d). He felt that many answers betrayed an unacceptable naivety in their treatment of the ethical matters involved. It is noteworthy that, as in real life, the problem to be addressed involved both matters of ethics and matters of law: the two are not the same and both are relevant here.

Marking scheme

		Marks
(a)	Internal review	8 marks
	External review including competition	4 marks
	Comparison between two companies	8 marks
		Maximum 20 marks
(b)	Advantages and disadvantages of each strategy	
	Selling distribution network	up to 6 marks
	Buying in tractors	up to 6 marks
	Setting up financial facility	up to 6 marks
	Product development	up to 6 marks
		Maximum 20 marks
(c)	Aspects to consider	up to 3 marks each
	Added-value	
	Consumer and governmental acceptability	
	Costs	
	Cultural fit	
	Operational fit	
	Financial acceptability	**Maximum 12 marks**
(d)	Discussion on Murphy's position	up to 3 marks
	Needs of stakeholders: for each stakeholder mentioned	up to 2 marks
		Maximum 8 marks
		Total 60 marks

Part (a)

Text reference. The topics mentioned in this answer are discussed in Chapter 7 of your BPP Study Text.

Top tips. The requirement says 'use academic models, wherever practical'. Do not get carried away with this: you should use models to guide your thinking and support your argument, but the chief requirement is to analyse the position the company funds itself in. Do not drag models in on a name-dropping basis, in the hope of a mark per mention: they must be relevant.

REPORT

To: Kenneth Murphy
From: Management consultant
Date: December 200X
Subject: Review of position of WAMC

I have been asked to review the current position of World-Wide Agricultural Machinery Company (WAMC) from the background information and summarised financial details provided to me. As part of this review, the performance of WAMC is also to be compared to that of Agricole Mecanique (AM). For this review I have used a SWOT analysis, whereby the position of the company is considered by looking at its strengths, weaknesses, opportunities and threats.

1   **Strengths**

WAMC is a **long established company** with a **strong brand**. It would appear that building of this brand name is continuous, as WAMC annually spends significantly more on marketing effort than AM.

WAMC has in recent years attempted to **modernise and rationalise** its business and has drastically cut its workforce from 2,500 in 1993 to just 700 currently. Although this caused great resentment and resistance, it was eventually seen as **necessary for the continued existence** of the company. The number of factories was also reduced from seven to three, with each of these factories producing a narrow range of products enabling specialisation to take place. These cost saving activities were consciously entered into but their effect has been somewhat disappointing so far: operating profit as a percentage of sales was only 2.1% in 2001 compared to 10% in 2000 and compared to over 14% in AM.

A further strength of WAMC is that it has its own **distribution network** of 10 freehold outlets spread regionally, which not only presumably reduce distribution costs, but, more importantly, are estimated to be worth of £15 million.

A final strength is that WAMC appears to have **low gearing**, with a ratio of debt to equity of only 52% compared to over 100% for AM. WAMC also appears to have a significantly lower cost of debt, with the interest payments during the year being 8.5% of its year end debt compared to 14.6% in AM.

2   **Weaknesses**

Clearly, the major problem with the company is **poor profitability**. The gross margin has decreased significantly, from 40% in 2000 to 35% in 2001, and is drastically lower than that of AM (47% in 2001). Although there have been attempted cost savings by redundancies and reorganisation of the factories, there is little evidence of reduced overall cost, with operating profit at only 2.1% of sales in 2001. Despite the reorganisation of the factories, it is likely that WAMC is operating with fairly dated machinery compared to the up-to-date manufacturing facilities of AM. Output per employee in 2001 was only £40,000 at WAMC compared to £49,000 at AM.

Product range and development are also problem areas. In 1993, a decision was made to stop producing tractor units; this led to a slump in sales and it became apparent that being unable to purchase this lead product from WAMC, customers were deciding not to buy the ancillary units either. There has traditionally been a lack of product development at WAMC and even now the company's expenditure on research and development is significantly below that of AM.

There has also been a general lack of detailed **product and market knowledge**; this has not helped the company with earlier strategic decisions.

3   **Opportunities**

As the managing director has clearly noted, there are opportunities that might be available for WAMC. Manufacturing capability has moved towards **more specialised products** and this may fit well with the specialist nature of the needs of most European farmers.

WAMC **owns the freeholds of its distribution outlets** and it is suggested that these could be sold for £15million. The injection of that amount of cash would certainly give WAMC a welcome breather while further reorganisation and strategies were carried out.

It has been noted that the end of manufacture of the tractor unit has been the cause of much of the loss of sales; however, it might be possible to rectify this problem by **sub-contracting** the manufacture of such units and selling them under the WAMC brand.

Other possible areas of development that have been recognised include **diversification** into the road building and repair industry and entry to the **finance market** by the provision of much needed credit finance to farmers.

A final potential opportunity for turning around the fortunes of WAMC is to merge with AM, which would appear to have some areas of competence that complement those of WAMC.

4   **Threats**

The threats that face WAMC largely relate to its customer base and its competitors. The problem of having an **incomplete product range** as a result of discontinuing the manufacture of tractor units has already been considered. The lack of innovation and investment in product development means that many of WAMC's products are seen as **old-fashioned**; are often **costly to repair** and are not as **flexible** as other machinery on the market. It has to be questioned whether WAMC currently has the ability to satisfy its customers' needs for less costly repairs and greater flexibility.

Competition is strong, with the large US car producers dominating the market.

5   **Conclusion**

It would appear that WAMC is not in a position to continue as it is and **will probably decline further into loss-making without significant changes**. It does not currently appear to be able either to satisfy potential customers' needs or to compete with direct competitors. However, the company does have a number of strategic opportunities and there has been some attempt at modernisation and reorganisation. Perhaps most importantly, WAMC has a long-established brand name, which in a conservative market such as farming should be of great value if it can provide its customers with what they require.

Part (b)

> **Top tips.** To tackle this part of the question you must first be absolutely clear in your own mind as to just what the strategies consist of and how they are different.

Potential strategies

A number of potential strategies for the future of WAMC have been identified by Kenneth Murphy and each of these will now be evaluated.

Sale of distribution outlets

The sale of the 10 distribution outlets could raise a much-needed £15 million for WAMC. This might be **reinvested**, perhaps in much-needed product and market development. However, these distribution outlets are an operational asset of the company, and have, presumably, eliminated the need to pay rent and been of benefit to customers. A detailed **cost/benefit analysis** should be carried out before any decision to sell is made. Selling the distribution outlets, although increasing cash immediately available, may have an undesirable long-term effect on the business that has not been foreseen.

Also, such a sale must also be considered in the light of the **potential merger** with AM. The marketing infrastructure represented by the distribution outlets may combine well with the research and development activities of AM.

Sub-contracting of tractor manufacturing

It is quite clear that the axing of the manufacture of **tractor units** in 1993 has been an important contributory cause of the company's current problems. However, the proposed move back into this market by sub-contracting manufacture but selling under the WAMC brand name needs careful consideration.

One of WAMC's major assets is its **brand name and reputation** as a long-standing manufacturer of farming equipment. If bought-in tractor units are to be marketed under the WAMC brand, the company must be certain that they are of sufficient quality and reliability. The relationship with the sub-contractor will therefore have to be close and trusting. Constant co-operation will be required on quality and also on other such matters as production scheduling, design changes and improvements.

A problem that WAMC might face with sub-contracting is the **reaction of its own workforce**. In recent years there have been almost 2,000 redundancies. Many redundant employees had worked for the company for their entire working lives. This caused major resentment and resistance at the time. If the company now returns to the tractor market but by sub-contracting rather than manufacturing, further resentment and resultant **productivity problems** may occur within the workforce.

Although it is clear that WAMC does need to return to this market, the **possible merger with AM** might be a much more satisfactory method of doing so, rather than sub-contracting and all of the problems associated with that.

Diversification

A further option is **diversification** in order to provide increased work for the factories. The area being suggested is equipment for the road building and repair industry. Despite the fact that this is likely to be a growth area, it is necessary to ask whether WAMC has the **expertise** to enter into this area of manufacture, which would not appear to be particularly related to its current products.

It is possible that this could become a profitable area of diversification for WAMC but it is certainly a **risky venture**. Both the technology and the public sector market are new to WAMC and the market itself could be volatile if there is a change in government plans. We have no information about competition in the market but it is likely to be well established, since the market has been in existence for a very long time; furthermore, the low-tech nature of the proposed products means there is **no technological barrier to entry**.

Although it is possible that this may be a new and profitable area for WAMC, there are also many risks and it may, in fact, serve merely to divert WAMC's attention and resources away from its core business, making the current situation worse rather than better.

Provision of finance to customers

It is no doubt correct that WAMC is losing business as it is not able to offer potential customers adequate credit facilities. However, it is questionable whether providing such facilities directly to customers is the best method. The plan is for WAMC to raise loans on its own account and then lend direct to customers. WAMC's gearing and interest costs are relatively low, but the company has **no experience in this finance provision role**: it is not a bank and should not expect to do well in such a very different business.

WAMC would do better to provide finance to its customers by acting as the **agent of an established finance house**.

Conclusion

The only one of these four strategies with any real merit is the possibility of the **sale of the distribution outlets**. This would provide the company with funds to be used in other areas. However, as well as any deleterious effect this may have on current sales, it would also mean losing an asset that could be an effective bargaining chip if the merger with AM were to go ahead.

The sub-contract manufacture of tractor units and the provision of finance to customers are both attempts to deal with perceived customer requirements. However, business strategy is about the *profitable* satisfaction of customer demand. It could be argued that both of these strategies are **more likely to increase the company's losses than to enhance profitability**.

Diversification could certainly form the basis of improved future profitability but it is also a **high risk**. WAMC should seek a strategy that involves less risk and exploits its existing competences.

Part (c)

> **Text reference.** The topics mentioned in this answer are discussed in Chapter 7 of your BPP Study Text.
>
> **Easy marks.** Your reading of the business press should have convinced you that a merger is a very risky strategy: most mergers fail to produce the improved results their promoters promised. This simple fact will be relevant to **any** merger scenario.

Factors required for the success of the merger

There are four main factors that will determine whether the merger between WAMC and AM is to be successful.

- Will the combined entity be **more profitable** than the original two separately?
- Is the merger **worthwhile** given the costs involved?
- Are the two companies **compatible** operationally, financially and culturally?
- Will **stakeholders** in each company be better off after the merger?

Profitability

A merger is only worthwhile if the combination of the two businesses is more profitable than the individual businesses were in total. The merging of the two companies should be considered in detail to ensure that there is **long-term growth potential** for the combined entity that is greater than their individual potentials. This will normally come about through **economies of scale** or other **synergies** arising from **complementary competences**. In this case, it would appear that the marketing expertise of WAMC might be complementary to the manufacturing and research and development activities of AM, but this may not be enough to ensure future profitability.

Costs

Although there may be clear and perceived benefits to a merger the costs involved must also be taken into consideration. The proposed terms of the merger may well involve significant further **redundancy, disposal and relocation costs**, as it is proposed that the majority of the manufacturing should take place in France.

Compatibility

The compatibility of the two companies must be considered in **operational** terms, **financial** terms and in terms of **culture** of the organisations. On first sight, it would appear that AM need an established brand name and the range of products of WAMC, while WAMC would in turn benefit from the manufacturing capability of the French company. There would also appear to be **potential synergies** in marketing and R&D; and WAMC may well benefit from the higher profit margins that AM can generate.

As far as the financial structure of the two companies is concerned, they are quite different, with the French company being **much more highly geared** than WAMC. This may mean greater variability in profit than the shareholders of WAMC have been used to.

Culturally, the two companies also appear to be quite **diverse**. Whereas WAMC is a long-standing company with an entrenched, unionised workforce, AM is a much younger and smaller company. The terms of the merger certainly appear to **favour the French company** and this may cause considerable problems with the workforce and management of WAMC, who have already seen considerable cut-backs and changes over recent years. The probability of a happy union of the two workforces would not appear to be high.

Stakeholders

The terms of the merger appear to favour AM. Their workforce is probably fairly safe as manufacturing is largely proposed to take place in France and most of the management positions are to be held by AM senior managers. This means that there are likely to be **considerable redundancies** in the UK amongst both the workforce and the senior management.

Shareholders are also threatened. Not only would the shareholders in WAMC be taking on additional risk in the form of the higher gearing of AM, but also, the aim is a share for share exchange at a time when the price of WAMC shares is low. This does not bode well for the wealth of WAMC shareholders.

Part (d)

Text reference. The topics mentioned in this answer are discussed in Chapter 4 of your BPP Study Text.

Top tips. Always take the highest possible moral position when dealing with any problem that has an ethical dimension. Your professional body is determined to enforce the highest standards.

Ethical considerations

Kenneth Murphy has been offered a significant number of shares in the merged company and a future management position if he is able to gain agreement for the merger when the price of WAMC shares is low. This is **clearly a corrupt proposal**. Legally, it is Kenneth Murphy's duty to act at all times in the interests of WAMC's shareholders and a strong ethical case could be made that he should be equally careful of the interests of other WAMC stakeholders. He is being asked to subordinate these interests to the **personal gain and security** that are being offered.

His major ethical problem here is that the proposed merger is very likely to have **significant negative effects** on a number of stakeholder groups within WAMC. If production is likely to take place largely in France, then it is likely that a majority of the UK **workforce** will be made redundant. This move from UK manufacturing will also have a knock on effect on **suppliers** and other companies within the local community. There is also a potential effect on **customers** in the UK, as transferring the majority of production to France may adversely affect the availability and cost of the products in this country.

Perhaps the most significant of all potential effects on stakeholders, however, is the effect on the **shareholders** of WAMC. The French company's plan, with the help of Murphy, is to carry out a share exchange when the price of WAMC shares is low. If Murphy plays a part in this then he is effectively defrauding his own company's shareholders. This is not only **unethical** but also **illegal**.

Kenneth Murphy is in a **position of trust** and his role is to act in the best interests of all of the stakeholders in WAMC. He is effectively being tempted by an offer that will guarantee his own personal security and well-being to the detriment of those it is his duty to protect.

48 Hair Care

Part (a)

Top tips. You will need to look carefully at the table of data in order to get a good grip on this question. You might find that SWOT would form a good basis for thinking about the information you are given.

Easy marks. The question calls for a report: make sure you write and set out your answer in a suitable way: the marking scheme does not offer any marks for doing this, but the marker will expect it.

It is clear from a glance at the data table that turnover, cost of sales and borrowing have all risen rapidly and are expected to continue to rise. Two minutes with a calculator will reveal the relative rates of increase, which are very significant indeed. A related point, and one that might not have occurred to you, is the change in the rate of interest on borrowings expected in the forecast period.

Examiner's comments. This part of the question was generally well answered, though more attention could have been paid to potential future problems. Too many candidates fail to analyse or apply the quantitative data properly: analysis should extend beyond the calculation of financial ratios.

			Marks
(a)	Analysis of quantitative data		
	Trend in costs		up to 3
	Level of debt		up to 4
	Range of products		up to 3
	Stock levels		up to 3
	Fixed assets		up to 2
			Maximum 12 marks
	Future developments		
	Exchange rates		up to 2
	Management succession		up to 2
	Relationship with competitors		up to 2
	Supplier rapport		up to 2
	Relationship with customers/branding		up to 2
			Maximum 8 marks
			Maximum 20 marks
(b)	Market penetration		up to 2
	Product development		up to 3
	Market development		up to 3
	Diversification		up to 3
	Focus		up to 3
	Acquisition		up to 4
	Strategic alliance		up to 4
			Maximum 20 marks
(c)	Profit decline		up to 3
	Debt levels		up to 3
	Complacency		up to 3
	Operational inefficiencies – ie stock levels		up to 3
			Maximum 10 marks
(d)	Primary activities	up to 1·5 marks each to maximum of 7·5 marks	
	Support activities	up to 1 mark each to maximum of 4·5 marks	
			Maximum 10 marks
			Total 60 marks

To:	Managing Director, Hair Care Limited
From:	Accountant
Date:	June 20X3
Subject:	**Hair Care Limited – current position and prospects**

1   **Current situation**

Trading

The last three years' trading results show **impressive growth in turnover**, which is forecast to continue into 20X3. Unfortunately, **cost of sales**, which is by far the largest expense item, has risen at an even faster rate; this trend is also forecast to continue. The effect of this disproportionate rate of increase has been ameliorated by lower rates of increase in other costs, but has led to **relatively slow growth in profits** as compared to the growth in sales. In fact, the operating profit percentage is forecast to be only 7.7%: in 20X0 it was 13%.

Costs

Cost of sales. The relative rise in cost of sales may be caused, at least in part, by the **expansion of the product range**, the number of lines having more than tripled since 20X0. It might be worth examining the margins achieved on each line to establish whether the product range might be trimmed. This may also have a desirable effect on the amount of capital tied up in **stocks**, which has increased more than 600% since 20X0.

Distribution and marketing. Distribution and marketing costs have risen much more slowly than cost of sales and slower even than turnover. While the level of marketing costs may be regarded as subject to some discretion, holding distribution costs down to an increase of only 67% when sales have more than tripled is a significant achievement.

Finance costs. The expansion of the business has largely been financed by borrowing. Total indebtedness is comfortably lower than the value of fixed assets alone, but the interest payments have risen to 4% of turnover and are expected to rise to 9% of the much increased turnover forecast for 20X3. This is partly because borrowing itself will double, but there is also an **increase in the rate of interest** forecast, presumably reflecting the bank's perception of increasing risk as the company's borrowing expands. This should be borne in mind if further expansion of premises is considered: leasing may turn out to be cheaper.

Administration. Administration remains the smallest category of cost, though these costs are expected to increase in line with turnover, by 50%, presumably as a result of the intended similar **growth in staff numbers**.

2 Issues for the future

2.1 Competition

At the moment, Hair Care is not significantly challenged by **competitor**s: larger hair products companies sell into the consumer market and smaller ones specialise in other product ranges. It would not be wise to plan for the future on the basis that this happy state of affairs will continue indefinitely. Even if the current rate of growth is not maintained, it will not be long before the company is challenged, either by a start-up business or by an established company seeking further growth. The company's relationship with the retail chemist chain will already have brought it to the attention of the larger players.

2.2 Business cycle

You have argued that your market segment is recession-proof. This is unlikely to be the case. You have not so far encountered a downturn. Much of your trade is in superior quality, branded products for which you are able to charge premium prices. In the event of a recession, it is likely that your customers would seek to **contain or reduce their costs by buying cheaper goods**: if you were able to supply them, your margins would be eroded; if you were not you would lose the business all together.

2.3 Suppliers

The expansion of your product range means that you now deal with more than three times the number of suppliers you bought from three years ago. Part of your success has been built on strong relationships with your suppliers: these relationships will be difficult to establish with the new suppliers simply because there are so many of them. This may affect the reliability of your **deliveries**, the **discounts** you receive and your access to newly developed **premium products**. These effects are particularly likely to occur if competitors enter your chosen markets.

2.4 **Management**

The company has expanded to a size many times larger than it was when it was set up, but the **management structure has remained the same**. It seems unlikely that this can continue much longer. The **volume of transactions** alone is likely to generate a scale of managerial work that two people cannot handle; there is also the whole field of **human resource management** to consider. Staff numbers are planned to increase by 50% in 20X3. Payroll administration, recruitment, selection, and other aspects of personnel management are likely to become more and more time consuming. It would also be appropriate to consider the potential for **ill-health** to affect the smooth operation of the business: having greater managerial capacity would provide the organisation with the **flexibility** to deal with absence through ill-health. It is probably time to think about taking on at least one person who can undertake some of the more routine management and administrative functions. This could also have the advantage of releasing some of your own time to allow consideration of **strategic issues** in greater depth.

2.5 **Currency exchange**

Most of your purchases are paid for in foreign currency. The dollar and euro exchange rates have been reasonably stable, but this may not be the case in the future. As the volume of your business expands, it may become practical for you to use your bank's services to **hedge** against unfavourable exchange rate movements.

3 **Conclusion**

Your business continues to expand, but your cost structures might benefit from close attention. This is particularly true of cost of sales and finance charges. Management structure is another matter that needs consideration. There are also a number of possible developments in the business environment that could affect the continuing success of the business. You should give some thought to the possibilities of recession, adverse exchange rate movements and increased competition.

Part (b)

Text reference. The topics mentioned in this answer are discussed in Chapter 7 of your BPP Study Text.

Top tips. This question lends itself to an answer based on the various basic strategic option models that you should be very familiar with. The scenario gives a lot of detail that is relevant when considering the various possible routes to growth, so a fairly careful answer plan would be a good idea here.

There is one aspect of the scenario that may have slightly confused you: we are told in the scenario that the subsidiary that became Hair Care Ltd sold its products 'to wholesalers and large retail chemist chains'. Later, we are told that major international companies sell similar products but 'not directly to the hairdressing salons as does Hair Care Ltd'. We must presume that the later information is more up to date: the Examiner's own answers make it clear that the company does, in fact, sell direct to salons. However, whether it still sells to wholesalers as well is uncertain. It is quite likely that it does and it is probably safest to assume this, though, unfortunately, to do so would rule out one area of market development that you might have been tempted to suggest.

Easy marks. *Ansoff's* product-market vector analysis makes a good starting point for this answer.

Examiner's comments. Far too many candidates failed to discuss longer-term strategies, concentrating instead on quick, tactical courses of action.

ANSWERS

To: Managing Director, Hair Care Limited
From: Accountant
Date: June 20X3
Subject: Hair Care Limited – possible development strategies

1 Current limitations

At the moment you have half of your chosen market, which must be accounted a dominant share. While there is still some potential for further organic growth in like-for-like sales, you are probably justified in doubting that this could be a major source of expansion. It is likely that you would have to base such growth on price competitiveness: you may be able to do this reasonably profitably if you can exploit purchasing economies of scale, but you may feel that there are more inviting routes to growth than further **market penetration** based on a **cost-focus**.

However, before leaving this topic completely, it is worth mentioning the possibility of a **differentiation focus** strategy. I have already remarked on the recent rapid growth in the number of products you offer and recommended a **review of profitability**: this might lead you to concentrate much of your attention on the **high margin items** you sell under your own brand. You could aim for a two component business: branded goods selling at high prices and your supply of own brand items in high volumes to your main retail chemist customer.

2 Product-market options

2.1 Product development

At the moment, you sell a range of hair care items to wholesalers and large retail chemist chains, mostly for salon use, and direct to the salons themselves; your product range includes goods sold both under your company's brand and some sold as own brand items by the country's leading chain of retail chemists. Possible scope for **product development** lies in the category of goods sold into your market by your smaller competitors, such as towels and razors. These items would complement your existing range. However, any future introduction of new products should only be contemplated in the light of the review of profitability already recommended.

It would be inappropriate for you to contemplate a move into **salon furnishings**, since these high-value items are so very different in nature from your existing range. You would probably have to establish **completely new supplier relationships** and the items themselves may incur significant costs in **fitting** and after sales service.

More adventurous product development, such as selling a line of cosmetics, would put you in competition with major international companies. You might be able to source low cost, unbranded supplies, but there could well be **product safety** issues to contend with. This option should not be discarded, but needs careful consideration.

2.2 Market development

There are two principal new markets you might consider.

First, you might consider providing other retail chemist chains with goods to sell under their **own brands**. You would, of course have to consider how this might affect your relationship with your existing retail chain customer. This would be low margin business, but you have already found that the volumes make up for this: an expansion should increase your purchasing power and enhance your margins by reducing your purchase costs. This strategy could also be applied to supermarket and department store chains.

Second, you might consider **international expansion**. This would require some careful market research to assess such things as distribution chains, competition and consumer preferences, but there is considerable potential here. Attendance at one of the many European hair care industry trade fairs would be a good way to start.

2.3 Diversification

Diversification is a high risk strategy and none of the options seems appropriate for you. A move into a completely new market with new products would not build on any of your strengths and would expose you to established competition. A **vertical move** up or down the value system has more to recommend it, since you would be able to build on your current market experience, but there would be significant disadvantages to such a move.

A move upstream into manufacturing would put you in competition with your current suppliers. You would not be operating on the same scale as them and therefore you would expect your costs to be higher. It is possible that you could find and exploit a **manufacturing niche**, perhaps producing a small number of similar lines that you currently have difficulty in sourcing, but this does not seem to offer much prospect for achieving your aim of continued substantial growth. If you contemplate manufacturing, you should certainly think in terms of off shore production, perhaps by entering into outsourcing agreements. This would significantly reduce the capital requirement.

A move downstream into **retailing** would be even more difficult. You have no experience of retail operations, so your bank would be unlikely to provide the capital to acquire a chain of outlets; this means that you would have to build the new business by **organic growth**, which would necessarily be a slow process. Such a move would require you to learn all the skills involved in retailing and to source a much larger range of products.

3 Methods of growth

3.1 Acquisition

I have already mentioned the relatively slowness of organic growth. More rapid growth can often be achieved by the **acquisition** of an appropriate existing business. This might be an attractive option for expansion within your existing markets and as an alternative to the product development route mentioned above. Acquisition could also be a route to rapid implementation of the international expansion and manufacturing niche strategies.

3.2 Joint venture/strategic alliance

A joint venture or strategic alliance might be an alternative route to expansion. The difference between the two concepts is that the former involves to creation of a new, jointly owned business entity, while the latter is based on the shared use of an asset, thus spreading its costs and creating scale economies from the increased rate of use. Either of these approaches could be a relatively low risk route to international expansion, for example. A joint venture might be arranged with an existing customer or supplier, while a form of strategic alliance might be created by the use of a foreign commercial agent.

The drawback of these vehicles from your point of view would be that you would have to share control, which might not be an attractive prospect.

4 Conclusions

Either a cost focus or a differentiation focus could be a route to further **market penetration**, though growth by these means would probably be slow.

There do not seem to be good prospects for expansion based on **product development**.

You may to look more closely at the two possibilities for **market development** I have described: further manufacturing for own brand retailers and a foreign venture. Acquisition or joint venture might be worth further examination as means to the latter end.

The only diversification strategy that seems worthy of further examination seems to be the development of a manufacturing niche. Acquisition could also be a means of implementing this idea.

Part (c)

> **Top tips.** In this requirement the Examiner emphasises 'the context of the case study scenario'. This is a pretty clear indication that your answer should not be confined to a discussion of theory!
>
> **Easy marks.** Significant increases in stocks and debt have taken place as part of Sam's pursuit of growth. The consequent increase in fixed costs makes the business much less resilient. Another obvious point to make is that Sam's management style, while highly suitable to a small business, is unlikely to become less appropriate as the business expands.

Much research has been done on why successful businesses decline and fail: *Altman's* **Z score** offers a rule of thumb for predicting failure from key financial ratios, while *Argenti's* **A score** makes a wider assessment of management structure and practice.

We have already noted that Sam's drive for expansion has led him to very significant increases in his borrowing and in the level of his stocks. The consequent rise in his **operational gearing** means that he will be poorly placed if his business turns out to be less recession-proof than he believes it to be. In any case, the profitability of his business appears to be declining, which will make servicing his debt more difficult. A **high level of gearing** and **overtrading** are two of the three specific management mistakes identified by Argenti: there seems to be some danger that Sam is on course to fall into these errors. He must pay close attention to his cash flows and reduce his stocks as far as possible, implementing the product line review already discussed.

Sam's desire to promote the growth of his business seems to be his principal strategic idea. Wisely, he has taken advice on possible future courses of action, but there must be some doubt about his ability to put them into action. He displays the drive, market knowledge and tactical agility of the **typical entrepreneur**; unfortunately, these qualities are rarely combined with the ability to plan and control the operations of the much larger business he aspires to.

Sam's business has grown to the point at which he needs good quality management support and advice, but he may not be **temperamentally suited** to working in this way. Argenti's analysis lists several symptoms of poor top management, all of which relate to a general situation of dominance by one powerful individual. Sam needs help and the business needs more structure and systems that will support its routine operations without hampering its agility and innovation.

Sam will also have to keep a close eye on the conditions in his chosen markets. He has been very fortunate in that he has encountered little competition so far. He should not count on this happy state of affairs continuing indefinitely: one of the major internationals may consider it worthwhile to attack his salon market, for example, perhaps by offering a wider range of products or better prices. It would be easy for a large company to **drive him out of business**. Similarly, his relationship with the large chemist chain for whom he produces own brand goods is unequal; they may decide to cut the margins they allow him in the same way that the UK supermarkets do to their suppliers.

Part (d)

> **Text reference.** The topics mentioned in this answer are discussed in Chapter 6 of your BPP Study Text.
>
> **Top tips.** The question emphasises Sam's success and it would make sense, therefore, to confine an answer to those parts of the value chain that have been managed in a way that contributes to that success. However, the Examiner's answer makes reference to problem areas, such as the lack of succession planning, so it is probably fair to conclude that a balanced picture is required.
>
> This is a good principle to follow: it is often hard to decide just what is relevant in an answer, but the implication here is that an over-strict interpretation of the question requirement is not a good idea. Do not be afraid to add the odd sentence or three that might seem to be marginal to such an interpretation.
>
> There is no need to draw the value chain diagram.
>
> **Easy marks.** Marketing and sales is an obvious place to start among the primary activities, as Sam is basically, a very successful salesman.

Primary activities

Sam is a very successful salesman and the **marketing and sales** activity of his company, resting in his hands as it does, must be regarded as a major source of the company's success. He has created good relationships with his key customers, not least by his determination to provide excellent service. He has also successfully established both the Hair Care brand, which offers enhanced margins and a bulk, own brand supply to a chain of retail chemists, which gives him volume sales and the advantages of bulk purchasing.

We might consider **operations** and both **inbound** and **outbound logistics** together. Sam has invested substantially in storage and packing facilities and his wife Annabelle has managed the company's staff so as to provide a high quality of service: we must presume that this includes accurate and prompt deliveries. All three of these activities form an important basis for the company's success.

The final primary activity is **service**, in the sense of after sales service. The company's products are generally too simple to require very much of this, but no doubt prompt attention to returns, when required, contributes to its overall reputation.

Secondary activities

Procurement is also an activity into which Sam has put considerable effort and from which the company derives great advantage. Sam sources his products entirely from outside the UK and has overcome problems of foreign exchange, international trade regulation and national culture to do so successfully, having negotiated a number of favourable prices.

Technology development at Hair Care has two aspects. The development of the product range continues apace, possibly to the extent that some rationalisation is required, as discussed earlier. This might be accounted a mixed success for this reason. The continuing development of systems and utilisation of resources (such as those in the warehouse) has allowed the company to expand its operations smoothly and without constraint. However, there is some concern about the level of debt and thus fixed costs that has developed. Overall, this activity continues to need careful management if it is not to become an important weakness.

Human resource management is also an activity worthy of some attention. Staff turnover has been low, which is a good sign, but staff numbers are expected to double over the next two years and it is unlikely that this happy state of affairs will continue. Annabelle will have to pay careful attention to recruitment and training and be prepared for a higher level of turnover as numbers increase. There is also the problem of managerial capacity already discussed: Sam needs increased managerial support of a high calibre.

Firm infrastructure in terms of specialist services such as legal advice is, no doubt, bought in as required. There is however, a growing need for more in-house capacity for such activities as planning, financial control and, possibly, as the scale of operations increases, quality management.

49 Polymat Tapes

Examiner's comments. The compulsory question is the key to passing the examination. Candidates who fail to achieve 30 marks on Question 1 find it difficult to gain sufficient marks from Section B to compensate for a poor performance on the compulsory question. The scenario was of a multi-product manufacturing company supplying a range of industrial tapes to a wide variety of industrial and commercial customers. Many of their customers were large manufacturers themselves. There was therefore an emphasis on business-to-business relationships.

Marking scheme

		Marks
(a)	Evaluation of company performance	Up to 3
	Evaluation of each product group	Up to 6 each
	Use of appropriate models	Up to 5
		Maximum 25 marks
(b)	Source of competitive advantage – generic strategy	Up to 3
	Alternative growth directions	Up to 6
	Alternative methods for growth	Up to 3
	Preferred strategy – justification	Up to 5
		Maximum 15 marks
(c)	Consideration of culture change	Up to 3
	Models for creating change	Up to 3
	Measures for implementing change	Up to 5
		Maximum 10 marks
(d)	Current product performance evaluation	Up to 2
	Current NPD process	Up to 2
	Creation of a formal process for New Product Development	Up to 5
	Feedback on new NPD process effectiveness	Up to 2
		Maximum 10 marks
		Total 60 marks

Part (a)

> **Text reference.** The topics mentioned in this answer are discussed in Chapter 6 of your BPP Study Text.
>
> **Top tips.** Here is an opportunity to use the BCG model and decide whether the product groups are 'dogs', 'cows', 'question marks/problem children' or 'stars'. Correct use of the financial data provided was essential in locating each product within the grid.
>
> **Examiner's comments.** Part (a) asked for an assessment of the performance of the product groups using appropriate models, particularly the BCG matrix. The industry structure in the scenario lent itself to an intelligent use of Porter's Five Forces model, and product life cycle analysis was often used to good effect. Candidates also used SWOT analysis which, when it is done well, and not merely as a listing exercise, is revealing about the firm's position.

To: Richard Johnson, Managing Director, Polymat Industrial Tapes Ltd
From: External consultant
Date: December 20XX

Introduction

There is cause for concern at PIT. At company level the return on sales is falling, with a disproportionate increase in fixed costs. Close analysis of the performance of the individual factories and product groups reveals further disturbing developments, as well as some cause for optimism.

Analysis of specific product groups

Cable Jointing Tapes

This product group is registering a sound increase in year-on-year sales, clearly exceeding the increase in the cost of sales with a consequent **improvement of the gross margin** from 40% in 2001/02 to a forecast 45% in 2003/04. There appears to be a link between the consistently high R&D spend and successful development of profitable products that meet customer requirements. **Market share** is high and consistent.

PVC Industrial Tapes

This group seems very stable, with gross margin again forecast at a healthy 45% in 2003/04 and a steady if slow growth in sales. The **decline in market share** does give cause for concern, perhaps reflecting the impact of low cost tapes. In addition, R&D expenditure is low, which seems to indicate that there is little prospect of product innovation to grow the market for the products of this division.

Paper Masking Tapes

Sales are declining and costs are increasing, particularly those associated with transport. **Market share** is being maintained, but costs cannot be allowed to spiral out of control in order to achieve this at any price. Despite the investment in a modern factory, this division is constrained by the terms of the operating licence with the US, and its inability to achieve an efficient low cost operation.

Models that could be used to analyse PIT's performance include the **BCG matrix**, which emphasises the relationship between market share and profitability. A company with a portfolio of products could expect a range of growth profiles in the various industries with which it is associated. There is little evidence however to suggest that PIT has any products in high growth sectors.

In terms of the three product groups, the Paper Masking Tapes group has a respectable market share compared to its main competitor, but it more closely resembles a 'dog' than a 'cash cow' because of its declining profitability and spiralling costs. It is difficult to see how this division could be turned around without radical cost control measures.

Using another model, closer analysis of the tape groups could suggest that PVC Industrial Tapes are reaching the **mature stage** of their **product life cycle**, with stagnant profits and static sales.

A respectable market share together with improving margins, supported by significant R & D, suggests that the Cable Jointing Tapes division has the potential to move into the 'star' category, assuming that market growth can be assured (there is nothing in the scenario however to indicate that this is possible).

Porter's generic strategies

Competitive strategy involves a choice between being the lowest cost producer (cost leadership), making the products different from competitors in some way (differentiation) or specialising in a segment of the market (focus, using cost leadership or differentiation). *Porter* believes that firms must choose one of these, or be regarded as 'stuck in the middle'. It could be said that PIT is 'stuck in the middle', with few if any claims to be a cost leader. Only in its Cable Jointing Tapes division does it have products differentiated to meet the needs of cable manufacturers.

PIT's products are aimed at a wide range of customers – from large multinationals to DIY enthusiasts and, consequently a large range of distribution channels are used. This has promoted inefficiencies: transport costs need to be brought under control and the value chain for each division needs examination for the benefits that are being delivered.

Information for management decision making – organisational knowledge

There is a lack of detailed management information on the **profitability**, or otherwise, of PIT's product range. The links between sales and marketing and the R & D teams seem *ad hoc* and underdeveloped and there is little co-ordination of the overall R & D effort. **Organisational knowledge** is not currently shared.

It should be noted in this context that knowledge and 'knowledge workers' are increasingly recognised as significant factors in the determination of competitive advantage, and PIT should consider the development of a system that encourages the sharing of its significant organisational knowledge. This will eliminate duplication of effort in accessing information, encourage a consistent approach to product management and facilitate employee co-ordination. This will be particularly valuable in the effort to **better understand customer requirements** and **promote innovation**.

Conclusion

Many of PIT's products are **mature**, and suffering from severe **price competition**. A strategy is needed to ensure the survival and growth of the company. The product life cycle is instructive in this regard: opportunities for innovation should be sought out to extend the life of products and create new ones.

Part (b)

> **Text reference.** The topics mentioned in this answer are discussed in Chapter 7 of your BPP Study Text.
>
> **Examiner's comments.** Part (b) gave the opportunity to discuss strategic options. Here the BCG matrix and the invest/harvest/divest options were relevant, together with a consideration of Ansoff's growth options. Useful consideration was often given to whether the value chain of the firm should stay the same, as there were clear prompts from the scenario to consider whether the centralised warehouse and in-house transport service were really adding value to the company's products. There was often a reluctance to choose a preferred strategy as requested.

Strategies need to be evaluated by PIT according to their **suitability** to the firm's strategic situation, their **feasibility** in terms of resources and competences and their **acceptability** to key stakeholder groups. From the scenario, it appears that radical change to either products or markets is unlikely to occur, but there is a need to establish which products can be developed, and for which customers.

Product market strategies involve the determination of which products should be sold in which markets, by market penetration, market development, product development and diversification. Any analysis of PIT's performance to date should lead to withdrawal from unprofitable markets, divestment of poorly performing products and a closing down of company activities which are adding little value, thereby releasing resources to be redirected to value-adding spheres of activity.

Examining each of the divisions in turn:

Cable Jointing Tape products look to offer the most likely opportunity for improved **market penetration** and **market development**, through links with cable manufacturing customers. There may be an opportunity to **develop PIT's brand** as part of an attempt to stave off aggressive US competition.

Paper Masking Tapes is a product group without much scope for improved performance. Its cost base is higher than its major competitor, it has significantly lower market share and its access to product and process innovation is limited because of the arrangement with the American manufacturer. In addition there is significant overcapacity, and tape supplied to the automobile industry is under **severe price pressure**. **Divestment** would be a sensible option.

PVC tape products look to be a **product group with some potential**, with healthy margins and sales increases. Competition is increasing from competitors with a lower cost base, but PIT has the advantage that its products already meet demanding quality standards so there may be resistance on the part of **satisfied customers** towards moving to a competitor. **Innovation** is likely to be a key differentiating factor in the future for this division, and the way to retain competitive advantage, but the question of whether product innovation in a mature market is a realistic strategy should be asked. Sustained competitive advantage may involve **process** (rather than product) **innovation**. Certainly, PIT needs to look closely at its **value chain** and its customer base.

PIT needs to review the value of operating its own **warehouse and transport system**, which together involve the commitment of significant resources. More evidence is needed on the precise benefit that such an arrangement brings for the company. The scenario indicates that it has merely added to overheads and done very little to add any value for customers or the company.

A range of strategic options is open to the company, but much more information is needed on revenue and costs. From the above analysis however is does appear that an exit from Paper Masking Tapes, closing the warehouse and outsourcing the transport function would contribute to a successful business strategy.

Part (c)

Text reference. The topics mentioned in this answer are discussed in Chapter 11 of your BPP Study Text.

Top tips. Part (c) was looking for ways the culture inside the firm could be changed - the process of change rather than any marketing actions and decisions. Culture and culture change has been a favourite area in previous papers.

Examiner's comments. Parts (c) and (d) were the parts which typically gave the most problems but offered the candidate an opportunity to think creatively about what was required. Lewin's force field analysis and change process was by far the preferred model for explaining how the process might be managed, and there was encouraging evidence of its being better understood and more effectively applied to the problem.

Culture at PIT is production led. This is evidenced by the use of graduate chemists, the organisational structure of the company into factories specialising in their own product range, and separate R & D programmes. There is no overall mechanism for reporting, for example, the performance of the various divisions in terms of customer satisfaction or detailed product/market analysis. R&D should be closely coordinated with marketing because customer needs, as identified by marketers, should be a vital input to new product development.

Favoured models for stimulating change such as is required here include *Lewin's* **force field analysis** and three stage change process (unfreeze, change, refreeze). It is important to recognise that there is likely to be resistance to any change, so the culture shift has to be well thought out and implemented.

Unfreeze is the most difficult stage of this process, concerned mainly with selling the need for a marketing orientation to the staff of PIT, who may regard it as unimportant. They need a **motive** for changing their attitudes – this may be provided by demonstrating the negative effects of a lack of adequate marketing focus for the future of the company. A failure to stimulate the market has certainly had a detrimental effect upon the performance of **Retardon**, and paved the way for competitors.

Change is mainly concerned with identifying the key features of a new marketing orientation, communicating it and encouraging it. The new ideas must be shown to work. **Refreeze** implies the consolidation or reinforcement of the new behaviour. This could involve an **action plan** including timescales for particular activities (such as staff training on how to use a new customer database), milestones and the allocation of responsibilities.

Measures to increase the exposure of all types of staff to marketing, and the setting up of appropriate customer information systems leading eventually to a proper customer database, will help. Marketing has a key role to play in the effective implementation of new products but requires these changes to information provision.

Part (d)

Examiner's comments. Part (d) was a deliberate attempt to give candidates the opportunity to be creative and move away from predictable and prescribed answers. Unfortunately, few candidates really thought through how a new product development (NPD) system might work. There were some good answers which took the evidence from the scenario and used it to good effect. The company had one breakthrough product which it was failing to develop properly.

Any organisation must have a system through which new ideas are managed. PIT needs a system through which new ideas can be screened and technologists, manufacturing and sales people can be brought together. Product ideas with the most potential can then be developed. The NPD process at PIT lacks detailed information on the performance of existing products, which in turn could show the need for new ones. Even the developments around its one breakthrough product, Retardon, are not encouraging, and action needs to be taken.

As noted in the answer to part (a), PIT's current separation into three factories and three product groups prevents an **integrated view of innovation** from being developed. There is currently no way of telling what percentage of revenue comes from new products, and no indication in the scenario as to how new products are developed, or how long such development takes. Are staff suggestions made, and acted upon? The company needs to ask itself whether it can continue to improve and create value for the future. This does not mean that innovation is pursued for its own sake: there should be clear understanding of what advantages a new product/service innovation is expected to deliver: increased market share, for example.

As noted in the answer to part (c), **customer needs**, as identified by marketers, should be a vital input to new product development. PIT is failing to use the information on customer needs brought back by its sales force in the NPD process. On the other hand, the R&D department might identify possible changes to product specifications, so that a variety of marketing mixes can be tried out and tested. It appears, however, that the employees in the various groups simply do not work together; and there is probably no real sense at ground level of the overall market objectives of the PIT company.

Innovation can be a major source of **competitive advantage** but it brings a burden of uncertainty, and of course, costs. Ultimately, the learning curve effect may bring cost advantages, but does require appropriate financial analysis. This also needs to be developed by PIT.

50 NMS

Part (a)

> **Text reference.** The topics mentioned in this answer are discussed in Chapter 3 of your BPP Study Text.
>
> **Top tips.** Notice the two parts to the requirement in this question: 'explain the purpose...' and 'evaluate...'. You may be of the opinion that mission statements are a once-fashionable, consultant-driven gimmick of little business value, or you may believe that only a clear understanding of mission can form a proper basis for business strategy. Arguments can be advanced for either point of view.
>
> Such arguments should form the basis of your response to the requirement to *evaluate*. However, before you plunge into this exciting debate, you must satisfy the requirement to *explain*. And you must explain with reference to NMS.
>
> **Easy marks.** This is an easy question: get the basics down: these will bring you the easy marks that all tutors will tell you are available in every question. Then, and only then, proceed to your wider discussion.
>
> **Examiner's comments.** This part of the question provided candidates with a positive start to their examination.

Marking scheme

		Marks
(a)	Mission statements	up to 2 marks each
	Identification of purpose, strategy, values and standards of behaviour	
	contribution to the strategic management purpose	
	communication to stakeholders	
	should reflect changing conditions	
	evaluation of contribution to NMS	up to 4 marks
		Maximum 10 marks

(b)   environmental analysis: up to 12 marks
      Porter's five forces model
      Supplier power – significant
      Buyer power – considerable – varies between two market segments
      Threat of new entrants – significant barriers
      Competitive rivalry – intense in components, favourable in network management systems
      Threat of substitutes – significant in hi-tech industry
      PEST analysis
      organisational analysis   up to 12 marks
      value chain analysis
      SWOT
      balanced scorecard
      strategic analysis   up to 6 marks
      emergent, entrepreneurial and opportunistic
      focused differentiation
      ad-hoc   **Maximum 25 marks**

(c)   Evaluation of each exit option against suitability, acceptability and feasibility tests   Up to 6 marks each
      Option 1 Recovery strategy and going public – high risk/return – long term option
      Option 2 Immediate sale – low risk/return – short-term option
      Option 3 Friendly acquisition – medium risk/return option   **Maximum 15 marks**

(d)   business-to-business marketing   up to 2 marks each
      bases for segmentation
      understanding buyer motivation
      identifying key decision makers
      differences from consumer goods marketing
      implications for the marketing mix   **Maximum 10 marks**
                                                                                                   Total 60 marks

---

Mintzberg tells us that mission 'describes the organisation's basic function in society, in terms of the products and services it produces for its clients'. This means that a company's mission provides the commercial logic for its strategy. The concept is usually extended to include three other basic parameters.

An organisation's **strategic scope** is defined by the boundaries its managers set for it. These boundaries may be set in terms such as geography, market, business method, or in any other way that defines the nature of the organisation. Some reference to IT in general and networks in particular may be appropriate for NTS. Such a statement of scope can be useful in strategic planning, as outlined below.

Policies and standards of behaviour should be specified. The mission needs to be converted into everyday performance. For example, a firm whose mission covers excellent customer service must deal with simple matters such as politeness to customers, speed at which phone calls are answered and so forth. NTS seems to have achieved some differentiation in terms of quality and value; a reference to this as a defining feature of the business might be appropriate.

A strong line should be taken on **values and culture**, particularly where **ethical matters** are concerned. The mission statement can lay down suitable principles of business; ideals of loyalty and commitment to stakeholder groups; and guidance for behaviour. A clear mission statement can help to create a work environment where there is a sense of common purpose.

For there to be a strong, motivating sense of mission, these elements must be mutually reinforcing.

Although the mission statement might be seen as a set of abstract principles, it can play an important role in the **planning process,** since plans should outline the fulfilment of the organisation's mission. Mission is therefore useful to the strategic process in several ways: it provides a focus for the **development** of plans and a set of criteria for the **evaluation and screening** of plans; it also promotes **consistency** in strategic decisions. Mission can also be used to influence the **implementation** of a planned strategy, *via* its effect on the culture and business practices of the firm.

Despite all this, there are those who see mission statements as being of little value. *Scott Adams*, creator of *Dilbert* has one of his characters define a mission statement as 'a long, complicated sentence that demonstrates management's inability to think clearly'.

An important problem with mission statements is that they are often intended merely for public consumption and are frequently **ignored in practice**. This leads to the use of imprecise generalisations about the company's aspirations for itself and its stakeholders. *Enron* was an excellent example: the company had high-sounding ideals that were very different from the methods it actually employed.

Another problem is that mission statements are sometimes produced in order to *rationalise* the organisation's existence to particular audiences. In other words, mission does not drive the organisation, but what the organisation actually does is **assumed to be a mission**.

One further comment may be particularly applicable to NTS: a very young company often has to live from day to day, trading more on its **agility** than on any coherent ideas about what it is trying to do. If Ray Edwards has clear ideas about the relevance of the various aspects of a mission statement might help him, then it might indeed do that. But there is little point in his writing one just because it **seemed like a good idea** when he was told about it on his strategic planning course.

Part (b)

Text reference. The topics mentioned in this answer are discussed in Chapter 5 of your BPP Study Text.

Toptips. With 25 marks allocated to it, this question requires a fairly detailed answer. Note the stated requirement to use 'appropriate models'.

The Examiner's marking scheme and suggested solution were loosely based on the environmental analysis, position audit and corporate appraisal phases of the rational model of strategy. The suggested solution made extensive use of the standard models such as PEST, the value chain and even the balanced scorecard.

The strategic analysis general approach is a good one, since it covers all the options, but it would be a good idea to be careful in your use of models: it is not necessary to work slavishly through them one by one. You should use models to illuminate and give structure to your arguments, not treat them as checklists with items to be ticked off. For example, using the five forces, there is nothing in the scenario about the bargaining power of suppliers, so it would be as well not to open this topic up at all – concentrate on the forces that are relevant, as we do in our answer below.

Make full use of the numerical information given in the question. It never requires advanced analysis techniques: ratios and percentages normally reveal much that is of interest. Where there is a sequence of annual figures as here, make sure that you understand what changes have taken place from year to year.

Examiner's comments. SWOT is not a model: it is a technique.

NMS – THE CURRENT STRATEGIC POSITION

A report prepared by A Consultant & Co

1 Introduction

NMS finds itself at something of a crisis in its existence and it is appropriate at this juncture to take a careful look at the company and its circumstances. Several years of profitable growth seem to be coming to an end as the economic downturn takes effect and, at the same time, issues of strategic management are beginning to require attention.

2 Revenues and costs

Revenue grew satisfactorily in the three years to 20X3. The significant reduction expected in 20X4 may be blamed on the current recession, but we would sound a note of caution here: we fear that a lack of attention to marketing and strategic planning may have contributed to the magnitude of the reduction. We have more to say about this later. A further noteworthy point is the **low level of export sales**, which have not exceeded 10% during the last three years; we would have anticipated a higher level in this highly globalised industry.

20X3 saw a small net loss on operations, while 20X4 is forecast to end in a much larger loss of £365k. Examination of summary financial data reveals that both **gross and net margins have declined seriously** as a result of increasing costs.

It is very likely that **committed costs** will erode margins during a period of falling sales and we see this effect clearly in the forecast level of overheads for 20X4: they will be higher than in 20X3, despite an 11% overall reduction in sales value. Administration, distribution and R&D costs will fall in 20X4, but of these three, only distribution will be lower than in 20X2, when the value of total sales was very close to the figure forecast for 20X4.

While this effect is to some degree inevitable, it may be that attention is needed to the level of expenses. One noteworthy point is the very great disparity between the level of spending on marketing and on R&D. The latter is, clearly, very important, but, as we point out below, important marketing-related activities **appear to have been neglected** and it may be that the bias here is excessive.

We can say with more certainty that something has gone badly wrong with **cost of sales**. In 20X1, gross margin was 45%; strong growth in sales in 20X2 was matched by a proportionate growth in cost of sales, gross margin being maintained at 45%. However, in 20X3, cost of sales rose by 21%, while the increase in total sales was only 11%. As a result, gross margin fell to 40%. This worrying trend is forecast to continue in 20X4, a decline in total sales of 10% being set against a fall in cost of sales of only 5%.

Once again, a comparison with 20X2 is revealing: total sales in 20X4 will be only £45k lower than in that year, but cost of sales will have risen by £550k. We submit that this situation should be examined in greater detail in order to establish what has gone wrong.

3 Management and organisational matters

There are several issues concerning the internal functioning of the company that give cause for concern.

3.1 Growth and structure

NMS has grown successfully overall and is now, by UK standards, a medium sized firm, turning over in excess of £6m annually and employing 75 full time staff. It has been experiencing the first crisis of *Greiner's* growth model, the crisis of **leadership**. Some progress has been made, in that a functional structure has been set up and some skilled managers have joined the company, but Ray Edwards has found that his entrepreneurial style cannot make up for a lack of robust and flexible systems for routine management. Similarly, at the strategic level, it is time for more sophisticated planning to replace Ray Edwards' rather **short-termist and opportunist approach**.

3.2   **Weaknesses**

We note three specific areas of organisational weakness.

Technical support

Technical support is a key success factor and the company has a good reputation in this area. However, its technical support operation is hampered by the **lack of a national network**, all support being delivered from the London base.

Forecasting and planning

The existing manual planning system requires an upgrade to improve the scheduling of production and purchases in order to reduce **production downtime** caused by component shortages. This problem is linked to deficiencies in sales forecasting, which, in turn are linked to the point made below.

Market research

A sales and marketing department now exists; the head of this department will need to give urgent attention to the problem of **market and sales forecasting**. This probably does not mean extensive and expensive independent market research activities, merely an improved effort to build customer relationships in order to improve awareness of their probable future needs.

4   **The business environment**

4.1   **The wider environment**

The most important aspect of the wider business environment to affect NMS is the **current recession**. This is affecting sales overall, but it offers some opportunity, in that customers will welcome innovations that reduce their costs. There is an obvious implication here for the focus of both development work and sales effort in the near future.

NMS operates in a **high-technology industry** and expends considerable effort in attempting to keep abreast of both industry developments and customer requirements. The company seems well-placed to maintain its position.

4.2   **The forces of competition**

NMS competes in **two separate markets**: data communications components and network management systems. There are important differences and some similarities between these markets.

Bargaining power of buyers

The OEM market consists of a number of large customers. NMS has less than one percent of this market and competes with more than twenty other suppliers. These factors alone would mean that buyer bargaining power relative to NMS was **high**. In addition to this general picture, NMS's **cannot afford to lose** the single customer that takes 40% of its sales; this customer is therefore in a very strong position. This market is also complicated by the need for regulatory approval for all products.

The network management market is less subject to the power of buyers. NMS is recognised as an effective supplier of customised equipment and commands margins in excess of 40%.

Competitive rivalry

The **large number of competitors** in the OEM market and the **instability** likely to result from shorter lifecycles will make this market highly competitive. NMS has a good reputation for quality but may be too small to achieve the high volume output required to permit competitive, low prices.

The position in the network management market is more benign, in that a totally standardised product is impractical, so volume of sales is less important. NMS seems well-placed here, particularly as its modular approach to design allows it to achieve some **economies of scale**.

Threat from new entrants

There are important **barriers to entry** to NMS's markets. Both markets are **knowledge intensive**. While there is room for innovative new entrants to create niche markets, customers are likely to value **experience** and **proven ability**. Also, even in low volume products, the **experience curve effect** is likely to give a cost advantage to established suppliers such as NMS.

In the OEM market, the requirement for **regulatory approval** imposes both cost and time penalties. However, there are certain to be many **standardised components** needed in such a market and producing the simpler ones would be a route in. Nevertheless, the need to compete on **price** and hence the need for **scale economies** would make it difficult for a small business to enter successfully, except a s a niche supplier as mentioned above.

The network management market seems equally difficult to enter. NMS has established its **brand** by close attention to technically superior products and customer service, which will tend to act as a barrier to entry. A further barrier to entry exists in the form of NMS's reputation for excellent **technical support**. To reproduce this would be costly.

Threat from substitute products

There is a generalised threat to NMS in the wide and rapid progress within its industry. New and potent IT systems are regularly developed, bringing both threats and opportunities. This is another aspect of the urgent requirement for NMS to improve its abilities to survey its competitive environment and assess the impact of developments within it.

Part (c)

Text reference. The topics mentioned in this answer are discussed in Chapter 8 of your BPP Study Text.

Top tips. This is a fairly unusual question in that the ability to write a good answer depends very much on an awareness of the way business works and hardly at all on theoretical knowledge of strategic management.

Nevertheless, the Examiner's own answer addresses each of the three proposed options in terms of **suitability**, **acceptability** and **feasibility**. This is a classic example of good use of a model: taking this approach will help you to ensure that you do not overlook anything in the scenario that might be relevant, since it will focus your attention on factors relevant to each of the criteria in turn. One could go further and say that this model is very useful for considering *any* possible course of action, not just those that might qualify under the heading 'strategy'.

The Examiner has been quite generous with the marks for this question as there is not actually a great deal to say about any of options proposed.

Examiner's comments. Many candidates seemed to have time management problems with this question and part (c) frequently received very little attention. The word 'options' is very important, since it implies a reasoned consideration of possible choices.

Ray's desire to investigate exit routes from his enterprise reflects both the difficulties it is facing and his reaction to them. It is worth remarking that, ideally, such an exit should be **planned well in advance** so that it can be achieved on the most advantageous terms. Ray is disappointed and upset and should be very careful to analyse his options rationally and as fully as possible.

A major consideration at any time must be the views of the **providers of finance** and this is doubly so in hard times such as those NMS is currently encountering. It is likely that the venture capitalists involved have already made their own exit plans and anything Ray proposes would have to satisfy their requirements. The banks will also have their own agenda and will look to their **security** before any other consideration.

The **first option**, a flotation as soon as possible, is rather vague. It would, presumably, initially entail managing for survival (as mentioned earlier) until the global economy picks up. The problem then would be for Ray to define just what he means by 'as soon as possible'. There are a number of routes to flotation and Ray would need some expensive advice as to the best course for his company. In any event, he is going to have to **achieve significant growth** and **sustained improvements in profitability** before flotation becomes a reasonable option. As soon as possible' is unlikely to be in the near future: Ray should think in terms of five to ten years.

The sustained growth necessary to make this option feasible implies **significant change** in NMS. The organisation will almost certainly have to **expand** and its **management structure and practices will have to be developed**. Ray has already become aware that 'muddling through' with informal systems and structures is no longer an option. Clear strategic direction is required and it is not actually apparent that Ray is the man to provide this.

Of the three exit options proposed this seems to be the **least realistic**, both because of the timescale involved and doubt about whether it is actually achievable.

The **second option**, a rapid sale, is more practical, but seems likely to offer **little comfort** to Ray. No doubt the offer made by the Finance Director and the General Manager was intended to be an opening bargaining position, but it seems unlikely that an objective valuation of the business would be significantly higher. Ray may be falling into the **classic layman's error** of thinking that the balance sheet value of his business has some relationship with its actual value in the real world. We do not have enough data to carry out even a tentative valuation of the business, but we might reasonably suggest that the **volatility of its profits** and the **high level of its indebtedness** would make it unattractive to a private purchaser, even one already involved in the industry that could see some prospects for achieving **synergy** with his existing operation. To walk away might well leave Ray with little more than small change, figuratively speaking.

This brings us to the **third option**, a sale to a large customer. This would presumably be an OEM customer, as it seems unlikely that one of the network systems customers would be interested in a business so very different from their own. This option is very similar to the second, in that it depends on a fairly immediate valuation. However, a large customer might see more potential in NMS than a private buyer, not so much because it would offer an element of backwards vertical integration but because of the **well-established R&D function**. This might, indeed, be the most attractive aspect of the business to such a buyer. On the other hand, such a purchaser would be likely to take a very careful look at the value of the business and might not offer any more than a small private buyer.

Part (d)

Text reference. The topics mentioned in this answer are discussed in Chapter 5 of your BPP Study Text.

Easy marks. This is actually a fairly easy question, depending as it does on the not very complex contrasts between the characteristics of the two aspects of marketing practice. However, if you have never come across the topic before, you might well find it difficult to work it out from first principles. Thinking about the four Ps of the marketing mix might have helped you to spot a few possible contrasts.

Examiner's comments. It is a matter of concern that so many candidates were unable to produce an answer this part of the question.

The nature of industrial or business-to-business (B2B) marketing may be contrasted with marketing to consumers under three main headings, each with its influence on the marketing mix.

Purchase decision-making

Most consumer purchasing decisions are taken by a **single individual**. Exceptions exist in the case of major purchases, such as a house or a car, and fashion items, where advice may be sought, but such purchasing decisions are relatively infrequent. Businesses organise their buying on a different basis. Larger items are normally only purchased after a complex process involving several people has taken place. The **decision-making unit** (DMU) will have several members who divide the various aspects of the purchase decision between them. Different people will recognise the need for a purchase, prepare the technical specification and give final approval for the purchase. Others may be involved at a distance, in such roles as selecting preferred suppliers, for example.

This complexity of decision-making has a particular effect on **promotion**. Consumer promotion can be **highly focussed** and designed to appeal to the target segment's emotions and personal interests. B2B promotion has to serve rather different purposes. In the case of the company's component sales, the creation of a good **catalogue** will be vital to ensure that designers and specifiers are aware of what the company's products are and what they can do. **Personal selling** will be important to achieve recognition as an authorised supplier. The highly customised nature of the company's network management systems will also demand a high standard of personal selling, since several members of the appropriate DMU may have to be convinced to make a purchase. This could involve senior managers and directors.

Purchase motivation

In wealthy, advanced economies, many consumer purchases are influenced by considerations such as lifestyle, image and entertainment value. Most industrial purchasing, on the other hand, is the result of a carefully established and defined operational need; it can be seen as involving greater **rationality** of thought. The members of the DMU will seek an **appropriate and rationally justifiable mix of quality, value for money, credit terms and delivery**.

This has clear implications for the marketing mix. The **product** must be designed to satisfy clear and specific criteria. **Price** must be competitive unless there is a clear differentiation that the customer values and even then, hard bargaining is likely. **Place**, in the form of distribution and delivery will be a fundamental part of the value offered. **Promotion** must emphasise the presentation of information rather than the creation of **emotionally-based brand values**, though brand values of quality and reliability will be important.

Segmentation

The rational nature of industrial purchasing influences **market segmentation**. Consumer products positioned and promoted to exploit fashion and lifestyle preferences and aspirations are sold into markets that are segmented on those bases. Industrial products are generally designed to match a range of technical specifications whose basic parameters are established from **rational market requirements**: this requires that industrial markets be segmented on such bases as size, product range, geographic location and technology used.

In the case of NMS, the company serves **two fairly distinct markets**: the OEMs and the end users of network components. It is probably unnecessary to segment the end user market at all: there are only two or three competitors, so it seems to be fairly small. The OEM market seems much larger, with a forecast value in Europe of $6bn in 20X3, so some segmentation might be useful, if only on a **geographic basis**. General class of component used might be another suitable basis. The point is that the segmentation base chosen should support the marketing mix in some way, perhaps by guiding priority for personal sales visits (the larger users) or choice of promotional method or content.

51 Elite Plastic Packaging

Part (a)

> **Text reference.** The topics mentioned in this answer are discussed in Chapter 18 of your BPP Study Text.
>
> **Top tips.** Unusually, the table of numerical information given in the scenario is very thin. Just about all you can conclude from it is that Elite Plastic Packaging seems to be doing quite well, maintaining steady and profitable growth, while the division and group of which it is part seem to be shrinking and becoming less profitable.
>
> This information is obviously important, but it is available almost by glancing at the table: previous exams incorporated tables that required you to do a little more digging if you were to make full use of the numbers given in a typical Question 1.
>
> By contrast, the Examiner's suggested solution to this part of the question makes it clear that he was expecting candidates to pick up on a number of qualitative factors in the scenario, including management style, business experience and personal judgement.
>
> **Easy marks.** No marks are allocated for report format in this exam, but it is worth spending a moment on a heading and thinking about report writing style: a little effort here may encourage the marker to be generous.

		Marks
(a)	Advantages and disadvantages of each option (four options)	up to 5 marks for each option
	Alternative 'hybrid' solutions	up to 3 marks
		Maximum 20 marks
(b)	Strategic management styles	up to 2 marks per style
	Cost and benefits of each style	up to 3 marks per style
		Maximum 15 marks
(c)	Use of Mintzberg's organisational configurations	up to 6
	Product v geographic divisions	up to 4
	Centralisation v decentralization	up to 4
	Global co-ordination v local independence and responsiveness	up to 4
		Maximum 15 marks
(d)	Relevant financial skills	up to 3
	Ability to see whole picture	up to 2
	Strategic management skills	up to 2
	Ability to be innovative	up to 2
	Implementation role	up to 3
		Maximum 10 marks
		Total 60 marks

From: A Consultant
To: J Wainwright

ELITE PLASTIC PACKAGING – MARKET ENTRY OPTIONS

You asked me to assess four options for a possible move by Elite Plastic Packaging (EPP) to operations on a global scale.

As well as the usual considerations of business strategy, your freedom of manoeuvre is constrained by the priorities of your Divisional and Group managers. These priorities include a **high degree of risk aversion** and an insistence on **careful and accurate budgeting**.

Current performance

EPP has achieved steady growth averaging six percent between 20X1 and 20X5 and has improved its operating margins from 33.1% to 40.3% over the same period. These leading indicators must be a source of satisfaction to you and ought to impress both Divisional and Group managers, especially as the performance of other parts of the Group seems to have been rather poor overall.

Your success is the result of a strategy that has included both successful **market penetration** and **product development** in the form of your smart packaging. Currently, you have 50% of the European market overall and must therefore probably anticipate some slowing of your company's rate of growth.

The global opportunity

You have identified important market opportunities for your smart packaging in both the Americas and in Asia, since potential competitors in those regions have failed to invest sufficiently in the new technology.

Overall strategic considerations

Sigma Group displays a high degree of risk-aversion generally and takes a short-term view of investment, applying a three-year payback hurdle to investment proposals. The Group Chairman was personally responsible for closing down a previous move towards global operations.

Sigma group thus has little experience of operations outside Europe. The very different **business and cultural conditions** that prevail in those regions must inevitably affect any consideration of potential global expansion.

Global expansion methods

You have identified four possible methods of exploiting your smart packaging on a global scale: licensing, subcontracting, acquisition and establishing your own manufacturing facilities. There is, of course, no reason why you should not employ different methods in different countries.

Licensing

Licensing is a **low-risk option** and would require little investment. It would require care to select a suitable licensee that could be relied on to exploit the technology fully. It would also require the provision of technical assistance to the licensee, at least initially. The financial return on the investment would be good, potentially offering a growing cash flow stream for little input. This would no doubt be attractive to the senior managers of Sigma Group.

The downside of licensing is **loss of control**: you would be in the hands of the licensee for the life of the contract and unable to drive growth by your own efforts. Such a deal would not give clear exposure to your brand and you would gain no experience of wider global management. There would also be **potential for dispute** with the licensee over the terms of the licence, both during the initial negotiations and subsequently.

Licensing should be seen as a long-term option, since a successful licensee will establish competences in all aspects of the business; should you wish at some future time to start up your own operation, you would be starting from scratch and meeting **competition you had yourself created**.

Subcontracting

Subcontract manufacturing would allow you to retain much more control over your operations while avoiding the need for heavy investment in manufacturing plant and staff. You would be able to retain control of the marketing mix and **build your brand** as you wish to.

On the other hand, you would be exposed to the **potential for error** in such matters as logistics and dealing with promotion in a new cultural setting. You would also lose much control over **quality and delivery** since day-to-day management of the production process would be in other hands.

An advantage of this approach is that is might be possible to contract with a privately owned firm that could be taken over after a few years. The owners of such a firm might welcome this as an **exit strategy**. Subcontracting might thus merge into acquisition.

Acquisition

The acquisition of a suitably skilled and equipped packaging company could form the basis for a **very rapid expansion into a new market**. No loss of control over marketing or manufacturing operations would occur. Selection of the target company would be the crucial process.

Acquisition of an efficient company is likely to be expensive as goodwill will have to be paid for: the alternative of buying a company in a distress sale carries a significantly greater degree of risk.

The downside to acquisition is the inherent difficulty of making it work. It is well known that high-profile acquisitions in the past have **consumed rather than created value** and some have brought the companies concerned close to failure. The major problems are **cultural**, but there are also likely to be operational issues relating to the integration of work, management restructuring and system compatibility. The last problem is particularly common with IT systems.

Sigma Group does not seem to be particularly acquisitive and the Chairman led a recovery programme based on unpicking a previous round of acquisitions. However, the accountants who seem to dominate the group might feel at home with a proposal based on **quantifiable costs and benefits**.

The green field option

Building up a business operation from scratch in a new market is a high risk option. It will be extremely expensive and will take a long time to become profitable.

Suitable premises will have to be built, staff engaged and trained and marketing operations started. This will require project management skills of a high order. If you were to take the green field option, you should not contemplate starting operations in both Asia and the Americas simultaneously. The cost would be very large indeed and you would not benefit from any **learning experiences** that might be gained on a single initial project.

The advantage of this option is that complete control is retained over all aspects of the venture. Also, it may be possible to reduce the total cost by taking advantage of government incentives to invest in certain countries and regions.

Conclusion

The four outlines above deal only in generalities and can be no more than a rough indication of initial considerations. I should be pleased to assist with more detailed evaluation of options in due course.

Part (b)

Text reference. The topics mentioned in this answer are discussed in Chapter 9 of your BPP Study Text.

Top tips. Any answer to this question needs to be rather heavy on theory. This is for two reasons: there is not a great deal of detail in the scenario to discuss; and there is quite a lot of relevant theory to talk about.

Easy marks. It is important to point out that the numerical data indicate that the Group Executive do not seem to be doing a good job.

Sigma Group is a **diversified conglomerate**, owning a number of disparate companies that operate more or less independently of one another. Such groupings are out of favour in the West, largely as a result of unimpressive performance. At one time, taking over an inefficient company and selling off under-utilised assets was a route to quick returns, but such opportunities have now largely disappeared and, anyway, the benefits of such reorganisation can only be achieved once and for all.

Current thinking is that the creation of groups is only appropriate if it can generate extra value through the effect of **synergy**. The argument that diversification **reduces shareholder risk** by creating a ready-made **portfolio** for investors does not impress: such diversification can be achieved by investors themselves through their choice of investments or through an investment trust and without the cost penalty of running a corporate headquarters.

Overall, the top management of Sigma Group do not seem to be doing a particularly good job. Indeed, the Group looks as if it is on the **verge of collapse**. Turnover has shrunk from £580m to £351m over a four year period and operating margins have almost halved from 10.8% to 5.7%. As a result operating profit has fallen from £63m to £20m. Jeff Wainwright of EPP might complain with justification that membership of the group is actually destroying the value his company creates, since EPP's most recent operating profit exceeded £21m.

Goold and Campbell researched the role of the centre in 16 British-based conglomerates. They concentrated on two main activities.

- Determination of overall strategy and the allocation of resources
- Controlling divisional performance

These roles they referred to as **planning influence** and **control influence**. The variation in these roles allowed the identification of eight distinct **strategic management styles**.

Planning influence was exercised in a variety of ways, but a fairly smooth spectrum of styles was observable, ranging from minimal, where the centre is little more than a holding company, to highly centralised, where the managers in the business units have responsibility only for operational decisions.

Control influence was exercised by the agreement of objectives, the monitoring of results and the deployment of pressures and incentives. This gave rise to three distinct categories of control influence: **flexible strategic**, **tight strategic** and **tight financial**.

Of the **eight strategic management styles** they defined, Goold and Campbell found that **three** of them were particularly common; each was associated with one of the three control influence categories mentioned above and with a different degree of planning influence.

Strategic management styles

Strategic planning. The strategic planning style is associated with **flexible strategic control influence** and a **fairly high degree of central planning influence**. The centre establishes extensive planning processes through which it works with business unit managers to make substantial contributions to strategic thinking, often with a unifying overall corporate strategy. Performance targets are set in broad terms, with an emphasis on longer-term strategic objectives. Such organisations build linked international businesses in core areas. Business units tend to follow bold strategies and often achieve above industry average growth and profitability

Strategic control. The strategic control style involves a fairly **low degree of planning influence** but **uses tight strategic control**. The centre prefers to leave the planning initiative to the business unit managers, though it will review their plans for acceptability. Firm targets are set for a range of performance indicators and performance is judged against them. The centre concentrates on rationalising the portfolio. Such companies achieve good profits but are less successful at achieving growth.

Financial control. The centre exercises influence almost entirely through the budget process. It takes little interest in business unit strategy and controls through profit targets. Careers are at stake if budgets are missed. Strategies are cautious and rarely global. Business unit managers tend to sacrifice market share to achieve high profits. As a result, these companies produce excellent profits, but growth comes mainly from acquisitions.

Sigma Group would seem to fit fairly precisely into the **financial controller style**. The Group Executive do not get involved with the strategy planning process, but they impose an extensive and demanding system of budgetary control over performance. However, as pointed out above, the Group's management do not seem to be achieving the excellent short-term results they aspire to.

Part (c)

Text reference. The topics mentioned in this answer are discussed in Chapter 9 of your BPP Study Text.

Top tips. It would be possible to answer this question quite well in terms of **organisational and national cultures**, pointing out that whatever method of entry into the new global markets is chosen, issues of the kind identified by *Hofstede*, for example, are bound to affect the way the organisation functions.

The Examiner's suggested solution makes it clear that he was actually thinking about **organisation structure** and, specifically, about structuring a rapidly growing international company.

This is not an unreasonable approach to take, since it is organisation structure that forms the framework upon which systems of communication, control and co-ordination may be hung.

Examiner's comments. The Examiner declared that 'structure is the key to implementing chosen strategies'. This will be worth bearing in mind for future exams.

We do not have any detailed forecasts for the size of the expansion Jeff Wainwright (JW) envisages, but we know that he has identified markets in both Asia and the Americas that are similar in size to the existing European market. We might assume that eventually two further businesses might be established, each on a scale similar to that of the current European operation. In other words, JW may be planning to **triple the size of his business by operating in two completely new regions**.

If this is the case, significant issues of control, co-ordination and communication are raised and these in turn make it necessary to consider the basic problems of **organisation structure**.

Organisation structure is the basic mechanism by which organisations are managed. Structure provides the channels of communication and co-ordination and the lines of authority and accountability through which control is exercised.

Archie Williams maintains a strongly expressed commitment to decentralisation as the best way to run Sigma Group. The extensive and complex system of budgetary control he imposes demonstrates that the Group is actually highly centralised, but this does not invalidate the principle.

If EPP does expand on the scale we have assumed, the process of such expansion is likely to impose **severe strains** on the Williams system. The monthly Divisional board meetings are likely to become dominated by the affairs of EPP, as indeed, may the deliberations of the Group Executive. JW will have little time to spare for such matters if he is to drive the planned expansion along and there is a risk that higher management will give only minimal attention to the other Group companies. However, given the current performance of the Group, this may actually be an advantage, freeing operating company MDs to spend more time on running their operations.

The solution to this problem is for EPP to be **allowed much greater freedom of action**, with monitoring restricted perhaps to quarterly reports against outline budget. The Group senior managers cannot be experts in everything, and the changing circumstances of the Group make a policy of decentralisation appropriate.

JW will also have to consider how he wants to run his expanding company. The scale we envisage implies two new operations, each comparable to what exists now, all three being widely separated geographically. If JW is to manage this much expanded structure, he is also likely to find that **decentralisation** will be appropriate. This is because any central system attempting to control the increased scale of operations would be **over-complex and unwieldy**. Regional autonomy would also prevent the emergence of major problems of **language and national or regional culture**.

JW will have to recruit or promote a **replacement for himself** to run the existing European business while he sets up the new global organisation. Eventually, on our assumptions, he will be managing three businesses, each as big as the one he runs now. He will therefore have to find two further managers to head his two new continental operations. The implication of all this for JW himself is that he will have to take an overview and will not be able to spend too much time on any one of his three businesses.

Each of the new companies will require its own internal structure and systems that must reflect local general and managerial culture. There will then be a requirement for an over-arching structure of proper systems of guidance and control for the total expanded business. Creation of this structure will be JW's principal task for the longer term.

Part (d)

> **Top tips.** The Examiner's own suggested solution uses a very good approach to this question: rather than talking about the role of the accountant generally and in Sigma group overall, it concentrates on EPP and the various routes it could take to expansion. This makes the exposition particularly relevant to Jeff Wainwright, directly addressing his scepticism.
>
> The suggested solution also mentioned the accountant as a member of *Mintzberg's* technostructure, and the importance of cost accounting for the basic decision on *Porter's* generic strategy.
>
> **Examiner's comments.** Simply listing typical accountancy roles produces a poor answer: there must be reference to the strategic decisions being taken by the Sigma Group.

From: A Consultant
To: J Wainwright

THE ROLE OF THE ACCOUNTANT IN STRATEGIC MANAGEMENT

Accurate quantification in money terms is the overall role of accountants generally. The area of accountancy that supports business operations is generally known as management accountancy and includes work relating to costs, investments and performance control systems. Detailed knowledge of **costs** is the main stock-in-trade of the management accountant and forms the basis of much of the rest of management accountancy generally.

It would not be possible to run a business without detailed and accurate accounting information, because **effective decision-making** is not possible without this basic data. A good example is **pricing**. While there are many influences on the price decision, it is obvious that overall, prices must exceed costs if the business is to survive. Even where a decision is taken to sell at a loss for good market-based reasons, costs should be considered so that the magnitude and sustainability of the loss is known.

Decisions concern the future. Accountants are not fortune-tellers, but they are able to deploy a number of techniques for making **reasonable forecasts of the future**. Where other techniques, such as sales forecasting, are used, it is the role of the accountant to calculate and assess their financial implications. The natural caution of the accountant should be balanced against the natural optimism of the entrepreneur.

Within Sigma Group, there appears to be a very heavy emphasis on detailed budgeting, financial control and short-term profit, which seems to be somewhat counter-productive. This partly reflects the extreme **risk-aversion** of the Group management. It is also an example of what can happen when financial disciplines become ends in themselves. The proper strategic role of accountancy is to **support the creation and management of strategies** of all types that will create value, not to stifle them.

If we examine your own hopes for expansion, we will see many examples of how accountancy might support them.

In the first place, it will be necessary to produce a detailed **budget and cash flow forecast** for the project. This will require the making of estimates and consideration of the interaction of the various business processes involved. The project will have to be **financed** and, while currency operations are a specialist role, the general implications of interest rates, exchange rates and hedging possibilities must be considered. New ventures in overseas locations involving unknown contractors and newly engaged staff must involve **high risks** of many types. Again, risk management is a specialist role, but the application of simple accounting controls on income, disbursements and assets will help to minimise the possibility of fraud. Finally, we might mention the need for an effective system of **performance monitoring** and control to be established if the new businesses are to be run effectively: this, again, is the role of the accountant.

One final overriding consideration is this: it is important that accountants understand that their work is not an end in itself and that they exist to **support the business**. It is equally important that non-accountant managers understand and make use of the support that their accountant colleagues can provide.

52 LRP

Part (a)

> **Easy marks.** It is not unusual for case studies to commence by asking you to analyse and comment on the setting. There are marks available here simply for reading, understanding and summarising. A little thought will then bring you a pass mark in that part of the question.

REPORT

LRP FASTENERS

Introduction

The aim of this report is to discuss the strategic value of LRP as an independent entity.

Background

LRP manufactures a wide range of fasteners, ranging from basic nuts and bolts to more sophisticated devices. It became part of the Stillwell Slim group in 1990. Its turnover in 2000 was £53.5m and its profit was £6.05m. It has plants in Ireland, Taiwan and the UK and sells its products globally.

Strengths and weaknesses

Overall, LRP is a **sound enterprise** and seems **properly managed**. Its average net profit margin over the last three years has been 11%, while turnover has grown steadily at about 4%. Overdraft has increased in line with the growth in turnover.

The company has a record of sensible **product innovation** and maintains a review of technical developments.

There is an appropriate emphasis on **quality** within the company. However, the industry benchmark reports indicate a disturbing upward trend in both **internal reject rate** and **customer returns**. These may be linked to recent productivity gains in that output volume may be being achieved at the expense of quality. This is an important point, especially in the market for the more sophisticated fasteners.

There are opportunities for further improvements to productivity. The average age of the plant is rising as time passes and now stands at 10.2 years. While an average gives no detail, it does indicate that if advantage is being taken of recent technical improvements there must be counterbalancing examples of very old machinery. The UK plant is in **particular need of investment**.

The introduction of **computer-based scheduling systems** (such as MRP2) is another possible route to improved efficiency. The value of WIP is a little higher than the industry average, indicating scope for improvements in **production control**.

The level of WIP, while higher than desirable, is fairly constant. However, over the last two years, there has been a significant **rise in stocks of finished goods**. These are now one fifth higher than the industry average. This rise may be associated with the parallel rise in customer returns, but that possibility is not a proper explanation. Rejected goods should be sold to less demanding customers, reworked or scrapped. They should not accumulate as stock. If they are saleable, with or without rework, their existence should be taken into account in works ordering procedures. This may be further justification for an improved production control system. A review of the saleability of stocks might be an interesting exercise, also.

Opportunities and threats

The **global market for fasteners is growing at about 4% annually** and LRP should be well placed to at least obtain its share of that growth. However, its **market share in basic fasteners has fallen** from almost 10% to less than 8½%. The reasons for this are not clear, but two important possibilities are apparent from the data available. The first is the possible falling-off in quality mentioned earlier. The second is the lack of a manufacturing facility in North America, where growth is higher than elsewhere but sales have remained almost constant over the last three years.

It should also be noted that while turnover growth in the European market has been fairly low at 3% and 2.6% in the last two years, the Rest of the World market has grown strongly in the same period, at 8.8% and 6.7%.

It is possible therefore that LRP's manufacturing facilities are **significantly mis-matched with its markets**, since it has two plants within the EU, none in the NAFTA and only one in the remaining part of the global economy, in Taiwan. Consideration should be given to the possibility of **manufacturing in North America**. The long term future of the two EU plants should also be reviewed.

Sales of higher-value fasteners have been **adversely affected** by the increase in competition resulting from the entry of TIG Products into the market. TIG have a **cost advantage** in that their manufacturing takes place in eastern Europe. Their current success shows that their quality and service must be appropriate. They are in a favourable position to serve the European market, both geographically and in price terms. TIG must be seen as a significant threat to LRP, at least in Europe. However, their ability to compete globally must be constrained by the same factors that hamper LRP, particularly the cost and delay associated with international delivery.

Conclusion

LRP is in reasonably good commercial health, but quality and production planning seem to be areas in which improvements might be possible.

In the longer term, the location of the company's manufacturing facilities should be reviewed in the light of its pattern of trade.

Part (b)

Text reference. The topics mentioned in this answer are discussed in Chapter 9 of your BPP Study Text.

Top tips. This part of the question is particularly useful because this organisational form is typical of most large companies. Many aspects of organisational management are drawn together in a consideration of the divisionalised conglomerate.

It is unusual, but not unknown, to be asked to discuss a theoretical topic in the exam.

Chandler showed that the conglomerate form can provide a very large organisation with a suitable compromise between centralisation and decentralisation. Centralised control through functional organisation becomes unwieldy and inefficient as organisations grow geographically or in terms of products and markets. The other extreme, a loosely linked group of independently managed firms owned by a holding company, fails to achieve any advantage or synergy.

The divisionalised conglomerate is based on combining a high degree of autonomy at the operating division (SBU) level with value-adding input from the strategic apex. High divisional autonomy allows the organisation to operate effectively over a wide range of product-markets. Divisional managers can concentrate on their own operations and markets thus becoming more effective in them. Autonomy also promotes a high degree of motivation.

Mintzberg shows that the strategic apex. has a range of roles that contribute to the success of the organisation.

Management of the strategic portfolio. Portfolio analysis is as applicable to SBUs as it is to products. A conglomerate needs a suitable range of product-market operations. The corporate HQ must decide the overall shape of the organisation, buying and selling divisions to achieve a balanced portfolio.

Control of financial resources. Corporate HQ controls major investment in the SBUs. Its detailed knowledge of their operations and prospects enables it to invest more profitably than the most efficient external market. SBUs often have their liquid assets centralised under a corporate treasurer for more efficient short-term investment. The size and stability of the organisation as a whole enhance its creditworthiness and allow it to raise funds in the capital markets more cheaply than the individual SBUs could.

Performance control. Corporate HQ designs and operates a performance measurement system that supports the roles above. The system also permits assessment of the performance of SBU management. The only real method the HQ can use to deal with unsuccessful management is to replace it. The design of the control system must take account of potential manipulation and must not encourage dysfunctional decision making. Members of the corporate HQ supplement the reporting system by making regular **personal visits** to SBUs.

Support services. Some functions may be organised centrally and provided on a charge-out basis to SBUs. Apart from the services of the HQ itself, these typically include R&D, HR, PR and legal services.

Part (c)

> **Text reference.** The topics mentioned in this answer are discussed in Chapter 4 of your BPP Study Text.
>
> **Top tips.** Ethical considerations are more prominent in the syllabus for Paper 3.5 than they were in its predecessor. This is emphasised by the fact that the pilot paper included an 8 mark question requirement on this topic. Always take a firm line and stand by the highest ethical positions.

Ethics is concerned with notions of right and wrong behaviour and is inevitably subject to dispute because of the wide range of cultural, legal, religious and professional influences. The question of price fixing is a common and practical problem for managers.

Johnson and Scholes define an organisation's **ethical stance** as the extent to which it will exceed its minimum obligation to stakeholders. To some extent that minimum obligation is defined by law. However, law and ethics are not congruent; they may in fact be opposed to one another, as is often the case in totalitarian states.

The first comment to make on the CEO's proposal is that collusive price fixing is illegal in most western jurisdictions and is therefore something that responsible managers should not countenance. However, it is a fundamental of economic theory that **oligopolies** rarely compete on price. Industry prices are 'sticky' and even when a price war breaks out, it does not usually last long. It is possible, in fact, for a kind of **non-collusive** price fixing to take place, often when there is an accepted **price leader**. This is not illegal. Whether or not it is ethical is anther question.

The CEO's proposal would be more difficult to deal with if such behaviour were legal in the region in question. Global organisations such as LRP and Stillwell Slim are subject to conflicting pressures from stakeholders in different parts of the world. For example, the use of child labour in developing countries can be seen either as a way for those countries to exploit a form of natural economic advantage, thereby contributing to their economic development, or as a shameful neo-colonialist practice. The water is muddied when it becomes apparent that employers of child labour may be ignoring basic health and safety standards while opponents may merely be seeking to protect domestic employment from competition.

To some extent, the problem of differing national legal standards is being eroded by the modern tendency for **extra-territorial legislation**. The USA has been most prolific with this, particularly in its efforts to promote economic sanctions against Cuba. Generally, such legislation has been limited to major wrongdoing, such as war crimes. However, in 1997, the OECD countries and five others adopted a convention to prohibit the bribery of foreign public officials. This is now making its way into UK law.

While corruption might be seen as more serious wrongdoing than price fixing, it is clear that a trend exists. It would be risky for any international company to behave in a way that was illegal in any of the countries where it has a presence.

A further refinement of LRP's ethical problem would arise if the legal position were different from what was generally acceptable to the ethical notions of the local society. For example, the success of Mr Berlusconi in Italian politics, despite his many brushes with the laws relating to corruption, has been attributed to a belief among the Italian electorate that such behaviour is an unavoidable part of the way their society works.

A very simple test for behaviour is the principle known as the **golden rule**, which is often stated as 'deal with others as you would like them to deal with you'. We are told that LRP has never been able to penetrate the regional market in question. If this has been the effect of trade association action that LRP has condemned as improper, it would clearly be cynical and ethically inappropriate to subscribe to the same behaviour when circumstances changed and it offered an advantage.

A final consideration is a practical one: the effect of bad publicity. Another simple ethical test for individuals is whether a particular course of action would be acceptable to their friends. For companies we might substitute 'stakeholders' for 'friends'. It may be that LRP's current and potential investors, customers, employees and business associates would have differing views on any given ethical question, but giving them due consideration would help to indicate a suitable solution to an ethical dilemma.

53 Screen Books

> **Top tips.** This question is a little dated now, set as it is in the time of the internet bubble, but it is still worth tackling since it brings together basic strategic ideas and the problems associated with innovation.

Part (a)

Screen Books began as a joint venture intended to harness the **direct sales potential of the Internet**. We are told that it was successful initially in that it grew in accordance with its business plan; its operating losses of £42,000 and £54,000 in 1996 and 1997 would fit this assessment, especially as turnover increased from £367,000 to £635,000 in these two years. We may assume both that the joint venture generated some synergistic effects and that the warehousing and distribution part of the business worked satisfactorily. **Fulfilment** was a common problem area for the Internet business model in the early days.

That being said, such a joint venture is not an obvious strategic choice for a publisher such as Jack Benfold Limited to take. In essence, it is an example of **forward vertical integration**, requiring skills in distribution and retailing. The alliance with John Rogers Books made the new venture possible. We gather that Mr Speight is prepared to be **open minded** in his strategic thinking, as indicated when he moved into the travel and cookery markets. From the point of view of John Rogers Books, the Screen Books venture fitted well with their existing business.

The sudden availability of huge amounts of capital in 1998 brought Screen Books into very different territory. There are two important issues here.

(a) **The band wagon effect of the Internet boom of the late 1990s.** There is no doubt that investing in the Internet became extremely fashionable. For many months, normal business considerations such as profitability, cash flow and prudent investment appraisal seemed no longer relevant. The boom rapidly became a classic bubble, with investors so anxious not to be left behind that they would pour money into any Internet-based venture.

Such profligacy on the part of providers of finance is contagious: managers began to think in more and more grandiose terms and less and less of fundamentals (like profitability and so on). In this atmosphere, the least plausible projects could flourish – for a time.

(b) **The screen-based device.** The new device was, in fact, quite a plausible idea and no more outrageous in technical or marketing terms than the Internet-connected refrigerators now in production, that are capable of organising their own re-stocking. However, it was a very risky venture.

It is actually quite difficult to classify the new product in terms of *Ansoff's* product-market growth vector matrix.

Penetration. It could be seen merely as a way of bringing more books to the existing market, though this is likely to be a minority view.

Product development. The strategy certainly contains an element of product development, particularly including the risk. 'Considerable technical development' was required, involving both in-house staff and research agencies. The investment in R&D was enormous, rising to a total that exceeded Screen Books' turnover in 1997. It is not possible to assess the inherent practicability of the idea, but it certainly represented a major step.

Market development. It is arguable that the Screen Books joint venture was merely a new way of reaching an existing market; that is, a new form of distribution rather than an example of market development. However, the LCD device would inevitably attract the attention of the particularly gadget-conscious market segment and sales potential might be well be slanted to this segment. It would certainly be appropriate to ensure that books and magazines dealing with computers and the Internet were well represented on Screen Books publications list.

Diversification. It is even possible to see the new device as an example of diversification, being both a new product and aimed at a new market.

This complexity of possible analyses reflects the complexity of the strategy itself. Such a strategy will inevitably make major demands on the top management of the company.

This brings us to **strategic implementation and control**. We are told that expenditure on both marketing and research has been higher than forecast and, indeed, the table of summary data gives the impression of lack of control over expenditure.

In the case of **marketing**, it is fair to comment that turnover has roughly doubled each year and this must inevitably require an increased marketing budget. Indeed, marketing spending *as a proportion of turnover* has fallen in the last three years. However, it still seems rather high. It would be interesting to establish the proportion of the marketing expenditure that was spent on salaries: the marketing headcount has also doubled each year, which would seem rather excessive.

Research and development expenditure seems to have been under greater control. Indeed, it is partly by comparison with the R&D expense that the growth in marketing expenditure seems so high. Nevertheless, spending on R&D has been very high in absolute terms. It is not possible to comment in detail on the R&D effort, but it is somewhat disturbing to hear of 'fundamental technical limitations' after more than £1.5 million has been spent over three years.

The disturbing feature of the Screen Books strategy is its close correspondence with a classic pattern of business failure: that is, escalating commitment to a single, major high-technology project that ultimately proves unworkable. The profligacy of the Internet bubble, mentioned above, appears to have undermined prudence and financial control to the extent that the continued existence of Screen Books appears to depend on the willingness of lenders to finance it. The ability of the basic Internet sales operation to support the current burden of loan finance must be questioned. Also, if the new product fails to materialise and it becomes necessary to write off much of the past development expenditure, lenders may take the first opportunity to salvage what they can by closing the business down.

In conclusion, we may say that Screen Books' strategy appears to suffer from failings in both intent and execution. It is questionable whether the plan for the new product was ever really feasible and it seems likely that its implementation lacked direction and control.

Part (b)

Text reference. The topics mentioned in this answer are discussed in Chapter 7 of your BPP Study Text.

Easy marks. A theoretical model helps here. We have based our answer on SWOT: generic strategies or product market vector could also have provided a basis for an answer. We recommend such a use of models because it guides your thinking and allows you to organise both your thoughts and the data given. It will also be worth a mark or two for basic knowledge.

1   **SWOT Analysis**

Strengths

The Internet retailing operation is fundamentally successful and has the crucial fulfilment capacity. While trading at a loss, the company has actually held its losses to not much more than the total of the apparently inflated spending on marketing and R&D. This implies that the basic retailing business is sound.

Extensive experience of both publishing and book retailing is available.

The screen-based device. It is debatable whether this is, in fact, a strength, but if any technical progress has been made it represents a knowledge asset that may have value, if only on disposal.

There would seem to be significant cash reserves. The flotation must have raised more than £12 million and cumulative operating losses amount to less than £3 million.

Weaknesses

The financial position is dubious. There are a number of elements to this.

- The **share price has collapsed**. This may be due partly to market panic, but also reflects the justified doubt about the viability of the new product. This is bound to bring pressure from shareholders and analysts.

- Ability to generate **positive cashflows** is somewhat suspect. While the basic retailing operation is assessed above as probably healthy, it is doubtful that it could generate enough funds to service the existing debt and make a reasonable profit. If it were to be expanded, this would require further marketing expenditure.

- Contracts have been let with external R&D agencies. These may require continuing payments.

The dot com bubble has burst. It will be very difficult for Screen Books to raise capital or even obtain a sympathetic hearing from existing providers. Internet retailing is no longer a fashion statement and has become little more than an alternative to catalogue shopping.

Opportunities

It is difficult to identify opportunities without further information, other than to say that Internet shopping is now accepted as routine by many customers.

Threats

The *Palm Pilot* type of personal organiser is the subject of continuing development and may make the new product unviable, even supposing it can be brought to market.

The current global economic slowdown would prejudice the launch of the new product.

2   **Comment**

Screen Books is subject to major uncertainty over its new screen-based product. If it is ultimately feasible to bring this to market, the company's strategic position will be very different from the one it would find itself in if it proves impracticable. The first priority therefore, is an **authoritative assessment of the project**. This should be carried out externally to ensure objectivity.

If the project is judged to be viable, the next thing to be assessed is whether or not it will be necessary to **raise more finance**. If it is, financial market conditions may mean that it becomes necessary to make an approach to another company in the same field with a view to some form of alliance or even outright sale of the project.

If it is felt that it is possible to bring the product to market with existing resources, it will be necessary to exert **stringent control over progress**.

Should the new product development be shown to be a dead end, Screen Books must **avoid escalating commitment**. It must cut its losses as fast as possible, restricting operations to Internet retailing. This will improve its cash flow position, but it is likely to reveal that the company is under-trading to a dangerous extent. It would be necessary to **expand profitable turnover** significantly in order to service existing debt and satisfy shareholders.

Internet trading may not hold the potential to achieve this. The principals in the joint venture must also consider using their available cash resources to **expand their more traditional operations**. The acquisition of more high street retail outlets is one possibility. There are legal and taxation implications here, relating to the form of the group and the three businesses, that will require detailed attention.

Any retail expansion will require significant **promotional expenditure**.

Part (c)

A research and development project such as Screen Books' must be carefully managed if it is to have the best chance of success. Poor or non-existent planning is a recipe for disaster. In particular, **objectives** must be clearly defined and **time and cost constraints** established. Project management teams often fail to exercise control under changing circumstances. A special problem exists with IT projects: the technical ability of IT staff is no guarantee of management skill.

When an organisation is highly dependent on the success of a single large project, it is particularly important that **effective strategic control** is exercised. In particular, regular performance reviews against planned targets should be held.

All projects are likely to be subject to difficulties that must be resolved.

(a)   **Teambuilding.** The work may carried out by a newly assembled team who must immediately be able to communicate effectively with each other. Arrangements must be made to manage the probable need to cut across functional boundaries within the organisation.

(b)   **Unexpected problems** There should be mechanisms within the project to enable these problems to be resolved during the time span of the project without detriment to the objective, the cost or the time span.

(c)   **Specialists**. Contributions made by specialists are of differing importance at each stage, but must be carefully managed.

(d)   **Unproven technology**. Estimating the project duration can be difficult when it involves new technology or existing technology at its limits. Screen Books' project almost certainly suffered from this.

(e)   **Over-optimism.** Costs are often underestimated by optimistic designers, particularly with new technology. Screen Books may well have suffered from this problem.

A development project often arises out of a perceived problem or opportunity. Screen Books' research arose because of the opportunities presented by the Internet and the availability of finance. Under these circumstances it is important that the **management process should begin immediately**. The problem should be analysed to establish its **precise nature** and to outline possible solutions. When it is determined that technological development is required, the project **objectives** and **success criteria** should be clearly specified and possible routes to achieving them explored.

It should be possible to break the forecast activity down into **stages**. This eases both the assessment of the required **resources** and the establishment of intermediate **objectives**. Subsequent control is greatly enhanced if there is clear understanding of what is to be done, by whom and when. A variety of management techniques may then be used to control projects, including **Gantt** charts and network analysis. Network planning facilitates management by exception by identifying, from the outset, those critical activities that might delay others.

The process of control should include regular **meetings** to review overall progress and undertake financial and quality **audit**. Review will be undertaken at more than one level of management, with those in immediate control of developments meeting perhaps once a week; a higher level review might take place each month and a strategic review perhaps quarterly.

The final stage of control is **post-audit**, which asks two questions.

- Did the project meet its objectives?
- Was the management of the project successful?

Screen Books has been concerned with a single major project. It is possible to make recommendations for organisations that are concerned with broader aspects of innovation.

R&D should **support the organisation's chosen strategy**. To take a simple example, if a strategy of **differentiation** has been adopted, it would be inappropriate to expend effort on researching ways of minimising costs, at the expense of work to create a differentiating feature.

Problems of **authority relationships and integration** arise with the management of R&D. The function will have to liase closely with marketing and with production, as well as with senior management responsible for corporate planning: its role is both strategic and technical.

Pure research or even applied research may not have an obvious **pay off** in the short term. Evaluation could be based on successful application of new ideas, such as patents obtained and the commercial viability of new products.

Research staff are usually highly qualified and profession-orientated, with consequences for the **style of supervision** needed and level of **remuneration** offered to them.

Encouraging innovation means trial and error, flexibility, tolerance of mistakes in the interests of experimentation, high incentives and so on. If this is merely a subculture in an essentially bureaucratic organisation, it will not only be difficult to sustain, but will become a source of immense political conflict. The R&D department may have an academic or university atmosphere, as opposed to a commercial one.

Intrapreneurship is entrepreneurship carried on within the organisation at a level below the strategic apex. The encouragement of intrapreneurship is an important way of promoting innovation. Such encouragement has many aspects.

(a)   Encouragement for individuals to achieve results in their own way without the need for constant supervision
(b)   A culture of risk-taking and tolerance of mistakes
(c)   A flexible approach to organisation that facilitates the formation of project teams
(d)   Willingness and ability to devote resources to trying out new ideas
(e)   Incentives and rewards policy that support intrapreneurial activity

54 Universal Roofing Systems

Part (a)

Text reference. The topics mentioned in this answer are discussed in Chapter 6 of your BPP Study Text.

Top tips. The requirement for this part of question 1 makes an explicit call for your answer to make use of 'an appropriate model'. The **value chain** is the obvious model to use, since providing 'a superior level of service' is just one example of the way in which companies succeed in their fundamental task of creating value for their customers: the value chain model may be used to analyse the ways in which any company does this.

Indeed, the **marking scheme** for this part is heavily biased towards this model, offering up to five marks for each of: primary activities, secondary activities, linking activities and value system. Up to a further five marks are also available for a discussion of the **distinguishing features of service businesses**. This last element of the mark allocation supports the view that a brief and relevant introduction to the subject under discussion is usually worthwhile.

The test for determining whether or not to provide such a technical introduction is to ask yourself how much you could say about the overall question topic that is both **relevant** and **appropriate at this level**. If you have nothing to say, get on with the main part of your answer; if you think there is a lot that could be said and you believe it is both relevant and that it is at an appropriate technical level, you are probably justified in spending a few minutes writing about it. However, do not lose track of time and spend longer on your scene-setting than is justified.

As always at this level, **judgement is required**.

Easy marks. Assuming you are familiar with the value chain and choose to use it, you ought to be able to score a couple of marks each for identifying the things that URS does that correspond to the primary and secondary activities; the links between them; and the value system.

Examiner's comments. The Examiner expected that the value chain would be used here and suggested that the balanced scorecard was a possible alternative. He cautioned that, while there may be no single best model to use in any question, some will be inappropriate and lead to candidates answering their own question, rather than the one actually asked.

The Examiner's suggested solution contained an unusual interpretation of the **inseparability** characteristic of services. This is usually understood to refer to the **simultaneity of production and consumption** of many services; the suggested solution dealt with inseparability in terms of the service being sold and performed by the same person. We do not recommend this approach.

As you will see, we do not consider inseparability in the classic sense to be a significant problem for Universal Roofing Systems.

		Marks
(a)	Value chain analysis:	
	Primary activities	up to 5 marks
	Support activities	up to 5 marks
	Linking activities	up to 5 marks
	Value system	up to 5 marks
	Features that distinguish services	up to 5 marks
		Maximum 20 marks

(b) Performance analysis:

Rate of sales growth	up to 4 marks
Cost behaviour	up to 4 marks
Profit margins	up to 4 marks
Staff	up to 4 marks
Owner/managers	up to 4 marks
Other measures	up to 4 marks
	Maximum 20 marks

(c) Implementation:

Strategy	up to 2 marks
Structure	up to 2 marks
Systems	up to 2 marks
Skills	up to 2 marks
Staff	up to 2 marks
Style	up to 2 marks
Shared values	up to 2 marks
Other implementation issues	up to 4 marks
	Maximum 15 marks

(d) Excellence: Peters & Waterman attributes up to 2 marks

Per attribute	
Other attributes	up to 4 marks
	Maximum 5 marks
	Total 60 marks

Universal Roofing Systems (URS) falls into the large category of businesses whose market offering includes both physical product and service elements. Despite the fact that they provide a tangible and significant physical product, Matthew and Simon Black have successfully differentiated their business by establishing superior standards of service. Services differ from physical products in ways that have important implications for how a business is run.

(a) **Intangibility.** There are no substantial material or physical aspects to a service. As mentioned above, URS provides a mix of tangible product and intangible service. To some extent, the quality of the services provided is reflected in the physical products, such as in the fit and finish of the roofing systems installed, but for other aspects of service, such as the provision of credit facilities, there is **no physical evidence for the customer to contemplate**. The implication of intangibility is that a satisfying purchase experience depends on the quality of the service provided, which in turn has implications for management and for HR practice in particular.

(b) **Inseparability.** The creation of many services cannot be separated from their consumption: an example is dental treatment. Associated with this is **perishability**: such services cannot be stored. This is not really a problem for URS: the installation service can, in fact, be **scheduled** to suit the convenience of the customer and the availability of supplies and labour, as can the provision of credit facilities, which are arranged during follow up visits by salespeople. The use of a flexible labour force is an advantage here, since the ability exists to trim capacity at periods of low demand, thus maintaining a high rate of **resource utilisation**.

(c) **Variability** or **heterogeneity.** It may be hard to attain precise standardisation of the service offered. The quality of the service may depend heavily on **who** delivers it and exactly **when** it takes place. For URS, there is a clear link here to the intangibility factor and its implications, which we have already discussed. In particular, the quality of workmanship achieved when roofing products are installed must be of a high and consistent standard.

(d)   **Ownership.** Services differ from goods in that they do not normally result in the **transfer of property**. The purchase of a service only confers **access** to a facility, not **ownership** of it. However, in the case of URS, the company's service revolves around a very substantial and long-lasting physical structure. We might reasonably expect customers to see the improvements made to the roofs of their houses as having very important property implications.

Porter's value chain model provides a useful basis for analysing the way URS carries on its business.

Inbound logistics is the activity concerned with receiving, storing and issuing **inputs to the operational systems**. It deals with physical assets and is therefore of principal importance in relation to physical products as opposed to intangible services. This is not exclusively the case, of course, since the provision of many services depends on physical inputs such as tools, consumables and fuel. In the case of URS, inbound logistics is primarily concerned with the PVC components needed in its roofing systems. These must be made available to the installation teams in the right quantities and at the right times.

Transportation of installers and supplies to sites will be an important aspect of this activity and a significant element of cost. The materials used are bulky rather than heavy, which will tend to extend the service life of the vehicles, so the choice of Mercedes vans for the transport fleet is justified on grounds of long-term reliability (as well as image). We know that URS has six showrooms in its region, with plans for nine more: a similarly distributed approach to stockholding may reduce installers' travelling time and enhance system flexibility.

With less than 1% of the UK PVC roofing market, URS is unlikely to have much influence over its much larger suppliers and will have to base its stock management on traditional lines rather than JIT. It must also be prepared for failures of service on the part of its suppliers, which also implies the holding of a certain level of stock.

Operations is the value activity that converts resources into a final product. This is where URS is able to generate much of the value it offers. In particular, its **standardisation of processes**, **innovative roofing design** and use of a **unique installation** stand increase the productivity of its installers, while the founders' **emphasis on a high quality of service** puts this aspect of value creation at the heart of the company's operations. The financial service offered by the company also falls under this heading and constitutes a significant part of the value it offers.

The value added by both the roof fitting and the financial service aspects of the company's operations is enhanced by effective **human resource management**. *Porter* includes this in the **support activities** of the value chain: we have already mentioned its importance in service provision.

There is no significant **outbound logistics** element in the URS value chain as delivery is part of the **operations** activity.

Marketing and sales provides the interface between the company and the customer. It thus creates value both by informing customers what the company can do for them and by informing the company about what customers need and want. URS has a sophisticated sales operation, making use of canvassers, sales representatives, showrooms and a full range of promotional methods. Discounts for immediate orders can work to the advantage of both customer and company, though they must be carefully controlled so that they do not become routine. The ability to offer credit rounds out the sales service, though it brings training and regulatory burdens under the Financial Services Act.

Marketing and sales also has an important linking role within the company. **Customer satisfaction** is fundamental to survival and growth and it is the marketing and sales people who should be closest to the customer. It is for them to feed **customer comments** on work that has been done back into the operational systems and to take a leading role in considering **possible future market and product developments** in discussion with the other functions.

Service in this context is **after sales service**. This makes a vital contribution to customer satisfaction. The company provides a unique ten year guarantee on its installations. By the nature of its product, URS has little opportunity for repeat selling to the same customer. This is a general characteristic of building services and explains to some extent the poor quality and dissatisfaction typical of the sector. However, good service and customer satisfaction is an important aspect of URS' business model and helps the company attract the 30% of its customers that come from personal recommendation. There are obvious links here with the marketing and operations activities and we would expect that in a company as small as URS the same people would be involved.

Support activities are emphatically not of secondary importance in creating sustainable competitive advantage. However, their significance is not perhaps as obvious in the short term as that of the primary activities. The brothers Black evidently understand this and seem to have given a large measure of attention to these activities.

Firm infrastructure is the activity that, among other things, manages the company's property portfolio, its finances and its vehicles. It is thus fundamental to several of the value-adding features we have identified and must be integrated with them. For example, financial constraints must be balanced against marketing validity in the selection, fitting out and operation of the company's showrooms. The financial and management information systems installed by Harry Potts form an important part of the firm's infrastructure.

We have already mentioned the importance of **human resource management** to a business with a high service content and the importance of linking it effectively with other activities. Selection, training, remuneration and other aspects of motivation must all be managed so as to produce staff who are both willing and able to provide exemplary service.

Technology development has been very important to the company's ability to create value. Despite the difficulty of involving their large suppliers in development, URS has used technology to improve and differentiate its offering: this was discussed earlier, in connection with **operations**.

Procurement as a function is usually distributed within an organisation, with **decision-making units** comprising members of more than one department or team. These people must work together effectively, maintaining commitment to overall goals rather than system goals. Routine re-ordering of supplies and components must be done efficiently, but the real value-adding opportunities in procurement lie in sourcing decisions. URS has found innovative designs and products that distinguish its roofing systems from the competition, while simultaneously keeping its materials costs under control.

Part (b)

Top tips. Questions requiring a strategic evaluation are very common in Part A of your exam. They are often pitched at the level of overall strategy, though the focus is occasionally narrower, as in December 2003, when a product portfolio review was called for.

It can be difficult to know quite where to start with a question of the broader type. Basically, there are two possible approaches.

The first is to run through a few **analytical models** (such as the five forces, the value chain, the competences concept and the various portfolio analysis approaches; the balanced scorecard could also be useful) and see if they are relevant to any of the material in the scenario. It is unlikely that a scenario will fit any of them particularly neatly, but you may find that it can be broken down into manageable chunks like this.

The second basic technique is to **go through the scenario** noting anything that seems to be of strategic significance, then arranging the facts with relevant comments so as to make a reasonable account. This approach is certainly worth using on the table of numerical data that always accompanies the Part A scenario: the computation of a few percentage changes from year to year and a few basic ratios such as gross profit can reveal much of interest.

You can, of course, use both of these approaches sequentially. In any event, you should ensure that you spend ten minutes or so giving careful consideration to the numbers. As indicated above, you will not normally be expected to carry out any complex calculations; the data will be of overall strategic significance.

The marking scheme for this question mentioned sales growth, cost behaviour, profit margins and the contributions made by the management and staff of the company.

Examiner's comments. Candidates seemed to find this part of the question quite difficult. The Examiner wondered if the requirement to 'strategically evaluate' might have been puzzling. He intended it to indicate that there was a need to go beyond a purely financial analysis.

URS is a small company, turning over less than £10m and having less than 1% of the potential national market. Not surprisingly, it has followed a strategy of **focus differentiation**: the company operates in one region only and, as discussed above, differentiates its product in a variety of ways related to service scope and quality. The directors have communicated their ideas about quality and service effectively and the company seems to have achieved the differentiation they sought. URS is now poised to move beyond its home region and build up a national presence.

URS has achieved **impressive growth** since the appointment of Mick Hendry in 2002 and the adoption of a business model based on that used in the PVC replacement door and window industry. The company achieved growth of 27% in total turnover in 2004. Most of this growth has come from the private housing sector; the achievement of commensurate growth in the commercial sector would have required the commitment of substantial extra resources that the company does not possess.

URS seems to have its **costs under control**. Its cost structure has changed markedly since 2002, with **total sales costs** approximately doubling as a proportion of turnover. However, there was also a massive increase in sales, which has continued in subsequent years. At the same time, there was an increase in **gross margin** from 44% in 2001 to 48% in 2002 and 49% in 2003. Gross margin in 2004 was 53% and is expected to remain at that level in the near to medium term future. **Net profit** was negative in 2002 as a consequence of the up front nature of the increased sales costs, but rose to 5.8% in 2004. Continuing increases are forecast, with 11.8% being expected for 2007. **Direct labour costs** seem to be reasonably stable, despite the expansion, which might have been expected to counteract any experience and learning effects.

In the context of labour costs, the company's **policy of using sub-contractors** for its roofing operations is worthy of mention. This practice has certainly helped the company to **manage its costs** but must inevitably limit its ability to achieve its desired standards of service. The sub-contractors work in teams of two, so they must be largely self-motivating and they must take considerable responsibility for the quality of the service provided. The problem is that their somewhat insecure status may **prejudice their commitment** to a high level of service provision.

There is also potential for **problems in after-sales service**. The **potential weakness** of the URS system is that rectification is carried out by the installers, who are paid by results. If these teams are paid to rectify the work they have not done properly, there is an obvious disincentive to getting things right first time. If they are not paid, there is an equally obvious disincentive to getting it right the second time. Managing the implications of this approach is likely to be rather difficult.

Part (c)

Text reference. The topics mentioned in this answer are discussed in Chapters 6 and 9 of your BPP Study Text.

Top tips. It is not unusual to find current ideas about strategic implementation to be less cohesive than those concerned with strategic analysis and strategic options. This is because **implementation covers such a wide and varied range of business activities**. You could approach this question in either of the ways we outlined in our tutorial note to part (b) above, but it is probably best to start with some ideas about just what is involved in implementation. The chapter headings from Part C of your BPP Study Manual would do, but perhaps not many candidates would have committed them to memory. We certainly don't advise such a memory exercise, but we think that you ought to be able to summon up a scratch list of implementation issues to check against the scenario.

Both the marking scheme for this question and the Examiner's suggested solution were built around the *McKinsey 7S model*, which you may be more familiar with in the context of culture or of internal analysis. The suggested solution also made use of *Greiner's* growth model, which is clearly relevant, and *Johnson and Scholes'* analysis of implementation issues into **structuring**, **enabling** (with resources and competences) and **change management**.

The fact that the marking scheme was based on the 7S model does not, of course, mean that other approaches would be disadvantaged. Valid points, properly explained, will always score good marks.

Strategic choice

A fundamental issue is whether or not the directors of URS have made **good basic strategic choices**. The industry is highly fragmented, with no firm having more than 3% of the market. URS is unlikely to find its growth constrained by powerful competition for some time, therefore, but the directors should give some thought to the longer term. This raises the question of the continued appropriateness of the differentiation strategy. They may have an opportunity to achieve **cost leadership**, with all its advantages, but if they are to do this they must avoid decisions that would close off the possibility. This means actively seeking economies of scale and, above all, maintaining close control of costs.

A second basic decision concerns the **market** the company has chosen. We must presume that a conscious and reasoned decision has been taken to give higher priority to the domestic housing market and to starve the commercial market of resources. If this is not the case, and the strategy has arisen by default, it would appear to be questionable.

The domestic market requires **intensive sales and marketing effort**: expanding it to a national scale will require major investment in showrooms and in the recruitment, selection and training of canvassers and salespeople. The commercial market, by contrast, appears to require much less marketing effort, since a single sale can cover many houses: the problem has been finding the (presumably operational) resources to exploit the opportunity. We must now ask whether the resources that would be required for significant expansion of domestic house operations would be better employed in the commercial market. This expansion could be within the home region at first, potentially generating cash to finance later national expansion.

Finance

The company's growth to date does not seem to have been hampered by the **working capital shortages that often accompany such rapid expansion**. However, this may not be the case in the future. We are not told very much about the company's financial resources or its relationship with its bank, but it must be remarked that adequate working capital is fundamental to any business operation. There will also be a requirement for significant capital investment in new premises and equipment and in the personnel costs mentioned earlier.

Structure and systems

URS is currently organised along **functional lines** but a **regional structure** is being considered. The functional approach is suitable for the company's current scale of operations and some form of regional structure is probably appropriate for a company operating nationally. The problem is how to move from the one to the other. Effectively, the current directors will have to duplicate the existing structure in each of the new regions they operate in. This will require the recruitment of managers and staff capable of doing the things the directors and their staff do now and the expansion of existing control and administrative systems.

It will also be necessary to provide a **management structure at the national level** to manage the regions. Perhaps the most difficult thing that Matthew and his colleagues will have to do will be to undertake a different and more challenging role themselves as the strategic apex of national operations. They may find this beyond their capacity.

Culture and change management

Matthew and Simon Black have been successful in putting customer service at the heart of their business. To some extent their ability to provide customer satisfaction has been the result of their careful **standardisation of work processes**, but there must also have been the successful development of a **culture of good service**. Such a culture is one of the most important assets a service business can have. It must be nurtured and defended against erosion by the side effects of other management priorities, such as cost reduction. The planned expansion, with its inevitable expansion of staff numbers has the potential to **dilute and even destroy this culture**. Matthew and Simon must make it their business to ensure that this does not happen; they will have to make sure they devote time to communicating their ideas to new and existing staff and make sure that their attention is not diverted by minor operational problems.

This brings us to the issue of **change management**. No specific changes are currently proposed to the way things are done at URS, but growth on the scale anticipated is bound to bring substantial change. New and improved **systems of reporting and accounting** will be required, almost certainly involving major developments in the company's IT systems. This is also likely to be true in marketing, where, for instance, a **national marketing database system** may be appropriate. Such developments imply new staff, new procedures and new problems.

There may be other issues, such as promotion, sideways moves, new responsibilities and even relocation for existing staff. These must be handled with great care if the current successful company is not to be dangerously disrupted. Careful planning will be required, overseen at board level, combined with clear ideas about how the various necessary changes are to be achieved.

Part (d)

Text reference. The topics mentioned in this answer are discussed in Chapters 3 and 16 of your BPP Study Text.

Top tips. As we point out below, 'excellence' is something of a dead end in thinking about business. Nevertheless, it continues to attract attention, not least from your Examiner.

The suggested solution for this question mentioned the balanced scorecard as a way of measuring excellence, but did not identify any of the material in the scenario as relevant to it. We might identify a good standard of customer service (customer perspective), healthy margins (financial perspective) and the development of the unique roofing stand (innovation and learning perspective).

Easy marks. A knowledge of the characteristics of excellence would be a good start here and a little reference to how the brothers have performed might give you three marks quite easily.

Examiner's comments. The Examiner also mentioned that the attributes of excellence include both 'hard' and 'soft' elements. This is, of course, a reference to the **McKinsey 7S** model (also to be laid at the door of Tom Peters), **which he seems to think is applicable to almost any business problem**. You should bear this in mind when you sit your exam.

Peters and Waterman popularised the idea of **excellence** in their book *In Search of Excellence*, originally published in 1982. The study is now regarded with some cynicism, partly because the methodology was not very scientific and partly because several of the companies it describes as excellent stumbled in later years. Nevertheless, its prescriptions still embody a great deal that is of value, though like most advice, it must be considered carefully in the light of the actual problem situation.

Peters and Waterman identified eight attributes in their excellent companies. However, these are not in themselves badges indicating excellence: they are characteristic ways of managing that will tend to provide the conditions in which excellence may be achieved.

A bias for action rather than analysis and procedure: this implies a willingness to take risks in order to achieve objectives. The Black brothers have demonstrated this attribute above all in their adoption of the PVC windows sales model; this has certainly been a success for them.

Closeness to customers in order to learn and promote loyalty: URS is differentiated by its customer service, but that is not really what is meant here. This attribute is really most relevant to businesses further back in the supply chain that need to build long-term relationships with their customers. Closeness to customers would become much more important to URS if the commercial market were more fully exploited.

Autonomy and entrepreneurship by organising in small units: URS is taking the first steps towards this by considering a regional basis of organisation.

Productivity through people: the principle here is to trust the people at the customer interface. URS has certainly done this with its employment of sub-contract installation teams and has enjoyed good customer relationships as a result.

Hands-on, value driven management: this is achieved by 'walking about' and shaping values. The Black brothers appear to have done this, particularly in their management and training of their installers.

Stick to the knitting: avoid conglomerate diversification and stick to competences. This is advice for large organisations and not really relevant to URS.

Simple flat structures, few administrative staff: it would seem that only now is there any likelihood of a move away from the classic 'simple' or 'entrepreneurial' flat structure described by *Mintzberg*.

Simultaneous loose-tight properties: this implies decentralisation supported by strong core values and is evident in the way installation is organised using small, largely independent teams.

55 Datum Paper Products

Part (a)

Text reference. The topics mentioned in this answer are discussed in Chapter 6 of your BPP Study Text.

Top tips. Unfortunately, there is no acknowledged model available that you could use as the basis of an answer to this requirement. However, you could make good use of the value chain model to establish relevant duplications, conflicts and complements in the two companies.

It is well established that a majority of acquisitions fail to achieve the synergy they appear to offer. You should be aware of this from your general reading of the business press. Perhaps the most obvious things to say about mergers is that the potential for synergy occurs when the combined business seems likely to create greater total value than its constituents do separately.

One possible approach to producing an answer is to use the suitability-acceptability-feasibility framework. The problem with this is that it begs the question somewhat, as nearly all the material available to us would have to be dealt with under the 'suitability' heading and thus leaves us little closer to getting a grip on the material.

One thing we can recommend is to start with the numerical data. With this sort of table, it takes very little time to analyse the operating statement into percentages of turnover and to calculate simple ratios such as gearing and sales per employee. Carrying out this kind of simple numerical analysis will get your mind moving in the right direction. A careful look at the data table also reveals a high level of dividends and a low charge for depreciation, a combination with clear potential for future decline as a result of a lack of investment.

Easy marks. Some things are fairly obvious from the data in the table: the two companies' markets would complement each other quite nicely and DPP is the more innovative of the two. Also, there is also a strong likelihood of problems over cultural matters generally and productivity in particular.

Examiner's comments. Caution was necessary here in terms of the number of models used and the depth of analysis.

Marking scheme

		Marks
(a)	Areas of strategic fit: customers, value chains, technology, systems, style etc.	up to 3 per point
	Areas of positive synergy and areas of negative synergy	up to 2 per point
		Maximum 20 marks
(b)	Shared values and mission, clear objectives, top management commitment, communication, cross organisational and functional teams etc	up to 2 marks
		Maximum 10 marks
(c)	Advantages and disadvantages of greenfield option	up to 2 per point
	Advantages and disadvantages of acquisition	up to 2 per point
		Maximum 15 marks
(d)	Identification of integration problems	up to 2 per point
	Selection of key performance indicators	up to 2 per point
		Total 60 marks

Strategic options

An acquisition is a major strategic step and should be evaluated using the same **suitability-acceptability-feasibility** framework as any other potential strategic option. In the case of an acquisition of Papiere Presse (PP) by DPP, the main considerations relate to suitability, or strategic logic, since we must assume that the necessary resources are available to make the purchase and that since DPP is a subsidiary operating company, its stakeholders will themselves be largely concerned with the suitability criterion. There is an obvious further potential acceptability hurdle, which is the reaction of PP's workforce, to which we will return.

Synergy

If the aim of strategy is to **maximise the value created by the business** organisation, the only justification for an acquisition is potential **synergy**: that is to say, a probability that, overall and in the longer term, the combined enterprise will generate greater value than the components would do separately. There are often immediate efficiency improvements that follow the merging of two businesses, but they are once and for all: the aim must be to create an organisation that will enjoy continuing advantages. Research indicates that a majority of mergers and acquisitions fail to do this, so there should be a heavy burden of proof laid on the promoters of such schemes.

DPP's strategic aims

DPP's medium-term strategic objective would seem to be **to survive the wave of consolidation** that seems likely as a result of falling demand and pressure for price reductions in the industry as a whole. Under these circumstances it will be only the most efficient operators that survive. Major factors will be **market share**, with its associated scale economies; **efficiency**, which means in effect strong downward pressure on costs; improvements in **customer service**; and **innovation**, with its potential for higher margins.

DPP and PP

We must assume that DPP is not planning to buy PP simply in order to take over its order book and then reduce industry capacity by closing it down: PP is quite successful: its operating profit percentage, at 11.8%, is slightly higher than DPP's own and it seems unlikely that all of PP's potential for value creation could be captured in this way. There is not even any guarantee that PP's existing customers would transfer their business to DPP.

DPP must therefore **seek synergy** from an acquisition.

Markets

There is a good fit between the two companies' **markets**. Half of DPP's sales, or almost £100m, are outside Europe, against PP's £4.5m. PP has 60% of the French market and 20% of the Italian, while DPP has only 10% and 8% respectively. DPP has 45% of the UK market, while PP has only 14%.

Operations

While PP's operating profit is very similar to that of DPP, the breakdown of costs is revealing. PP's gross margin is only 25%, compared to 37.5% for DPP. A major cause of this discrepancy must be PP's **significantly lower productivity**: we are told that its manufacturing manning levels are higher than DPP's; its turnover per person employed is only £120,000, compared with DPP's £156,400; and its absenteeism rate is twice that of DPP.

This is a point of great importance, bearing in mind both our remarks above about the need for efficiency and the French national attitude to productivity and job protection. The potential for damaging disputes seems very significant.

Fixed assets

DPP should look more closely at PP's plant and machinery. We know that **the technology is dated**. This is borne out in the very low figure of 1.1% of turnover charged for depreciation by PP, compared with DPPs 5.1%. This would constitute another obstacle to improved efficiency.

The fixed asset picture is particularly interesting in the light of the **high level of dividends** paid by PP. Dividend cover is only 1.33, while DPP's is 2.23. The Truffaud family are taking money out of PP at a rate that is eroding its ability to continue to operate.

Innovation

DPP's **superior record of innovation** is borne out by its record of patents granted, its sales from products less than five years old and its much higher relative level of R&D expense (2.3% of turnover compared with 0.6%). This would actually provide some synergy in that DPP's strength would compensate for PP's weakness.

Customer service

Philippe and François Truffaud have established for PP a reputation for a level of customer service that exceeds that enjoyed by DPP. This is the single **greatest asset** that PP might bring to a merger of the two companies' operations and the one that has the greatest longer term potential to add value. It is, however, questionable whether this alone would justify an acquisition, since the **language** and **other cultural differences** between the companies may make it very difficult to transfer the PP approach. Ken Drummond might do better to seek a home-grown solution, possibly strengthening his company by recruiting service oriented and experienced managers to supplement his existing team.

IT systems

It would be difficult to reconcile the two companies IT systems. This represents a **negative synergy** that could by itself preclude an acquisition: the cost if integration might be excessive, while to continue to run separate operations would seriously hamper the realisation of any potential synergies.

HRM

PP's three plants are heavily unionised. We are not told of DPP's approach to industrial relations, but it seems almost inevitable that there would be a clash with the French unions over productivity. It simply would not be worth DPP's while to acquire PP unless there were **potential to improve the productivity of the French plants**.

Culture

We have already mentioned the problems of language and working practices at the PP plants. There are also likely to be **significant cultural differences** arising from the contrast between DPP's status as a UK subsidiary of a very large conglomerate and PP's as a privately owned French independent.

Part (b)

> **Text reference.** The topics mentioned in this answer are discussed in Chapters 7 and 11 of your BPP Study Text.
>
> **Top tips.** This question talks in terms of steps to be taken but it is not just about how to manage change: the various well-known approaches to change management are relevant, but there is more to producing a good answer than that. Judging from his suggested solution and marking scheme, the Examiner also seems to expect you to suggest, at least in outline, the essential cultural features that the change process should aim to produce. The McKinsey 7S would provide a good alternative basis for an answer here, especially as the Examiner seems to be very fond of this model.
>
> **Easy marks.** *Hofstede* and *Lewin* are obvious references to make; as are pace, manner and scope and possibly force field analysis.
>
> **Examiner's comments.** Generally, this question was well answered.

Integrating the operations of PP with those of DPP would certainly require significant changes to the way things are done in both companies. However, such is the magnitude of the differences between the companies (not least the languages they use), it would be appropriate to confine a programme of change to essentials, at least to begin with. Basically, the companies should aim to **rationalise their products and markets**; to spread PP's **tradition of customer service** into DPP; and to bring PP's **productivity** up to the level achieved by DPP. The processes associated with **innovation** could usefully be left in DPP's care for the time being.

Overlaying these changes will be the creation of a degree of **shared culture**, with common values and ideas about the company's mission. Management structures will have to be merged and this will have an effect on lower levels in the organisation. An integrated top management structure will be required and it may not be possible for places to be found for all those currently employed at this level. Workforces at plant level will remain separate, but their **working practices** will have to change if the benefits of the acquisition are to be achieved.

At the managerial level, it will be relevant to consider *Hofstede's* findings: The managers of PP, a French company, are likely to display greater degrees of '**power distance**' and '**uncertainty avoidance**' than those of DPP, an apparently 'Anglo' company, though their '**individualism**' and '**masculinity**' may be less. If significant differences are identified, it maybe necessary to attempt to adjust them.

Probably the most important feature of any programme of change is **top management commitment**. This may be a problem area in an acquisition where the inevitable management restructuring is bound to lead to some disappointment and frustrated ambitions. Nevertheless, it will be essential for Ken Drummond to provide strong and effective leadership if the change programme is to move forward.

Lewin's three stage '**unfreeze – change – refreeze**' model of change management may be useful in planning and implementing the necessary changes. This starts with the need to challenge existing preconceptions about the way things should be in order to create a receptive frame of mind in those undergoing the change. Lewin is also associated with the **force field analysis** approach to the introduction of change, which may be useful at this stage. The aim here is to strengthen the forces promoting desirable change, while simultaneously weakening those opposing it.

The process of introducing the necessary changes is often considered under the three headings of **scope**, **manner** and **pace**.

Scope is the extent of change required: we have already suggested that this should initially be minimised.

The **manner** in which change is implemented is crucial if people are to accept it rather than resist it. Coercion is really only an option in a crisis. Tactics such as participative decision-making, negotiation, education, and persuasion can be used.

Pace is linked to scope: the more there is to do, the longer it is likely to take since there has to be adequate time for proper communication, dealing with queries and problems and the introduction of new ways of doing things. In the case of PP's heavily unionised plants, the challenge of improving productivity is likely to take a long time to deal with.

Part (c)

Advantages of the greenfield site option

Cost savings

The entire paper making industry is under heavy pressure to cut costs. The **operating cost savings** available from moving production to an Eastern European country must be a major reason for DPP to do so. A major element of the potential for cost saving must come from the much lower labour costs prevalent in Eastern Europe. It difficult to forecast how long these countries will retain this advantage as they become more prosperous, but it is likely to last beyond any reasonable strategic planning horizon.

An associated advantage is the generally high level of **educational attainment** in the countries of Eastern Europe, which should assist the recruitment of competent staff.

Financial incentives

In addition to cost savings, there is the prospect of receiving significant EU and government **incentives** for setting up operations in a currently depressed area. Such incentives typically include tax advantages, soft loans, subsidised or nil rental of premises and outright grants. Any of these would help with the inevitable costs of moving a large production operation to another country.

Concentration

DPP currently operates four plants. We are told that each of the four plants manufactures a different part of the total product range but not whether this split is inevitable or even desirable. A move to a greenfield site may offer an opportunity to **consolidate** some aspects of production and other operations and to achieve some **economies of scale**.

Currency

Most new EU members have adopted the euro as their currency. Siting the new operation in such a country would be an advantage for that part of DPP's sales made into the Eurozone, in that currency translation, charges and risks would not be issues. On the other hand, sales into the UK would be made more complicated for the same basic reason. Unfortunately, we do not know how much of the 50% of its sales that go to European markets is broken down between the UK and the eurozone, so we do not know if this would actually represent a net benefit.

IT systems

A new single site operation could be built from the ground up and could include a single, integrated IT **enterprise resource planning** system, with all its advantages for planning, control and knowledge management

Disadvantages of the green field site option

Lack of infrastructure

We are told that potential sites lack suppliers, distributors and logistical support. **Logistics** is likely to be a major concern: as a manufacturing company, DPP will have to obtain its raw materials and other supplies and move its output to its customers all over the world. Reliable **transport links** will be essential for its operations. A related consideration would be the extent of any cost differential caused by the location of the new site: it is likely that average delivery distances would increase if production were moved to Eastern Europe, with consequent increases in transport costs.

The lack of local suppliers may not be a major concern if inputs can be reliably moved from current suppliers to the new site, but here again, transport infrastructure will be very important.

Government policy and practice

DPP will be affected by the extent of **bureaucratic drag** said to be present in potential host countries. Since the company's markets are in the West, it need not be particularly concerned about government intervention in local markets, but the prospect of intervention in its own operations is more worrying. The **stability of government policy** would also be a concern, though all the countries in contention are members of the EU, so a reasonable level of stability could be expected.

Productivity

While Eastern European workers generally have proven themselves to be willing and productive workers, it is likely to take some time to build up the **experience** needed to achieve overall high levels of productivity. It would probably be desirable to relocate at least some of the existing UK supervisory managers, if they could be persuaded to move: there should be no major problem in doing this because of the UK's stand on free movement of labour within the EU.

Existing UK plants

Since the motive for a move to Eastern Europe would be to **reduce costs**, we must assume that most of the UK operation would be shut down. This would involve the company in significant expense associated with **redundancy** and possibly with work involved in closing down existing premises. There is also the possibility of a damaging industrial dispute to consider.

It seems likely that the **design function** would be retained in the UK at least in the short term, as this would probably be the most difficult part to transfer or replace.

Top tips. If you decided to consider the advantages and disadvantages of the French option as well, you might mention low productivity; high cost labour; good infrastructure; good and well-established market relationships; heavy labour market regulation; and the currency issue.

Part (d)

From:	Accountant
To:	Ken Drummond
Date:	June 20X5

Integrating an acquisition

You asked for a report on potential problems with integrating an acquisition. Historically, acquisitions have failed to achieve the benefits forecast for them and this, generally has been because of failures to integrate effectively.

IT systems

IT systems are fundamental to the operations of most companies and critical to many. There can be little synergy if the two parts of the new organisation continue to operate as they did before because of **incompatibility of systems**. **Scale economies** are much more difficult to achieve, **overall control data** is not readily accessible and **knowledge** cannot be pooled effectively. Several approaches can be taken to integration, including the commissioning of a totally new system and extension of one system to cover both elements of the new organisation. Measure of progress are set in terms of system availability and functioning and might include the number of workstations with access to the combined management system and the number of elements of that system in place. These elements would include compatibility of functions such as email and intranet and preparation of routine reports.

Rationalisation of assets and operations

An acquisition is likely to lead to opportunities to rationalise assets such as plant by concentrating work in a reduced number of locations. In the case of an acquisition of PP by DPP, for example, it would seem likely that **productivity** could be improved by closing at least one of the French plants and transferring the work to the more up to date and productive UK sites. Similar consolidation might be carried out with sales teams, transport fleets and stock-holding facilities.

Key measures of progress would depend on the setting of **targets** for what was to be achieved and the creation of a suitable plan for achieving it. In the case of a rationalised field sales force, for example, it might be decided to reduce headcount by a combination of redundancy and natural wastage, while reallocating the remaining staff. This would have to be done in stages and the completion of each stage could be reported in terms of staff numbers remaining, area coverage achieved and, to monitor effectiveness, sales per head of sales staff.

Culture

Organisational culture is often regarded as a source of problems during the integration phase. As already discussed above, DPP and PP have clear differences in culture, most of which arise from the facts of their national origins. Perhaps the most important example of the practical impact of a cultural impact of a cultural difference is the unionisation and rate of absenteeism at PP's sites. The French economy generally is highly productive, but these two elements lead to a suspicion that what might be called a **Theory X culture** prevails within these plants. If this is the case, it will be a difficult task to improve the performance of these establishments. Practical targets might include the negotiation of a suitable agreement with the local unions and simple measure such as those already in place to measure absenteeism and individual productivity.

56 Churchill Ice Cream

Part (a)

Text reference. The topics mentioned in this answer are discussed in Chapter 7 of your BPP Study Text.

Top tips. Clearly, the first thing you have to do here is to decide just what you think Churchill's strategy is. Equally clearly, you are not going to find that the way the company has gone about its business can be easily slotted into a single theoretical category, other than, perhaps, focussed differentiation. Remember, strategy has many aspects and Churchill ice cream seems to have had a go at a fair number of them. The Examiner is using the term 'strategy' in its widest sense here and we are interested in any aspect of what the senior management of the company consciously decides to do.

Be prepared to discuss the company's activities from the various points of view presented by the strategic models you are familiar with. You do not have to cover these in an ideal order or discern any pervasive theme. There is plenty to say.

Take careful note of part (d) of this question. This illustrates the importance of reading all the way through the question requirements before you start your answer. In this case, it would have been very easy to comment at some length on the failure of the overseas ventures in your answer to part (a) and then find you had stolen your own thunder and had nothing left to say in part (d). A sympathetic marker might give you some credit, but your aim must be to make the marker's job as easy as possible.

Easy marks. You should have noticed that the company displays a significant degree of vertical integration. There are standard text book arguments for and against this approach that lend themselves to Churchill's particular situation.

Examiner's comments. This requirement was answered well, generally speaking.

		Marks
(a)	Advantages of current strategy including: Control obtained through vertical integration Value chain linkages Closer to the final customer Strategy difficult to imitate New product innovation easier Reduced buyer power Flexibility in meeting varying demand levels	up to 2 per feature
	Disadvantages of current strategy including: Increased level of resource/capabilities needed Internal competition between manufacturing and retail sides of business Increased operation/organisational complexity Growth function of number of ice cream stores Cost implication of varying levels of demand	up to 2 per point
	Performance analysis	up to 6
	Use of models where appropriate including: Value chain/system Five forces analysis Ansoff's growth matrix	up to 5
		Maximum 20 marks

(b)   Suitability   up to 6
        SWOT analysis
        Gap and 'fit' analysis
        Resource/capability analysis

        Acceptability   up to 6
        Risk and return analysis
        Screening process
        Stakeholder analysis – owners v managers

        Feasibility: up to 6
        Funds availability
        Resource/capabilities availability

        Compatibility of three strategic goals   up to 5
                                                                                                            Maximum 20 marks

(c)   Identification of current marketing mix   up to 2 per element

        Changes to the mix for each goal including: up to 3 per goal
        Becoming leading national brand – product innovation,
        premium pricing strategy, national availability, and national promotion
        sales of £25 million – higher take home sales,
        increasing product range, national availability,
        Increased advertising
        Penetration of supermarkets – own label brands,
        lower prices, national distribution, promotion support

                                                                                                            Maximum 15 marks

(d)   Analysis and explanation for failure of the international strategy including: up to 2 per point
        Ethnocentric approach
        Differences in customer buyer behaviour
        Cultural differences
        Failure to understand risk
        Resources overstretched

                                                                                                            Maximum 5 marks
                                                                                                            Total 60 marks

In **generic strategy** terms, Churchill is a **focussed differentiator**. The company has established a geographical niche in the London area for its outlets and distinguishes itself from its competitors both by its emphasis on the quality of its ingredients and recipes and by its vertical integration of the production and distribution of its ice creams.

Differentiation is the obvious strategy for a company of Churchill's size. **Cost leadership** can only be attempted when there is favoured access to resources or technology or, more commonly, sufficient volume to generate significant **economies of scale**. Churchill has neither of these advantages so, like most small and medium sized enterprises, it has pursued differentiation.

Differentiation by quality is a common ambition, but difficult to achieve, particularly in service businesses, since it requires unrelenting attention to detail. Services cannot be prepared in advance of delivery, so there is no way that they can be subjected to traditional methods of quality control by inspection. The service company's reputation is largely dependent on the performance of its staff.

However, Churchill is only partly a service business. The company appears to have made the use of **high quality ingredients** the main source of differentiation in its manufacturing operation, and there is no reason why this should not be part of a satisfactory strategy, especially as premium ice cream is now a well-established product for adults in the UK.

The company seems to have had some success with its ice cream parlour operation also. In terms of *Lynch's* market options matrix, this constitutes **vertical integration**. This is a subcategory of **diversification** in *Ansoff's* growth vector model.

Diversification is commonly regarded as the **most risky** of the four basic options in the Ansoff model since it involves the greatest degree of new and unfamiliar activity. However, Churchill has established its ice cream parlours alongside its manufacturing operation and they constitute an established part of its business.

Vertical integration may bring **specific strategic advantages**.

In terms of *Porter's* **five forces**, downstream vertical integration may be a way to reduce the bargaining power of customers. It is not necessary to monopolise distribution for this reduction to take place: a large enough volume of profitable sales to consumers may lead other distributors to feel that they must have the product in their sales portfolio.

Marketing may be assisted. Churchill's distribution of its products through its own retail outlets should enable it to establish a closer and more knowledgeable relationship with its customers. This should assist its pursuit of its generic strategy of **focus differentiation**.

Churchill's ice cream parlours extend its **value chain** downstream to the customer, allowing it to capture much of the value created by the various ice cream distribution channels. Seventy percent of its sales are made to its own stores, so this is a very important feature of its strategy.

Synergy may be achieved. A merger or acquisition creates synergy when assets are used more efficiently than they were by the individual organisations separately. Improved efficiency of material assets is probably easier to achieve in horizontally integrated companies than in vertically integrated ones, since there is a greater chance that specific assets will be of use to different parts of the merged organisation. A good example would be shared use of distribution facilities. The points we make above about Churchill's ice cream parlours are all connected to the difficulty of achieving synergy through vertical integration.

There are likely to be some opportunities for the creation of **managerial and administrative synergies**, however, in such areas as IT, HRM and finance. There is also the likelihood that **new product development** will be assisted by the immediate availability of test markets in the owned stores.

There are also reasons to be cautious about a strategy of **vertical integration**.

There is a significant degree of **operational and organisational complexity** in such a strategy. The **management skills** involved in running the stores are significantly different from those required for manufacturing; possibly even to the extent that **competing factions** might develop within the company. The two parts of the organisation are likely to focus **conflict** over resources and a partisan approach might be taken, with managers in the manufacturing and retail elements each regarding the other operation as something of a distraction.

There is also a significant **cost** involved: the outlets themselves must be financed, equipped, stocked, staffed and managed. In the case of franchised stores, these costs are met by the franchisees, but more than two thirds of Churchill's stores are owned by the company. Also, the six to one ratio of sales volume, compared with the forty to eighteen ratio of owned to franchised stores, would seem to indicate that the owned stores must be **significantly larger** operations. The owned stores must achieve at least the same ROCE as the manufacturing operation if they are to be regarded as worthwhile.

Performance indicators

> **Top tips.** The numerical information given in the three tables of the scenario is quite interesting and prompts a number of observations and questions; unfortunately, not all of the latter can be answered.
>
> This need not discourage you from making suitable comment, even if it amounts to no more than pointing out the puzzles and the areas in which more information would be required if they were to be resolved.
>
> Note that 'net assets' would appear on a balance sheet prepared under UK GAAP and would be equal to 'capital and reserves'; it would not appear on a balance sheet prepared under IAS.

We are told that sales of ice cream are both seasonal and heavily influenced by summer temperatures; the table of numerical data shows that total ice cream sales shows no clear pattern of change. Under these circumstances, Churchill has done quite well to increase its sales each year, though it is important to note that the **rate of growth has declined** from 8.5% in 2003 to 2.5% in 2005 and is forecast to decline further to 1.8% in 2006.

Annual growth in cost of sales is also declining, though at a slower rate than the decline in turnover. The actual increases in 2003 and 2004 were greater than the corresponding increases in revenue, and this is forecast to occur in 2006. In 2005, the increases were identical. The company is thus experiencing an **erosion of its operating (gross) profit**, which has declined from 9.3% of turnover in 2002 to 5.6% forecast in 2006. Indeed, gross profit has declined in absolute as well as percentage terms, falling from £1,310k in 2002 to £1,040k in 2005 and £940k forecast in 2006.

The income statement shows only one expense other than cost of sales applied to produce net profit: product development. This seems to be **very expensive**, amounting in total to slightly less than 40% of operating profit for the years 2002 to 2005.

Net profit is itself very low, having declined from 6.9% in 2002 to 2.8% in 2004. It showed a small recovery to 4.5% in 2002, but is forecast to decline again to 2.6% in 2006.

The typical Churchill **product cost card** provided is interesting. It indicates a target profit percentage of just ten percent. We are not told what the cost item 'overheads' includes, but even if it is restricted to variable or factory overheads and the profit figure is thus gross rather than net, it is still ambitious: as discussed above, gross profit has not been as high as ten percent overall in the years for which we have data.

The value of **fixed assets** has declined from £10,910k in 2002 to £8,880 in 2005. Were this trend to continue for more than a few more years, it would represent a possibly damaging decline in the employment of modern technology: as a result, both serviceability and productivity might be expected to suffer.

The data shown as **net assets** is also interesting. This is, presumably, equal to capital and reserves. One would therefore expect to see this value increasing as profits are added to reserves. However, despite a small rise in 2003, it has declined from £4,810k in 2002 to £4,300k in 2005. Such a decline would be expected if the company were making **losses**, as these would be charged against reserves. However, the company is profitable. The only other charge that might be made against reserves would be a write-down of assets that had previously been revalued upwards: in the absence of any information to indicate that this might be a possibility, we are driven to the conclusion that Churchill's directors make a practice of **paying dividends out of reserves**.

Part (b)

> **Text reference.** The topics mentioned in this answer are discussed in Chapter 8 of your BPP Study Text.
>
> **Top tips.** Both the Examiner's marking scheme and his own suggested solution assume that you will answer this requirement using the well-known criteria of **suitability**, **acceptability** and **feasibility**. These criteria are, of course, primarily used to assess not strategic *goals* but strategic *options;* that is, possible courses of action. However, their use to assess these goals is reasonable, especially as penetration of the supermarket sector might indeed be seen as a strategic option rather than as a goal.
>
> The lesson is that you must think fairly widely when considering a question requirement and be prepared to use the basic models in imaginative ways. Here, because the question asks about strategic goals, you might have been tempted to answer largely in terms of **stakeholder expectations**, perhaps with additional comment on the **compatibility** or otherwise of the three stated goals. This would have been a good start, and might have led you to consider **resource implications**. However, the Examiner's approach has the advantage that it relates the three goals very clearly to the company's general strategic circumstances through the **suitability** criterion.
>
> **Easy marks.** Obvious points to discuss are the **ambitious nature** of the goals; the **thin margins** to be expected from distribution through the major supermarkets; and the probable **high cost of effective promotion** of the brand.
>
> **Examiner's comments.** Some candidates confused the three elements of the suitability – acceptability – feasibility model. This is a very serious error to fall into.

The five year strategic goals set by Richard Smith are first, to establish Churchill as the leading premium ice cream brand in the UK; second, to build turnover to £25M and third, to penetrate the supermarket sector.

We can use *Johnson and Scholes'* three appraisal criteria of **suitability**, **acceptability** and **feasibility** to structure and guide our further consideration of these goals.

The criteria

Suitability is judged in terms of the **overall strategic situation**. A strategy would achieve a high degree of suitability if it exploited strengths, seized opportunities, avoided threats and overcame weaknesses. It would fit well with existing plans, fill any gaps detected by gap analysis and suit the organisation's culture and way of doing things.

Acceptability lies in the perceptions of key stakeholder groups and is particularly dependent on assessment of **risk and reward**. At the moment, these are the members of the Churchill family that own the company and make a contribution to its management, Richard Smith, who has a significant personal commitment, the new Sales and Marketing Director and the company's bank, since significant finance will be required for the envisaged expansion.

Feasibility is a matter of resources. The fundamental resource is **money**, since it can be used to obtain any other material resources that may be required. It can also be used to obtain skilled labour, but the skill and experience of **human capital** is difficult to buy in: generally, it must be developed in-house over an extended period of time. Richard Smith has set three **ambitious goals**: each of them will require the commitment of significant sums of **money** and the deployment of a considerable degree of **management skill**.

The goals

The aim of becoming the UK's leading premium ice cream brand seems to qualify as **suitable**, though the five year time scale is very optimistic. Actually, this goal might well be a good choice as the company's overall long-term **mission**. It seems likely that a natural emotional commitment to the company will make this goal **acceptable** to stakeholders, but there must be doubts about its **feasibility**.

Churchill has achieved a high level of brand awareness in its region but to extend that awareness to the rest of England alone will require **extensive promotional expenditure**; the cost would be significantly increased if the whole of the UK were the chosen arena. It does not seem likely that the company will be able to finance a major and sustained **marketing communications campaign** from its existing resources. Also, it faces strong competition from its two main competitors. To become market leader will be extremely difficult.

The **turnover target** fits well with the brand target and could be seen as a stage along the route to brand leadership. It represents overall growth of just 50%, but this is **ambitious**, given the current rate of growth in the UK premium ice cream market: that growth has been driven by the advertising of the two US owned chains and they may be expected to seize most of it. Churchill's **reluctance to advertise** and its **logistic failures** will prevent it from gaining much extra market share. It is difficult to regard this goal as either suitable or feasible, even in the medium term, though, in principle, it would be acceptable to stakeholders. Expansion based on 'more of the same' with, perhaps, additional ice cream parlours and an expansion of sales to major public events outside the London region would be a reasonable route to a smaller degree of increased turnover. It might be difficult to finance extra retail outlets, but the company is familiar with the franchise method and could utilise it more extensively.

There is likely to be a general internal consensus on the idea of distribution through **supermarkets**, since John Churchill and Richard Smith seem to be in agreement on it, but this goal is of **questionable suitability and feasibility**. At the moment, Churchill is little more than a **niche player**, differentiated on quality of ingredients. While it might be easy enough to obtain supermarket distribution on a trial basis, permanent stocking would depend on the achievement of **satisfactory volume sales**. This would require not only a major increase in production capacity, but also the ability to deliver at the right place and at the right time. Given the failings of its current production control and logistic systems, Churchill might find this beyond its abilities to achieve. It is likely that it would also find it difficult to finance the major plant expansion that would be required.

A further problem with this goal is that a major supermarket chain would **seek to deprive the company of most of the value it creates**, either by demanding very large **discounts** on Churchill branded ice cream or by insisting that Churchill produce an **equivalent own-brand**.

In general, we may say that stakeholders generally are likely to be sympathetic to the pursuit of expansion, but are likely to look more carefully at the detailed methods chosen. The **problems of implementation** that we have already noted are likely to be of concern to all significant stakeholder groups. In particular, the requirement for extensive new **financial commitments** means that the ability of the company to deliver on its ambitions will be examined very carefully. There is some potential for **conflict between stakeholder groups** here, in that shareholders may be required to provide more capital or accept restrictions on dividends in order to fund the proposed expansion.

Part (c)

Text reference. The topics mentioned in this answer are discussed in Chapter 7 of your BPP Study Text.

Top tips. Questions about the marketing mix tend to be fairly easy because the model is little more than a list of important market-related factors. If you are able to deploy a little business awareness and background knowledge you should be able to tackle such questions with reasonable confidence. Remember the important basic rule that the various elements of any marketing mix should be mutually supporting.

The basic 4Ps and the extra 3Ps for services can usually be applied to a scenario to produce a list of sensible ideas and comments. In fact, the checklist below (which is far from exhaustive) should give you something to say about most question settings.

Product Mix, quality, packaging, enhancements
Price Penetration or skimming for new products, image
Promotion Brand management, integration of media
Place Relationship with distributors, forward integration, discounts, reliability of delivery
People Crucial to quality of service, training, motivation
Processes Efficiency, standardisation, computerisation

Physical evidence Ambience, evidence of ownership

Easy marks. Before you can recommend changes, you really have to establish the important features of Churchill's existing marketing mix. Indeed, the marking scheme offers you up to two marks per element for doing just that. However, it is unlikely that you would receive a pass mark on this question for doing that alone.

Examiner's comments. Some answers were unacceptably vague as a result of failing to relate the various strategic options to the marketing mix as required.

Product

At the moment, Churchill has a **premium product** in its ice cream and, judging by the cost of fitting them out, in its **ice cream parlours** too. The latter might be regarded as an aspect of **place**, or distribution, but they are worthy of consideration under this heading since they form part of the **enhanced product** or total consumer product experience. John Churchill places great emphasis on the quality of the ingredients and packaging used. There is also an additive-free range of products. These are good points of **differentiation** for the company.

Pursuit of Richard Smith's **three strategic goals** has implications for Churchill's products. The brand leadership and turnover targets will certainly require the company to continue with its **product development** effort: we are told that this is a key activity in the ice cream market. A wide range of flavours and sizes will be essential if sales are to be maximised. Supermarket placement would also benefit from this, but the main area for consideration is whether the company wishes to manufacture **own brand** ice cream for the supermarkets. This would provide high volume sales but at the price of losing both control over the product and much of the potential margin. However, this might be a way of building up manufacturing capacity with a view to future expansion of Churchill brand sales.

Price

Churchill's current pricing policy is **curious**. 'At least £1 cheaper than our rivals' is **not consistent** with the long-established policy of providing a superior product. This approach is not only likely to **confuse the customer**, since the price and the quality of the product say different things, it is also **hurting Churchill's revenues and profitability**. Nationally, the luxury ice cream market seems to be an oligopoly and it would be sensible for Churchill, as a relatively small player, to **follow the lead** of the larger ones on pricing. A case could be made for charging a **premium to emphasise the product quality**, but a competitive price is probably the safest policy at the moment. This would work for the brand and turnover objectives and probably for the supermarket objective as well.

Promotion

The company has a great deal of promotional work to do if it is to make significant progress towards any of its objectives. There is no advertising at the moment, the only promotional activity being sponsorship of sporting events in London. As already mentioned, both the brand leadership goal and the turnover goal are likely to require **considerable expenditure** on promotion. Advertising and point of sale promotion will certainly be required. The role of sponsorship is possibly less clear: Churchill really needs the advice of experts in branding if it is to get the best effect from its promotion spending. In brief, it will be necessary to create a positive **brand image** and to **position** the brand relative to the competition by promoting a suitable range of **brand values**. This is very skilled work.

The supermarket distribution objective may complicate the promotion problem. Churchill will need to be sure that its chosen supermarket partners do not undermine the brand values it is trying to create by, for example, using its products as loss leaders or by failing to display them correctly. It will be necessary to achieve a degree of co-operation on such matters and on promotional spending to which both manufacturer and distributor make contributions.

Place

Churchill has a major problem with distribution at the moment, in that its lack of a management information system has led to shortages and delays in delivery to its retail outlets. There can be no prospect of successful expansion until the company has a robust logistic system that is capable of handling the anticipated growth.

A further matter is the provision of branded cold display containers. *Mars* set the standard for this when it introduced its ice cream *Mars* bar in 1988. Branded refrigerators are now common for premium ice cream products and the company will have to decide whether it wishes to go down this route. The expense will be significant and there may be a problem of acceptance by distributors, but such exclusive displays can provide strong enhancement to brand values such as exclusiveness, quality and luxury.

Service aspects

Churchill's products have a high physical content, but the service marketing mix 3Ps are highly relevant to the company's ice cream parlours. If the company wishes this aspect of its business to grow in step with its other activities, it will have to pay significant attention to recruiting, training, motivating and rewarding its **people**, to the **physical evidence** of its ice cream parlours ambience, and to the **processes** it uses in all of its operations.

Part (d)

Text reference. The topics mentioned in this answer are discussed in Chapter 18 of your BPP Study Text.

Top tips. Five mark requirements are rather unusual in this exam. The scenario offers some basic information on what went wrong with Churchill's international ventures and the question wording invites you to speculate to some extent. If you are familiar with the basic ideas of international strategy, there is therefore quite a lot you might say on this topic, so the Examiner has been rather mean in offering a maximum of five marks. Make sure you manage your time properly and do not write too much.

Easy marks. The scenario tells us clearly that Churchill has attempted to sell its UK product in Germany, Italy and the US without making any adjustment for local taste and has suffered the consequences, even where it has had complementary local products to enhance its offering. You should score at least one mark simply for making this point.

Examiner's comments. The main problem candidates had with this requirement was time management. Some answers were too long.

The failure of the venture into New York is probably attributable, in part at least, to inadequacies of planning. Churchill made its entry with its existing business model and made no adjustments for **local conditions**. These could have affected matters as simple as the selection of flavours available and portion sizes, or might have been more difficult to accommodate. It certainly seems that the standard Churchill ice cream parlour, originally based on a US model though it is, did not appeal to New Yorkers' taste.

The failure of this approach is not a very surprising outcome. Such an **ethnocentric** approach is unlikely to succeed in premium consumer market. Also, it was very ambitious to start operations with not one but two expensive outlets in a particularly expensive metropolitan area. We might reasonably question the quality of the market research, if any that preceded this move. More important, however, is what this episode reveals about the thinking of those responsible for running the company.

The ventures in Germany and Italy may have failed for similar reasons, but the fact that they were based on the acquisition of established businesses suggests that the situation may have been more complicated than this. We are told that differences in taste and customer buying behaviour were insurmountable, so we might conclude that too much emphasis was placed once again on trying to transplant the standard Churchill model.

There is also the possibility that both the European and US the ventures were under-resourced. They were undertaken on a fairly large scale and it may be that too much capital was sunk in the initial investments, and not enough retained to make necessary adjustments to the way things were done.

Mock Exams

ACCA

Paper 3.5

Strategic Business Planning and Development

Mock Examination 1

Question Paper	
Time allowed	**3 hours**
This paper is divided into two sections	
Section A	ONE compulsory question to be attempted
Section B	TWO questions ONLY to be attempted

DO NOT OPEN THIS PAPER UNTIL YOU ARE READY TO START UNDER EXAMINATION CONDITIONS

SECTION A – This question is compulsory and MUST be attempted

Question 1

Dr John Clarkson is currently Managing Director of BlueSky Analysis Ltd, a research company which obtains data gathered from satellite observations, analyses this data and then sells the information to client organisations. During the 1980s Clarkson had been employed by the United Kingdom's Ministry of Defence, to interpret military data obtained from satellite surveillance. With the end of the Cold War and the change in political regimes in the early 1990s Clarkson believed that the demand for this military intelligence would decline and he accordingly set up BlueSky Analysis Ltd to utilise the technology which he understood and to adapt it for peaceful applications. Together with four other scientists he formed the company in 1992. These five scientists were the only shareholders. Most of the work was then focused on obtaining new customers, and as the technology had, until then, been primarily used for highly confidential military information gathering there were few other potential competitors. It was now possible to buy from both military and civil satellite owners data obtained from a variety of sources. This data could be usefully interpreted and could provide valuable information on a wide range of topics including climate change, crop forecasts, soil conditions and mineral deposits. The potential customers for such information were mainly governmental agencies, operating both nationally and internationally, including organisations such as the United Nations Food and Agricultural Organisation. Many mining and oil exploration companies also found the information invaluable in helping to select geographical locations for exploration and development.

The initial growth was rapid. The company had to employ more scientists and within two years the company had grown to number about 45 employees including 15 clerical staff. It was an attractive company for the scientists to work for. There was little management structure. Each analyst worked on an individual client's project, specialising on either a geographical area or on a specific industry such as mining, helping to identify the location of mineral deposits. The analysts could concentrate solely on scientific work and were not diverted into administrative activities involving long meetings and planning programmes. Staff turnover was very low. All the scientists required was a project to work on and secretarial support to prepare reports for clients. Otherwise they usually worked alone. Clarkson was the Managing Director, but all five shareholders took in turn to carry out the necessary but, in their opinion, mundane administrative tasks required in any company – personnel, purchasing, finance and marketing activities. They did employ some junior staff or used outside agencies to carry out the routine tasks such as payroll and book-keeping. Even recruitment was contracted out to an agency. These five senior managers were also totally responsible for the critical task of obtaining contracts. However they, like most of the scientists, were at their happiest when they were focusing on the analytical work for clients and not being managers.

Unfortunately, this informal style and structure did not run smoothly. Although the company provided a good social and challenging work environment, it was inevitable that this analyst-led approach should lack direction and that errors in administration would create problems with clients. There was inadequate integration and teamwork within the company, with most of the scientists working independently on their own projects. The five senior scientists began to spend much of their time 'fire-fighting' – correcting mistakes which should never had occurred. Fortunately the company was still a leader in this small specialist field and so did not lose much business to merging competitors.

However by late 1997 it was apparent that this loose management structure was inhibiting the growth of the company. The market for data collection and analysis was becoming more global and competitors were eroding BlueSky's market position. Its projects were frequently going over budget and many were taking too long to complete. A lack of cohesion and cooperation between the analysts with the company meant that when such delays occurred other staff members could not help to sort out the problems. Furthermore, as the senior managers acted as intermediaries between the client and the scientist responsible for their particular research contract, any negotiations for changes in requirements tended to be lengthy and confusing. The problem was that a move towards greater discipline and structure, necessary for keeping work on target and profitable, was likely to alienate the analysts who enjoyed their independence.

In early 1998 the senior management, now facing declining orders, decided that they could not continue in such an undisciplined manner. They were approached by a much larger company from the USA, United Data Systems (UDS), whose main business was as a software company, providing information systems for major clients throughout the world. These contracts were with both public and private sector clients ranging from automobile manufacturers to governmental tax agencies. UDS was accustomed to dealing with multi-million pound contracts, serviced by specialist teams, and accordingly had the infrastructure and systems to suit such a business. The company employed in excess of 3,000 employees world-wide, with almost half being in support but non-operational roles, compared with a total of 90 employees at BlueSky in 1998. Recognising their lack of interest in administration, Clarkson and his four fellow shareholders agreed to the acquisition by UDS, but still maintained a significant share of the equity. Although technically UDS now owned BlueSky it was not seeking to absorb it. The larger company, seeking to diversify into more innovative areas, saw BlueSky as providing the expertise and access into a rapidly expanding and lucrative market. They did not wish to destroy the research-centred culture of BlueSky because the company's success depended upon the scientists' continued good will and commitment. They agreed to allow the smaller company to continue operating as a subsidiary company in an innovative manner – no large company bureaucracy being imposed upon the scientists. However UDS would now require that all new contracts be investigated by themselves for financial attractiveness. A charge was levied from the centre for this service. This meant that all contracts, regardless of size, were now sent to the headquarters in the USA. This was intended to ensure that BlueSky did not accept contracts where they could not complete on time or which were not profitable.

However this fusion of cultures did generate unforeseen problems. BlueSky had been accustomed to managing smaller contracts with lower margins but now UDS was seeking to impose financial criteria on them which were more suitable for a larger company with a bigger infrastructure to support UDS also had a more formalised system of contract vetting which took time to complete. There was dissatisfaction in both BlueSky and UDS as BlueSky's scientists were seeing contracts being lost and the parent company was not seeing the growth it had expected when it acquired the subsidiary. In addition some of BlueSky's long-standing clients were becoming increasingly worried by the further reduction in quality and service they were receiving. Clarkson was summoned to the USA headquarters to discuss the future of BlueSky. He feared that the proposed solution would be to integrate BlueSky more closely into UDS, by making it an operating division, with both strategy and operations being dependent upon UDS's central control, rather than by allowing it the greater freedom it currently had as a subsidiary company.

Details of the performance and financial position of BlueSky Analysis Ltd can be found in Table 1 below.

Table 1 Financial Data

	1997	1999
	(last full year as an independent company)	(first full year as a subsidiary of UDS)
	£	£
Sales Revenue	4,400	4,350
Cost of Sales	3,400	3,250
Expenses	300	480
of which – marketing	100	80
– administration	200	400
Operating profit	700	620
Value of contracts in progress or on order book (31 December)	1,300	750
Employees	85	93
Fixed assets	750	600
Average value of contracts	45	90
Percentage of contracts not on cost or time	37	45

Required

(a)   Identify and explain the problems which are now being faced by BlueSky Analysis Ltd, operating as a subsidiary company of UDS.   **(15 marks)**

(b)   If BlueSky is integrated fully into UDS it is probable that there will be a clash of cultures. Using models of your choice to support your arguments:

     (i)   Comment on the current differences in culture, explaining the main factors which cause these differences;   **(10 marks)**

     (ii)   Explain the ways in which the management at UDS might minimise the conflict which may arise from the cultural differences.   **(10 marks)**

(c)   Clarkson, fearing an imposed solution by UDS which would be unwelcome to both employees and clients of the BlueSky subsidiary, has decided to put forward his own solutions.

Provide a brief report for Clarkson which he will present to the senior management of UDS, suggesting how the current situation might be improved.   **(15 marks)**

(d)   With reference to BlueSky identify and explain the main factors that can cause a project to fail to meet its original objectives.   **(10 marks)**

(Total = 60 marks)

SECTION B – TWO questions ONLY to be attempted

Question 2

Klypso Corporation is a medium-sized regional company, producing and distributing fruit flavoured, carbonated drinks. In recent years it has seen a rapid decline in its sales to local stores and supermarkets. There are two main reasons for its poor performance. Firstly the major corporations, selling cola drinks have developed global brands which are now capturing the youth market which is seeking more 'sophisticated' products. Secondly the sales outlets are no longer willing to provide shelf space to products which are not brand leaders, or potential leaders in their product category.

The Managing Director (MD) of Klypso believes that the company needs a drastic turnaround if it is to survive. The soft drinks industry has become too competitive, and the bottling technology too expensive to warrant new investment. However the company feels that its greatest strength is its knowledge and access to distribution channels and therefore its opinion is that it should still stay within the food and drinks industry. Whilst on a fact-finding mission to the United States of America he MD was attracted by a new chocolate confectionery product which claims to provide high energy contact but with low fat. This seemed to be a successful combination of attributes for those consumers, mainly active participants in sporting activities, who were concerned with their diet but who enjoyed an occasional treat. The product has been developed and is owned by a relatively unknown confectionery company in California. The company has agreed to provide Klypso with a licensing contract for manufacture and sales of the product within Klypso's own country.

The MD is convinced that the secret to success will be in the marketing of the product. The company has suffered in its drinks business because it did not develop a distinctive and successful branch. The new product is also unknown in Klypso's own country. In order to get national recognition and acceptance from the major retail outlets the product will need considerable promotional support. As the company has very little experience or expertise in promotional activity it was decided to use a marketing consultancy to provide guidance in developing a promotional plan.

Klypso, being a medium-sized company, has only a limited budget. It will have to focus upon a new and national market instead of its traditional, regional stronghold. It has to develop a new brand in a product area with which it is not familiar. Before committing itself to a national launch Klypso has decided to trial the product launch in a test market.

Required

You have been appointed to act as the business consultant as part of the marketing consultancy team assisting Klypso.

(a) Present a report to the management of Klypso recommending and justifying the types of promotional activity that could be used to support the launch of the new product. **(14 marks)**

(b) Which factors need to be considered to ensure that the test market produces results which can be reliably used prior to the national launch? **(6 marks)**

(Total = 20 marks)

Question 3

Alan Ormerod, the senior partner at ASG, a medium sized UK based accounting firm, was worried. The firm had developed an active policy towards the recruitment of graduates from various academic disciplines who were then sponsored to take professional accounting qualifications. The graduate trainees were given a week's induction course into the firm and then placed on a six month training programme organised by the personnel department. The programme consisted of six weeks spent in each of the main areas of the firm's business – taxation, auditing, business services and financial planning, so that they could get an overview of the firm's activities and the services provided to clients. At the end of the six month training period they were assigned to one of the main areas of business as assistant accountants.

The programme had been in existence for many years and had the support of the senior partners in the firm and also the personnel department, whose budget reflected both the time taken by the graduates in training and the number of graduates on the programme. Unfortunately, there was no clear consensus amongst the partners about what, precisely, the graduate trainees should be able to do on completion of the programme. Successful completion of the programme was important to the graduates as it signalled the end of their probationary period and was linked to a significant rise in salary. The graduate trainees, however, were not happy. They felt that the lack of clarity over what precisely they should be able to do and the time taken to move them through areas of the firm which were of little interest to them was affecting their morale and commitment to the firm. Even more significant was the number who either failed to complete the training programme or who left to join one of ASG's rivals. Despite this problem, the partners insisted that to get a full appreciation of the firm the graduates needed the full six months training experience.

Alan was perplexed as to how he could reconcile the traditional view of training taken by the partners with the needs of the graduate trainees and their desire for a more focused and shorter period of training. The firm certainly needed committed, well motivated graduate accountants to meet the increased expectations of clients and the competition from rival firms.

Required

(a) Examine the change theories and models which could help Alan understand the conflict between the partners and the graduate trainees. **(12 marks)**

(b) Recommend an action plan whereby the differing attitudes of the partners and graduate trainees could be reconciled. **(8 marks)**

(Total = 20 marks)

Question 4

Matthew Sanders is the Operations Director of Chestlands Insurance Ltd. Chestlands is a medium-sized company, operating in a specific niche within the financial services sector. It has found a reasonably profitable segment focusing on the lower income end of the personal insurance market. Its customers are generally unskilled workers, single parent families or older people with poor pensions. The common factor is that they all have little discretionary income. Most other financial companies see this segment as being unattractive and unlikely to yield high profits and as a result Chestlands have had few competitors. By concentrating on this one segment it can obtain economies of scale, particularly in collection and administration. Furthermore it does not need to provide a wide portfolio of products as most other financial companies are obliged to.

Most of the business is for cheap insurance policies to cover future contingencies – the cost of essential household repairs, furniture and even funerals. These clients generally have insufficient money to pay for these types of bill out of current income and therefore they need to save for them. Unfortunately some of them do not have bank accounts and so savings have to be collected in a more direct manner. Others, with bank accounts, rarely use them for saving, and it is not unknown for these accounts to be mismanaged. The company uses agents who make weekly calls at the clients' homes to collect their payment. These agents also are responsible for seeking new business by following up enquiries from potential customers who have heard of Chestlands through advertising in the local newspapers or from word-of-mouth recommendations from other customers. Because the company inevitably works on low margins the payment to these agents is low and a significant proportion of it is commission based. Consequently this 'salesforce' is mainly unskilled and turnover is high.

Recently Sanders has received an increasing number of complaints from his customers and new business has been declining. Existing customer have not renewed policies and there have been fewer new customers. The complaints have centered around the sales staff, involving incomplete and unfinished documentation, missed appointments, financial irregularities and an aggressive attitude towards selling new policies. Sanders is aware that his company is only profitable because it has volume sales in a focused market. Any loss of business will damage his company's reputation and profits. He has come to the conclusion that quality is the key to recovery and so he has decided to implement a system of checking the paper work so as to ensure a more acceptable level of delivery. He feels confident that this will solve the problem.

Required

(a)   Discuss whether Sanders' proposed solution will correct the problems currently being experienced by Chestlands. **(10 marks)**

(b)   It has been suggested to Sanders that a system of Total Quality Management should be introduced into Chestlands.

Describe the actions which must be undertaken within the organisation to ensure that this quality initiative is successfully implemented. **(10 marks)**

(Total = 20 marks)

Answers

DO NOT TURN THIS PAGE UNTIL YOU HAVE
COMPLETED THE MOCK EXAM

A plan of attack

We discussed the problem of which question to start with earlier, in 'Passing the 3.5 exam'. Here we will merely reiterate our view that question 1 is nearly always the best place to start and, if you do decide to start with a Section B question, **make sure that you finish your answer in no more than 36 minutes**.

Question 1 is a good example of the kind of question the Examiner has occasionally set in the past, in that the numerical data is rather limited and the emphasis is on narrative and concept. The requirements include references to culture, conflict and projects, but requirements (a) and (b), worth 15 marks in total, are very open-ended and give little hint as to how you should proceed. You must pause and think carefully about you are going to deal with these requirements.

We would recommend that you tackle the four requirements of question 1 in the order in which they appear, since there is an element of continuation in the first three, at least. Requirement (d) will to some extent stand by itself, so you could deal with it first if you really wanted to, but if you do, make it absolutely plain to the marker where it starts and stops: markers will generally expect answers to appear in the same order as the requirements.

Question 2 is a little longer and a little simpler than is now typical in Paper 3.5 exams. The scenario is largely illustrative and the requirements are not as closely linked to its details as is likely to be the case in future exams. Nevertheless, sometimes the Examiners set a question of this type and you must be prepared to answer it. The preparation of a solution does require a **sound knowledge of basic marketing activity** and this is a very popular topic with the Examiner. If you decide to tackle this question, it would be as well to do it early on and get it out of the way.

Question 3 is very much a game of two halves. Requirement (a) is quite helpful in that it makes very clear the theoretical knowledge you will have to deploy if you are to deal with it properly. There is really no point attempting this question if you do not have a reasonable understanding of change theories – unless you are desperate for a third question and think you might pick up a few marks with some sensible suggestions for requirement (b). That second requirement is, of course, very different in its nature: there is no specific model that would provide you with a template for an action plan, so you will have to think hard and be as practical as you can.

Question 4 is rather specialised and requires a certain amount of analysis, particularly in requirement (a). Also, it is unusual in the order in which the requirements appear: it is more common for the theory-based part to come first and be followed by the more open-ended, judgement-based element. Despite all of that, however, this could be a good choice if you are confident in your knowledge of quality topics.

SECTION A

Question 1

Part (a)

> **Top tips.** This part of the question places a premium on your ability to analyse the given data – there is little scope for the introduction of theory. Questions like this are easier to tackle if you have experience of the way businesses are run. Unfortunately, few students have much experience of that type. It is important that you both cultivate an awareness of what is happening in your own organisation and supplement that awareness by reading the business pages of your newspaper and other, more specialised publications, such as *The Economist*.

BlueSky and UDS are two very different companies. The only things they have in common are **project-based activity** and **high technology** and even here there are important differences: UDS deals in IT exclusively while BlueSky provide a wide range of environmental information from satellite imagery; BlueSky's projects are much smaller than those of UDS. Add to these differences the more obvious factors of company size, nationality and managerial approach and it becomes clear that the two companies are extremely ill-matched.

This poor match is evident in the very different way the two companies have been accustomed to do their business. To some extent the difference is **cultural**, but it also appears in basic management practice, particularly where **marketing** is concerned. The five senior scientists have been essentially dilettante in their approach to their market and to administration. Their business succeeded initially because they were exploiting a new product. The emergence of better-run competitors revealed the company's management inadequacies

BlueSky finds itself in a managerial straitjacket that has done little about its fundamental problems. All that was needed was an injection of senior management competence in order to address two main problem areas:

- Poor project control resulting in missed deadlines and cost overruns
- Lack of prompt attention to changes in client requirements

Both problems could have been tackled by the appointment of scientifically competent but market oriented project managers. In fact, an extra layer of management has been imposed with the result that a much higher percentage of contracts now overrun on cost or time.

The new procedure of contract vetting by UDS appears to have **reduced the informal flexibility** that was one of BlueSky's strengths. The average value of contracts has doubled, as has administrative expense, perhaps indicating an emphasis on larger customers with more formal procedures. This would be the influence of UDS at work, accustomed as they are to thinking in terms of multi-million pound IT contracts. It is probably an inappropriate approach for BlueSky.

Turnover has fallen slightly and appears likely to fall further, judging from the state of the work-in-progress and order book. This may be partly the result of a market perception of falling ability to give a satisfactory service. There has also been a reduction in marketing expenditure, which has perhaps contributed to the falling order book.

BlueSky is now in an unenviable position. Its order book is shrinking; competition is mounting; its reputation is in decline; and its new business model is at odds with its culture.

Part (b)

> **Text reference.** The topics mentioned in this answer are discussed in Chapters 3 and 11 of your BPP Study Text.
>
> **Easy marks.** Up to half of the marks for this part of the question were available for outlining and applying a suitable theoretical model. The two we use were mentioned by name in the marking scheme. Whenever you hear the word 'culture' reach for *Harrison's* typology: it will probably be relevant. If not *Hofstede* may help.

Cultural differences

As outlined above, BlueSky and UDS are very different organisations. BlueSky is a pleasant place for scientists to work, offering great independence and a minimal burden of administration. In terms of *Harrison's* classification of organisations it is closest to the **existential** type, which exists for the benefit of its members rather than its members serving the ends of the organisation. Such an organisation depends on the talent of the principal members; management is largely dependent on their continuing consent to being managed. Staff whose roles are purely managerial or administrative are likely to have lower status than those whose work forms the core of the organisation's activities. The culture in this type of organisation is likely to support professionalism, individualism and a very light hand on the managerial reins.

BlueSky is also identifiable in *Mintzberg's* typology as a **professional bureaucracy.** It has an operating core of highly trained professionals who require no real supervision: indeed they would be highly likely to reject attempts to control their work. Power is based on expertise and the work processes are too complex for supervision by any form of technostructure.

There is a great contrast with UDS, which is a large organisation run in a rational and systematic fashion. We are not told very much about UDS, but we may deduce that it displays at least some of the characteristics of Mintzberg's **machine bureaucracy**, with importance attached to formal control systems, documentation and standardisation. No doubt there is also a degree of the flexibility required to manage large projects, so we may see UDS as exhibiting a combination of the characteristics of the machine bureaucracy and the **adhocracy**, or in Harrison's terms, of the **role culture** and the **task culture**.

Thus, there is no head on clash between the cultures of the two companies, but we may expect there to be frequent instances of **mismatch**. UDS is more likely top call for routine reports, for instance, and to have set administrative procedures.

These cultural differences arise largely from the **scale of operations**. It will have been possible for co-ordination of effort in BlueSky to have existed largely on a basis of **mutual adjustment**. UDS, however, is far too large for such a system, and even though the company is used to team-working methods, overall financial control and the need to deliver on time and to specification will have made some degree of central control inevitable. This will have knock-on effects. Some proportion of the technical staff working in each company would be unhappy with the prevailing ethos in the other: there will be BlueSky scientists who resent any control at all, just as there will be UDS managers who are disappointed in BlueSky's rather chaotic arrangements. Management style will be rather different, being more formal and probably rather better in UDS, more tentative, informal and amateurish in BlueSky.

The other main influence on culture is likely to be **nationality**. We are not specifically told that BlueSky is a UK company, but it appears clear that it is. UDS, on the other hand, is stated to be a US company. Without descending into stereotypes, we may anticipate some differences of approach and attitude as a result.

Change management

The integration of BlueSky into UDS implies a significant change management problem. Minimising the clash of cultures will be part of this process. There are a number of models that might be applied, at least in part, to such a process of change.

The **Gemini 4Rs** framework for planned strategic change aims to cover all the important components of the organisation's identity. Each of the four dimensions of the process has three components.

Reframing involves fundamental questions about what the organisation is and what it is for. This is very relevant to BlueSky's situation.

- **Achieve mobilisation**: create the will and desire to change.
- **Create the vision** of where the organisation is going.
- **Build a measurement system** that will set targets and measure progress.

Restructuring is about the organisation's structure, but is also likely to involve cultural changes.

Revitalising is the process of securing a good fit with the environment and so is less relevant to the cultural aspect of BlueSky's problem

Renewal ensures that the people in the organisation support the change process and acquire the necessary skills to contribute to it. The components here may be of value to BlueSky.

- **Create a reward system** in order to motivate.
- Build individual learning.
- Develop the organisation and its adaptive capability.

The change process

Lewin/Schein's three stage approach to changing human behaviour is relevant hare. It may be depicted thus.

| UNFREEZE existing behaviour | $\longrightarrow$ | Attitudinal/ behavioural change | $\longrightarrow$ | REFREEZE new behaviour |

Unfreeze is the most difficult stage of the process, concerned mainly with 'selling' the change, with giving individuals or groups a **motive** for changing their attitudes, values, behaviour, systems or structures.

If the need for change is immediate, clear and necessary for the survival of the individual or group, the unfreeze stage will be greatly accelerated. It is likely that the scientific staff at BlueSky will be unsympathetic to the notion of change, however.

Unfreezing processes need four things.

(a) **A trigger.** A crisis is an effective trigger, so BlueSky is part-way there.
(b) Someone to **challenge** the existing behaviour pattern. This could be the present MD.
(c) The involvement of **outsiders.** UDS can act here.
(d) Alterations to the **power structure**. To some extent this has started, in the form of the UDS control of contracts.

Change is mainly concerned with identifying what the new, desirable behaviour should be, communicating it and encouraging individuals and groups to adopt it. The new ideas must be shown to work.

Refreeze is the final stage, implying consolidation or reinforcement of the new behaviour. Positive reinforcement (praise, reward) or negative reinforcement (sanctions applied to those who deviate from the new behaviour) may be used.

Peter Honey suggests that each of the sources of resistance to change identified below can be dealt with in a different way.

Cause	How to deal with it
Parochial self-interest	**Negotiation** (eg offer incentives to those resisting on grounds of self-interest).
Misunderstanding	This is best dealt with by **educating and reassuring** people. Trust has to be earned.
Different viewpoints of the situation	Change can be promoted through participation and by **involving potential resisters**.
Low tolerance of change	Force the change through and then **support** the new behaviours it requires. People may have to be coerced (by carrot and stick methods) to adopt the new methods.

When dealing with resistance to change, managers should consider three aspects of the change.

- Pace
- Manner
- Scope

Pace of change

The more gradual the change, the more time is available for questions to be asked, reassurances to be given and retraining (where necessary) embarked upon.

Presenting the individual concerned with a *fait accompli* may short-circuit resistance at the planning and immediate implementation stages. However, it may cause problems later.

The manner of change

The manner in which the changes at BlueSky are introduced will be important for their success. Talking through areas of conflict may lead to useful insights and the adapting of the programme of change to advantage. The change will have to be sold, particularly to the scientific staff. Information should be sensible, clear, consistent and realistic.

Scope of change

The scope of change should also be carefully reviewed. Total transformation would be more difficult than moderate innovation. It may be possible to minimise the impact of the change of BlueSky's status.

> **Top tips.** This is likely to be a difficult part of the question for most candidates since there is little in the way of theory to prop an answer up on. A good response requires careful reading of the question, business awareness and calm thought: these are all, unfortunately, factors that may be in short supply in the examination hall.

Part (c)

To: UDS Vice-President for Operations
From: J Clarkson, Managing Director, BlueSky Analysis Limited
Date: 6 June 200X
Subject: **BlueSky Analysis Limited**

Introduction

Since becoming a subsidiary of UDS, BlueSky Analysis Limited (BSL) has not developed as well as we hoped it would. While turnover has remained more or less constant, operating profit has fallen significantly, largely because of the doubling of administrative expense. The rate of generation of new business has fallen markedly, with a significant deterioration in the value of our order book.

Diagnosis

The intention when BSL and UDS became linked was that BSL should retain its innovative and flexible technical approach while having grafted on to it some of UDS's expertise in the acceptance and management of contracts. Unfortunately, the necessary balance has not been struck. UDS contract vetting has proved administratively expensive and tended to reject small but potentially profitable contracts. At the same time, the individualistic approach of BSL's staff has hampered the proper management of the larger projects we have undertaken.

Future improvements

A different approach is needed to the management of BSL, an approach that will combine flexibility with discipline across the company. At the moment, discipline seems confined to the contract vetting function and flexibility to the technical staff.

It would seem appropriate that those responsible for the strategic control of BSL should deploy more flexibility of approach, while a greater degree of co-ordination should be applied to the work of the technical staff.

The contract vetting criteria applied by the central staff at UDS should probably be modified to allow more projects to be accepted. At the same time, the technical staff must work in a more controlled way, especially where the larger contacts are concerned.

Recommendation

BSL needs an injection of on-site senior management skill. This could be achieved by seconding managers from UDS to BSL. These managers would have responsibility for contract approval and overall project management. They should be people who understand both the financial imperatives of wider strategy and the motivation of the scientific staff. They should be skilled in financial management but sufficiently intelligent and open-minded to be credible in the eyes of the scientific staff at BSL. There is probably a need for a chief executive and two project managers.

At the same time, the scientific staff will have to undergo a process of education, above all to lead them to accept that the way we do things has to change. This should, perhaps, be the first task for the new executives. The requirement for an improved system of project management and budgetary control should be explained to them and there should be an introduction to the necessity of controlled and effective team working, especially with regard to quality and delivery. The overall aim of this process of development would be to inculcate a proper degree of commercial awareness but without constraining the creativity and scientific credentials of the specialists.

John Clarkson

Managing Director

Part (d)

Easy marks. The Examiner's marking scheme for this question appeared to be a condensed version of the relevant section of the BPP Study Manual, to the extent of including some identical wording. Our paragraph headings indicate the areas to be awarded marks in the marking scheme.

Project management is a distinct branch of management expertise with its own problems and techniques. Many projects go wrong: this is usually manifested as a failure to complete on time, but this outcome can arise for a variety of reasons.

Unproven technology

Then use of new technological developments is likely to be a feature of any project. The range of such developments extends from fairly routine and non-critical improvements, through major innovations capable of transforming working practices, costs and time scales, to revolutionary techniques that make feasible projects that were previously quite impracticable. As the practical potential of a technical change moves from minor to major, so too moves its potential to cause disruption if something goes wrong with it. A classic example is Rolls Royce's attempt to use carbon fibre in the design of the RB211 engine in the early 1970s. Not only did the project fail to meet its objectives, its failure led to the company's financial failure, which necessitated its rescue by government.

Changing client specifications

It is not unusual for clients' notions of what they want to evolve during the lifetime of the project. However, if the work is to come in on time and on budget, they must be aware of what is technically feasible, reasonable in their aspirations, prompt with their decisions and, ultimately, prepared to freeze the specification so that it can be delivered. The failure of the TSR2 aircraft project forty years ago was in large part caused by major, unrealistic changes to specification.

Note that the term 'client' includes *internal* specifiers.

Politics

This problem area includes politics of all kinds, from those internal to an organisation managing its own projects, to the effect of national (and even international) politics on major undertakings. Identification of a senior figure with a project; public interest and press hysteria; hidden agendas; national prestige; and political dogma can all have deleterious effects on project management. **Lack of senior management support** is an important political problem.

Poor project management

This comes in several guises

- **Over optimism**. This can be particularly troublesome with new technology. Unrealistic deadlines may be accepted, for instance, or impossible levels of performance promised.

- **Over-promotion of technical staff**. It is common for people with a high level of technical skill to be promoted. Only then is it made clear that they lack management and leadership ability. This is a particular problem with IT projects.

- **Poor planning**. Realistic timescales must be established, use of shared resources must be planned and, most fundamental of all, jobs must be done in a sensible sequence.

- **Poor control**. Progress must be under continuous review and control action must be taken early if there are problems. The framework of control must provide for review at all levels of management and prompt reporting of problems.

SECTION B

Question 2

> **Top tips.** In part (a) we have given quite a lot of introductory information, before dealing with actual promotion. You must do this if you are asked for a *report*, but, clearly, it should not overwhelm the rest of the answer. Answering part (b) would be made easier by the general awareness which comes from reading the business press.
>
> **Easy marks.** Notice the double requirement in part (a) to both recommend and to justify. We have listed five promotional methods, which seems reasonable. We would expect that a half mark would be available simply for naming each method and another half mark for a few words that demonstrate that you know what it is. Probably up to four marks would be available for each method discussed: with one of these scored as outlined above, another would be available for a very simple initial account of its application; the rest would come for more complex ideas. Look at our paragraph on advertising to see how we move from the basic to the more complex idea.
>
> **Examiner's comments.** The Examiner noticed a strong contrast in the quality of the answers submitted to this question. Most candidates produced good answers to part (a), demonstrating a sound knowledge of promotional activities. However, answers to part (b) were disappointing, frequently confusing test marketing with product testing.

Part (a)

REPORT

From:	Sharpe & Keene, Marketing Consultants
To:	Managing Director, Klypso
Date:	1 January 200X
Subject:	Promotion for new confectionery product

Introduction

Klyso has a new low-fat, high-energy confectionery product, licensed from the USA, which it intends to market nationally. The product will be aimed at a niche market: health and exercise conscious consumers. Klyso's core competence is in access to retail distribution channels in its region. To exploit this and expand to national distribution, it will be necessary to establish a national brand. Klyso's promotional budget is small, so expenditure must be carefully planned and controlled. It is intended that national launch should be preceded by test marketing.

Aim

The aim of this report is to recommend and justify appropriate promotional methods for the test launch of the new product.

Promotional objectives

The product must be promoted to two groups; the distributors and the ultimate consumers. The distributors will not be prepared to stock the product unless they believe it will generate turnover. The product is new to this country. The initial objectives therefore will be to raise awareness of the product and its brand name among both consumers and distributors and to persuade the consumers to try it.

Success in these objectives can be measured first by a brand recognition survey and second by interpretation of the value of sales and sales returns.

The target market

The target market has been identified as physically active people who enjoy an occasional treat.

Promotional methods

The name of the new product has not yet been decided, nor has its packaging been designed. These are therefore tentative suggestions which may need modification. The overall theme is the product's contribution to an active lifestyle.

Advertising

The limited budget means that wide media coverage is inappropriate. Specialist magazines dealing with popular participation games and pastimes will provide the most precise targeting, combined with posters at recreational facilities which have shops and cafes. A life-style approach should be used, emphasising that the product enhances a healthy, active way of life.

Direct sales

There will be a major role for direct selling in the approach to distributors, who will expect help with merchandising and any problems at the time of product launch.

Public relations

This product is tailor made for sponsorship. Possibilities include financing training for a young athlete with national representative potential and promoting a local amateur league in an active game such as squash, soccer or rugby. When the time comes for national launch, endorsement by a well-known sports person may be appropriate. Thought should be given to that now, as such relationships should be undertaken for the long term.

Sales promotion

The distributors must be convinced to stock the product: high initial discounts will be necessary. Consumers must also be persuaded to try the product. The slightly tacky traditional sales promotion measures such as money-off and buy one get one free are inappropriate; a percentage of revenue put into a good cause such as coaching for school children might be more appropriate.

Conclusion

The new product must be promoted to both distributors and consumers. A closely targeted life-style approach will make the best use of the limited budget. Adequate provision must be made for the assessment of the effectiveness of the launch and the promotion in particular.

Part (b)

Test marketing is an important part of the **new product development process**. It obtains information about how the test market reacts to the new product and the other marketing mix elements associated with it. The aim is to extrapolate these results to the national market so that the product's prospects can be assessed. Consumer test markets are usually selected geographically, with the area covered by a regional television company used as a basis.

Clearly, it is essential that the test market should be as representative of the national market as possible, so that the correct conclusions may be drawn. The following aspects of the chosen test market should be considered in this context.

- The **structure of the population in demographic terms** such as age and social class distributions; size of ethnic minorities and religious denominations; and number of urban and rural households, should be similar to the national population.

- The **economic characteristics** should be typical; a permanently depressed area such as South Yorkshire would be as inappropriate as one in a permanent boom such as South East England.

- **Distribution channels** should be representative.

- **Promotional media** should be similar to those available nationally.

There are other considerations for test marketing.

- The test must run long enough for reliable results to be obtained. In the case of Klypso's new product, this probably means at least three cycles of ordering by distributors.

- The test market should be reasonably **isolated from the rest of the nation**. This helps to prevent competitors finding out about the new product and gives more representative results.

- Ideally, there will be a **control area**, that is, one which is not subject to the experimental stimulus. This allows the effects of extraneous developments such as economic changes to be assessed.

Question 3

Marking scheme

		Marks
(a)	Sources and causes of conflict:	Up to 2 per point
	Conflicting goals	
	Differing group norms reflecting different attitudes and beliefs	
	Traditional pattern of training	
	Power differences	
	Self interest	
	Different perceptions of costs/benefits of change	
	Change theories and application of them to problem analysis	Up to 6
		Maximum 12 marks
(b)	Creation of an action plan:	Up to 2 per point
	Elements in the plan	
	Desired results against agreed criteria	
	Guidelines for progression against agreed goals	
	Resources available for graduate trainees to draw on	
	Accountability for achieving results and time of evaluation	
	Consequences of meeting or not meeting training goals	**Maximum 8 marks**
		Total 20 marks

Part (a)

Alan has to reconcile the **attitudes and ambitions** of groups with very different views of the training and development process that the graduates should undergo. The main groups (partners and graduate trainees) are important stakeholders in ASG as they develop their careers over time. They will bring different attitudes and beliefs about the training process. The potential for fresh and different ways of thinking, brought in by the graduates, is much needed in the changing competitive environment. The partners want to retain traditional training methods. It is also important to recognise that the personnel department may **reinforce the partners' position** through their professional convictions of the benefits of the training programme (which they will have helped to design and will to a certain extent be responsible for).

ASG is, in Mintzberg's terms, a professional bureaucracy, where the qualified accountants have considerable discretion in their work, and skills are standardised. The graduate training programme is of course a key method to achieve such skills. This is coupled with professional exams. The partners are convinced that the graduates should have go through exactly the same training process as they themselves did.

Change may be incremental or transformational, and management may choose to take a proactive or reactive role. *Johnson and Scholes* have written about the change process and how to manage it effectively, and suggest the model of change shown below.

Nature of change

Management role	Incremental	Transformational
Proactive	Tuning	Planned
Reactive	Adaptation	Forced

Certainly the partners response to date has been **reactive**, and the nature of change **incremental** (affecting only part of the firm's activities). This implies from the above grid that a process of **adaptation** needs to occur.

The *Lewin/Schein* three stage model of the change process (unfreeze, change, refreeze) could be used in conjunction with **force field analysis**, which identifies the forces driving the change and those which are restraining it. The drivers for change come from the graduates, who want to complete their training quickly and get into 'real' work with a significant salary increase. The restraining forces are the traditional views of the partners, with the added support of the personnel department, which add up to a strong interest group that creates a powerful inertia holding up any change process.

Part (b)

Currently the trainees and partners do not see eye to eye on the requirements of the training programme. The trainees want it to be quick and effective, whereas the partners seem to justify the process through the assumption that if the trainees go through the same experience as themselves, the outcome will automatically be graduate accountants who are able to meet the modern business challenges facing ASG.

Any action plan will need the participation of all parties in resolving the conflict, and will involve a **process of negotiation**. It should contain the following elements.

1 **Desired results**, clearly specifying the skills the graduates should be able to demonstrate on conclusion of the programme, should be clarified as a first step. This needs the full participation of the partners if there is to be a clear vision of what needs to be achieved, but the more discretion they can allow the graduates in the way the results are achieved, the more motivated they are likely to be. It would be very valuable if recently qualified trainees were invited to assist with this process, having gone through the training and possibly **identified weaknesses and strengths** first hand.

2 Once the results of the programme have been clearly identified, it needs to be driven through. This often involves a **change agent**, and this role may be taken up by Alan, whose role will be to make sure that the programme is successfully promoted and implemented. It will involve ongoing identification of any problem areas (part of reviewing and monitoring training progress), and will need the full support of all functions within ASG that may have a hand in delivering the training programme. Advice and information will have to be provided to trainees and partners alike. It needs to be continually emphasised that the old training methods are no longer appropriate for ASG.

Question 4

> **Top tips.** This is quite a common type of question: the scenario describes a problem and a possible solution: then you are asked to comment. You need to form an opinion and be able to back it up with sensible remarks based on both theory and business reality. It will normally be fairly clear to the well-prepared student what the best solution is.

Part (a)

> **Text reference.** The topics mentioned in this answer are discussed in Chapter 12 of your BPP Study Text.
>
> **Easy marks.** Up to half of the marks available for this part of the question were awarded for a discussion of the theoretical background to quality issues. Of the remainder, most were awarded for dealing with the HRM implications of the new policy.

A **system of checking** is an obvious measure to deal with errors, especially those of procedure, and is routinely used in tasks such as aircraft operations **where performance must be highly standardised**. A system of checking the paperwork will address some of the unsatisfactory occurrences that Chestlands Insurance has suffered. Incomplete documentation will be detected at an early stage; financial irregularities and mis-selling may also be affected for the better.

Nevertheless, simple checking is probably **not the best way** to address the current quality problems. The process of checking would not add value to correctly completed documentation but it *would* increase costs and the complexity of operations. **Checking is something to be avoided if possible**.

A more modern approach to quality would be to take steps to **eliminate the creation of errors**. This is the **quality assurance** approach, rather than the quality control approach, which depends on inspection or quality checking. Quality assurance requires that members of staff **accept responsibility for the quality of all aspects of their work**. Such an approach would address all of the problems now apparent in Chestlands Insurance's operations.

However, taking the quality control approach would require **significant changes** to the company's management of its human resources, since success would be dependent upon the motivation and skill of the individual employee.

(a)   It would be necessary to review the **recruitment policy** so that only people with suitable personal qualities started work.

(b)   Identifiable **poor performers** would have to go, preferably by natural wastage, but by dismissal if necessary.

(c)   **Effective training** would be required, both for new recruits and for existing staff who were not working satisfactorily.

(d)   The **remuneration policy** should be reviewed. There should be incentives that promote the behaviour the company needs. At the moment, the large element of commission will tend to encourage dubious selling practices and poor attention to documentation. An adjusted system, with a higher level of basic pay, would encourage sales people to take a longer-term view of their customers. A performance related bonus could include an element of penalty for inadequate documentation.

It will be difficult to strike the right balance between the need for more effective staff and the need to hold down costs, but a quality assurance approach is the best way to approach the problem.

Part (b)

> **Text reference.** The topics mentioned in this answer are discussed in Chapter 12 of your BPP Study Text.
>
> **Easy marks.** This part of the question gives an example of a requirement that can be satisfied in several ways. One or two marks would be available for a whole range of relevant points. In addition to the matters we discuss, you might also mention the need for a training programme and the long-term commitment that would be required.

Total Quality Management (TQM) is an extension of the quality assurance approach to every activity in the organisation, with the aim of ensuring complete customer satisfaction both externally and *internally*. Quality lies in the eye of the consumer and this applies as much to those products that are consumed *within* the organisation as to those that are marketed externally. Total Quality Management thus views the organisation as an integrated whole and quality as an organisation-wide concern.

TQM is more of a philosophy of business than a collection of techniques. A high degree of commitment is necessary if it is to be implemented. Senior management, in particular, must support its introduction and promote the necessary changes. This can be a particularly difficult thing to achieve, since it demands changes of practice, not just lip service. A TQM initiative can also be expensive, especially if there is much training to undertake. It is necessary to take a long view and maintain the momentum of the programme over the longer term.

Staff at lower levels must be prepared to accept responsibility for their performance and to undergo appropriate training. A problem Mr Sanders will have to solve is the likelihood that staff will expect greater remuneration in return for improved performance and for accepting greater responsibility. In the longer term, improved productivity and quality should pay for these extra costs.

The development of a TQM programme inevitably requires the participation of the workforce. They have the greatest knowledge of the details of the work and they will see the effects of changes first. Quality circles are a possible technique for promoting their continued input. Participation in development is also likely to encourage internalisation of the principles of the new approach.

It will not be enough to rely on the positive motivational effects of participation to ensure compliance with the aims of the new approach. Work procedure should be reviewed with a view to simplification and standardisation, both of which will improve performance. Also, the philosophy must be supported by improvements in control and discipline to ensure that poor performance is checked.

ACCA

Paper 3.5

Strategic Business Planning and Development

Mock Examination 2

Question Paper	
Time allowed	3 hours
This paper is divided into two sections	
Section A	ONE compulsory question to be attempted
Section B	TWO questions ONLY to be attempted

DO NOT OPEN THIS PAPER UNTIL YOU ARE READY TO START UNDER EXAMINATION CONDITIONS

SECTION A – This question is compulsory and MUST be attempted

Question 1

The Ace Bicycle Company (ABC) is a private UK company, based within the United Kingdom and managed by Colin Doncroft, the grandson of its founder. The shares are totally owned by the family, with Colin and his wife controlling just under half of the shares, the rest being held by other members of the family. The company was started in 1935, producing bicycles for the general market. These bicycles were targeted mainly at people who could not afford to buy motor vehicles – then a relative luxury – but who needed transportation to get them to work or for local travel. Initially the company was a regional producer focusing on markets in Central England but over the next 60 years ABC transformed itself into a national company. ABC took advantage of changes in fashion and periodically introduced new models focusing on different market segments. Its first diversification was into making racing bicycles, which still account for 20% of its volume output. Most of these bicycles are very expensive to produce. They are made of specialist light-weight metals and are often custom-built for specific riders, most of the sales being made on a direct basis. Members of amateur cycling clubs contact the company directly with their orders and this minimises distribution costs, so making these machines more affordable to the customers. ABC's reputation has been enhanced by this highly profitable product. The company has seen no reason to change its branding policy and these products are still sold under the 'ABC' brand name.

During the 1980s the company responded to the demand for more sporty leisure machines. Mountain bikes had become the fashion and ABC designed and produced some models which appealed to the cheaper end of the market. These products, although robust and stylish, were relatively cheap and were aimed at families with teenage children and who could not afford to spend large sums of money on the more sophisticated models. The company is currently selling nearly 30% of its output to this market segment. Most of the sales are through specialist bicycle shops, although about 25% of these mountain bikes sales are made through a national retail chain of bicycle and motor vehicle accessories stores. Apart from those sold via this retail network, under the retail brand name, the mountain bikes were also sold under the ABC brand. With the advent of fitness clubs the company saw and opening for the provision of cycling machines for the health club and gymnasium market. These machines were sold at a premium price but they still accounted for less than 5% of total volume sales of the company. The main product group for the company was still its basic bicycle – it is the entry model for most families who are buying bicycles for teenagers and for those people who still use bicycles as a means of transportation as distinct from seeing them as entertainment or fun machines. The product is standardised, with few differentiating features, and as such can be produced relatively cheaply. About 75% of this segment is sold through the same national retail chain mentioned above with reference to mountain bike sales. These bicycles in fact are built for the retail chain and marketed under their brand name. This appears to be advantageous to ABC because it guarantees them a given level of business without their being responsible for either distribution or promotion. This segment, however, is now seeing increasing competition from cheaper overseas imports.

The company had historically made reasonable profits and most of these were re-invested in the company's production facilities, increasing capacity substantially. However, throughout the late 1990s, ABC has seen its market being eroded. Sales have fallen gradually, mainly because the total United Kingdom market for bicycles has been in decline, but also because of increased competition from foreign suppliers. The high value of sterling has encouraged imports. Surprisingly, during this period ABC actually increased its share of domestic output. This is due to the fact that it has been prepared to accept lower margins so as to maintain sales and, in addition, a few UK producers had decided to exit the market and move into other, more attractive product lines.

By early in the year 2000 the company has seen its profits continue to fall. It now has a debt to the bank of £4 million, having been unable to pay for all recent, new capital expenditure out of retained earnings. (Table I gives some financial information about the recent performance of ABC.)

There are now very few UK manufacturers of bicycles who concentrate solely on producing bicycles. Most have a diversified portfolio and can count on other product groups to support the bicycle sector when demand is poor. However, ABC has continued to focus entirely on this specialised product range. It is surviving basically because it has built up a strong reputation for reliable products and because the Doncroft family has, until recently, been content with a level of profits which would be unacceptable to a public company that had external shareholders to consider. However, it is now becoming apparent that unless some radical action is taken the company cannot hope to survive. The bank will now only make loans if ABC can find a suitable strategy to provide it with a higher and more acceptable level of profit. If the company is to retain its independence (and it is questionable whether any company will really want to acquire it in its current position) it has to consider radical change. Its only experience is within the bicycle industry and therefore it appears to be logical that it should stay in this field in some form or other.

Colin Doncroft has examined ways to improve the profitability of the company. He is of the opinion that if ABC becomes more successful it could become a desirable acquisition for other companies. However, currently the company will not attract bidders unless it is at a low price. Doncroft has looked at the profile of his products and wonders whether any rationalisation could help to improve performance. He has also decided to look at the potential for overseas marketing. Having examined statistics on current world production and sales statistics he has identified that the real growth areas for bicycles are in the Far East. China alone supports a bigger market for bicycles than the whole of Europe and North America. India and Pakistan have also developed a significant demand for bicycles. Doncroft decided to visit some of these markets and he has returned full of enthusiasm for committing ABC to operate in these Far Eastern markets or in India and Pakistan. Whilst Doncroft considers that exporting from the UK might be a viable option, he has become increasingly attracted to manufacturing in the Far East, particularly in China. He believes that transportation costs could prove to be a disadvantage to exporting for ABC. He estimates that costs for shipping and insurance could add about 15% to the final selling price. Furthermore, he is concerned about the discrepancy between labour costs in the United Kingdom and in China. Wage rates, including social costs in China appear to be about 30% of those in the UK and these costs account for approximately 25% of the total production costs.

Colin Doncroft has summoned a meeting of all the shareholders to persuade them to agree to plan to manufacture, or at least assemble bicycles in the Far East. The other shareholders are not quite so enthusiastic. They feel that this strategy is too risky. The company has never been involved in overseas business and now they are being asked to sanction a strategy which by-passes the exporting stage and commits them to significant expenditure overseas. Colin is convinced that the bank will loan them the necessary capital, given the attractiveness of these overseas markets. The other shareholders are more in favour of a gradual process. They want to improve the position within the United Kingdom market first rather than leap into the unknown. They also believe that diversification into other non-bicycle products might be less risky than venturing overseas. They know the UK market but overseas is an unknown area. Colin has decided that it is time he sought some professional advice for the company. A management consultant, Simon Gaskell, has been retained. He is a qualified accountant who also has an MBA from a prestigious business school.

Table I: Information concerning ABC's current sales and financial performance

Financial Year April/March	1998/1999	1999/2000	2000/2001 (forecast)
Mountain Bikes			
volume	18,000	17,500	16,500
direct costs £000	2,070	2,187.5	2,145
revenue £000	2,610	2,625	2,475
Standard Bicycles			
volume	27,000	26,200	25,000
direct costs £000	2,160	2,096	2,075
revenue £000	2,430	2,227	2,125
Racing Bicycles			
volume	11,000	1,500	11,750
direct costs £000	4,950	5,750	6,227.5
revenue £000	6,875	7,475	7,931.25
Exercise Bicycles			
volume	2,800	2,800	2,700
direct costs £000	756	840	837
revenue £000	910	980	945
Indirect costs £000: inc.	1,225	1,730	1,890
Distribution	175	200	250
Promotion	300	280	240
Administration and other	750	850	1,000
Interest on loan	-	400	400
Profit before tax £000	1,664	703.5	301.75

Required

Acting in the role of Simon Gaskell:

(a) Write a report, evaluating the current strategies being pursued by the Ace Bicycle Company (ABC) for its different market segments, using appropriate theoretical models to support your analysis. **(24 marks)**

(b) Identify and explain the key factors which should be taken into consideration before ABC decide on developing manufacturing/assembly facilities in China. **(12 marks)**

(c) Write briefing notes to the shareholders, explaining the advantages to the company of concentrating solely on the production of bicycles and also the opportunities which may be available by pursuing a strategy of diversification. **(12 marks)**

(d) Using the example of the ACE Bicycle Company to support your views, identify the benefits of:

(i) organic growth **(4 marks)**
(ii) acquisitions **(4 marks)**
(iii) joint developments **(4 marks)**
    as a preferred means of developing the business in China.

(Total = 60 marks)

SECTION B – TWO questions ONLY to be attempted

Question 2

All organisations have objectives in some form or another. The methods of setting these objectives vary depending on the nature of the organisation. After they have been set and an appropriate period of time has elapsed, organisations should assess to what extent their objectives have been achieved.

Two organisations with very different characteristics set strategic objectives and evaluate their achievement. The two organisations are

- A publicly-funded local administrative authority which provides housing, education, social and road maintenance services for an area within a country, and

- A multi-national conglomerate company (MNC).

Required

(a)   Explain the differences between how the local administrative authority and the MNC should set their strategic objectives. **(8 marks)**

(b)   Discuss how each organisation should assess how well it has performed in respect of the attainment of its strategic objectives. **(12 marks)**

(Total = 20 marks)

Question 3

Elite Fabrics (EF) is a medium-sized manufacturer of clothing fabrics. Historically, EF has built up a strong reputation as a quality fabric manufacturer with appealing designs and has concentrated mainly on the women's market, producing fabrics to be made up into dresses and suits. The designs of the fabric are mainly of a traditional nature but the fabrics, almost all woven from synthetic yarns, include all the novel features which the large yarn producers are developing.

Three years ago EF decided that more profit and improved control could be obtained by diversifying through forward integration into designing and manufacturing the end products (ie clothes) in-house rather than by selling its fabrics directly to clothing manufacturing companies.

EF's intention had been to complement its fabric design skills with the skills of both dress design and production. This had been achieved by buying a small but well-known, dress design and manufacturing company specialising in traditional products, targeted mainly at the middle-aged and middle-income markets. This acquisition appears to have been successful, with combined sales turnover during the first two years increasing to £100 million (+ 34%) with a pre-tax profit of £14 million (+ 42%). This increased turnover and profit could be attributed to two main factors: firstly the added value generated by designing and manufacturing end-products and secondly, the increased demand for fabrics as EF was more able to influence their end-users more directly.

In the last financial year, however, EF had experienced a slow down in its level of growth and profitability. EF's penetration of its chosen retail segment - the independent stores specialising in sales to the middle-class market - may well have reached saturation point. The business had also attempted to continue expansion by targeting the large multiple stores which currently dominate the retail fashion sector. Unfortunately the buying power of such stores has forced EF to accept significantly lower, and potentially unacceptable, profit margins. The management team at EF believes that the solution is to integrate even further forward by moving into retailing itself. EF is now considering the purchase of a chain of small, but geographically dispersed, retail fashion stores. At the selling price of £35 million, EF would have to borrow substantially to finance the acquisition.

Required

(a)   Consider how the EF strategy of integrating forward into dress manufacturing has affected its ability to compete. Use an accepted model as a framework for analysis.   **(10 marks)**

(b)   EF's potential expansion into retailing presents both advantages and disadvantages to the company. Evaluate the consequences of such a move for the business and assess the change in competences which would be required by the newly expanded business.   **(10 marks)**

(Total = 20 marks)

Question 4

Natalia Norman is a designer and manufacturer of knitwear clothing. She has based her designs on ethnic patterns, inspired by clothing she has seen in Central Asia. She has sourced her products both from these Asian regions – Uzbekistan and Kazakhstan – as well as from small factories in parts of the United Kingdom. Her products, though stylish, are relatively cheap, but her marketing strategy is totally passive. She has a web-site and most of her sales are reactive, responding to orders over the internet. The resultant sales and, in particular, profits have been disappointing and so she has hired a marketing consultant to give her some advice. The following are extracts from the consultant's report.

'Your product, although distinctive, is insufficiently unique. The designs have no patents nor copyright and because the production technology is so simple and inexpensive there are few barriers to entry. Competition is all too prevalent. Your promotion is too general. It focuses on no specific market. By relying on the internet your advertising is rather indiscriminate and you have failed to create a loyal following and your image is diffused with little opportunity for building brand awareness. There is a failure within distribution. Most consumers wish to see, handle or try on products before making a purchase, particularly if the products do not already have a well-established reputation and/or a brand name. In your case the only exposure your products have is via the world-wide web. Your pricing structure is too cost-based. You are able to source your products cheaply but your margins are too low to provide you with the necessary capital to reinvest if the business is to develop profitably in the future.

You have failed to establish yourself in the market place as a dominant player. Too many of your business decisions are reactive and often too late to have adequate impact. You are following market trends and not attempting to lead them.'

Natalia is naturally disturbed by the criticisms which this report has levelled at her company's operations and has decided that she must be more positive in her actions. In particular she has decided that her marketing efforts must be more focused and she must pursue more proactively her competitive activities.

Required

In order to focus her company's marketing efforts more precisely Natalia has decided to segment the market for knitwear products.

(a)   Suggest potential bases for segmenting this knitwear market and discuss the benefits which a more focused segmentation could bring to the company.   **(12 marks)**

(b)   Evaluate strategies which Natalia might pursue as a market follower to make her knitwear company more competitive.   **(8 marks)**

(Total = 20 marks)

Answers

**DO NOT TURN THIS PAGE UNTIL YOU HAVE
COMPLETED THE MOCK EXAM**

A plan of attack

We discussed the problem of which question to start with earlier, in 'Passing the 3.5 exam'. Here we will merely reiterate our view that question 1 is nearly always the best place to start and, if you do decide to start with a Section B question, **make sure that you finish your answer in no more than 36 minutes**.

Question 1 is quite typical of the sort of thing you are likely to find in the exam. Its only unusual feature is its strong international flavour. You should not allow this to put you off, as the actual technical implications are minimal. The tabulated numerical data present two immediately obvious routes into analysis: year on year comparison and product line comparison. Five minutes calculator work along these lines will give you lots of ideas for comment in requirement (a). Twenty four marks are available for this part of the question and there is plenty to say. Note the use of the word 'report' in the requirement and act accordingly.

There are several models and theories you could make use of to help you to deal with requirement (b), including the various aspects of environmental analysis and even the suitability-acceptability-feasibility framework for assessing strategic options. However, you can produce a perfectly acceptable answer without using any of them if you can identify the relevant material in the setting.

Parts (c) and (d) are heavily biased towards theory but you must relate it carefully to the circumstances of the company.

Question 2 is very easy and would make a very good choice for your first Section B question, but only if you are sufficiently knowledgeable about the general organisational background. Candidates for this exam tend to be a little unsure of themselves when dealing with questions about non-commercial organisations, but there is little here to worry about since the topic of objectives is fairly easy to discuss from a general awareness of the nature of the public sector. This question follows the usual pattern of two linked parts, with the second requirement building logically on the first. It is noteworthy that the marks are quite heavily biased towards part (b).

Question 3 needs an answer that combines a careful analysis of the detail in the setting with the ability to apply theory relating to the value system and vertical integration. There is lots of opportunity to earn good marks, but this would be a difficult question to answer well if you do not have the theory in the forefront of your mind.

Question 4, coincidentally, is also about the clothing industry but approaches it from a completely different direction. Marketing is one of the Examiner's favourite topics and this is a fairly typical question. Note the appropriate split of marks between requirement (a) and requirement (b): segmentation is a more fundamental topic that the market position strategies referred to in (b). Overall, this is probably a more accessible question than Question 3.

SECTION A

Question 1

Part (a)

> **Text reference.** The topics mentioned in this answer are discussed in Chapter 6 of your BPP Study Text.
>
> **Top tips.** Do not be daunted by a single requirement worth twenty four marks. This indicates that there is plenty to say. Work methodically and plan your answer so that if flows logically from section to section. Also, take care: the mark allocation amounts to almost a quarter of your available time. Do not get carried away and spend too long on part (a)!
>
> **Examiner's comments.** The examiner pointed out that an answer could have been based on other theoretical models, such as the product life cycle or *Ansoff's* product/market growth vector matrix. However, the BCG approach does seem particularly useful here for assessing ABC's portfolio.

REPORT

To:	Colin Doncroft, Managing Director
From:	Simon Gaskell, Management Consultant
Date:	December 2000
Subject:	Evaluation of Ace Bicycle Company strategies

Introduction

This report is designed to consider the different **strategies** that Ace Bicycle Company (ABC) is following in its different markets and to **evaluate each of these individual strategies** given the information provided for the last two years and the current year's forecast figures .

In overall terms ABC has seen a **decline in demand** for its products, with demand expected to fall by 5% over the period. Although revenue is expected to increase in 2000/01 the direct costs are an increasingly large proportion of sales revenue and are expected to reach 84% of revenue in the current year, a rise of 14% over the period. Together with a dramatic expected increase in indirect costs of 54% over the period this has caused a significant fall in profits to an expected, and unacceptable low, of just 2%.

ABC has **four distinct market sectors** – racing bicycles, mountain bikes, health clubs and basic bicycles – with distinctly different strategies being followed for each market therefore I will consider each market in turn.

Background

ABC is a private, family owned company which is now a national producer of bicycles. Some of its products are sold under its own brand name whereas others are sold through a national retail chain under its retail brand name. Over the last few years ABC has seen its **market being eroded** with **increasing competition** from cheaper overseas imports. The overall UK market for bicycles is in decline and this has been made worse by the high value of sterling encouraging imports from foreign suppliers. However during this period ABC has been able to increase its share of domestic output by accepting lower profit margins in order to maintain sales. ABC concentrates its efforts solely on the bicycle market and has a **strong reputation** for reliable products.

Each individual market that ABC operates in will now be considered in turn in the light of this background information.

Racing bicycles

ABC has been making racing bicycles for many years and this area currently accounts for approximately 20% of its volume output and almost 60% of its sales revenue. This is the only sector of ABC's business where the volume of sales is expected to **increase** this year. This sector is by far the **most profitable** of ABC's market areas, but even though anticipated revenue has increased by 15% over the period considered, the **direct costs** of production have outstripped this with an expected increase of 25%. However, this area still remains profitable and although the bicycles are expensive to produce, some being custom made, the **distribution costs** in this sector are minimised by the policy of taking direct orders from amateur cycling clubs. These racing bicycles are marketed under the ABC brand name and have enhanced ABC's reputation.

ABC appears to have followed a successful strategy of **premium pricing** in this market and has **differentiated** the product by the policy of producing custom made bicycles. Despite the cost increases, the margins in this sector are still healthy with clear potential for volume and revenue growth. Any potential for increasing UK market share in this area or diversifying into sales of racing bicycles overseas should seriously be considered as this is clearly the most successful part of the current business.

This area of the business could be described as a **cash cow** according to the BCG growth-share matrix as ABC's market share is relatively high and the market is growing slowly.

Mountain bikes

ABC moved into this fashion area in the 1980s producing relatively cheap models and currently this sector accounts for 30% of ABC's output but only 16% of revenue. The volume of **sales is expected to decline by 8%** over the period considered and **revenue to decline by 5%**. However direct costs of production have increased each year and are anticipated to be 87% of revenue for mountain bikes in the current year. Despite increases in costs and decreases in revenue this sector remains **relatively profitable** in relation to other market sectors of the business.

About 75% of these mountain bike sales are made under the ABC brand name through **specialist bicycle shops**. The remainder of the sales are made through a **national retail chain** of bicycle and motor vehicle accessories stores under the retailer's own brand name.

ABC's pricing policy of charging relatively low prices for the mountain bikes is a strategy of **penetration pricing**; however, in order for this to be successful, ABC needs to be able to **compete on costs**. The increases in direct costs will tend to invalidate this policy as ABC does not appear to have the production capacity to achieve the **economies of scale** necessary to maintain profit margins as sales volumes decline and cheaper foreign imports pose a threat.

As ABC has been so successful in its premium pricing policy in the racing bike market, and the majority of the mountain bikes are also marketed under the ABC brand name, the company should consider **moving away from the low price market** for mountain bikes. If the mountain bikes produced are promoted as being of high quality based upon the well-respected **brand name** of ABC in the racing bike market, the company may be able to attract customers prepared to pay a higher price due to the quality of the product.

This area of ABC's business certainly appears to have potential but if changes in both the stabilisation of costs and marketing and pricing policy are not made it would appear that profits from this sector will continue to decline.

Exercise bicycles

The health club market for **exercise bicycles** plays only a small part in ABC's business currently with less than 5% of total volume sales. As this is a **niche market** it is possible to have a **premium pricing policy**; this sector has been consistently profitable over the period, although margins have reduced to an expected 11% for the current year. Part of the reason for the fall in profitability is, as with other areas of the business, the **escalation of costs** which in the current year represent 88% of the sales value of the exercise bicycles.

This market sector is different from ABC's other areas as it is a **diversification** into a different line of business. The exercise bicycles will have some similarities to the other bicycles manufactured but the market characteristics are very different. Health clubs are a completely different type of customer from those for the other sectors. Sales volume is expected to show a slight fall in the current year since ABC do not produce a full range of exercise equipment, which the market seems to prefer in its suppliers. Therefore ABC might consider **diversifying** into production of **other fitness equipment** such as running machines and cross trainers. This market appears to be potentially profitable but currently ABC is too small a player to take advantage of it in full.

Basic bicycles

The main product of the group, the basic bicycle, accounts for about 45% of the output volume and is therefore still the **core of the business**. However, the **margins** in this area are the main cause of ABC's overall fall in profitability. Sales volume has decreased by 7% over the past two years but sales revenue has fallen by even more, at 12%, as a result of reducing price in an attempt to maintain sales levels in the face of **increasing competition** from cheaper overseas imports. In the current year the margin has fallen to 2.4%, a drop of almost 80% over the two years. Two years ago the production cost per bicycle was £80 but this has increased to £83 per bicycle in the current year. In addition to this the selling price has reduced from £90 two years ago to £85 currently.

About 75% of these bicycles are supplied to a national retail chain supplying bicycles and motor accessories and marketed under the chain's own brand name. As ABC is heavily dependent upon the retail chain it may be that the retailer is forcing prices down using its **buying power**.

ABC's strategy in this market appears to have been one of competing on **both cost and price**. Unfortunately, it appears not to have worked. Prices are coming down and costs are rising. This area of the business is now being **subsidised** by the other more profitable but smaller markets.

There is no real brand association with the basic bicycles as the majority are sold under the retailer's brand name. Therefore it might be difficult for ABC to disassociate itself from the retailer and sell directly, although it may be possible to build on the brand association from the racing bicycle market. According to the BCG growth-share matrix the basic bicycle market could be categorised as a **dog** as the UK market in this area does not appear to be growing and ABC appear to have a relatively low market share.

If ABC is to improve profitability in this market it must decrease costs, probably move away from dependence on the retailer and attempt to **differentiate its product** in some way. Withdrawal from this market could be considered although as it is such a significant element of the business this may be a **dangerous strategy** and should only be considered when all other options have been examined.

Indirect costs

A further worrying area of the business is in the **escalating indirect costs**. Over the two years there has been a staggering increase of 54% in total indirect costs. **Distribution costs** are up by 43% although this may be understandable given the nature of the direct sales of the racing bicycles and exercise bicycles.

Administration costs have also increased by 25% over the last two years which, given the decrease in sales volumes, appears unusual.

Promotion costs have, however, fallen and this must be **rectified** if ABC is to capitalise on its brand name and increase sales volumes.

Loan interest is unavoidable but worryingly high as in the current year **interest cover is only 1.75 times**, a potentially dangerous level.

Conclusion

ABC currently has a wide range of strategies, a premium pricing policy for racing bicycles and exercise bicycles, and an attempt to be a cost leader at the lower end of the market with its basic and mountain bikes. **Production costs** must be brought under control before any rationalisation of strategies can be considered.

It would appear that ABC's strengths lie in its **strong reputation and brand** association in the racing bicycle market. If this can be extended to the **mountain bike market** and a premium pricing policy introduced here with **market differentiation based upon the quality of the product**, then this could produce significant improvements in the mountain bike market.

A further potentially successful market is that of the **health club equipment** if the production range can be extended. The basic bicycle market could be improved with more control of direct costs but as the UK market is not expanding and the strategy has been one of cost leader, which has not succeeded, then it may be necessary to consider withdrawal from this market.

It would appear that the future of ABC lies with the **quality products** as ABC does not appear to have the production capacity to achieve the cost economies necessary for a successful cost leader strategy at the lower end of the market.

Part (b)

> **Top tips.** To some extent our answer is unstructured, addressing salient points in no particular order. If you prefer a more structured approach, you could use the PEST and five forces concepts to produce something like an environmental analysis. You would have to cover the same ground, but you may find this approach more fruitful if you are wondering just how to get started.

When considering any potential investment many factors must be taken into account but when considering such a major change in strategy as the managing director is proposing then there must be a **wide ranging review** of the key factors.

Operations

Let us first consider the **operational aspects** of the development of a manufacturing or assembly facility in China. The proposal is based upon the **large demand** for bicycles perceived in the Far East, the **cheaper labour** which would reduce **production costs** and the reduction in **transportation costs**.

As far as the demand for bicycles is concerned, the view of the market appears to be that of the managing director and there is no evidence that any **market research activities** have been carried out. What type of bicycles are in demand in China and can ABC produce bicycles that satisfy this demand? If the bicycles required are not the same as those currently manufactured by ABC there may be significant costs involved in re-design and changes to the manufacturing processes.

The **labour cost** aspect must be put into perspective. Labour costs only account for 25% of the total production cost therefore the cheaper labour would only lead to a maximum decrease in production costs of 17.5%. The labour issue should be considered further – how does the **productivity** of bicycle manufacturing employees in China compare to that in the UK. If productivity is significantly lower in China then this could **wipe out any cost benefit**.

The **transportation costs** of bicycles from the UK to China are obviously significant. However, if the proposed facility is set up in China instead there are still likely to be significant transportation costs since China covers a vast area and demand is likely to be spread widely. This internal transportation cost should not be ignored.

ABC must consider other operational aspects of setting up a manufacturing facility in China. Can the correct **components** be purchased at a competitive price and be delivered on time? What type and amount of **marketing expenses** will there be? ABC must also question its **ability to run** such an operation as it has no experience in even trading with other countries, let alone setting up a full scale operation in one, particularly one as distant and unknown as China.

Finance

ABC must also consider **financial aspects**. ABC has very low profit levels currently and a large debt outstanding. How does it propose to **raise the finance** necessary for such a major investment? Would the finance be raised in this country or in China? Are there opportunities for a UK company to raise major finance in China? Would a joint venture with a Chinese company be a viable option?

Further financial problems will concern the **remittance of funds back to the UK** and any **foreign exchange risks** that ABC may face. Many countries restrict the amount of their currency that can be taken out of the country and as ABC is so short of funds it will clearly require any profits to be remitted back to the UK. ABC should also consider the foreign exchange risks that are associated with any form of trade with foreign countries. If the Chinese currency moves against sterling then ABC could be subjected to large foreign exchange losses.

Risk

Political risk is a further important area that should be considered. How stable is the Chinese government? What is their attitude to foreign investors, are they encouraged or are there sanctions which will make operations more difficult and expensive?

Analysis

Many of the key factors involved in this proposal can be addressed through a **SLEPT analysis** (social, legal, economic, political and technological aspects). Analysis of social factors will help to define the market, determine the type of bicycle required and clarify the potential customer and method of marketing and sale. Legal factors will include dealing with suppliers, contracts for setting up a factory and employment issues. Economic factors will help to define the demand structure, inflation rates, interest rates and availability of finance. Political issues will be of great importance in a country such as China which has large state control. From the technological viewpoint, particularly if there is a demand for ABC's more high-tech products, such as the racing bicycle, does the technology exist in China or must it be exported?

Part (c)

Briefing notes on advantages of concentration on bicycle production or diversification

Advantages of concentrating on bicycle production

- ABC has been in the bicycle manufacturing business for many decades and therefore has the **skills and competences** necessary to operate in this area. These skills might not necessarily be easily transferred to other markets such as production of other fitness equipment.

- The fact that ABC specialises in the production of bicycles, albeit of different types, would argue that the company obtains some **economies of scale** from just this type of production. As direct costs are increasing there is some doubt about these economies of scale but diversification into another field may reduce margins even more.

- *Peters and Waterrman* would argue that ABC should stick to its **core activities** and not be side-tracked into other areas in which it has limited experience. This will also be of benefit in developing value chain relationships.

- By remaining within the bicycle industry the ABC **brand name** can be cultivated. Its value in other sectors must be doubted.

- Concentration on a single market would be the only real way to achieve **market leadership** which the PIMS studies show to be the main factor in achieving above-average profits.

Advantages of diversification

- If the bicycle market is in decline or faced with significant competition from cheaper foreign imports then there may be **gains to be made in other markets**.

- Other markets, such as the health and fitness club market, may offer higher gains than the bicycle market although the **risks** may also be greater because of factors such as changes in technology.

- If ABC were to **diversify**, this would reduce the **risk** of becoming involved in an individual market area that may decline and would give ABC **greater flexibility** to deal with changes in fashion and technology.

- It is possible that ABC could use its current **distribution networks** in order to market a different range of products.

- **New products** may have greater potential to provide technological or commercial advantages to the company.

Conclusion

The theory behind diversification for large companies is that there is no need for a company to do this simply to reduce the risk of just being in one industry as the shareholders are quite capable of doing this on their own behalf by owning a portfolio of shares. However for a private family owned company that is experiencing problems with profitability, a move into a new area is enticing. For ABC, given its core expertise, diversification should only be considered if it is believed that there are no future gains to be made from its current markets and that moves into non-core areas are likely to be successful.

Part (d)

> **Text reference.** The topics mentioned in this answer are discussed in Chapter 7 of your BPP Study Text.
>
> **Easy marks.** There is little in the scenario that you can use in this answer, so you may proceed more or less on a text book basis, which is generally easier than applying knowledge to scenario problems.

(a) **Organic growth**

Organic growth means setting up the operation purely with ABC's own resources. The benefits of such an approach are:

- Since ABC would provide all of the resources for the investment, the development can be scheduled according to its **own timetable** rather than that of a partner.

- Organic growth tends to be slower than setting up a joint venture and will be less of a **drain on the resources** of ABC, since it can set its own pace.

- As ABC is setting up the venture on its own **all profits will accrue to ABC** and do not need to be shared with any partner.

- As ABC is not reliant on any other party it will be able to expand its own **competences and knowledge**.

- The development can to take place in an orderly manner with no pressures from third parties to introduce products early. ABC will be in control and can introduce its products to the market **as and when it deems appropriate**.

- There is no need for ABC to **integrate with a partner**, either organisationally or culturally.

- Organic growth is likely to mean **higher motivation for employees and managers** as they are in control of the operation without input from any other party.

(b) **Acquisition**

- A further way of setting up the operation in China would be to acquire a bicycle manufacturer in China. The benefits of this approach are:

- The project can get **started more quickly** as the acquired company will already have the infrastructure in place and the expertise and resources required.

- This approach may be **cheaper than organic growth** if the cost of setting up the operation from scratch was going to be very high. Also, an acquisition can sometimes be self-financing; this occurs if unwanted parts of the acquired entity can be sold at a profit.

- ABC has no experience of trade in China and therefore by acquiring a company already operating there they are also effectively **acquiring the knowledge and expertise required**.

- ABC may find that there are **barriers to entry into the market by organic growth** such as access to distribution outlets, building a brand name or obtaining necessary licences; by acquiring an already operational company ABC may be able to avoid these problems.

(c)   **Joint developments**

A further method of entering the Chinese market is to enter into some sort of joint venture with a Chinese organisation. The benefits of such a joint development are:

- The **cost of the investment would be reduced** as it would be spread between ABC and its partner.

- The **risk would also be lower** as it would be shared with the partner – if the venture were unsuccessful ABC would have less investment to lose.

- In many countries foreign operations are **treated with suspicion** by government and customers alike – if a joint venture with a Chinese organisation is set up then this would make the operation more politically and commercially acceptable.

- ABC should be able to enter the market much more **rapidly** in a joint venture than by organic growth.

- ABC will obtain the benefit of the partner's **market knowledge** and access the partner's current customer base and supplier network.

- By entering into a joint venture the partner is **avoided as a direct competitor**.

SECTION B

Question 2

Part (a)

The **rational planning model** starts with the mission statement as the basis for the development of objectives. The mission statement denotes values, and the organisation's rationale for existing. Objectives are the quantified embodiments of the mission, and include measures such as profitability, timescales and deadlines. In practice, most organisations set themselves quantified objectives in order to enact the mission, using the **SMART** acronym.

The MNC will have as its main financial objective the interests of its **shareholders**, narrowly defined as **profit maximisation**, in order to reward shareholders for the risks that they take. Financial objectives would include the following.

- Profitability
- Return on investment (ROI) or return on capital employed (ROCE)
- Share price, earnings per share, dividends
- Growth

Growth in shareholder value is the yardstick by which most companies measure their success. This takes precedence over other growth objectives such as size, market share and so forth.

Private sector organisations have **other stakeholder groups**, with employees being of particular significance. However, their interests are generally subordinated to the overriding demands of commercial success and indeed, survival.

Local administrative authorities do not set objectives with the aim of achieving profit for shareholders, but they are being increasingly required to apply the same disciplines and processes as companies which are oriented towards straightforward profit goals. Business strategy issues are just as relevant to a local authority as they are for an MNC operating with a profit motive.

Having said that, whilst the basic principles are appropriate for the public sector, **differences** in how the public and private sectors apply these principles should not be forgotten.

Objectives for the local administrative authority will concentrate on achieving a particular response from target markets, and embody **social priorities**. **Efficiency** (getting the most output for the level of input) and **effectiveness** (meeting the objectives set) are particularly important in the use of public funds. Objectives related to these may even be set by central government.

There are no buyers in the public sector, or shareholders to satisfy. Instead, the local authority has a number of different **stakeholders**, particularly those in the local community who are to benefit from the housing, education, social and road maintenance services that they provide. Possible objectives for the local authority follow on from this and include the following. They are sometimes directly comparable with the objectives of an MNC.

- Surplus maximisation (equivalent to profit maximisation)
- Revenue maximisation (as for a commercial business)
- Maximising the use of facilities and services
- Matching the capacity available to the demands for it
- Cost recovery
- Satisfying staff
- Satisfying clients

Part (b)

The CIMA definition of **performance measurement** can be applied to both public and private sector organisations. It is 'the process of assessing the proficiency with which a reporting entity succeeds, by the economic acquisition of resources and their efficient and effective development, in achieving its objectives. Performance measures may be based on non-financial as well as financial information.'

Performance measurement communicates the objectives of the company and concentrates efforts towards those objectives. There are a number of key areas to consider when determining the approach to adopt towards performance evaluation in a given set of circumstances, and these can be used to discuss how the local administrative authority and the MNC should assess how well they have performed.

(a) **What is evaluated?**

This is a key question for both organisations. Some approaches concentrate on the performance of the organisation as a whole, while others look at strategic business units, divisions or functions. The local authority will want to assess the performance of its key service areas, while the MNC will be looking at profitability over a certain time period.

(b) **Who wants the evaluation?**

The MNC may base its assessment upon the viewpoint of a single group, primarily its investors and, by extension, the market. Their reactions will impact its share price. The local authority will be concerned about the maintenance of positive relations with its interested 'publics' which will include the clients for its services, the government and interest groups.

(c) **What are the objectives of the organisation?**

Is there a single goal, or many goals? Are the goals short or long term? Are they directly measurable? There is likely to be a mix of these for both organisations. The long term goal of the MNC could be to expand its operations into many more countries over the next ten years, while the local authority may be planning to open several more schools in that time. Short term objectives for the MNC may include divesting certain non-core businesses. The local authority may be trying to secure additional funding. All of these objectives will require different methods of assessment and control.

It must be remembered that objectives are likely to need revision and updating, so measurement of progress towards their attainment is an ongoing process which will need systematic reporting.

(d) **Are quantitative or qualitative measures appropriate?**

Measures must be relevant to the way that the organisation operates, and managers themselves must believe that the indicators are useful. Controlling activities is complicated for the local authority by the difficulty of judging whether non-quantitative objectives have been met. In a business such as the MNC, measures such as the level of sales, profit or ROI can indicate progress towards the achievement of objectives. This cannot be the case when the services are not sold but are provided to meet social needs. Improving services and increasing the satisfaction of those using them are likely to be important goals.

It is not always easy to measure the quality of output in public services. For example, league tables of exam results have been established to enable identification of those schools which get the best results. Housing services may be assessed by the length of waiting lists for accommodation.

(e) **What targets are used to assess performance?**

Measures are meaningless unless they are compared against something. Common sources of comparison for both organisations could include historic figures, standards/budgets, similar activities carried out by different local authorities, organisations or divisions, indices and trends over time.

Value for money audits can be seen as being of particular relevance in not-for-profit organisations. Such an audit focuses on economy, efficiency and effectiveness. These measures may be in conflict with each other. To take the example of higher education, larger class sizes may be economical in their use of teaching resources, but are not necessarily effective in creating the best learning environment.

Question 3

Part (a)

Forward integration into dress manufacture and its effect on competitive ability

Forward vertical integration is often justified as it enables the firm to do three things

(a) Earn more of the profit available in the value chain

(b) **Control marketing and pricing strategy** (eg Benetton) – the firm can ensure it maintains the image of quality and exclusivity

(c) **Control usage of the product**

EF's main motivation has been to earn more profit. In this, the incorporation of an **in-house clothing design team** has enabled it to increase its profits.

EF has thus extended the value chain. Previously, the process of adding value was simply a matter of designing and producing cloth. Dressmakers then creamed off the value added from turning the cloth into dresses and suits. A consequence is that EF's customer has changed from being the trade customer to being the end consumer. The operations process in the value chain is now more complicated, because **what were previously two value chains in a value system have now become one.**

The firm's success may lead its directors to consider that vertical integration has no drawbacks, hence their suggestion to enter retailing.

The drawbacks of EF's approach

(a) EF has **restricted its market** to the middle aged and middle income market. This is probably a sensible strategy for a clothing design company, but not for a fabric manufacturer. EF has put more eggs into one basket.

(b) EF has **precluded the possibility of other ways of increasing fabric sales**, by exporting for example.

(c) The **dress design company is limited** in its use of fabrics to what EF supplies. Its designers may resent the restrictions and lack of freedom.

(d) EF has to support **two different production operations** – spinning/weaving the fabrics, on the one hand, and dress manufacture on the other. There are thus two sets of machinery and two workforces.

(e) Capacity may not be matched properly. EF will have increased warehousing costs if it needs to manufacture cloth ahead of retail demand.

(f) There are other minor administrative issues such as **transfer pricing**. However, it should not be too difficult to compare cloth prices with competing products on the market.

Forwards vertical integration has made it harder to compete with **other yarn manufacturers**, and EF is now competing for fickle consumers who face many other offers.

Part (b)

Forward vertical integration into retail outlets

EF is proposing copying *Laura Ashley* and *Benetton* in having exclusive outlets for its own products. The intention is to earn more of the value in the value system.

Advantages

(a)   EF would have **total control over production, pricing and marketing**. It could develop a precise marketing strategy that further differentiates the product, enabling an even more targeted focus on its desired customer base. Moreover, it will have more freedom to develop marketing messages and integrate its marketing strategy.

(b)   EF will also be able to ensure that its products are available and visible, and are not competing in the same clothes racks as other competitors – thereby **avoiding price comparisons**. In other words, EF will not depend on retailers' professional buyers to order or display its products.

EF will **become fully informed of its target market.** It may be able to make clothes to order, if customer measurements can be transmitted electronically to the factory: this would be an example of **mass customisation.**

Drawbacks

(a)   EF will acquire a range of high street properties, with management problems of their own. **Debt service** will eat into any extra profits that are made on clothing sales.

(b)   **Higher risk.** If EF's clothes go out of fashion, the stores will become an expensive liability. Owning a chain of retail outlets involves a much higher proportion of fixed costs than cloth and clothing manufacture. Much depends on the location of the shops.

(c)   If EF products are exclusively sold in its own shops, **EF may forgo the sales it would have made at the department stores**. EF might be better advised to bite the bullet and accept that it will have to accept the high customer bargaining power with the stores.

(d)   EF will need to produce a wide enough range of products to encourage customers to enter. EF may have to supplement its own wares with others by other suppliers – will it be able to do so cost-effectively?

Competences

(a)   As EF is acquiring the chain, it will inherit the many competences needed, providing both that it can keep the staff and that EF's managers integrate the acquisition in a sensitive way.

(b)   Stock management for many small retail stores will be quite complicated. EF may well inherit systems currently employed in the acquired company.

(c)   EF needs to understand high street retailing, display, and merchandising (ensuring a suitable range of clothes is available in the right volumes and at the right time).

(d)   EF needs a more responsive distribution system.

(e)   EF is now running three different types of business. To benefit from economies of scale it may need a performance monitoring system for each business.

Question 4

Top tips. A common problem for candidates in the Paper 3.5 examination is the **application** of their theoretical knowledge to question scenarios. In this answer we show in *italics* those parts that constitute application of theory to the specific problems represented by the scenario.

Marking scheme

		Marks
(a)	Bases of segmentation:	
	Geographic	up to 2
	Socio-demographic	up to 2
	Behavioural	up to 2
	Psychographic	up to 2
	Benefits of segmentation:	
	Focus on differing needs	up to 3
	Better use of marketing mix	up to 3
		Maximum 12 marks
(b)	Follow closely (reactive me-too)	up to 4
	Follow at a distance	up to 2
	Follow selectively (niche)	up to 4
		Maximum 8 marks
		Total 20 marks

Part (a)

Text reference. The topics mentioned in this answer are discussed in Chapter 5 of your BPP Study Text.

Top tips. The great advantage of careful market segmentation is that it permits a precise determination of the marketing mix variables. This saves money and allows the firm to make best use of its competences.

Easy marks. Part (a) is about segmentation methods. This idea less well known than some of the strategic theory you have come across, such as, say, *Porter's* generic strategies, so there are going to be some marks simply for enumerating some suitable bases. Part (a) is worth twelve marks overall, which can be expected to break down into six for suggesting the bases and six for saying why segmentation is a good idea, or possibly five and seven respectively. Thus we might expect three marks for proposing three bases and saying a little about the relevance of each, with another two (or possibly three) for deeper discussion. Our discussion of each of the bases we have chosen illustrates this approach, progressing from the name of the base through its relevance to its wider implications or applications.

*Segmentation would be Natalia's first step towards a more active relationship with her existing and potential customers. If she knew who they were in more detail she could design her market offering in a way that would improve her own **efficiency** while also providing increased **customer satisfaction**.*

The simplest form of segmentation is probably **geographical**. *Natalia's potential market could be very simply split into domestic and overseas, for instance. Indeed, she probably does this already, in a sense, since she must make appropriate arrangements for the extra complications of shipping to foreign customers. Geographical segmentation would be necessary if Natalia wished to sell in other ways than via the Internet, perhaps by issuing catalogues, since the styles of knitwear offered would have to appeal to varying local tastes.*

BPP
LEARNING MEDIA

Geographical segmentation becomes much more useful when it is combined with demographic information. *This geo-demographic segmentation would enable Natalia to target segments defined by such variables as place, age, sex, income and social class. A consideration of these variables might for instance lead her to concentrate her marketing effort on older, affluent people in specific metropolitan areas. This would have immediate implications for design, quality, promotion, price and distribution.*

Psychographic segmentation analyses the market according to personality and lifestyle. *This might be difficult for Natalia to use, but if she could, perhaps by continuing to employ her marketing consultant, it might offer important advantages in the areas of design and promotion in particular.*

A further segmentation variable is customer **behaviour**. This includes such matters as sensitivity to changes in the marketing mix variables, purchase frequency and magnitude and how the product is used. *This approach might be useful to Natalia. For example, she might find that some of her designs are frequently bought by women for their menfolk. This might have important implications for design and sizing.*

The benefit of accurate market segmentation is that it permits a more precise specification of the marketing mix variables, so that they are shaped to conform to the needs of the target segment or segments.

Product. Different segments will probably require different products. When the size of each segment, its product requirements and their costs are known, it will be possible both to estimate the most profitable segment to attack and to specify fairly precisely the nature of the products needed to do so. *Natalia might find, for instance, that she needed to adjust her designs to make her range more recognisable and coherent.*

Price. Pricing decisions are fundamental to trade and very difficult to take. It is very easy to set prices too high, so that customers are put off, or too low, so that potential profit is lost. The problem is compounded by the complex messages about quality, exclusivity and value that can be sent by price levels and changes to them. *At the moment, Natalia's products are relatively cheap and this is preventing her from generating the funds needed for expansion: she may find that she can charge more for some of her knitwear.*

Promotion. *Natalia's consultant has identified her promotion efforts as insufficiently focused, which has led to a diffuse image and little brand awareness. Detailed knowledge of the characteristics of her target segments will allow Natalia to develop the accuracy of her promotion. She may find, for example, that a large market exists which is unwilling to use the Internet at all and so remains in ignorance of her products.*

Place. *Natalia's distribution is currently largely via her web site. This limits her potential market to those who are both confident in the use of computers and interested in original design knitwear. It is likely that a much larger market could be served through a more traditional approach using prestige clothing outlets. This could be established by careful consideration of the results of the segmentation exercise.*

Part (b)

> **Text reference.** The topics mentioned in this answer are discussed in Chapter 7 of your BPP Study Text.

The **market follower** accepts the status quo and thus **avoids the cost and risk associated with innovation** in product, price or distribution strategy. Such a **me-too** strategy is based on the leader's approach. This can be both profitable and stable. However, it is very easy for this strategy to come to depend entirely on charging lower prices. As the follower is unlikely to have the scale economies that accrue to the market leader, this means accepting a much lower level of profit

To be consistently successful, the market follower must not simply imitate. The follower should **compete in the most appropriate segments**, maintain its **customer base** and ensure that its **turnover grows** in line with the general expansion of the market. *Natalia could attempt to do this by exploiting the originality of her designs, thus effectively differentiating her market offering and justifying higher prices. The development of her brand image will be a necessary precondition for success with this strategy.*

An important problem for the market follower is that it may constitute an **attractive target** for market challengers seeking growth by acquisition, or indeed for the market leader seeking to extend control over the market. *An agreed turnover may, in due course, be a suitable way for Natalia to realise the equity in her business; however, assuming that she wishes to maintain her independence of operations for the foreseeable future she must control her costs and exploit appropriate opportunities to achieve differentiation. Otherwise, cash flow difficulties may force her to sell out.*

ACCA

Paper 3.5

Strategic Business Planning and Development

Mock Examination 3

December 2006

Question Paper		
Time allowed		**3 hours**
This paper is divided into two sections		
Section A	ONE compulsory question to be attempted	
Section B	TWO questions ONLY to be attempted	

DO NOT OPEN THIS PAPER UNTIL YOU ARE READY TO START UNDER EXAMINATION CONDITIONS

SECTION A – This question is compulsory and MUST be attempted

Question 1

Introduction

Tony Masters, chairman and chief executive of the Shirtmaster Group, is worried. He has recently responded to his senior management team's concerns over the future of the Group by reluctantly agreeing to appoint an external management consultant. The consultant's brief is to fully analyse the performance of the privately owned company, identify key strategic and operational problems and recommend a future strategy for the company. Tony is concerned that the consultant's report will seriously question his role in the company and the growth strategy he is proposing.

Group origins and structure

Tony's father, Howard Masters, set up Shirtmaster in the 1950s. Howard was a skilled tailor and saw the potential for designing and manufacturing a distinctive range of men's shirts and ties marketed under the 'Shirtmaster' brand. Howard set up a shirt manufacturing company with good access to the employee skills needed to design and make shirts. Howard had recognised the opportunity to make distinctive shirts incorporating innovative design features including the latest man-made fibres. In the 1960s London was a global fashion centre exploiting the UK's leading position in popular music. Men became much more fashion conscious, and were willing to pay premium prices for clothes with style and flair. Shirtmaster by the 1960s had built up a UK network of more than 2,000 small independent clothing retailers. These retailers sold the full range of men's wear including made-to-measure suits, shirts and matching ties, shoes and other clothing accessories. Extensive and expensive TV and cinema advertising supported the Shirtmaster brand.

The Shirtmaster Group is made up of two divisions – the Shirtmaster division which concentrates on the retail shirt business and the Corporate Clothing division which supplies workwear to large industrial and commercial customers. Corporate Clothing has similar origins to Shirtmaster, also being a family owned and managed business and is located in the same town as Shirtmaster. It was set up to supply hardwearing jeans and workwear to the many factory workers in the region. The decline of UK manufacturing and allied industries led to profitability problems and in 1990 the Shirtmaster Group acquired it. Tony took over executive responsibility for the Group in 1996 and continues to act as managing director for the Shirtmaster Division.

Shirtmaster division – operations and market environment

By 2006 the UK market for men's shirts was very different to that of the 1960s and 1970s when Shirtmaster had become one of the best known premium brands. In a mature market most of Shirtmaster's competitors have outsourced the making of their shirts to low cost manufacturers in Europe and the Far East. Shirtmaster is virtually alone in maintaining a UK manufacturing base. Once a year Tony and the buyer for the division go to Asia and the Far East, visiting cloth manufacturers and buying for stock. This stock, stored in the division's warehouse, gives the ability to create a wide range of shirt designs but creates real problems with excessive stock holdings and outdated stock. Shirtmaster prides itself on its ability to respond to the demands of its small retail customers and the long-term relationships built up with these retailers. Typically, these retailers order in small quantities and want quick delivery. Shirtmaster has to introduce new shirt designs throughout the year, contrasting with the spring and autumn ranges launched by its competitors. This creates real pressure on the small design team available.

The retail side of the shirt business has undergone even more fundamental change. Though the market for branded shirts continues to exist, such shirts are increasingly sold through large departmental stores. There is increasing competition between the shirt makers for the limited shelf space available in the departmental stores. Shopping centres and malls are increasingly dominated by nationwide chains of specialist clothing retailers. They sell to the premium segment of the market and are regarded as the trendsetters for the industry. These chains can develop quickly, often using franchising to achieve rapid growth, and are increasingly international in scope. All of them require their suppliers to make their clothes under the chain's own label brand. Some have moved successfully into selling via catalogues and the Internet. Finally, the UK supermarket chains have discovered the profitability of selling nonfood goods. The shirts they sell are aimed at value for money rather than style, sourced wherever they can be made most cheaply and sold under the supermarket's own label. Small independent clothing retailers are declining both in number and market share.

The Shirtmaster division, with its continued over-reliance for its sales on these small independent retailers, is threatened by each of the retail driven changes, having neither the sales volume to compete on price nor the style to compete on fashion.

The Shirtmaster division's international strategy

Tony's answer to these changes is to make the Shirtmaster brand an international one. His initial strategy is to sell to European clothing retailers and once established, move the brand into the fast growing consumer markets in Asia and the Far East. He recognises that the division's current UK focus means that working with a European partner is a necessity. He has given the sales and marketing manager the job of finding major retailers, distributors or manufacturers with whom they can make a strategic alliance and so help get the Shirtmaster range onto the shelves of European clothing retailers.

Corporate Clothing division – operations and market environment

Corporate Clothing has in recent years implemented a major turnaround in its business as the market for corporate clothing began to grow significantly. Corporate Clothing designs, manufactures and distributes a comprehensive range of workwear for its corporate customers, sourcing much of its range from low cost foreign suppliers. It supplies the corporate clothing requirements of large customers in the private and public sectors. Major contracts have been gained with banks, airlines, airports and the police, fire and ambulance services.

The Corporate Clothing division supplies the whole range of workwear required and in the sizes needed for each individual employee. Its designers work closely with the buyers in its large customers and the division's sales benefit from the regular introduction of new styles of uniforms and workwear. Corporate employers are increasingly aware of the external image they need to project and the clothes their employees wear are the key to this image. Corporate Clothing has invested heavily in manufacturing and IT systems to ensure that it meets the needs of its demanding customers. It is particularly proud of its computer-aided design and manufacturing (CAD/CAM) systems, which can be linked to its customers and allows designs to be updated and manufacturing alterations to be introduced with its customers' approval. Much of its success can be attributed to the ability to offer a customer service package in which garments are stored by Corporate Clothing and distributed directly to the individual employee in personalized workwear sets as and when required. The UK market for corporate workwear was worth £500 million in 2005. Evidence suggests that the demand for corporate workwear is likely to continue to grow.

The Corporate Clothing division also has ambitions to enter the markets for corporate clothing in Europe and recognises that might be most easily done through using a suitable strategic partner. There is friendly rivalry between the two divisions but each operates largely independently of the other. Over the past 10 years the fortunes of the two divisions have been completely reversed. Corporate Clothing now is a modest profit maker for the group – Shirtmaster is consistently losing money.

Shirtmaster Group – future strategy

Tony is determined to re-establish Shirtmaster as a leading shirt brand in the UK and successfully launch the brand in Europe. He sees a strategic alliance with a European partner as the key to achieving this ambition. Though he welcomes the success of the Corporate Clothing division and recognises its potential in Europe, he remains emotionally and strategically committed to restoring the fortunes of the Shirtmaster division. Unfortunately, his autocratic style of leadership tends to undermine the position of the senior management team at Shirtmaster. He continues to play an active role in both the operational and strategic sides of the business and is both well known and regarded by workers in the Shirtmaster division's factory.

The initial feedback meeting with the management consultant has confirmed the concern that he is not delegating sufficiently. The consultant commented that Tony's influence could be felt throughout the Shirtmaster division. Managers either try to anticipate the decisions they think he would make or, alternatively, not take the decisions until he has given his approval. The end result is a division not able to meet the challenges of an increasingly competitive retail marketplace, and losing both money and market share.

Table 1 – Financial Information on the Shirtmaster Group (£ million)

	2003	2004	2005	2006 Budget	2007 Forecast	2008 Forecast
Total sales	25.0	23.8	21.4	23.5	24.4	26.7
UK sales	24.5	23.2	21.0	22.7	23.4	24.7
Overseas sales	0.5	0.6	0.4	0.8	1.0	2.0
Cost of sales	17.7	16.8	15.2	16.3	16.8	17.8
Gross profit	7.3	7.0	6.2	7.2	7.6	8.9
Marketing	1.7	1.5	1.2	1.7	1.9	2.2
Distribution	1.6	1.4	1.2	1.4	1.5	1.9
Administration	1.8	1.8	1.7	1.9	1.9	2.1
Net profit	2.2	2.3	2.1	2.2	2.3	2.7
Shirtmaster division						
Total sales	14.8	12.6	10.3	11.7	12.0	13.5
UK sales	14.3	12.0	9.9	10.9	11.0	11.5
Overseas sales	0.5	0.6	0.4	0.8	1.0	2.0
Cost of sales	11.1	9.8	8.2	9.1	9.4	10.1
Gross profit	3.7	2.8	2.1	2.6	2.6	3.4
Marketing	1.5	1.3	1.0	1.5	1.7	2.0
Distribution	1.2	1.0	0.8	0.9	1.0	1.3
Administration	1.3	1.2	1.1	1.2	1.2	1.3
Net profit	(0.3)	(0.7)	(0.8)	(1.0)	(1.3)	(1.2)
Stock	2.0	2.2	3.0	2.7	2.5	2.0
Employees	100	100	98	98	99	100
Corporate Clothing division						
Total sales	10.2	11.2	11.1	11.8	12.4	13.2
Cost of sales	6.6	7.0	7.0	7.2	7.4	7.7
Gross profit	3.6	4.2	4.1	4.6	5.0	5.5
Marketing	0.2	0.2	0.2	0.2	0.2	0.2
Distribution	0.4	0.4	0.4	0.5	0.5	0.6
Administration	0.5	0.6	0.6	0.7	0.7	0.8
Net profit	2.5	3.0	2.9	3.2	3.6	3.9
Stock	0.9	1.0	0.8	0.8	0.9	1.0
Employees	84	84	80	79	77	75

Required

(a)   Assess the strategic position and performance of the Shirtmaster Group and its divisions over the 2003-2005 period. Your analysis should make use of models where appropriate.   **(20 marks)**

(b)   Both divisions have recognised the need for a strategic alliance to help them achieve a successful entry into European markets.

Critically evaluate the advantages and disadvantages of the divisions using strategic alliances to develop their respective businesses in Europe.   **(15 marks)**

(c)   The Shirtmaster division and Corporate Clothing division, though being part of the same group, operate largely independently of one another.

Assess the costs and benefits of the two divisions continuing to operate independently of one another.
          (15 marks)

(d)   Family owned and managed businesses often find delegation and succession difficult processes to get right.

What models would you recommend that Tony use in looking to change his leadership and management style to create a culture in the Shirtmaster Group better able to deal with the challenges it faces? **(10 marks)**

(Total = 60 marks)

SECTION B – TWO questions ONLY to be attempted

Question 2

Good Sports Limited is an independent sports goods retailer owned and operated by two partners, Alan and Bob. The sports retailing business in the UK has undergone a major change over the past ten years. First of all the supply side has been transformed by the emergence of a few global manufacturers of the core sports products, such as training shoes and football shirts. This consolidation has made them increasingly unwilling to provide good service to the independent sportswear retailers too small to buy in sufficiently large quantities. These independent retailers can stock popular global brands, but have to order using the Internet and have no opportunity to meet the manufacturer's sales representatives. Secondly, UK's sportswear retailing has undergone significant structural change with the rapid growth of a small number of national retail chains with the buying power to offset the power of the global manufacturers. These retail chains stock a limited range of high volume branded products and charge low prices the independent retailer cannot hope to match.

Good Sports has survived by becoming a specialist niche retailer catering for less popular sports such as cricket, hockey and rugby. They are able to offer the specialist advice and stock the goods that their customers want. Increasingly since 2000 Good Sports has become aware of the growing impact of e-business in general and e-retailing in particular. They employed a specialist website designer and created an online purchasing facility for their customers. The results were less than impressive, with the Internet search engines not picking up the company website. The seasonal nature of Good Sports' business, together with the variations in sizes and colours needed to meet an individual customer's needs, meant that the sales volumes were insufficient to justify the costs of running the site.

Bob, however, is convinced that developing an e-business strategy suited to the needs of the independent sports retailer such as Good Sports will be key to business survival. He has been encouraged by the growing interest of customers in other countries to the service and product range they offer. He is also aware of the need to integrate an e-business strategy with their current marketing, which to date has been limited to the sponsorship of local sports teams and advertisements taken in specialist sports magazines. Above all, he wants to avoid head-on competition with the national retailers and their emphasis on popular branded sportswear sold at retail prices that are below the cost price at which Good Sports can buy the goods.

Required

(a)   Provide the partners with a short report on the advantages and disadvantages to Good Sports of developing an e-business strategy and the processes most likely to be affected by such a strategy.   **(12 marks)**

(b)   Good Sports Limited has successfully followed a niche strategy to date.

Assess the extent to which an appropriate e-business strategy could help support such a niche strategy.

(8 marks)

(Total = 20 marks)

357

Question 3

Clyde Williams is facing a dilemma. He has successfully built up a small family-owned company, Concrete Solutions Ltd, manufacturing a range of concrete based products used in making roads, pavements and walkways. The production technology is very low tech and uses simple wooden moulds into which the concrete is poured. As a consequence he is able to use low skilled and low cost labour, which would find it difficult to find alternative employment in a region with high unemployment levels. The company has employed many of its workforce since its creation in 1996. The company's products are heavy, bulky and costly to transport. This means its market is limited to a 30-mile area around the small rural town where the manufacturing facility is located. Its customers are a mix of private sector building firms and public sector local councils responsible for maintaining roads and pavements. By its nature much of the demand is seasonal and very price sensitive.

A large international civil engineering company has recently approached Clyde with an opportunity to become a supplier of concrete blocks used in a sophisticated system for preventing coast and riverbank erosion. The process involves interlocking blocks being placed on a durable textile base. Recent trends in global warming and pressure in many countries to build in areas liable to flooding have created a growing international market for the patented erosion prevention system. Clyde has the opportunity to become the sole UK supplier of the blocks and to be one of a small number of suppliers able to export the blocks to Europe. To do it he will need to invest a significant amount in CAM (computer aided manufacturing) technology with a linked investment in the workforce skills needed to operate the new technology. The net result will be a small increase in the size of the labour force but redundancy for a significant number of its existing workers either unwilling or unable to adapt to the demands of the new technology. Successful entry into this new market will reduce his reliance on the seasonal low margin concrete products he currently produces and significantly improve profitability.

One further complication exists. Concrete Solutions is located in a quiet residential area of its home town. Clyde is under constant pressure from the local residents and their council representatives to reduce the amount of noise and dust created in the production process. Any move into making the new blocks will increase the pollution problems the residents face. There is a possibility of moving the whole manufacturing process to a site on a new industrial estate being built by the council in a rival town. However closure of the existing site would lead to a loss of jobs in the current location. Clyde has asked for your help in resolving his dilemma.

Required

(a)   Using models where appropriate, advise Clyde on whether he should choose to take advantage of the opportunity offered by the international company.   **(12 marks)**

(b)   Assess the extent to which social responsibility issues could and should affect his decision to move into the new product area.   **(8 marks)**

(Total = 20 marks)

BPP
LEARNING MEDIA

Question 4

David Silvester is the founder and owner of a recently formed gift packaging company, Gift Designs Ltd. David has spotted an opportunity for a new type of gift packaging. This uses a new process to make waterproof cardboard and then shapes and cuts the card in such a way to produce a container or vase for holding cut flowers. The containers can be stored flat and in bulk and then simply squeezed to create the flowerpot into which flowers and water are then put. The potential market for the product is huge. In the UK hospitals alone there are 200,000 bunches of flowers bought each year for patients. David's innovative product does away with the need for hospitals to provide and store glass vases. The paper vases are simple, safe and hygienic. He has also identified two other potential markets; firstly, the market for fresh flowers supplied by florists and secondly, the corporate gift market where clients such as car dealers present a new owner with an expensive bunch of flowers when the customer takes delivery of a new car. The vase can be printed using a customer's design and logo and creates an opportunity for real differentiation and impact at sales conferences and other high profile PR events.

David anticipates a rapid growth in Gift Designs as its products become known and appreciated. The key question is how quickly the company should grow and the types of funding needed to support its growth and development. The initial financial demands of the business have been quite modest but David has estimated that the business needs £500K to support its development over the next two years and is uncertain as to the types of funding best suited to a new business as it looks to grow rapidly. He understands that business risk and financial risk is not the same thing and is looking for advice on how he should organise the funding of the business. He is also aware of the need to avoid reliance on friends and family for funding and to broaden the financial support for the business. Clearly the funding required would also be affected by the activities David decides to carry out himself and those activities better provided by external suppliers.

Required

(a) Provide David with a short report on the key issues he should take into account when developing a strategy for funding Gift Designs' growth and development. **(10 marks)**

(b) Using models where appropriate, what are likely to be the critical success factors (CSFs) as the business grows and develops? **(10 marks)**

(Total = 20 marks)

Answers

DO NOT TURN THIS PAGE UNTIL YOU HAVE
COMPLETED THE MOCK EXAM

A plan of attack

We discussed the problem of which question to start with earlier, in 'Passing the 3.5 exam'. Here we will merely reiterate our view that question 1 is nearly always the best place to start and, if you do decide to start with a Section B question, **make sure that you finish your answer in no more than 36 minutes**.

Question 1 is largely straightforward and of the type we are quite used to. The well-prepared candidate should be able to tackle it with some confidence. The only requirement that might cause some head scratching is requirement (b), which revolves around the idea of strategic alliances. This is not a very prominent topic in the syllabus and you might have some difficulty in finding enough to say about it within the rather specialised context of the scenario. Nevertheless, you should not have too much difficulty in obtaining a pass mark in this question.

Question 2 is, unfortunately, of a type the Examiner tends to set, in that requirement (b) amplifies an aspect of requirement (a). You would have to take care, therefore, that you did not steal your own thunder by dealing with the topic of requirement (b) while responding to requirement (a), thus leaving yourself with nothing to say when you came to deal with requirement (b). Also, e-commerce is a **somewhat specialised topic**, so, overall, you may prefer the other two Section B questions to this one.

Question 3 is more attractive in that it is concerned with the mainstream topics of **strategic options** and **social responsibility**. The only quibble you might have is that the scenario content appears a little biased towards requirement (b), while the marks are biased towards requirement (a). This is unfortunate, but if you are confident in your basic analysis and options models, as you should be, you should not finds it too much of a problem. We like this question.

Question 4 is also fairly attractive, if a little specialised in business strategy terms. However, you should be able to produce a good answer to requirement (a) without too much difficulty, since it is really about a mainstream accounting topic. Requirement (b) might cause you a little difficulty, since it can actually be very difficult to isolate critical success factors in practice. One common pitfall is to fail to be sufficiently specific and propose factors that are actually quite generic, such as 'customer service'. If you avoid this error and look more deeply, it then becomes difficult to establish precisely which aspect of, say, customer service is critical – if any. However, despite this note of caution, we recommend this question, with the proviso that your answer to requirement (b) must make it absolutely clear that you know what a critical success factor is, so that you are sure of the easy marks.

SECTION A

Question 1

Part (a)

> **Top tips.** Our answer includes the figures so that we can highlight some key trends – you may not have provided this information in such a format for your answer, and indeed you would not have been expected to in the exam due to time constraints. An understanding of the key trends, however, is what the question is all about and you must be capable of analysing the separate performances of the two divisions. Your findings are likely to inform your answers to later parts of the question.

	2003	2004	2005	2006 Budget	2007 Forecast	2008 Forecast
Overall Shirtmaster Group:						
Total sales	25.0	23.8	21.4	23.5	24.4	26.7
UK sales	24.5	23.2	21.0	22.7	23.4	24.7
Trend		-5%	-9%	8%	3%	6%
Overseas sales	0.5	0.6	0.4	0.8	1.0	2.0
Cost of sales	17.7	16.8	15.2	16.3	16.8	17.8
Cost of sales %	71%	71%	71%	69%	69%	67%
Gross profit	7.3	7.0	6.2	7.2	7.6	8.9
Gross profit %	29%	29%	29%	31%	31%	33%
Marketing	1.7	1.5	1.2	1.7	1.9	2.2
Distribution	1.6	1.4	1.2	1.4	1.5	1.9
Administration	1.8	1.8	1.7	1.9	1.9	2.1
Other costs %	20%	20%	19%	21%	22%	23%
Net profit	2.2	2.3	2.1	2.2	2.3	2.7
Net profit %	9%	10%	10%	9%	9%	10%
Shirtmaster division:						
Total sales	14.8	12.6	10.3	11.7	12.0	13.5
UK sales	14.3	12.0	9.9	10.9	11.0	11.5
Trend		-19%	-19%	10%	1%	5%
Overseas sales	0.5	0.6	0.4	0.8	1.0	2.0
Cost of sales	11.1	9.8	8.2	9.1	9.4	10.1
Cost of sales %	75%	78%	80%	78%	78%	75%
Gross profit	3.7	2.8	2.1	2.6	2.6	3.4
Gross profit %	25%	22%	20%	22%	22%	25%
Marketing	1.5	1.3	1.0	1.5	1.7	2.0
Distribution	1.2	1.0	0.8	0.9	1.0	1.3
Administration	1.3	1.2	1.1	1.2	1.2	1.3
Other costs %	27%	28%	28%	31%	33%	34%
Net profit	(0.3)	(0.7)	(0.8)	(1.0)	(1.3)	(1.2)
Net profit %						
Stock	2.0	2.2	3.0	2.7	2.5	2.0
Employees	100	100	98	98	99	100

	2003	2004	2005	2006 Budget	2007 Forecast	2008 Forecast
Corporate Clothing division:						
Total sales	10.2	11.2	11.1	11.8	12.4	13.2
Trend		*10%*	*-1%*	*6%*	*5%*	*6%*
Cost of sales	6.6	7.0	7.0	7.2	7.4	7.7
Cost of sales %	*65%*	*63%*	*63%*	*61%*	*60%*	*58%*
Gross profit	3.6	4.2	4.1	4.6	5.0	5.5
Gross profit %	*35%*	*38%*	*37%*	*39%*	*40%*	*42%*
Marketing	0.2	0.2	0.2	0.2	0.2	0.2
Distribution	0.4	0.4	0.4	0.5	0.5	0.6
Administration	0.5	0.6	0.6	0.7	0.7	0.8
Other costs %	*11%*	*11%*	*11%*	*12%*	*11%*	*12%*
Net profit	2.5	3.0	2.9	3.2	3.6	3.9
Net profit %	*25%*	*27%*	*26%*	*27%*	*29%*	*30%*
Stock	0.9	1.0	0.8	0.8	0.9	1.0
Employees	84	84	80	79	77	75

As demonstrated by these figures and ratios, the performance of the Shirtmaster Group is a composite of two very different performances by the totally separate divisions. These divisions are operating in very different markets, with very different strategies and very different results. For the group as a whole, sales have declined to 2005 and net margins are struggling to get into double figures.

The Shirtmaster division is **dragging down the performance of the entire group**. The overall group net profit margin of 10% in 2005 masks the fact that the Shirtmasters division suffered a net loss, while Corporate Clothing recorded a net profit margin of 26%.

Using the information from the scenario to consider the Shirtmasters value chain, for example, Tony Masters' strategy of being an integrated shirt manufacturer carrying out all the activities needed to design, manufacture and distribute its shirts is in doubt, because most of its competitors have recognised the commercial sense in **outsourcing production to cheaper and more flexible manufacturers overseas**. There is no competitive advantage in retaining production in the higher cost UK, particularly when the company has no other point of differentiation (such as recognised high style or fashion) for its products.

The premium end of the shirt market, its historical focus, has changed since the days of Shirtmasters' earlier success and the division now needs to change to respond to a new **market structure** with **new participants in the value system**. As can be seen from the above analysis, Shirtmasters' reliance on small retailers has seen the costs of its support activities (marketing, distribution and administration) take up a huge part of its turnover. Trips to buy cloth from foreign suppliers have resulted in large stocks of expensive cloth, around a month's worth of sales being held at any one time. Meeting the demands of its many small customers is therefore having a real impact on marketing, manufacturing and distribution costs.

Making reference to Porter's five competitive forces, the key ones at work are the **rivalry between the shirt makers**, and the increased **buying power of customers** in the industry – the specialist retail outlets and supermarkets. To accommodate these forces, Shirtmasters may have to consider the possibility of making own brand shirts for the supermarkets so that it can expand its market.

The effect of these problems is revealed in selected aspects of performance, when compared to the Corporate Clothing division:

	Shirtmaster division	Corporate Clothing division
Sales growth to 2005	Slowing	Increasing
Gross margin	Lower	Higher and sustained
Sales per employee	Modest	Improving
Marketing etc expenses	Out of control	Acceptable levels
Stock levels	Too high	More modest
Net margins	Negative	Positive
Market share	Minimal, stagnant	Growing
Product innovation	Nil	Customer focus
Process innovation	Nil	Investment in technology
Customer base	Declining	Growing

The measures above reflect a **balanced scorecard approach** to performance analysis. On all measures, Corporate Clothing is a stronger performer and this must be due to its **focus on the customer**, through its willingness to embrace the realities of its market, invest in appropriate technology and take close note of customer needs. The contrast with Tony's 'pet' division, Shirtmasters, could not be more stark, and should serve to impress upon the senior management of the group the need to give more strategic responsibility to managers possessing the necessary detachment to manage Shirtmasters more effectively.

Marking scheme

	Marks
Shirtmaster Group position and performance	up to 3 marks
Eg Static sales; low margins; little synergy	
Shirtmaster division	up to 10 marks
Value chain comments	
Stock levels, procurement	
Customers segment served declining	
High marketing etc costs	
Corporate Clothing division	up to 10 marks
Better customer focus	
Growing market	
Positive margins	
Use of models	up to 3 marks
	Maximum 20 marks

Part (b)

Top tips. Begin your answer by defining a strategic alliance, and outlining its advantages and disadvantages. We have concentrated upon the suitability of a joint venture for this answer. Apply the advantages and disadvantages to the circumstances of Shirtmakers and Corporate Clothing and use your answers to part (a) to examine the suitability of each company. You should answer large scenario questions in order, as your answers to one part may inform the content of a later part, as is the case here.

Johnson and Scholes define a strategic alliance as 'where two or more organisations share resources and activities to pursue a strategy'. Alliances can be particularly attractive to smaller firms such as Shirtmakers, or where expensive new technologies or markets are being developed and the costs can be shared. One particular form of strategic alliance is the joint venture, whereby two or more firms join forces for manufacturing, financial and marketing purposes and each has a share in both the equity and the management of the business.

Particular advantages to Shirtmakers and Corporate Clothing of the pursuit of such an alliance are the following.

(a)   **Share costs**. As the capital outlay is shared, joint ventures can be especially attractive. The joint operation may lead to economies of scale that mean that costs can be reduced.

(b)   **Cut risk.** A joint venture can reduce the risk of government intervention if a local firm is involved.

(c)   Alliances provide **close control** over marketing and other operations, as both companies have a strong interest in ensuring that processes are effective.

(d)   Overseas joint ventures provide **local knowledge**. Alliances are commonly entered into where, as in this scenario, a company is seeking to expand overseas.

(e)   **Synergies.** One firm's production expertise, for example, can be supplemented by the other's marketing and distribution facility. In this way, particular competences can be exploited for the good of the whole alliance.

(f)   **Learning.** Alliances can also be a learning exercise in which each partner tries to learn as much as possible from the other, particularly about local markets.

(g)   **Technology.** New technology offers many uncertainties and many opportunities. Such alliances provide funds for expensive research projects, spreading risk.

(h)   **The alliance itself can generate innovations** and be a learning exercise for all participants.

(i)   The alliance can involve **testing the firm's core competence** in different conditions, which can suggest ways to improve it.

When choosing the type of alliance to pursue, the following factors need to be considered by Shirtmakers and Corporate Clothing.

What benefits are going to be offered by collaboration?

•   Which partners should be chosen?
•   Is the environment favourable to a partnership?
•   What activities and processes will have to be set up?
•   Are there any other alliances within the industry?

Johnson and Scholes argue that for an alliance to be successful there needs to be a **clear strategic purpose** and **senior management support**; **compatibility** between the partners; time spent defining **clear goals**, governance and other organisational arrangements; and **trust** between the partners that together they can get the job done.

The major disadvantage of joint ventures is that there can be **major conflicts of interest**. Disagreements may arise over profit shares, amounts invested, the management and control of the alliance, and overall strategy. Shirtmakers and Corporate Clothing would need to make sure that such issues are clearly set out and agreed at the beginning to avoid damaging clashes later.

The Shirtmaster and Corporate Clothing divisions have very different experience and business conditions to offer any potential partner. Shirtmaster may struggle to attract a partner with its current product and strategy, particularly its insistence on **retaining manufacture in the UK** when most competitors now source from cheaper markets in Europe and the Far East. Its dwindling network of low volume small retail customers, and the processes by which it manages its stock and designs would appear to many potential partners and European retailers to be anachronistic. By contrast, the Corporate Clothing division seems to be much more favourable as a potential partner. The market for corporate workwear is growing, and the company employs sophisticated systems coupled with a superior customer service record. This could be repeated in Europe if the right partner could be found.

	Marks
Definition of strategic alliance	1 mark
Advantages of successful strategic alliances, eg: Economies of scale Specialisation and synergies Learning from partners and developing competences	up to 6 marks
Disadvantages of strategic alliances, eg: Conflicts of interest and disagreement	up to 3 marks
Application to Shirtmasters/Corporate Clothing	up to 5 marks
	Maximum 15 marks

Part (c)

Top tips. This is a complex question. The existence of the two divisions largely reflects the origins of the two family businesses, and the divisions have grown and developed separately. Think about the advantages and disadvantages of divisionalisation and how these are currently manifested in the Shirtmasters group. Does divisionalisation make sense for the management of these businesses? Their products may be along the same lines, but their trading conditions and circumstances are very different.

Divisionalisation has some advantages, notably **focusing the attention of subordinate management** on business performance and results. It therefore can provide a good training ground for junior managers in the individual divisions. It also enables proper concentration on particular product-market areas – in this case, shirts and workwear.

Problems can arise, as in this scenario, with the **power of the head office**, and **control of resources**. It appears that Tony Masters has more emotional commitment, and presumably more management time, to devote to Shirtmaster at the expense of Corporate Clothing.

Mintzberg believes there are inherent problems in divisionalisation, many of which are actually those of conglomerate diversification. In the Shirtmaster group, it could be that each business might be better run independently. The different businesses might offer different returns for different risks which shareholders might prefer to **judge independently**.

There does not appear to be any common effort between the divisions, with no sharing of resources apparent from the scenario details. While both are in the clothing market, their respective value systems run very differently. Information systems are also likely to operate independently. This may be leading to **duplication of effort** and **waste of resources**.

If divisionalisation is to operate effectively, divisional management should be free to use their authority to do what they think is right for their part of the organisation. This is not happening in the Shirtmaster division, and the time has come for Tony Masters to allow his management team to **develop strategy** to drive the company forward, perhaps with the necessity to take some tough decisions that he appears incapable of making. Performance in both divisions needs to be clearly identified and controlled, and resources channelled to those areas showing potential.

Each division must have a potential for growth in its own area of operations. It seems that only Corporate Clothing can satisfy this test in current trading conditions.

Divisions should exist side by side with each other. If they deal with each other, it should be as an arm's length transaction. There should be no insistence on preferential treatment to be given to one particular unit. While there is no suggestion in the scenario that this is happening, Tony Masters' favouring of the Shirtmaster division in more subtle ways is having an effect upon performance.

Using the BCG matrix it is possible to classify the Shirtmaster division as a 'dog' with low market share, in a market with little growth. It needs refreshed management to take it forward and find new markets. The Corporate Clothing division, by contrast, has a small share of a growing market, and this potential also needs to close management.

Marking scheme

	Marks
Advantages of divisions operating independently: eg performance monitoring, manager training	up to 5 marks
Disadvantages of divisions operating independently: eg no sharing of resources/skills Duplicated costs	up to 5 marks
Effective divisionalisation eg management initiative encouraged not stifled	up to 5 marks
	Maximum 15 marks

Part (d)

> **Top tips.** This answer concentrates upon the McKinsey 7S model. You may have used others in your answer. For example, the work of Edgar Schein on leadership and its relationship with organisational culture is well documented (and mentioned by the ACCA's own model answer).

The link between organisational leadership and culture can be seen most strongly in the influence of a founding entrepreneur upon the culture of the organisation. Leaders such as Tony's father start up their companies with a strong vision of the product that they want to make, the customer that they wish to serve and the type of organisation that they want their company to be. Tony is now clearly influenced by such a cultural legacy, and to this end he has found it difficult to relinquish his dominant role.

The McKinsey 7S model shows the links between how an organisation such as Shirtmakers operates and the behaviour of individuals within it. The founder or leader is the main influence on the central **shared values** of the firm. If we analyse the other interdependent features of the model that affect organisational performance – strategy, structure, systems, skills, staff and style – it is clear that Tony is heavily involved in these areas too, chiefly because of his **reluctance to delegate**. This reluctance will eventually hamper the success of the Shirtmakers Group.

Three of the elements within the McKinsey model are considered 'hard'.

(a) **Structure.** The organisation structure determines division of tasks in the organisation and the hierarchy of authority from the most senior to junior. Tony's influence is felt throughout the organisation but he appears to be more committed to the Shirtmasters division than to Corporate Clothing.

(b) **Strategy.** Strategy is way in which the organisation plans to outperform its competitors, if it is a business, or how it intends to achieve its objectives. Tony appears to be heavily involved here and does not allow his staff to have enough input to the strategy formulation process.

(c) **Systems.** Systems include the technical systems of accounting, personnel, management information and so forth.

These 'hard' elements are easily quantified or defined, and deal with facts and rules.

369

However, the McKinsey model suggests that certain 'soft' elements are equally important.

(a)   **Shared values** are the guiding beliefs of people in the organisation as to why it exists. These were laid down by Howard Masters and remain very important to Tony.

(b)   **Staff** are the people in the organisation. They have their own complex concerns and priorities.

(c)   **Style** is another aspect of the corporate culture, which includes the shared assumptions, ways of working and attitudes of management. Tony is well regarded and respected by his staff, particularly on the factory floor, but he does not have the **correct balance** between being a respected manager and allowing his senior staff to develop their own strategic management skills. He is able to do this on occasion, as demonstrated by the responsibility that he has given his sales and marketing manager to research potential alliance partners, but he will need to go further if his autocratic leadership style is to adapt and soften.

(d)   **Skills** are those things that the organisation does well. The market for corporate workwear, for example, appears to be a success for the group because of its commitment to the appropriate technology and customer service levels. It would appear from the scenario that Tony is far more 'hands-off' here than he is with the Shirtmasters division. Both divisions require his attention and appropriate management.

The importance of the 'soft' elements for success was emphasised by Peters and Waterman in their study of **excellent** companies.

Changing the culture of an organisation is not an easy task. If it is accepted that leadership is 'the process of influencing others to work willingly and to the best of their capabilities' then Tony has a huge task ahead of him to adapt his style and lead Shirtmakers as it faces various market challenges and tries to establish itself as an international brand by working with a European partner in both of its divisions.

Marking scheme

Marks

Models linking leadership and culture:
Eg McKinsey 7S model
'Excellence' model

Up to 5 marks for explanation/features
Up to 5 marks for application to Shirtmaster

Maximum 10 marks

Section B

Question 2

Part (a)

> **Top tips.** This question puts e-commerce firmly into a strategic context. IT and the Internet pervade the modern business organisation and so it should be possible for you to offer sensible comments upon this basis. The main advantages and disadvantages of an e-business strategy that you put into your answer must be applicable to Good Sports' own business situation. It is not a foregone conclusion that involvement in e-commerce will be unequivocally beneficial. There a several strategic issues to consider – such as the familiar framework of 'suitability, acceptability and feasibility'. Porter's generic strategies are also brought into this question, and you should have little difficulty discussion 'niche' for the 8 available marks.

REPORT

To: Alan and Bob, Good Sports Limited
From: Strategic consultant
Date: December 20XX
Subject: E – Business strategy

Introduction

Very few businesses can afford to ignore the **potential of the Internet** for driving forward strategy and activity. The markets that Good Sports operates in are being affected by the development of e-business. Small enterprises such as this one can gain access to customers on a global scale, which only relatively recently would have been viewed as impossible. In many ways the advantages and disadvantages of e-business can be viewed from the perspective of the customer.

Advantages of an e-business strategy

Through the integration and acceleration of standard business processes via highly sophisticated IT systems (order placing, stock control, dispatch and so on), attention to customer needs, and communication with them, can be much quicker.

Although the Internet has a global reach, its benefits are not confined to large organisations. Good Sports can move into a global marketplace.

Websites can provide new channels of communication, linked with customer databases which can be analysed to provide much greater insights into consumer buying behaviour.

Increased quantities of data, and more sophisticated methods of analysing it, mean that greater attention can be paid to customising product offerings to more precisely defined **target customers**.

Disadvantages of an e-business strategy

E-commerce presents completely new problems of management and organisation, not least because it needs the **involvement of specialists**. There may be a lack of in-house expertise.

A detailed cost/benefit analysis should be undertaken. It may even be decided that costs exceed the benefits of setting up the e-business operation.

New technology installed by Good Sports will need to **link up with existing business systems**, so the resources needed (money, time and effort) should not be underestimated.

Processes

For Good Sports, e-business will probably be a **supplement** to its traditional retail operations, with the website forming a supplementary channel for communication and sales. Even so, its development is likely to have wide implications and involve and affect several functions, and so should be managed at the highest level. It is also necessary that it conform to the standard criteria for any strategic choice: suitability, acceptability and feasibility. Precise objectives for this new strategy need to be set. The company will need to go back to basics and ask itself some fundamental questions such as:

- What do customers want to buy from us?
- What business are we in?
- What kind of suppliers might we need?
- What categories of customer do we want to attract and retain?

Assuming that these questions can be answered satisfactorily, new technology can be introduced to connect electronically with employees, customers and suppliers to help drive the strategy forward.

Part (b)

With a **niche strategy**, a firm concentrates its attention on one or more particular secure segments (or niches) of the market, and does not try to serve the entire market. Good Sports has pursued such a strategy, seeking to serve a local market for less popular sports, in a way that insulates it from competition against the major high volume retailers who are concentrating on the more popular sports such as football.

In this way, Good Sports has been able to ensure that it **does not spread itself too thinly** in the market for sporting goods. There is nothing in the scenario to suggest they have reached saturation point in their chosen niche market. The question then needs to be asked whether it makes strategic sense for Good Sports to invest in online transaction capability to continue to serve (and develop) its market.

It is recognised that one of the key features of e-business is that it brings far greater **price transparency**, with customers being able to shop around for the cheapest deal using the vast information resources available on the Internet (either from other companies, or other customers). The customer has become far more powerful. There is a theory that customers expect goods and services to be discounted when sold online (and indeed, many are) since they are aware that administrative costs are likely to be lower than in more traditional forms of distribution. Good Sports will need to find out how likely this is to happen with their customers, and whether there are competitors who are offering lower prices on the same range of goods. This should be easy to find out using market research and a search of competitor sites.

Such customer involvement however could provide a mechanism for **increasing customer loyalty**, for example by targeting particular groups and finding out more about their sports activity and spending habits. This can be done via online questionnaires or surveys, and could lead to the identification of new niche markets, currently not served by any competitors, that can be developed (such as new types of sports equipment to be included in the product range; new services). As indicated in the answer to part (a), Good Sports needs to go back to basics and consider all the costs and benefits that could be associated with offering such enhanced online capability to its chosen niche market.

		Marks
(a)	*Advantages of Good Sports developing an e-business strategy:*	up to 5 marks
	Improved processes for better customer service	
	Global marketplace	
	Greater communication; more information	
	Disadvantages of developing an e-business strategy:	up to 5 marks
	Lack of in-house skills and competences	
	Cost/benefit analysis	
	Expensive investment	
	Processes	up to 2 marks
		Maximum 12 marks
(b)	*E-strategy supporting Good Sports' niche strategy*	up to 3 per point
	Customers' own awareness	
	New sports	
	Better understanding of customers	**Maximum 8 marks**
		Total 20 marks

Question 3

Top tips. Easy marks are on offer in part (a) for application of recognised models. We have used PEST analysis in our answer, as there are several obvious 'environmental' elements pointed out in the scenario. We also consider the use of SWOT and 'suitability, feasibility and acceptability'. In part (b), use your understanding of the term 'corporate social responsibility' (such as the Johnson and Scholes definition) to frame your answer, particularly in terms of the importance of stakeholders.

Part (a)

This scenario highlights the many factors that may need to be considered when making strategic decisions. The PEST framework can be used to analyse the environment. Use of PEST will indicate to Clyde the various risks and influences upon his decision, and help him decide upon its suitability or otherwise for his business.

An initial PEST analysis would indicate the following.

Political/legal

The local council is likely to be **split** between supporting Concrete Solutions for its employment opportunities and other contributions that it makes to the local economy (such as payment of rates and supply of product) and responding to the pressure from residents who object to the noise and pollution from it activities. The council in the rival town is likely to welcome any relocation of the business to its own site, but is likely to have the same pollution concerns. Legal limits on poisonous emissions must be considered.

Economic

The decision to take up the opportunity with the new company would involve **redundancies** in the local community, which already has high unemployment levels. For Concrete Solutions, however, an entire **new market** would be opened up and would reduce the current reliance on a relatively slow and seasonal local economy.

Social

Redundancies would have an impact on the social framework of the local area.

Technology

The current processes are very low-tech, but this new opportunity would require **significant investment** in new CAM technology, with a trained workforce to operate it. This would be a fundamental change to the usual business environment that Concrete Solutions operates in. The **resource implications** of the new opportunity are therefore very significant.

Such a move can be viewed as a related diversification – 'development beyond the present product market, but still within the broad confines of the industry…[it]…therefore builds upon the assets or activities which the firm has developed' (Johnson & Scholes). A detailed SWOT is likely to be necessary, along the lines of the following.

Strengths

Familiarity and experience with basic product

Weaknesses

- Experience to manage the new (larger) operation, with international expertise and new technology required
- Low skill; low tech operation – low barriers to entry
- Small company; limited (seasonal) market
- Small margin
- Resource constraints

Opportunities

- Increased profitability with new venture
- Expanded markets and new product
- Exposure to new technology and new partners

Threats

- Development of competitor products
- Legislation against pollution

This quick initial analysis would seem to indicate that the current operations of Concrete Solutions are a source of several weaknesses that the company could start to overcome by its involvement with the new venture.

As a major strategic option there is also a need to address issues of its suitability, acceptability and feasibility.

Suitability

The opportunity seems to solve some of the problems associated with the current **product range**. The new blocks can be sold all year round and into a much wider geographical market area. This will lead to increased profitability and possible exposure to new opportunities.

Acceptability of the new venture to both Concrete Solutions and the various stakeholders involved (employees, local residents, local councilors, new venture partner) is more complicated to assess. Clyde may find stakeholder mapping and scenario building useful in coming to a decision. As the owner of the business he needs to assess the **risk** involved against the likely **returns**.

Feasibility

New resources and skills will be needed, but with the support of the partner this may not be problematic.

Part (b)

Johnson and Scholes see **corporate social responsibility** as 'concerned with the ways in which an organisation exceeds the minimum obligation to stakeholders specified through regulation and corporate governance'.

Businesses both large and small are subject to **increasing expectations** that they will exercise social responsibility. This is an ill-defined concept, but appears to focus on the fulfilment of obligations to society in general, such as (in Clyde's case) the creation or preservation of employment and the consideration of environmental improvement or maintenance. A great deal of the pressure is created by the activity of **pressure groups** and other interested stakeholders, and is aimed at businesses because they are perceived to possess the resources to solve such problems.

There is no doubt that many businesses have behaved irresponsibly in the past, and it is very likely that some continue to do so. Small firms such as Concrete Solutions are therefore not exempt from the requirement to consider issues of social responsibility when making strategic decisions. The **impact** of such decisions upon all interested parties becomes crucial up front, in order to avoid damaging a company's reputation later.

A consideration of Concrete Solutions' **stakeholders** is therefore needed. Clyde is entitled to distinguish between 'contractual' and specified stakeholders (customers, suppliers, employees) who have a legal relationship with Concrete Solutions, and 'community' stakeholders – such as local residents and councillors – who do not have the same legal status. For the latter, the trade-off between the creation of skilled jobs, the necessity for redundancies and the possibility of increased pollution in the local area will need to be made, probably after negotiations between all the parties concerned.

The decisions are not easy ones to make. A decision by Clyde to bow to pressure and not increase his investment in new operations, for example, may protect local jobs and conserve resources in the short term, but will affect the **long term ability** of Concrete Solutions to compete effectively and may hand opportunities to his competitors.

Marking scheme

		Marks
(a)	Assessing the opportunity:	
	Environmental appraisal	up to 5 marks
	SWOT analysis	
	Criteria for assessing option – suitability, acceptability and feasibility	up to 3 marks each
		Maximum 12 marks
(b)	Social responsibility dimensions	up to 3 marks each
	Definition	
	Corporate social responsibility – compatibility with business strategy	
	Stakeholders	
	Short v long term	
		Maximum 8 marks
		Total 20 marks

BPP LEARNING MEDIA

Question 4

> **Top tips.** In this answer to part (a), the key model relating to organisational growth, formulated by Greiner, has been used, linked to the product life cycle. The identification of critical success factors (part (b)) can be difficult. Remember that they need to be critical, not just 'nice to have'. Getting the product on to the market in the first place must be a fundamental milestone.

Part (a)

REPORT

To: David Silvester, Gift Designs Ltd
From: Strategic consultant
Date: December 20XX
Subject: Funding strategy for Gift Designs Ltd

Gift Designs has the potential for developing a **highly successful product** with its cardboard vase, but as with all forms of strategy evaluation there are risks attached. The task facing the company is to reduce the risk of this chosen course.

As you are aware, there are several kinds of risk, and you realise the difference between **financial risk** (the risk to shareholders – at the moment, yourself – caused by debt finance having first call on company profits) and **business risk** (the general risk of the company not succeeding because of many factors in the business environment – competitors for example).

Linking business risk to **financial risk** is important – in the early stages of the life of any company business risk (of failure) is high, so it is important to have a low financial risk. Funding the business is essentially deciding the balance between debt and equity finance, and equity offers lower financial risk. The need to pay interest to debt providers might prevent capital growth, as well as constrain any necessary investment. As Gift Designs grows and develops, so the balance between debt and equity can change.

This analysis can be related to the **product life cycle**, which states that the profitability and sales of a product can be expected to change over time. The new cardboard vase will take some time to find acceptance, and there will be a **slow growth in sales initially** as the product establishes itself. The vase may even make a loss as production technology and other start up costs create high unit costs. This all equates to a **high business risk**.

As the market for the vase grows, sales (and profits) will rise more sharply and unit costs will fall. Eventually if this trend continues then the vase will enter the mature phase of the product life cycle where the rate of sales growth slows down, but it is a relatively long period, and profits are good. Debt finance at these later stages presents less of a financial risk than at earlier stages of the life of the business. Indeed in maturity, the business should be able to generate significant retained earnings of its own to finance further development, even beyond the £500k that is being envisaged for investment over the next two years.

Part (b)

Critical success factors (CSFs) 'are those factors on which the strategy is *fundamentally* dependent for its success'. If these factors are achieved, then the strategy (and the company) should be successful. Each CSF should have relevant performance indicators identified. For a new product, for example, these could be such measures as 'trial rate' or 'repurchase rate', which will demonstrate that the new cardboard vase is a success with customers.

- There are four general sources of CSFs.

- The industry that the business is in – how likely is it that a new product will succeed? Does it have many competing/substitute products?

- The company itself and its situation within the industry - does Gift Designs already have a high profile? Do its products already have a strong reputation?

- The environment (consumer trends, economy, political factors) -

- Organisational factors – does David have the capacity to get the new vase onto the market quickly?

Many success factors when a new product is involved will of necessity be linked to customer needs and expectations, in order that sales targets are met.

One of the first critical success factors to consider will be the time taken to develop and launch the new vase. Being first to market will be critical for success, and a patent should be sought so that the innovation is protected. After that, the vase can be customised for the various markets that have been identified – hospitals (standard design, large volume) and corporate (bespoke designs, lower volume, higher quality and customization, such as the incorporation of promotional logos).

Greiner indicated the different stages a growing business goes through in his **organisation life cycle model**. The model assumes that as an organisation ages, it grows both in size and the diversity and range of its activities. Different problems and factors are thereby associated with each stage.

In phase 1 of the model, the organisation is in a stage which Greiner calls 'growth through creativity'. Gift Designs is in this stage. The company is small, and is managed in a personal and informal way. David is actively involved in the operations and innovations, with a limited product range. He planning to carry out most of the functions himself, but the time will come when he needs to **delegate or outsource** some of the key activities associated with manufacture and distribution, for example. As the company develops and grows, David is going to need to delegate and accept that collaboration will be the only way to cope with increased workloads, and make sure that Gift Designs manages its value chain and adds value.

Marking scheme

		Marks
(a)	*Identification of key issues: up to 3 per issue*	
	Linking business risk to financial risk – start-up finance, growth, maturity and decline	
	Developing an appropriate funding strategy – debt v equity	
	Using appropriate models – product life cycle	
		Maximum 10 marks
(b)	*Critical success factors and performance indicators: up to 2 per point*	
	Critical success factors identified	
	Greiner's model – relate to David's role in business	
		Maximum 10 marks
		Total 20 marks

Part 3 Examination – Paper 3.5
Strategic Business Planning and Development

June 2006 Answers

1   (a)   The case scenario gives a five-year insight into the growth and development of Churchill Ice Cream. Throughout its history it has followed a strategy of in-house manufacture, retailing largely through the company's own shops and, to a lesser extent, through franchising. This vertically integrated strategy gives more control, which is particularly important given its use of fresh ingredients and emphasis on premium product quality. But it exposes Churchill to the twin problems of both manufacturing and retailing a product which is highly seasonal in demand and equally vulnerable to the vagaries of the British summer. In fact, there is a close correlation between the average summer temperature and the volume of ice cream consumed. The case, therefore, provides us with an opportunity to develop an understanding of the implications of a company's pattern of vertical integration for competitive advantage and the strategic development of the company. Clearly, if key activities and capabilities are kept inside the company, this makes imitation far more costly and complex. The question is whether Churchill Ice Cream has developed a unique format that delivers competitive advantage and superior performance. John Churchill would almost certainly argue that through its retail operation it gains a unique insight into its customers' needs and desires. With premium ice cream we are dealing with a luxury product increasingly bought by consumers looking to indulge themselves. One of the problems of being both a manufacturer and retailer is where you decide to place the emphasis – commitment of resources to one area almost inevitably leads to resources being constrained in the other. There is evidence in the case to suggest that Churchill Ice Cream with its newly-built factory is tending to favour the manufacturing side of the business. But with ice cream stores costing £100K to fit out and needing constant refurbishment this places a heavy investment load on the company.

A company's make or buy decisions therefore profoundly affect the shape and scope of the company and the types of competitive advantage. In Porter's generic strategy terms, Churchill Ice Cream is looking to be a focused differentiator able to earn (though there is less evidence of its strategy working) above average returns through its focus. This belief in and commitment to a vertically integrated strategy almost certainly reflects the beliefs and values of the Churchill family. In terms of Porter's five forces, the ownership of its own shops has in the past given it some protection from the need to sell through the large supermarket chains and the consequent impact on the company's profit margins. As indicated above, this should provide the company with some unique insights into customer buying behaviour, but unfortunately the delay in introducing a new management information system prevents full advantage being taken of this information. Churchill also maintains control over its distinctive ice cream recipes and this helps forestall integration strategies by either suppliers or retailers. There is no evidence in the scenario to suggest any significant supplier power although their reliance on the company owned shops might mean commercial property owners may be able to exert some power. In terms of new entrants, the company's heavy reliance on the London region makes them vulnerable to similar retail formats being opened in other parts of the UK. The presence of two major US manufacturers with their own ice cream stores may offer a real threat. Certainly ice cream is very much a global product and foreign manufacturers may find the UK a very attractive market to enter.

The company is facing significant competitive rivalry and its competitive strategy based upon differentiation comes from its product ingredients and manufacturing expertise, the development of a regional brand name, control of the point of sale and, more recently, product innovation with a market very responsive to it increasing the product range. Churchill, through its vertical integration, presents a different product experience to the customer and this helps to shelter it from the major manufacturers and powerful supermarkets.

However, there are some downsides – the seasonal pattern of demand implies an under use of manufacturing and retailing capacity for a significant part of the year. Churchill has done little to reduce the impact of a highly seasonal demand. Overall, therefore, the company has adopted a distinctive vertically integrated strategy which has supported its desire to be different and has major implications for the capabilities needed in the business and the type of resources required.

There are some conflicting performance indicators – both financial and non-financial – which require an explanation. Churchill Ice Cream seems to have a quality product and a good reputation, albeit only a regional one. Their sponsorship of major sporting events is a high profile achievement, but there is little point achieving such exposure if customers can only buy the product once a year! As a family business they have shown an ability to survive, but have a miniscule share of a major market. There is some growth of sales, unfortunately at a declining rate, but the return on sales is consistently poor. Comment has already been made on their regional presence, but the progress with opening new stores is modest to say the least and not moving them into becoming a national brand.

Perhaps more disquieting is their failure to move the retail format abroad. Their international strategy is commented on below but they have had two costly failures to date and yet seem committed to proving they can operate abroad. It would be interesting to know what has been learned from these two international ventures. In terms of the efficiency of business processes there is the comment that they have a new purpose built factory and that their products are 'supplied quickly and directly'. This performance is not currently having any significant impact on costs and profits.

From the information given in the retail sales index the performance of the ice cream industry is not very exciting. However, Churchill Ice Cream is clearly located in the premium segment of the market and the growth of sales of US owned competitors supported by huge advertising budgets has led to significant growth of the premium sector. Therefore, Churchill Ice Cream sales growth looks less impressive seen against an overall growth for the premium sector market. Equally worrying is their relative failure to get their product and brand accepted by the supermarkets. The supermarkets are dominant and squeezing sales through the more traditional outlets. Again, Churchill Ice Cream's lack of a national brand presence may be limiting their ability to get into the supermarkets' ice cream cabinets.

Finally, the firm is in an interesting transition phase from being family owned and managed through to being professionally managed. There is little evidence to date of this transition having any significant impact on performance.

(b) The three strategic goals are to become the leading premium ice cream brand in the UK; to increase sales to £25 million; and to achieve a significant entry into the supermarket sector. On the basis of performance to date these goals will certainly be stretching. All three strategies will involve significant growth in the company. Johnson and Scholes list three success criteria against which the strategies can be assessed, namely suitability, acceptability and feasibility. Suitability is a test of whether a strategy addresses the situation in which a company is operating. In Johnson and Scholes' terms it is the firm's 'strategic position', an understanding of which comes from the analysis done in the answer to the question above. Acceptability is concerned with the likely performance outcomes of the strategy and in particular whether the return and risk are in line with the expectations of the stakeholders. Feasibility is the extent to which the strategy can be made to work and is determined by the strategic capability of the company reflecting the resources available to implement the strategy. It is interesting to see that the three growth related goals are compatible in that becoming the leading premium brand will involve increased market penetration, product development and market development. If achieved it will increase sales and necessitate a successful entry into the supermarket sector. Time will be an important influence on the success or otherwise of these growth goals – five years seems to be a reasonable length of time to achieve these ambitious targets.

Suitability – Churchill is currently a small but significant player at the premium end of the market. This segment is becoming more significant and is attractive because of the high prices and high margins attainable. This is leading to more intense competition with global companies. One immediate question that springs to mind is what precisely does 'leading brand' mean? The most obvious test is that of market share and unless Churchill achieve the access to the supermarkets looked for in the third strategic goal, seems difficult to achieve. If 'leading brand' implies brand recognition this again looks very ambitious. On the positive side this segment of the ice cream market is showing significant growth and Churchill's success in gaining sponsorship rights to major sporting events is a step in the right direction. The combination of high price and high quality should position the company where it wants to be. Achieving sales of £25 million represents a quantum shift in performance in a company that has to date only achieved modest levels of sales growth.

Acceptability – as a family owned business the balance between risk and return is an important one. The family to date has been 'happy' with a modest rate of growth and modest return in terms of profits. The other significant stakeholder group is the professional managers headed up by Richard Smith. They seem much more growth orientated and may be happier with the risks that the growth strategy entails. The family members seem more interested in the manufacturing side than the retailing side of the business and their bad previous experiences with growing the business through international market development may mean they are risk averse and less willing to invest the necessary resources.

Feasibility – again this is linked to how 'leading brand' is defined. If as seems likely the brand becomes more widely known through increasing the number of company owned ice cream stores then a significant investment in retail outlets will be necessary. Increasing the number of franchised outlets will reduce the financial resources required but may be at the expense of the brand's reputation. Certainly there would seem to be a need for increased levels of advertising and promotion – particularly to gain access to the ice cream cabinets in the supermarket chains. This is likely to mean an increase in the number of sales and marketing staff. Equally important will be the ability to develop and launch new products in a luxury market shaped by impulse buying and customers looking to indulge themselves.

Overall, becoming the leading brand of premium ice cream may well be the key to achieving the desired presence in the supermarket ice cream cabinets, which in turn is a pre-requisite for increasing company sales to £25 million. So the three strategic goals may be regarded as consistent and compatible with one another. However each strategic goal will have to be broken down into its key elements. For example in achieving sales of £25 million what proportion of sales will come from its own ice cream stores and what proportion from other outlets including the supermarkets? Sales to date of Churchill ice cream are dominated by impulse purchases but in achieving sales of £25 million penetrating the take home market will be essential. Finally, what proportion of these take home sales will be under the supermarkets own label brands? Over reliance on own label sales will seriously weaken Churchill's desire to become the leading national brand of premium ice cream. It looks to be an ambitious but attainable strategy but will require a significant planning effort to develop the necessary resources and capabilities vital to successful implementation of the strategy.

(c) Each of the strategic goals will have a profound impact on the marketing mix as it currently exists. As each goal affects the market position of Churchill developing an appropriate marketing mix will be the key to successful implementation of the overall growth strategy. The **product**, the brand and the reputation it creates are at the heart of the company's marketing strategy. Their focus on the premium segment of the market seems a sensible one and one which allows a small family-owned business to survive and grow slowly. Evidence suggests this is a luxury indulgence market reflecting changing consumer tastes and lifestyles. Managing the product range will be a major marketing activity. While the core products may develop an almost timeless quality there will be a need to respond to the product innovations introduced by its much larger competitors. The company's emphasis on the quality of its products resulting from the quality of its ingredients is at the heart of its competitive advantage. Growing the product range will also bring the danger of under performing products and a consequent need to divest such products. Packaging is likely to be a key part of the products' appeal and will be an area where constant innovation is important.

Pricing raises a number of issues. Why is Churchill's core product priced at £1 less than its immediate competition? What is the basis on which Churchill prices this product? Each of the methods of pricing has its advantages and disadvantages. Using cost plus may create an illusion of security in that all costs are covered, but at the same time raises issues as to whether relevant costs have been included and allocated. Should the company price in anticipation of cost reductions as volume increases? Should the basis for pricing be what your competitors are charging? As a luxury product one would assume that its demand is relatively price inelastic: a significant increase in price e.g. £1 would lead to only a small reduction in quantity demanded. Certainly, profit margins would be enhanced to help provide the financial resources the company needs if it is to grow. One interesting issue on pricing is the extent to which it is pursuing a price skimming or price penetration policy – evidence from the scenario suggests more of a price skimming policy in line with the luxury nature of the product.

Place is an equally important issue – the vertical integration strategy of the company has led to company-owned shops being the main way customers can buy the product. At the same time, this distribution strategy has led to Churchill's sales being largely confined to one region in the UK – although it is the most populous. If Churchill has a desire to grow, does it do this through expanding the number of company owned and franchised outlets or look for other channels of distribution in particular the increasingly dominant supermarket chains? Each distribution strategy will have significant implications for other elements in the marketing mix and for the resources and capabilities required in the company.

Finally, **promotion** is an interesting issue for the company. The relatively recent appointment of a sales and marketing director perhaps reflects a need to balance the previous dominance of the manufacturing side of the business. Certainly there is evidence to suggest that John Churchill is not convinced of the need to advertise. There are some real concerns about how the brand is developed and promoted. Certainly sponsorship is now seen as a key part of the firm's promotional strategy. The company has a good reputation but customer access to the product is fairly limited. Overall there is scope for the company to critically review its marketing mix and implement a very different mix if it wants to grow.

The four Ps above are very much the 'hard' elements in the marketing mix and Churchill in its desire to grow will need to ensure that the 'softer' elements of people, physical evidence and processes are aligned to its ambitious strategy.

(d) The two international strategies pursued to date are through organic growth (the stores in North America) and acquisition (the companies in Germany and Italy). Neither seems to have worked. Here there seem to be some contradictions while global tastes and lifestyles are argued to have developed – convergence of consumer tastes lies at the heart of this – but this does not seem to have benefited Churchill. One questions the learning that these two unfortunate experiences have created. Of the three core methods of achieving growth, namely organic, acquisition and joint venture, only joint venture remains to be tried.

The reasons for the international failures are clearly complex but one could argue that the strategy has been curiously naïve. Certainly, it has pursued a high-risk strategy. Exporting, perhaps through identifying a suitable partner, might create the learning to lead to a more significant market entry. There is a need to understand local tastes; indeed the whole of the marketing mix in the chosen market(s), and decide on appropriate strategy. A strategy based upon the acquisition of companies and their consequent development represents a large investment of capital and requires considerable managerial attention and expertise. Equally, the attempt to use the Churchill domestic format of opening its own stores creates both a major financial commitment and the need to manage a radically different operation. One must seriously question whether Churchill has these capabilities within a family-owned business. Clearly there are differences between the ice cream markets in various countries, though the emergence of global brands suggests some convergence of tastes. Such differences reflect differing cultures, tastes and competitive behaviour in each country. The lesson from Churchill's international initiatives is that national differences need to be carefully understood. There is little evidence that Churchill has understood these differences or indeed learnt from them.

2 (a) To: David Gould

From:

Writing a business plan is a critical stage in moving an idea for a business into a reality. The reality includes presenting a convincing case to potential financers of the business, be they banks or venture capitalists. The key ingredients include clearly saying what you plan to do and why people should want to buy your particular service. Experts warn of starting with a detailed cash flow and then working backwards to make the numbers fit. You should regard the business plan as a management tool and not simply a sales document. Again, the advice is to make credible and achievable projections; it is better to exceed low targets than fail to achieve over-ambitious ones. Many business plans are based on deeply flawed research. Key to your business success will be the size of your target market. There is much evidence to suggest that it is the make-up of the team presenting the plan and their commitment rather than the business idea itself that will determine whether the necessary financial support is made.

Clearly, you need to say how much money you require and why. Again the advice is not to be afraid to ask for large amounts if your business requires it. Linked to how much you want is a clear statement of the return the investor or lender will get – how much of the equity are you willing to give or what security can you offer the lender? Figure are important and you need projected cash flows, profit and loss accounts and balance sheets for at least three years ahead. Potential investors and/or lenders are likely to be impressed by a plan which clearly indicates where the major risks are to be found and the strategies available to handle such risks.

There needs to be a clear statement of the major steps and milestones on the way to achieving your goals. Where are you now, where do you intend to be and how are you going to get there. One expert argues there are three elements of the plan itself – an executive summary pulling together the key points in your proposal, secondly the plan itself and finally an 'elevator pitch', a one paragraph description that explains the business in the time it takes to go up in a lift.

In summary, your business plan should contain an executive summary as explained above, the objectives of the business, including key financial targets and the philosophy of the business, the target market and relevant forecasts, the range of products/services, the marketing strategy linked to the target markets, resource availability, people and organisation involved, performance measurement to measure progress towards stated objectives and a summary of financial information.

One final point is to remember that no business plan ever was carried out exactly! In many ways it is the quality of the thinking the plan includes and the actual process through which it is developed that will determine success.

Yours,

(b)   Clearly, there is a link between the ability to write a business plan and the willingness, or otherwise, of small firms to carry out strategic planning. Whilst writing a business plan may be a necessity in order to acquire financial support, there is much more question over the benefits to the existing small business, such as Gould and King, of carrying out strategic planning. One of the areas of greatest debate is whether carrying out strategic planning leads to improved performance. Equally contentious is whether the formal rational planning model is worthwhile or whether strategy is much more of an emergent process, with the firm responding to changes in its competitive environment.

One source argues that small firms may be reluctant to create a strategic plan because of the time involved; small firms may find day-to-day survival and crisis management prevents them having the luxury of planning where they mean to be over the next few years. Secondly, strategic plans may also be viewed as too restricting, stopping the firm responding flexibly and quickly to opportunities and threats. Thirdly, many small firms may feel that they lack the necessary skills to carry out strategic planning. Strategic planning is seen as a 'big' firm process and inappropriate for small firms. Again, there is evidence to suggest that owner-managers are much less aware of strategic management tools such as SWOT, PESTEL and mission statements than their managers. Finally, owner-managers may be reluctant to involve others in the planning process, which would necessitate giving them access to key information about the business. Here there is an issue of the lack of trust and openness preventing the owner-manager developing and sharing a strategic plan. Many owner-managers may be quite happy to limit the size of the business to one which they can personally control.

On the positive side there is evidence to show that a commitment to strategic planning results in speedier decision making, a better ability to introduce change and innovation and being good at managing change. This in turn results in better performance including higher rates of growth and profits, clear indicators of competitive advantage. If Gould and King are looking to grow the business as suggested, this means some strategic planning will necessarily be involved.

3   (a)   Environmental Analysis

Clearly, both the macro-environment and the industry environment facing Airtite are becoming more challenging and scanning the environment and understanding the relative significance of the challenges is a key step in developing a future strategy to deal with it. Many models and tools and techniques are available to assess the size of the competitive threats facing Airtite. One of the earlier scanning models looks to measure whether the environment an organisation faces is becoming more complex and more dynamic. Evidence from the scenario suggests both are occurring and this means it is becoming increasingly difficult to predict the future nature of competition from what has happened in the past. Airtite's future is linked to an increasingly global environment and many conflicting and contradictory factors require the company to develop a process through which these factors are considered on a regular and systematic basis.

Johnson and Scholes suggest there are five steps in terms of environmental analysis:

Step 1   Audit of environmental influences

Step 2   Assessment of the nature of the environment

Step 3   Identification of the key environmental forces

Step 4   Identification of competitive position

Step 5   Identification of the principal opportunities and threats

Systematic consideration of each of these steps leads to an understanding of the strategic position of the firm.

A PESTEL analysis is part of the process of environmental appraisal and it is important for John to recognise those parts of its environment it can influence. All too often firms can regard themselves as 'victims' of the chosen environment, failing to recognise that through their strategic decisions they can profoundly change the competitive environment for their current or potential competitors. A good PESTEL analysis inevitably links into an informed SWOT analysis. In both instances it is necessary to isolate the key forces causing environmental change – simply creating a long list of factors may simply convince you of your inability to change the situation.

Once having decided which are the critical factors, it is then necessary to decide on the likelihood of a particular environmental change occurring and the significance of its impact on the firm. Matching the competitive capability of the firm against the attractiveness of the business sector Airtite is operating in will provide an understanding of the firm's competitive position and the options open to it. Many other models and tools and techniques are available, including Porter's five forces, product life cycle analysis and scenario building to generate alternative strategic responses.

(b)   Carrying out a systematic PESTEL analysis is a key step in developing alternative scenarios about the future. Johnson and Scholes define scenarios as 'detailed and plausible views of how the business environment of an organisation might develop in the future based on groupings of key environmental influences and drivers of change about which there is a high level of uncertainty'. In developing scenarios it is necessary to isolate the key drivers of change, which have the potential to have a significant impact on the company and are associated with high levels of uncertainty. Development of scenarios enables managers to share assumptions about the future and the key variables shaping that future. This provides an opportunity for real organisational learning. They are then in a position to monitor these key variables and amend strategies accordingly. It is important to note that different stakeholder groups will have different expectations about the future and each may provide a key input to the process of developing scenarios. By their very nature scenarios should not attempt to allocate probabilities to the key factors and in so doing creating 'spurious accuracy' about those factors. A positive scenario is shown below and should provide a shared insight into the external factors most likely to have a significant impact on Airtite's future strategy. For most companies operating in global environments the ability to respond flexibly and quickly to macro-environmental change would seem to be a key capability.

The scenario as illustrated below, clearly could have a major impact on the success or otherwise of Airtite's strategy for the future. The key drivers for change would seem to be the link between technology and global emissions, fuel prices and the stability of the global political environment. Through creating a process which considers the drivers which will have most impact on Airtite and which are subject to the greatest uncertainty, Airtite will have a greater chance of its strategy adapting to changing circumstances.

Example of scenarios using the PESTEL framework – positive scenario

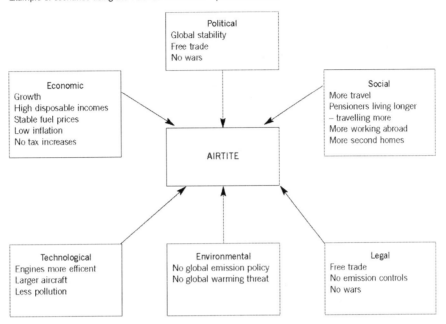

4   (a)   To: Paul Simpson – HR Manager

From:

Human Resource Planning and Global Imaging's future growth

I will use this report to highlight the main phases in HR (human resource) planning and then deal with the specific HR activities, which will be needed to support the achievement of the growth strategy.

There are four major stages in creating a human resource plan. Firstly, auditing the current HR resources in Global Imaging, as a relatively young company one could anticipate it having a relatively young labour force many of whom will be professionally qualified. Secondly, the planned growth will require a forecast of both the number and type of people who will be needed to implement the strategy. Thirdly, planning will be needed on how to meet the needs identified in the forecast – how do we fill the gap in between the human reources we currently have and those needed to fulfil the plan? Finally, there will be the need to control those resources in terms of measuring performance against the goals set.

The key activities to achieve the growth goals will be:

Recruitment, selection and staffing – here the key issues will be to recruit the necessary additional staff and mix of suitably qualified workers. The growth of the company will create management succession issues including the two managing directors, who are looking to exit the business in the foreseeable future. The rate of growth will also make it necessary to manage significant internal transfers of people in the company as new positions and promotion opportunities are created.

Compensation and benefits – the start up phase of a company's life is often a stage where a formal reward structure has not been created. It also may be necessary to meet or exceed the labour market rates in order to attract the necessary talent. As the firm grows there will be a need to ensure that the firm is competitive in terms of the rewards offered, but there is an increasing need to ensure equity between newcomers and staff already employed in the firm. These pressures will normally lead to the creation of a formal compensation structure.

Employee training and development – here there is a need to create an effective management team through management development and organisational development.

Labour employee relations – here there is a need to establish harmonious labour relations and employee motivation and morale.

Overall, the HR implications of the proposed growth strategy are profound and there is a significant danger that failure to link strategy and the consequent HR needs will act as a major constraint on achieving the strategy.

Yours,

(b) It is important to note that there is nothing in the nature of the activities carried out by HR staff and departments that prevents outsourcing being looked at as a serious option. Indeed, amongst larger companies the outsourcing of some parts of the HR function is already well under way, with one source estimating that HR outsourcing is growing by 27% each year. Paul, therefore, needs to look at the HR activities identified above and assess the advantages and disadvantages of outsourcing a particular HR activity. Outsourcing certain parts of the recruitment process has long been accepted, with professional recruitment agencies and 'head-hunters' being heavily involved in the advertising and short listing of candidates for senior management positions. Some HR specialists argue that outsourcing much of the routine personnel work, including maintaining employees' records, frees the HR specialist to make a real contribution to the strategic planning process. One study argues that 'HR should become a partner with senior and line managers in strategy execution'.

If Paul is able to outsource the routine HR activities this will free him to contribute to the development of the growth strategy and the critical people needs that strategy will require. In many ways the HR specialist is in a unique position to assess current skills and capabilities of existing staff and the extent to which these can be 'leveraged' to achieve the desired strategy. In Hamel and Prahalad's terms this strategy is likely to 'stretch' the people resources of the company and require the recruitment of additional staff with the relevant capabilities. Paul needs to show how long it will take to develop the necessary staff resources as this will significantly influence the time needed to achieve the growth strategy.

Outsourcing passes on to the provider the heavy investment needed if the company sets up its own internal HR services with much of this investment now going into web-based systems. The benefits are reduced costs and improved service quality. The downside is a perceived loss of control and a reduced ability to differentiate the HR function from that of competitors. Issues of employee confidentiality are also relevant in the decision to outsource.

Part 3 Examination – Paper 3.5
Strategic Business Planning and Development

June 2006 Marking Scheme

			Marks
1	**(a)**	advantages of current strategy including:	up to 2 per point
		control obtained through vertical integration	
		value chain linkages	
		closer to the final customer	
		strategy difficult to imitate	
		new product innovation easier	
		reduced buyer power	
		flexibility in meeting varying demand levels	
		disadvantages of current strategy including:	up to 2 per point
		increased level of resource/capabilities needed	
		internal competition between manufacturing and retail sides of business	
		increased operational/organisational complexity	
		growth function of number of ice cream stores	
		cost implication of varying levels of demand	
		performance analysis	up to 6
		use of models where appropriate including:	up to 5
		value chain/system	
		five forces analysis	
		Ansoff's growth matrix	
			maximum 20
	(b)	suitability:	up to 6
		SWOT analysis	
		gap and 'fit' analysis	
		resource/capability analysis	
		acceptability:	up to 6
		risk and return analysis	
		screening process	
		stakeholder analysis – owners v managers	
		feasibility:	up to 6
		funds availability	
		resource/capabilities availability	
		compatibility of three strategic goals	up to 5
			maximum 20
	(c)	identification of current marketing mix	up to 2 per element
		changes to the mix for each goal including:	up to 3 per goal
		becoming leading national brand – product innovation,	
		premium pricing strategy, national availability and national promotion	
		Sales of £25 million – higher take home sales,	
		increased product range, national availability,	
		increased advertising	
		penetration of supermarkets – own label brands,	
		lower prices, national distribution, promotion support	
			maximum 15
	(d)	analysis and explanation for failure	up 2 per point
		of the international strategy including:	
		ethnocentric approach	
		differences in customer buying behaviour	
		cultural differences	
		failure to understand risk	
		resources overstretched	
			maximum 5
			Total 60

			Marks
2	**(a)**	key features of a business plan:	up to 2 per feature
		executive summary	
		purpose, philosophy and objectives	
		financial targets	
		target market and forecasts	
		product/service range	
		marketing strategy	
		resource availability and funding needed	
		people and organisation	
		performance measurement and milestones	
		summary of financial information	
			maximum 12

	(b)	advantages of strategic plans:	up to 5
		speedier decision making	
		change management capability enhanced	
		better performance	
		longer term focus	
		surfaces assumptions	
		disadvantages of strategic plans:	up to 5
		time involved	
		flexibility reduced	
		planning skills not available	
		tools and techniques not known	
		information disclosure	
			maximum 8
			Total 20

3	**(a)**	PESTEL analysis including:	up to 2 per variable
		political – increasing government control	
		economic -- trends in disposable income	
		social – ageing population	
		technological – more efficient aircraft	
		environmental – tighter emission control	
		legal -- global agreement on emissions	
		assessing impact and uncertainty	up to 3
			maximum 12

	(b)	Key features in using a scenario:	up to 5
		identifying high impact/high uncertainty factors in environment	
		identifying different possible futures by factor	
		building scenarios of plausible configurations of factors	
		links to Airtite's strategy	up to 5
			maximum 8
			Total 20

			Marks
4	(a)	identification of key stages in HR plan:	up to 3 per activity
		audit of current HR resources	
		forecast of future needs	
		planning to fill identified 'gap'	
		measuring performance against goals set	
		linkages with growth strategy	up to 4
			maximum 12
	(b)	advantages of outsourcing HR:	up to 5
		freedom to contribute to strategy	
		reduced HR administration costs	
		focus on critical HR competences for growth strategy	
		improved service levels	
		disadvantages of outsourcing HR:	up to 5
		loss of control	
		confidentiality issue	
		long term dependence on outside provider	
		adverse workforce reaction	
			maximum 8
			Total 20

Part 3 Examination – Paper 3.5
Strategic Business Planning and Development

December 2006 Answers

1 (a) The Shirtmaster Group is performing poorly by any standards and this reflects the poor strategic position of a major part of the group – namely the Shirtmaster division. Using a 5-forces and value chain analysis we can see that the chosen strategy of being an integrated shirt manufacturer carrying out all the activities needed to design, manufacture and distribute its shirts is now seriously open to question. Most of its UK competitors have recognised the need to source shirts from low cost manufacturing countries. Shirtmaster, in the shape of Tony Masters, seems to be alone in thinking that by maintaining a UK manufacturing capability this will give it some competitive advantage. The economics of the industry have changed dramatically with foreign shirt makers able to supply both the quality of shirt required in the premium shirt market and at prices that would enable Shirtmaster to radically improve its profit margins. The division seems to be in the classic 'stuck in the middle' position having neither the volumes to achieve cost leadership or the skills to differentiate itself in the market as it has in the past. Its strategic choice has been to concentrate on the premium end of the shirt market but this focus strategy is now under considerable challenge.

The two key forces at work seem to be the intensity of rivalry between the shirt makers and the increased buying power of their customers – the retail outlets for their shirts. The Shirtmaster division has remained heavily dependent on its small independent retailers, who themselves are under threat from the specialist clothing retailers and the supermarkets. There is a pressing need to analyse the changes taking place in the value chain underlying the shirt business. There is no evidence to suggest that Shirtmaster is willing to make shirts under the own label brands of the dominant retailers.

The Shirtmaster division's reliance on small independent clothing retailers is having significant cost effects on its value chain. In terms of in-bound logistics Tony's expensive trips to buy cloth from foreign suppliers is resulting in large stocks of expensive cloth. Meeting the individual demands of its many small customers must have a real impact on its manufacturing and distribution costs. Marketing expenses supporting the Shirtmaster brand are both significant and yielding decreasing returns. In terms of the support activities, questions need to be asked at the infrastructure and HR levels in terms of Tony's influence over strategy and operations, at the technology level in terms of their apparent lack of investment in CAD/CAM systems compared with the Corporate Clothing division and the procurement strategy has already been questioned.

The net result of these problems is revealed in the financial performance compared to the Corporate Clothing division:

	Shirtmaster division	Corporate Clothing division
Sales growth	declining	increasing
Manufacturing efficiency/gross margin	low and falling	higher and sustained
Labour productivity/sales per employee	modest	improving
Marketing expenditure	relatively high	relatively low
Stock holding	relatively high	modest
Net margins	low/negative	modest/positive
Market share	minimal	small but growing
Innovation – product	stalled	customer driven
Innovation – processes	little evidence	significant
Divisional co-operation and learning	minimal	minimal
Customer segment	declining	growing

The measures above reflect a balanced scorecard approach to overall performance and clearly the Corporate Clothing division's results bring the problems of the Shirtmaster division into even more focus – comparisons are odious! Corporate Clothing is operating in a more attractive market and through close attention to its customers' demands is enjoying modest growth and profitability. Looking after a small number of large industrial customers and integrating its value chain with theirs has had positive results. All parts of its value chain/system seem to be involved in providing a superior service to its customers. One could point in particular to the link between its technology and its manufacturing operations as a critical area for success, and its willingness to hold stock the customer wants and has paid for, shapes its outbound logistics with workwear supplied to the individual employee.

Overall the performance of the Shirtmaster Group is a composite of two very different performances achieved by the separate divisions. These divisions are operating in very different markets with very different strategies. At present there is little or no synergy between the two divisions and they add very little value to one another.

(b) Johnson and Scholes define a strategic alliance as 'where two or more organisations share resources and activities to pursue a strategy'. There are a number of types of alliance ranging from a formal joint venture through to networks where there is collaboration but no formal agreement. The type of strategic alliance will be affected by how quickly market conditions are changing – swift rates of change may require flexible less formal types of alliance and determine whether specific dedicated resources are required or whether the partners can use existing resources. Johnson and Scholes argue that for an alliance to be successful there needs to be a clear strategic purpose and senior management support; compatibility between the partners at all levels – this may be complicated if it is a cross-border alliance; time spent defining and meeting performance expectations including clear goals, governance and organisational arrangements; and finally trust both in terms of respective competences and trustworthiness.

The advantages that may be gained by a successful strategic alliance include creating a joint operation that has a 'critical mass' that may lead to lower costs or an improved offer to the customer. It may also allow each partner to specialise in areas where they have a particular advantage or competence. Interestingly, alliances are often entered into where a company is seeking to enter new geographical markets, as is the case with both divisions. The partner brings local knowledge and expertise in distribution, marketing and customer support. A good strategic alliance will also enable the partners to learn from one another and develop competences that may be used in other markets. Often firms looking to develop an e-business will use an alliance with a partner with experience in website development. Once its e-business is up and running a firm may eventually decide to bring the website design skills in-house and acquire the partner.

Disadvantages of alliances range from over-dependence on the partner, not developing own core competences and a tendency for them not to have a defined end date. Clearly there is a real danger of the partner eventually becoming a competitor.

In assessing the suitability for each division in using a strategic alliance to enter European markets one clearly has to analyse the very different positions of the divisions in terms of what they can offer a potential partner. The earlier analysis suggests that the Shirtmaster division may have the greater difficulty in attracting a partner. One may seriously question the feasibility of using the Shirtmaster brand in Europe and the competences the division has in terms of manufacturing and selling to large numbers of small independent UK clothing retailers would seem inappropriate to potential European partners. Ironically, if the management consultant recommends that the Shirtmaster division sources some or all of its shirts from low cost manufacturers in Europe this may provide a reason for setting up an alliance with such a manufacturer.

The prospects of developing a strategic alliance in the Corporate Clothing division are much more favourable. The division has developed a value added service for its corporate customers, indeed its relationship with its customers can be seen as a relatively informal network or alliance and there seems every chance this could be replicated with large corporate customers in Europe. Equally, there may be European workwear companies looking to grow and develop who would welcome sharing the Corporate Clothing division's expertise.

(c) The Shirtmaster Group has decided to structure itself using two divisions who are dealing with very different markets, customers and buying behaviours. In so doing the intention is to provide more value to the customer through a better understanding of their needs. The existence of the two divisions also reflects the origins of the two family businesses. Mintzberg in his work on organisation design and structure sees divisional configurations as being appropriate in relatively simple and static environments where significant strategic power is delegated from the 'strategic apex' to the 'middle line' general managers with responsibility for the performance of the division. Indeed one of the benefits cited for divisionalised companies is their ability to provide a good training ground in strategic decision making for general managers who can then progress to senior positions at company headquarters. Tony Masters' reluctance to delegate real strategic decision making power to the senior managers in the Shirtmaster division may be preventing those managers developing key managerial skills.

Using the Boston Box model one could classify the Shirtmaster division as a 'dog' with low market share in a market exhibiting change but little growth. The Corporate Clothing division, by contrast, can be regarded as a 'problem child' having a small share but of a growing market. Porter's 'better-off test' needs to be met – are the two divisions better off being in the same Group? As it stands there seems little synergy between the two divisions – there seems to be little evidence of the two divisions sharing resources or transferring skills or learning between the two divisions. Their two value chains and systems are both separate and different though on the face of it there are many activities that are similar. Operating independently may encourage healthy competition between the two divisions and consequently better performance through better motivated staff. Specialised competences such as Corporate Clothing division's on-line response to customer orders and design changes are more easily developed within a divisionalised structure. Performance can be clearly identified and controlled and resources channelled to those areas showing potential. However, this may be at the expense of costly duplication of resources and an inability to get the necessary scale to compete in either of their separate markets. Certainly the lack of co-operation between the divisions in areas such as information systems may lead to higher costs and poorer performance.

(d) Much has been written on the links between leadership and culture and in particular the influence of the founder on the culture of the organisation. Schein actually argues that leadership and culture are two sides of the same coin. Tony's father had a particular vision of the type of company he wanted and importance of product innovation to the success of the business. Tony is clearly influenced by that cultural legacy and has maintained a dominant role in the business though there is little evidence of continuing innovation. Using the McKinsey 7-S model the founder or leader is the main influence on the development of the shared values in the firm that shapes the culture. However, it is clear from the scenario that Tony through his 'hands-on' style of leadership is affecting the other elements in the model – strategy, structure and systems – the 'hard' factors and the senior staff and their skills – the 'soft' factors – in making strategic decisions.

Delegation has been highlighted as one of the problems Tony has to face and it is a familiar one in family firms. Certainly there could be need for him to give his senior management team the responsibility for the functional areas they nominally control. Tony's style is very much a 'hands-on' style but this may be inappropriate for handling the problems that the company faces. Equally, he seems too responsible for the strategic decisions the company is taking and not effectively involving his team in the strategy process. Style is seen as a key factor in influencing the culture of an organisation and getting the right balance between being seen as a paternalistic owner-manager and a chairman and chief executive looking to develop his senior management team is difficult. Leadership is increasingly being seen as encouraging and enabling others to handle change and challenge and questioning the assumptions that have influenced Shirtmaster's strategic thinking and development to date. The positive side of Tony's style of leadership is that he is both known and well regarded by the staff on the factory floor. Unfortunately, if the decision is taken to source shirts from abroad this may mean that the manufacturing capability disappears.

Tony should be aware that changing the culture of an organisation is not an easy task and that as well as his leadership style influencing, his leadership can also be constrained by the existing culture that exists in the Shirtmaster Group. Other models that could be useful include Johnson and Scholes' cultural web and Lewin's three-stage model of change and forcefield analysis. Finally, Peters and Waterman in their classic study 'In search of excellence' provides insights into the close relationship between leadership and creating a winning culture.

2 (a) To: Good Sports Limited
       From:

E – Business strategy

Clearly the markets that Good Sports operates in are being affected by the development of e-business and its experiences to date are mixed to say the least. In many ways the advantages and disadvantages of e-business are best related to the benefit the customer gets from the activity. Firstly, through integrating and accelerating business processes e-business technologies enable response and delivery times to be speeded up. Secondly, there are new business opportunities for information-based products and services. Thirdly, websites can be linked with customer databases and provide much greater insights into customer buying behaviour and needs. Fourthly, there is far greater ability for interaction with the customer, which enables customisation and a dialogue to be developed. Finally, customers may themselves form communities able to contact one another.

There is considerable evidence to show how small operators like Good Sports are able to base their whole strategy on e-business and achieve high rates of growth. The key to Good Sports survival is customer service – in strategic terms they are very much niche marketers supplying specialist service and advice to a small section of the local market. The nature of the business means that face-to-face contact is crucial in moving customers from awareness to action (AIDA – awareness, interest, desire and action). There are therefore limits to the ability of e-business to replace such contact.

Yours,

(b) Good Sports has pursued a conscious niche or focus differentiation strategy, seeking to serve a local market in a way that isolates it from the competition of the large national sports good retailers competing on the basis of supplying famous brands at highly competitive prices. Does it make strategic sense for Good Sports to make the heavy investment necessary to supply goods online? Will this enhance its ability to supply their chosen market?

In terms of price, e-business is bringing much greater price transparency – the problem for companies like Good Sports is that customers may use their expertise to research into a particular type and brand of sports equipment and then simply search the Internet for the cheapest supply. Porter in an article examining the impact of the Internet argues that rather than making strategy obsolete it has in fact made it more important. The Internet has tended to weaken industry profitability and made it more difficult to hold onto operational advantages. Choosing which customers you serve and how are even more critical decisions.

However the personal advice and performance side of the business could be linked to new ways of promoting the product and communicating with the customer. The development of customer communities referred to above could be a real way of increasing customer loyalty. The partners are anxious to avoid head-on competition with the national retailers. One way of increasing the size and strength of the niche they occupy is to use the Internet as a means of targeting their particular customers and providing insights into the use and performance of certain types of equipment by local clubs and users. There is considerable scope for innovation that enhances the service offered to their customers. As always there is a need to balance the costs and benefits of time spent. The Internet can provide a relatively cost effective way of providing greater service to their customers. There is little in the scenario to suggest they have reached saturation point in their chosen niche market. Overall there is a need for Good Sports to decide what and where its market is and how this can be improved by the use of e-business.

3 (a) The dilemma faced by Clyde shows the complex nature of strategic decisions, even within a small firm like Concrete Solutions. There is a need for Clyde to undertake a strategic appraisal, and identify the various stakeholders affected by his decision and their relative power and interest. The appraisal should involve both a PESTEL and stakeholder analysis to identify the key environmental factors affecting the opportunity – as shown in the table.

Factors:	Stakeholder analysis:
Political – local council – opposition	Council: High interest and moderate power
Rival council – support	Rival council: as above
Economic – reduced disposable income	
Social – higher local unemployment	Employees: High interest/low power
	Council: as above
Technological – not significant	
Environmental – higher pollution	Council: as above
Legal – limits on noxious emissions	Environmental agencies: High interest/moderate power

For Concrete Solutions the move into the new product can be viewed as a related diversification – namely new market and new product with the attendant risk involved. Clyde will have to assess the resource implications of the move. A considered

SWOT analysis, including his personal liability to manage the strategic change would be useful. There may be a significant investment in new technology and employee training to make the new blocks. In effect he will be forming a strategic alliance with the international company and making significant changes to both the value chain and value system. There will be no need to invest in sales and marketing as this will be the responsibility of its larger partner. As a major strategic option there is a need to address issues of its suitability, acceptability and feasibility. In terms of suitability the option seems to address many of the strategic problems attached to his current product range. It is a product that can be sold all year round and into a much wider geographical market area. It is in terms of acceptability that the dilemma reveals itself and the impact on the different stakeholders involved – he may find stakeholder mapping and scenario building useful in coming to a decision. As the owner of the business he needs to assess the risk involved against the likely returns. Feasibility looks reasonably sound – new resources and skills will be needed but affordable and achievable with the support of the partner.

(b) Recent corporate scandals have increased the critical awareness of the need for business to operate ethically and in a socially responsible way. This is seen largely in the context of large firms and their governance but as the Concrete Solutions scenario shows small owner-managed firms are not immune from taking difficult decisions that have differing and significant impacts on the firm's stakeholders and their expectations. Johnson and Scholes see corporate social responsibility as 'concerned with the ways in which an organisation exceeds the minimum obligation to stakeholders specified through regulation and corporate governance'. They argue it is useful to distinguish between contractual stakeholders including customers, suppliers and employees, who have a legal relationship with an organisation and community stakeholders – such as local communities – who do not have the same degree of legal protection as the first group. Clyde's local community and its representatives will face a dilemma – jobs v pollution – not an easy choice! Clearly there will be considerable negotiation between the key stakeholders and Clyde as the owner/manager should act ethically and with integrity in reaching a decision having profound effects for all parties concerned.

4 (a) To: David Silvester
From:

Funding strategy for Gift Designs Ltd

Clearly you have identified a real business opportunity and face both business and financial risks in turning the opportunity into reality. One possible model you can use is that of the product life cycle which as a one-product firm is effectively the life cycle for the company. Linking business risk to financial risk is important – in the early stages of the business the business risk is high and the high death rate amongst new start-ups is well publicised and, consequently, there is a need to go for low financial risk. Funding the business is essentially deciding the balance between debt and equity finance, and equity offers the low risk that you should be looking for. As the firm grows and develops so the balance between debt and equity will change. A new business venture like this could in Boston Box terms be seen as a problem child with a non-existent market share but high growth potential. The business risks are very high and consequently the financial risks taken should be very low and avoid taking on large amounts of debt with a commitment to service the debt.

You need to take advantage of investors who are willing to accept the risks associated with a business start-up – venture capitalists and business angels accept the risks associated with putting equity capital in but may expect a significant share in the ownership of the business. This they will seek to realise once the business is successfully established. As the business moves into growth and then maturity so the business risks will reduce and access to debt finance becomes feasible and cost effective. In maturity the business should be able to generate significant retained earnings to finance further development. Dividend policy will also be affected by the stage in the life cycle that the business has reached.

Yours,

(b) David even at this early stage needs to identify the critical success factors and related performance indicators that will show that the concept is turning into a business reality. Many of the success factors will be linked to customer needs and expectations and therefore where David's business must excel in order to outperform the competition. As an innovator one of the critical success factors will be the time taken to develop and launch the new vase. Being first-to-market will be critical for success. His ability to generate sales from demanding corporate customers will be a real indicator of that success. David will need to ensure that he has adequate patent protection for the product and recognise that it will have a product life cycle. There look to be a number of alternative markets and the ability to customise the product may be a CSF. Greiner indicates the different stages a growing business goes through and the different problems associated with each stage. One of David's key problems will be to decide what type of business he wants to be. From the scenario it looks as if he is aiming to carry out most of the functions himself and there is a need to decide what he does and what he gets others to do for him. Indeed the skills he has may be as an innovator rather than as someone who carries out manufacture, distribution, etc. Gift Designs may develop most quickly as a firm that creates new products and then licences them to larger firms with the skills to penetrate the many market opportunities that are present. It is important for David to recognise that turning the product concept into a viable and growing business may result in a business and a business model very different to what he anticipated. Gift Designs needs to have the flexibility and agility to take advantage of the opportunities that will emerge over time.

Part 3 Examination – Paper 3.5
Strategic Business Planning and Development

December 2006 Marking Scheme

Marks

			Marks
1	(a)	Shirtmaster Group position and performance; Static sales Low margins Little synergy in Group	Up to 3
		Shirtmaster division: 'Stuck in the middle' – brand performance Sourcing strategy Customers segment served declining High stocks and distribution costs Value system declining in importance	Up to 10
		Corporate Clothing division: Differentiated product Growing market Positive profit margins Value chain integrated with customers' value chain	Up to 10
		Use of models	Up to 3 maximum 20
	(b)	Advantages of successful strategic alliances: Economies of scale and scope Co-specialisation and synergies Attaining 'critical mass' Learning from partners and developing competences	Up to 2 per point
		Disadvantages of strategic alliances: Over dependency on partner Failure to develop own core competences No end date to partnership Creation of a competitor	Up to 2 per point
			maximum 15
	(c)	Costs of divisions operating independently: Duplicated costs No sharing of resources/transfer of skills No shared learning Competition for resources	Up to 2 per point
		Benefits of divisions operating independently: Development of necessary competences Ability to serve distinctive market needs Motivation and accountability Risk reduction Allows measurement of divisional performance	Up to 2 per point
			maximum 15
	(d)	Models linking leadership and culture: McKinsey 7-S model Cultural web Lewin's change model 'Excellence' model	Up to 3 per model
			maximum 10 **Total 60**

				Marks

2 **(a)** Advantages of Good Sports developing an e-business strategy: — Up to 7
Improved processes allowing better customer service
Opportunity to develop information based new products and services
Greater insight into customer behaviour
Greater interaction and customisation
Customers creating own communities

Disadvantages of developing an e-based strategy: — Up to 7
Costs exceed benefits
Inappropriate to nature of service provided
Lack of in-house skills and competences
External Internet 'experts' use inappropriate language and systems

maximum 12

(b) E-strategy supporting Good Sports' niche strategy: — Up to 3 per point
Better levels of service possible
New niches developed
Better understanding of customer needs
Focused promotion and communication

maximum 8
Total 20

3 **(a)** Assessing the opportunity:
Environmental appraisal and stakeholder analysis — Up to 5
SWOT analysis
Criteria for assessing option – suitability, acceptability and feasibility — Up to 3 per criterion
maximum 12

(b) Social responsibility dimensions; — Up to 3 per point
Stakeholders – power, interest and conflict
Governance issues – purpose of the business; short v long term
Corporate social responsibility – compatibility with business strategy

maximum 8
Total 20

4 **(a)** Identification of key issues: — Up to 3 per issue
Linking business risk to financial risk – start-up finance, growth, maturity and decline
Developing an appropriate funding strategy – debt v equity, dividend policy
Using appropriate models – product life cycle, BCG etc

maximum 10

(b) Critical success factors and performance indicators: — Up to 2 per point
Stages of growth – Greiner's model – own role in business
make v buy
value chain and value system
growth matrix – market development, market penetration, product development and diversification

maximum 10
Total 20

Review Form & Free Prize Draw – Paper 3.5 Strategic Business Planning and Development (1/07)

All original review forms from the entire BPP range, completed with genuine comments, will be entered into one of two draws on 31 July 2007 and 31 January 2008. The names on the first four forms picked out on each occasion will be sent a cheque for £50.

Name: _____   Address: _____

_____

_____

How have you used this Kit?
(Tick one box only)

☐ Home study (book only)

☐ On a course: college _____

☐ With 'correspondence' package

☐ Other _____

Why did you decide to purchase this Kit?
(Tick one box only)

☐ Have used the complementary Study text

☐ Have used other BPP products in the past

☐ Recommendation by friend/colleague

☐ Recommendation by a lecturer at college

☐ Saw advertising

☐ Other _____

During the past six months do you recall seeing/receiving any of the following?
(Tick as many boxes as are relevant)

☐ Our advertisement in *Student Accountant*

☐ Our advertisement in *Pass*

☐ Our advertisement in *PQ*

☐ Our brochure with a letter through the post

☐ Our website www.bpp.com

Which (if any) aspects of our advertising do you find useful?
(Tick as many boxes as are relevant)

☐ Prices and publication dates of new editions

☐ Information on product content

☐ Facility to order books off-the-page

☐ None of the above

Which BPP products have you used?

Text	☐	Success CD	☐	Learn Online	☐
Kit	☑	i-Learn	☐	Home Study Package	☐
Passcard	☐	i-Pass	☐	Home Study PLUS	☐

Your ratings, comments and suggestions would be appreciated on the following areas.

	Very useful	Useful	Not useful
Passing ACCA exams	☐	☐	☐
Passing 3.7	☐	☐	☐
Planning your question practice	☐	☐	☐
Questions	☐	☐	☐
Top Tips etc in answers	☐	☐	☐
Content and structure of answers	☐	☐	☐
'Plan of attack' in mock exams	☐	☐	☐
Mock exam answers	☐	☐	☐

Overall opinion of this Kit   Excellent ☐   Good ☐   Adequate ☐   Poor ☐

Do you intend to continue using BPP products?   Yes ☐   No ☐

The BPP author of this edition can be e-mailed at: glennhaldane@bpp.com

Please return this form to: Nick Weller, ACCA Publishing Manager, BPP Learning Media Ltd, FREEPOST, London, W12 8BR

Review Form & Free Prize Draw (continued)

TELL US WHAT YOU THINK

Please note any further comments and suggestions/errors below.

Free Prize Draw Rules

1   Closing date for 31 July 2007 draw is 30 June 2007. Closing date for 31 January 2008 draw is 31 December 2007.

2   Restricted to entries with UK and Eire addresses only. BPP employees, their families and business associates are excluded.

3   No purchase necessary. Entry forms are available upon request from BPP Learning Media Ltd. No more than one entry per title, per person. Draw restricted to persons aged 16 and over.

4   Winners will be notified by post and receive their cheques not later than 6 weeks after the relevant draw date.

5   The decision of the promoter in all matters is final and binding. No correspondence will be entered into.